HISTORICAL PERSPECTIVES:
A Reader & Study Guide
Volume I, Fourth Edition

Abigail Press   **Wheaton, IL 60187**

HISTORICAL PERSPECTIVES:
A Reader & Study Guide
Volume I, Fourth Edition

Louise A. Mayo
County College of Morris
Randolph, New Jersey

Randolph Hollingsworth
Kentucky Virtual University
Frankfort, Kentucky

Thomas D. Matijasic
Big Sandy Community & Technical College
Prestonsburg, Kentucky

Jackyn Purple Rhodes
SUNY Morrisville
Morrisville, New York

Doug Cantrell
Elizabethtown Community & Technical College
Elizabethtown, Kentucky

Abigail Press   **Wheaton, IL 60187**

Design and Production: Abigail Press
Typesetting: Abigail Press
Typeface: AGaramond
Cover Art: Sam Tolia

HISTORICAL PERSPECTIVES:
A Reader & Study Guide
Volume I, Fourth Edition

Fourth Edition, 2004
Printed in the United States of America
Translation rights reserved by the authors
ISBN 1-890919-32-2

ABOUT THE AUTHORS

Louise Mayo is the Chairperson of the Department of History/Political Science at County College of Morris, Randolph, NJ, where she has been a professor for the past twenty-four years. She is the author of *The Ambivalent Image* (1988) and numerous articles and papers in the fields of women and minority history. She has an M.A. from Cornell University in Modern European and Russian History and a Ph.D. from City University of New York in American History, specializing in immigration and minority history. She teaches courses in Twentieth Century America, History of American Women, History of Minorities, History of American Cities and Suburbs, and Civil War and Reconstruction.

Randolph Hollingsworth received her B. A. from Vassar College and her M. A. from Colgate University. She began teaching in a central New York public junior high school, went to Zimbabwe to teach secondary school to the newly independent Africans, and then returned to Kentucky, her birthplace. Two years after starting the Ph.D. in history at University of Kentucky, she quit to teach full-time at Lexington Community College. Ten years later, she returned to her graduate studies and graduated in 1999 with a speciality in the American South focusing on nineteenth century women. She was selected for the Commonwealth Humanities Postdoctoral Fellowship during which she continued her research. Currently she is an administrator in the Kentucky Commonwealth Virtual University.

Jacklyn Purple Rhodes has a B.A. and M.A.T. from Binghamton University. She teaches American History at the State University of New York College at Morrisville. In addition to teaching at SUNY-Morrisville for the past 15 years, she has also been involved with projects aimed at helping disadvantaged urban students. At the present time, she is the acting director of an inner city program aimed at educating at-risk high school students in Syracuse, New York.

Thomas D. Matijasic earned a B.A. from Youngstown State University, a M.A. from Kent State and a Ph.D. in History from Miami University. He is currently a Professor of History at Big Sandy Community and Technical College in eastern Kentucky. Dr. Matijasic has received four Great Teacher Awards and five NISOD Awards for teaching excellence. He has served as President of the Kentucky Association of Teachers of History and is a member of the Kentucky Historical Society. In 1994, Governor Brereton Jones appointed him to a seat on the Kentucky Heritage Council. He was re-appointed twice to the Council by Governor Paul Patton. Dr. Matijasic has published more than twenty articles and thirty book reviews. He also contributed a chapter to *The Western Dream of Civilization*, Vol. I, published by Abigail Press.

Doug Cantrell is an Associate Professor of History Elizabethtown Community College in Elizabethtown, Kentucky, where he has taught for 13 years. He holds a B.A. from Berea College in History and Political Science, an M.A. from the University of Kentucky, and has completed 30 hours toward the Ph.D. He is the author of numerous journal and encyclopedia articles in the field of immigration and ethnic history. Professor Cantrell also teaches Kentucky and American History courses on the web and is the social science discipline leader for the Kentucky Commonwealth Virtual University. He is listed in *Who's Who in America, Who's Who in the World,* and *Who's Who in the South and Southwest,* He is a former editor of the *Kentucky History Journal* and past president of the Kentucky Association of Teachers of History.

Contents in Brief

Contents

Chapter One

THE DISCOVERY OF
THE AMERICAS

The European discovery of America was both the product of and a stimulus to the creation of a global system of international trade. Christopher Columbus was himself the product of the newly emerging system of trade. For centuries his Genoese ancestors had engaged in a lucrative trade in spices with Arab merchants who participated in the thriving commerce along Asia's Silk Road. For much of his life, he sailed on Portuguese ships that explored the west coast of Africa in search of a new water route to the Far East. In the end, he would seek a short, trans-Atlantic route to China as a means to enrich the royal treasury of the Spanish monarchy.

Columbus was almost certainly not the first European to stumble upon the Americas. Early European ventures were short lived and had little impact upon Native Americans. Columbus would begin the Spanish conquest of the New World and a permanent European presence.

The Spanish conquistadors and other European explorers, who followed in their wake, would find a wide variety of Native American cultural groups inhabiting the diverse ecosystems of the New World. In the Valley of Mexico, the Aztecs had established a wealthy and highly centralized empire based around the great city of Tenochtitlan. Aggressive and powerful, the Aztecs forced the subject peoples of their empire to provide them with tribute and captives for religious sacrifice.

To the south of the Aztec Empire, Mayan farmers had developed a system of writing, mapped the stars, developed an accurate calendar, and built ceremonial centers. In the Andes Mountains of modern Peru, the Inca displayed remarkable craftsmanship in the production of tools, weapons and ornaments. Their wealth in gold and silver was amazing by any standard.

Using a combination of gunpowder, horses, disease, and internal dissent, the Spaniards ruthlessly conquered all three of these well-developed Native American civilizations. Expropriating the wealth of the Aztecs and the Inca, the conquistadors turned Spain into the most powerful nation in Europe. The wealth of the Americas also helped transform the European economy from a manorial-based agrarian system into a dynamic capitalism centered on expanding trade.

North of the Rio Grande River, Native Americans would demonstrate their ability to adapt to virtually any environment. In the woodlands, east of the Mississippi River, Native Americans would develop a mixed economy of hunting, fishing, gathering, and agriculture, which allowed them to support semi-permanent villages, yet remain in harmony with their natural surroundings. The great mound building cultures of the Midwest were already in decline when the first Europeans entered the region. Still, the tribes of the Ohio and Mississippi River Valleys would carry on their legacy of trade, agriculture and craftsmanship.

West of the Mississippi, on the prairie and Great Plains, semi-nomadic tribes hunted large herds of bison. In the dry mountain valleys of the Southwest, the Pueblo cultures farmed irrigated fields near their adobe apartment houses. The Amerindians of the Pacific Northwest relied upon the harvest of salmon to develop prosperous communities in their rain-soaked habitat.

The Spaniards would be the first Europeans to impose a political and social system on the people of the New World. The Spanish Empire was based upon a hierarchy of race and privilege. Worthy conquistadors were awarded control over the land and the people who lived on the land. In exchange for the gift of European civilization, the natives were to labor for the benefit of their Spanish landlords. In areas like the Caribbean, where the Native Americans died too quickly, slaves from Africa were imported to labor on sugar plantations.

Other European powers followed the Spanish to the New World. Portugal established a plantation system in Brazil based upon the production of sugar. The English crown would finance attempts to discover a Northwest Passage to the Far East. Later, English merchants formed joint stock companies in order to promote overseas trade. After several unsuccessful attempts, the English would establish the settlement of Jamestown in Virginia. The French and the Dutch would both establish fur-trading outposts in North America in the early seventeenth century.

In the exchange of disease and products that resulted from the European invasion of the Americas, Europeans benefited far more than Native Americans. Old World diseases like smallpox, measles and influenza decimated the Native American population. The death toll from these epidemics was so great that they sometimes led Native Americans to call into question their religious beliefs. It also made them more vulnerable to their enemies. European livestock destroyed Amerindian farm fields and the alienation of property by settlers was a concept foreign to most Native American nations.

By contrast, American crops like corn, beans, and the potato improved the diet of Europeans. The gold and silver of Mexico and Peru enriched the economy of Europe and stimulated further capitalist expansion. Rice, sugar, and coffee were introduced into the Americas by Europeans but only at the expense of Native Americans, who were forced to work as plantation laborers. Europeans manufactured products often replaced Native American crafts and made the Amerindians economically dependent on Europeans.

Within a century of Columbus' first visit to the Caribbean, millions of Native Americans had died of European diseases. Great civilizations lay in ruins. Tens of thousands of Native Americans and Africans were enslaved and toiled for the benefit of European masters.

IDENTIFICATION: Briefly describe each term.

Christopher Columbus

Arawaks

Paleo-Indians

Motecuhzoma II

Tenochtitlan

Mayan

Aztec

2

Inca

Cahokia

Chief Deganawida

Ferdinand of Argon

Isabella of Castille

The Silk Road

Prince Henry the Navigator

Protestant Reformation

Humanism

Johann Gutenberg

Marco Polo's *Travels*

Leif Ericson

L'Anse aux Meadows

Treaty of Tordesilles

Conquistadors

Hernando Cortez

Francisco Pizarro

Encomienda system

Bartolome de las Casas

Hacienda system

John Cabot

Sir Humphrey Gilbert

Martin Frobisher

Sir Walter Raleigh

Roanoke Island

Melungeons

Sagadahoc

Samuel de Champlain

Quebec

Henry Hudson

Timbuktu

Guinea

Smallpox

Maize

THINK ABOUT:

1. In many regions of the New World, Native Americans were anxious to trade with Europeans. Had Europeans restricted themselves to peaceful trade, would they still have had a negative impact upon Native American cultures?

2. What do you admire most about the Native American cultures that you have studied? Explain your answer.

"EXPLAINING THE REPUTATION OF CHRISTOPHER COLUMBUS,"
by Jack Weatherford

During the late twentieth century, historians reexamined the lives of heroic figures from new perspectives. The explorations of Columbus helped to usher in a new era of prosperity for Western Europe. Unfortunately, his voyages had a negative impact on the lives of Native Americans. Jack Weatherford is an anthropologist at Manchester College in Minnesota. This essay was reprinted with the permission of WESPAC, the parent organization for Clergy and Laity Concerned (CALC).

Christopher Columbus' reputation has not survived the scrutiny of history, and today we know that he was no more the discoverer of America than Pocahontas was the discoverer of Great Britain. Native Americans had built great civilizations with many millions of people long before Columbus wandered lost into the Caribbean.

Columbus' voyage has even less meaning for North Americans than for South Americans because Columbus never set foot on our continent, nor did he open it to European trade. Scandinavian Vikings already had settlements here in the eleventh century, and British fisherman probably fished the shores of Canada for decades before Columbus. The first European explorer to thoroughly document his visit to North America was the Italian explorer Giovanni Caboto, who sailed for England's King Henry VII and became known by his anglicized name, John Cabot. Cabot arrived in 1497 and claimed North America for the English sovereign while Columbus was still searching for India in the Caribbean. After three voyages to America and more than a decade of study, Columbus still believed that Cuba was a part of the continent of Asia, South America was only an island, and the coast of Central America was close to the Ganges River.

Unable to celebrate Columbus' exploration as a great discovery, some apologists now want to commemorate it as the great "cultural encounter." Under this interpretation, Columbus becomes a sensitive genius thinking beyond his time in the passionate pursuit of knowledge and understanding. The historical record refutes this, too.

Contrary to popular legend, Columbus did not prove that the world was round; educated people had known that for centuries. The Egyptian-Greek scientist Erastosthenes, working for Alexandria and Aswan, already had measured the circumference and diameter of the world in the third century B.C. Arab scientists had developed a whole discipline of geography and measurement, and in the tenth century A.D., Al Maqdisi described the earth with 360 degrees of longitude and 180 degrees of latitude. The Monastery of St. Catherine in the Sinai still has an icon — painted 500 years before Columbus – which shows Jesus ruling over a spherical earth. Nevertheless, Americans have embroidered many such legends around Columbus, and he has become part of a secular mythology for schoolchildren. Autumn would hardly be complete in any elementary school without construction-paper replicas of the three cute ships that Columbus sailed to America, or without drawings of Queen Isabella pawning her jewels to finance Columbus' trip.

This myth of the pawned jewels obscures the true and more sinister story of how Columbus financed his trip. The Spanish monarch invested in his excursion, but only on the condition that Columbus would repay this investment with profit by bringing back gold, spices, and other tribute from Asia. This pressing need to repay his debt underlies the frantic tone of Columbus' diaries as he raced from one Caribbean island to the next, stealing anything of value.

5

After he failed to contact the emperor of China, the traders of India or the merchants of Japan, Columbus decided to pay for his voyage in the one important commodity he had found in ample supply—human lives. He seized 1,200 Taino Indians from the island of Hispaniola, crammed as many onto his ships as would fit and sent them to Spain, where they were paraded naked through the streets of Seville and sold as slaves in 1495. Columbus tore children from their parents, husbands from wives. On board Columbus' slave ships, hundreds died; the sailors tossed the Indians bodies into the Atlantic.

Because Columbus captured more Indian slaves than he could transport to Spain in his small ships, he put them to work in mines and plantations which he, his family and followers created throughout the Caribbean. His marauding band hunted Indians for sport and profit—beating, raping, torturing, killing, and then using the Indian bodies as food for their hunting dogs. Within four years of Columbus' arrival on Hispaniola, his men had killed or exported one-third of the original Indian population of 300,000. Within another 50 years, the Taino people had been made extinct {editors note: the old assumption that the Taino became extinct is now open to serious questions}—the first casualties of the holocaust of American Indians. The plantation owners then turned to the American mainland and to Africa for new slaves to follow the tragic path of the Taino.

This was the great cultural encounter initiated by Christopher Columbus. This is the event we celebrate each year on Columbus Day. The Untied States honors only two men with federal holidays bearing their names. In January we commemorate the birth of Martin Luther King Jr., who struggled to lift the blinders of racial prejudice and to cut the remaining bonds of slavery in America. In October, we honor Christopher Columbus, who opened the Atlantic slave trade and launched one of the greatest waves of genocide known in history.

Source: http:\\www.hartford-hwp.com/taino/docs/columbus.html

HOW WELL DID YOU UNDERSTAND THIS SELECTION?

1. Did Columbus prove that the world was round?

2. How did Columbus attempt to repay his debt to the Spanish crown?

"THE CHRISTOPHER COLUMBUS CONTROVERSY: Western Civilization vs. Primitivism,"
By Michael S. Berliner

The reevaluation of Columbus and other European explorers has stimulated a lively debate between liberal and conservative historians. Conservatives believe that to reinterpret American history from a non-Western perspective is by nature an attack on the values of Western Civilization. Michael S. Berliner, Ph.D., is the executive director of the Ayn Rand Institute in Marina del Rey, California.

Columbus Day approaches, but to the "politically correct" this is no cause for celebration. On the contrary, they view the arrival of Christopher Columbus in 1492 as an occasion to be mourned. They have mourned, they have attacked, and they have intimidated schools across the country into replacing Columbus Day celebrations with "ethnic diversity" days.

The politically correct view is that Columbus did not discover America, because people had lived here for thousands of years. Worse yet, it's claimed, the main legacy of Columbus is death and destruction. Columbus is routinely vilified as a symbol of slavery and genocide, and the celebration of his arrival likened to a celebration of Hitler and the Holocaust. The attacks on Columbus are ominous, because the actual target is Western civilization.

Did Columbus "discover" America? Yes – in every important respect. This does not mean that no human eye had been cast on America before Columbus arrived. It does mean that Columbus brought America to the attention of the civilized world, i.e., to the growing, scientific civilizations of Western Europe. The result, ultimately, was the United States of America. It was Columbus' discovery for Western Europe that led to the influx of ideas and people on which this nation was founded – and on which it still rests. The opening of America brought the ideas and achievements of Aristotle, Galileo, Newton, and the thousands of thinkers, writers, and inventors who followed.

Prior to 1492, what is now the United States was sparsely inhabited, unused, and undeveloped. The inhabitants were primarily hunter-gatherers, wandering across the land, living from hand-to-mouth and from day-to-day. There was virtually no change, no growth for thousands of years. With rare exception, life was nasty, brutish, and short: there was no wheel, no written language, no division of labor, little agriculture and scant permanent settlement, but there were endless, bloody wars. Whatever the problems it brought, the vilified Western culture also brought enormous, undreamed-of benefits, without which most of today's Indians would be infinitely poorer or not even alive.

Columbus should be honored, for in so doing, we honor Western civilization. But the critics do not want to bestow such honor, because their real goal is to denigrate the values of Western civilization and to glorify the primitivism, mysticism, and collectivism embodied in the tribal cultures of American Indians. They decry the glorification of the West as "Eurocentrism." We should, they claim, replace our reverence for Western civilization with multi-culturalism, which regards all cultures as morally equal. In fact, they aren't. Some cultures are better than others; a free society is better than slavery; reason is better than brute force as a way to deal with other men; productivity is better than stagnation. In fact, Western civilization stands for man at his best. It stands for the values that make human life possible: reason, science, self-reliance, individualism, ambition, productive achievement. The values of Western civilization are values for all men; they cut across gender, ethnicity, and geography. We should honor Western civilization not for the ethnocentric reason that some of us happen to have European ancestors but because it is the objectively superior culture.

Underlying the political collectivism of the anti-Columbus crowd is a racist view of human nature. They claim that one's identity is primarily ethnic: if one thinks his ancestors were good, he will supposedly feel good about himself; if he thinks his ancestors were bad, he will supposedly feel self-loathing. But it doesn't work; the achievements or failures of one's ancestors are monumentally irrelevant to one's actual worth as a person. Only the lack of a sense of self leads one to look to others to provide what passes for a sense of identity. Neither the deeds nor misdeeds of others are his own; he can take neither credit nor blame for what someone else chose to do. There are no racial achievements or racial failures, only individual achievements and individual failures. One cannot inherit moral worth or moral vice. "Self-esteem through others" is a self-contradiction.

Thus the sham of "preserving one's heritage" as a rational life goal. Thus the cruel hoax of "multicultural education" as an antidote to racism: it will continue to create more racism.

Individualism is the only alternative to the racism of political correctness. We must recognize that everyone is a sovereign entity, with the power of choice and independent judgment. That is the ultimate value of Western civilization, and it should be proudly proclaimed.

Source: Ayn Rand Institute's Media Link Department
              http://www.aynrand.org/medialink/

HOW WELL DID YOU UNDERSTAND THIS SELECTION?

1.   Does Dr. Berliner believe that Columbus discovered America?

2.   How does Berliner view revisionists who attempt to view Columbus from a non-Western perspective?

"PARRIS ISLAND'S FIRST EUROPEAN VISITORS"

During the sixteenth century, as Europeans explored the coast of North America, there were isolated attempts to plant settlements. Most of these attempts ended in failure, and little evidence remains of these abortive colonial ventures.

The area on and around Parris Island [South Carolina] was called Port Royal by the French, Santa Elena by the Spanish and again Port Royal by the British. It was here that the Empires of Europe met in battle for the New World. The harbor was first explored by the Spanish in 1520, and in 1525, the Spanish seafarer Pedro de Queyo named the region Santa Elena. Though impressed by the spacious harbor, the Spanish did not establish any permanent settlement until the 1560s when they returned to Santa Elena to combat French incursions.

The threat to the Spanish domain came from a French squadron led by Jean Ribaut who was searching for settlement sites for French Protestants known as the Huguenots, and for a military base where French vessels could attack the Spanish treasure fleets. Santa Elena Sound, which he named Port Royal, seemed to fulfill both requirements.

Ribaut arrived off Parris Island in 1562, and established what he hoped would be a permanent colony. After building Charlesfort, named after the French King, Charles IX, Ribaut returned to France for additional supplies and settlers, leaving 28 men behind. Unfortunately, a fire destroyed much of the fort's provisions and the Frenchmen survived only with the help of local Indians. Hardship, monotony and the cruel discipline of their commander led to mutiny. The soldiers killed their commander, abandoned Charlesfort, constructed a vessel and sailed back to France.

The Spanish Settlement of Santa Elena

When the Spanish authorities learned of Charlesfort, they immediately dispatched a warship to destroy the French fort, but when they arrived they found the fort abandoned. To protect their claims, the Spanish decided to organize settlements along the east coast of North America. A large Spanish armada was organized under the command of Pedro Menendez, but before it was ready to sail, a second French expedition established a new colony, Fort Caroline, on the St. John's River near present day Jacksonville, Fla. When Menendez arrived off the Florida coast, he found the French fort protected by a naval squadron under Ribaut's command. Realizing that the French were too strong to attack by sea, Menendez sailed down the coast and built a military base at St. Augustine, Fla. From there, he marched overland to attack Fort Caroline while, simultaneously, Ribaut sailed his squadron to attack St. Augustine. Both movements were caught by natural phenomena unfamiliar to Europeans, a hurricane. Despite the storm, or perhaps by using the storm as cover, Menendez's men surprised and destroyed Fort Caroline, while Ribaut's squadron was wrecked on a barrier island near St. Augustine. Here Menendez captured and executed Ribaut and the other French survivors.

With his enemies defeated, Menendez then sailed up the coast and established the city of Santa Elena on Parris Island in 1566. This city became the home of nearly 500 Spaniards and served as the capital of Spanish Florida from 1568 to 1576, when Indian attacks forced a brief evacuation. The Spaniards returned in 1577 and built a larger city that survived until 1587, when English raiders forced the Spaniards to evacuate and move to St. Augustine.

On the site of the French and Spanish settlements is the Tile Monument. In front of the monument is a set of tiles that were given to Parris Island by the Order of the Ocean Sea, a Spanish organization that promotes the history of Spanish colonization. The tiles commemorate the Spanish colony on Parris Island and the friendship between the United States and Spain.

Located on the rear of the monument are four information panels detailing the history of the site as well as a plaque dedicated to the archaeologists who have worked on the site. Mounted above the plaque is a brick taken from a Spanish pottery kiln located near the golf course club house. This kiln is the oldest known European pottery kiln discovered in the United States. When excavated it was found to contain many unique pots that gave tremendous insight to the lifestyle of the Spanish settlers.

Near the monument is Fort San Marcos, the Spanish fort that defended Santa Elena from 1577 to 1587. Concrete blocks mark the fort's outline. In the center of the fort is a monument to Jean Ribaut and the French Huguenots. For centuries Ribaut's Charlesfort was confused with the Spanish fort, and in 1926, after an archaeological excavation seemed to prove that the site was Charlesfort, the marker was dedicated. But excavations carried out by the South Carolina Institute of Archaeology and Anthropology have confirmed that the site is that of Fort San Marcos. Archaeologists now place the site of Charlesfort within the remains of San Felipe, a later Spanish fortification.

Source: Parris Island World Wide Web Site created by Sergeants Andre Martinez, Parris Island Information Systems Management Office, and William M. Lisbon, Parris Island Public Affairs Office (Summer 1997). http://parrisisland.com/eurofirst.htm

HOW WELL DID YOU UNDERSTAND THIS SELECTION?

1. Why did the French create a post on Parris Island?

2. Why did the Spanish city on Parris Island fail to survive?

The European conquest of the New World was often bloody and cruel. Many Europeans felt that the lives of non-Christian natives were of little value. Some even questioned whether Native Americans had "souls." Bartolome' de Las Casas believed that they did, and he bravely wrote of Spanish atrocities in the Caribbean in the hope of defending Native Americans against future abuse.

In the year 1492, the West-Indies were discovered, in the following year they were inhabited by the Spaniards: a great company of the Spaniards going about 49 years agoe. The first place they came to, was Hispaniola, being a most fertile Island, and for the bignesse of it very famous, it being no less then six hundred miles in compass. Round about it lie an innumerable company of Islands, so throng'd with Inhabitants, that there is not to be found a greater multitude of people in any part of the world. The Continent is distant from this about Two hundred miles, stretching it self out in length upon the sea side for above Ten thousand miles in length. This is already found out, and more is daily discovered. These Countreys are inhabited by such a number of people, as if God had assembled and called together to this place, the greatest part of Mankinde.

This infinite multitude of people was so created by God, as that they were without fraud, without subtilty or malice, to their natural Governours most faithful and obedient. Toward the Spaniards whom they serve, patient, meek and peaceful, and who laying all contentious and tumultuous thoughts aside, live without any hatred or desire of revenge; the people are most delicate and tender, enjoying such a feeble constitution of body as does not permit them to endure labour, so that the Children of Princes and great persons here, are not more nice and delicate then Children of the meanest Countrey-man in that place. The nation is very poor and indigent, possessing little, and by reason that they gape not after temporal goods, neither proud nor ambitious. Their diet is such that the most holy Hermite cannot feed more sparingly in the wildernesse. They go naked, only hiding the indecencies of nature, and a poor shag mantle about an ell or two long is their greatest and their warmest covering. They lie upon mats, only those who have larger fortunes, lye upon a kinde of net which is tied at the four corners, and so fasten'd to the roof, which the Indians in their natural language call Hamecks. They are of a very apprehensive and docible wit, and capable of all good learning, and very apt to receive our Religion, which when they have but once tasted, they are carryed on with a very ardent and zealous desire to make a further progress in it; so that I have heard divers Spaniards confesse that they had nothing else to hinder them from enjoying heaven, but their ignorance of the true God.

To these quiet Lambs, endued with such blessed qualities, came the Spaniards like most cruel Tygres, Wolves and Lions, enrag'd with a sharp and tedious hunger; for these forty years past, minding nothing else but the slaughter of these unfortunate wretches, whom with divers kinds of torments neither seen nor heard of before, they have so cruelly and inhumanely butchered, that of three millions of people which Hispanola it self did contain, there are left remaining alive scarce three hundred persons. And for the Island of Cuba, which contains as much ground in length, as from Valladolid to Rome; it lies wholly desert, untili'd and ruin'd. The Islands of St. John and Jamaica lie waste and desolate. The Lucayan Islands neighboring toward the North upon Cuba and Hispaniola, being above Sixty or thereabouts with those Islands that are vulgarly called the Islands of the Gyants, of which that which is least fertile is more fruitful then the King of Spains Garden at Sevil, being situated in a pure and temperate air, are now totally unpeopled and destroyed; the inhabitants thereof amounting to above 500000 souls, partly killed and partly forced away to work in other places: so that there going a ship to visit those parts and to glean the remainder of those distressed wretches, there could be found no more than eleven men. Other Islands there were near the Island of St. John more then thirty in number, which were totally made desert. All which Islands, though they amount to such a number containing in length of ground the space of above Two thousand miles, lie now altogether solitary without any people or Inhabitant.

Now to come to the Continent, we are confident, and dare affirm upon our own knowledge, that there were ten Kingdomes of as large an extent as the Kingdome of Spain, joyning to it both Arragon, and Portugal, containing above a thousand miles every one of them in compass, which the unhumane and abominable villanies of the Spaniards have made a wilderness of, being now as it were stript of all their people, and made bare of all their inhabitants, though it were a place formerly possessed by vast and infinite numbers of men; And we dare confidently aver, that for those Forty years, wherein the Spaniards exercised their abominable cruelties, and detestable tyrannies in those parts, that there have innocently perish'd above Twelve millions of souls, women and children being numbered in this sad and fatall list; moreover I do verily believe that I should speak within compass, should I say that above Fifty millions were consumed in this Massacre.

As for those that came out of Spain, boasting themselves to be Christians, they took two several waies to extirpate this Nation from the face to the Earth, the first whereof was a bloudy, unjust, and cruel war which they made upon them: a second by cutting off all that so much as fought to recover their liberty, as some of the stouter sort did intend. And as for the Women and Children that were left alive, they laid so heavy and grievous a yoke for servitude upon them that the condition of beasts was much more tolerable.

Unto these two heads all the other several torments and inhumanities which they used to the ruine of these poor Nations may be reduced.

That which led the Spaniards to these unsanctified impieties was the desire of God, to make themselves suddenly rich, for the obtaining of dignities & honours which were no way fit for them. In a word, their covetousness, their ambition, which could not be more in any people under heaven, the riches of the Countrey, and the patience of the people gave occasion to this their devillish barbarism. For the Spaniards so contemned them (I now speak what I have seen without the least untruth) that they used them not like beasts, for that would have been tolerable, but looked upon them as if they had been but the dung and filth of the earth, and so little they regarded the health of their souls, that they suffered this great multitude to die without the least light of Religion; neither is this lesse true then what I have said before, and that which those tyrants and hangmen themselves dare not deny, without speaking a notorious falshood, that the Indians never gave them the least cause to offer them violence, but received them as Angels sent from heaven, till their excessive cruelties, the torments and slaughters of their Country-men mov'd them to take Armes against the Spaniards.

Of Hispaniola

In the Island of Hispaniola, to which the Spaniards came first, these slaughters and ruines of mankinde took their beginning. They took away their women and children to serve them, though the reward which they gave them was a sad and fatal one. Their food got with great pain and dropping sweat, the Spaniards still consumed, not content with what the poor Indians gave them gratis out of their own want; One Spaniard consuming in one day as much as would saffice three families, every one containing ten persons. Being thus broken with so many evils, afflicted with so many torments, and handled so ignominiously, they began at length to believe that the Spaniards were not sent from Heaven. And therefore some of them hid their Children, others their Wives, others their Victuals in obscure and secret places; Others not being able to endure a Nation that conversed among them with such a boysterous impiety sought for shelter in the most abrupt and inaccessible mountains. For the Spaniards while they were among them did not only entertain them with cruel beating them with their fists, and with their staves, but presumed also to lay violent hands upon the Rulers and Magistrates of their Cities; and they arriv'd at that height of impudence and unheard of boldnesse, that a certain private Captain scrupled not to force the Wife of the most potent King among them. From which time forward they began to think what they might take to expell the Spaniards out of their Countrey. But good God! What sort of Armes had they? Such as were as available to offend or defend as bulrushes might be. Which when the Spaniards saw, they came with their Horsemen well armed with Sword and Launce, making most cruel havocks and slaughters among them. Overrunning Cities and Villages, where they spared no sex nor age; neither would their cruelty pity Women with childe, whose bellies they would rip up, taking out the Infant to hew it in pieces. They would often lay wagers who should with most dexterity either cleave or cut a man in the middle, or who could at one blow soonest cut off his head. The children they would take by the feet and dash their innocent heads against the rocks, and when they were fallen into the water, with a strange and cruel derision they would call upon them to swim. Sometimes they would run both Mother and Infant, being in her belly quite through at one thrust.

They erected certain Gallowses, that were broad but so low, that the tormented creatures might touch the ground with their feet, upon every one of which they would hang thirteen persons, blasphemously affirming that they did it in honour of our Redeemer and his Apostles, and then putting fire under them, they burnt the poor wretches alive. Those whom their pity did think fit to spare, they would send away with their hands half cut off, and so hanging by the skin. Thus upbraiding their flight, Go carry letters to those who lye hid in the mountains and are fled from us.

This Death they found out also for the Lords and Nobles of Land; they stuck up forked sticks in the ground, and then laid certain perches upon them, and so laying them upon those perches, they put a gentle fire under, causing the fire to melt them away by degrees, to their unspeakable torment.

One time above the rest I saw four of the Nobles laid upon these perches, and two or three other of these kinde of hurdles furnished after the same manner; the clamours and cries of which persons being troublesome to the Captain, he gave order that they should be hang'd but the Executioner whose name I know, and whose parents are not obscure, hindred their Calamity form so quick a conclusion, stopping their mouthes, that they should not disturb the Captair, and still laying on more wood, till being roasted according to his pleasure, they yeelded up the ghost. Of these and other things innumerable I have been an eye-witnesse; Now because there were some that shun'd like so many rocks the cruelty of a Nation so inhumane, so void of piety and love to mankinde, and therefore fled from them to the mountains; therefore they hunted them with their Hounds, whom they bred up and taught to pull down and tear the Indians like beasts: by these Dogs much humane bloud was shed; and because the Indians did now and then kill a Spaniard, taking him at an advantage, as justly they might; therefore the Spaniards made a Law among themselves, that for one Spaniard so slaine, they should kill a hundred Indians.

Source: *Tears of the Indians* by Bartolome' de Las Casas

HOW WELL DID YOU UNDERSTAND THIS SELECTION?

1. In the view of de Las Casas, what motivated Spanish cruelty regarding the native peoples of the Caribbean?

2. What motivated de Las Casas to report on Spanish atrocities in the New World?

The pre-Columbian Native Americans of the eastern Woodlands left behind dramatic remains of their culture in the form of temple and burial mounds. Many of these sites are now protected and administered by the National Park Service. Sylvia Flowers in a Park Ranger at Ocmulgee National Monument in Georgia.

Around AD 900, a group of newcomers evidently arrived rather suddenly in Central Georgia. Archeologists call these people Mississippians because their way of life, or culture, is thought to have originated in the Mississippi River Valley. They constructed a large town on the Macon Plateau near the Ocmulgee River at present-day Macon, Georgia. Though there are no written records, they left many objects (artifacts) and features in the soil which tell a little about how they lived. Six miles from their huge ceremonial center on the Macon Plateau, these Early Mississippians built another large village. Several smaller sites belonging to this "Macon Plateau" culture once existed near the Ocmulgee River's Fall Line, where the natural resources of the hilly Piedmont and the flatter Coastal Plain overlap.

MOUNDS AND BUILDINGS:

These early people of the Mississippian Period constructed a series of earth mounds built for public ceremonies important to religion and politics. These flat-topped, pyramidal mounds were raised in layers at intervals over the years and suggest intricate social relationships. The largest mound, known as the Great Temple Mound supported at least three wooden structures and a stepped ramp ascended to its summit. The Funeral Mound contained log tombs in its lowest level. Other burials were placed in each of the mound's seven levels. Some contained elaborate copper and shell ornaments suggesting high status, but most had no accompanying artifacts.

Several earthlodges were built. The most elaborate lodge has been reconstructed. Around the wall of this structure is a raised clay bench with 47 molded seats. Three additional seats are located on a large bird-shaped platform. The people who meet here were probably the group's leaders. Under one mound, archaeologists found "rows of hilled up dirt" that were obviously remnants of an ancient agricultural field. It has been theorized that this area, known as the "corn field," may have been a sacred seed patch. Partially surrounding the Macon Plateau town were two parallel lines of deep pit-like trenches. They may have been borrow pits from which soil was taken for mound construction, provided a defensive line, delineated the ceremonial portion of the town, or served some yet unknown purpose.

SOCIAL AND POLITICAL ORGANIZATION:

Mississippian society was organized into complex political structures called "chiefdoms," which consisted of several towns. Each village had a chief, but these may have been subservient to a more powerful Priest-Chief in another town. Each family and clan had a rank or position within the society, possibly determined by how closely related they were to the chief. The Chief and his family were entitled to exotic goods which emphasized their importance or status and may have been buried with them when they died.

SUBSISTENCE:

The people of the Macon Plateau town have been called Master Farmers. They grew and stored corn, beans, squash, pumpkins, sunflowers, and tobacco. They cultivated their fields with tools of wood, bone, and stone. The harvests were collected in baskets. Animals such as raccoon, turkey, rabbit, beaver, squirrel, turtles, and deer were hunted. Skins were tanned to make clothing and no part of the animal was wasted. Deer may have been hunted in several ways. A lone hunter could camouflage himself with the hide of a deer in order to approach the animals. Fires might have been set in the woods to drive the deer into open areas. The final kill was made with bows and arrows.

ARTISTIC EXPRESSION:

Women constructed pots by coiling and modeling local clays. These vessels were used for storing food and drink. This early Mississippian pottery was made in many sizes and shapes suited to a variety of everyday and ceremonial uses. Decoration was in the form of effigies (images or representations of people or animals). Designs were woven into baskets and fabric. Stone, wood, bone, shell and other materials were probably utilized, though unfortunately, organic material does not survive well in the moist, acidic soil of the Southeast. Based on evidence from other archaeological sites and upon historic accounts of the Indians, people decorated themselves with shell gorgets, beads, tattooing, paint, elaborate hairdos, feathers and many types of ear ornaments.

RECREATION:

A favorite game was "chunkey" which was played with a disc-shaped stone and a striped pole or wooden spear. After rolling the stone, a player tried to toss his spear close to where he thought the stone would stop rolling. Stickball, very similar to the modern game of lacrosse, was also played. Wooden "racquets" were used by the players from two opposing teams to throw a small leather ball down a large playing field. Points were scored when the ball was thrown between two vertical posts at each end of the field. Stickball was usually played between two rival towns and sometimes was a method of setting arguments.

DECLINE OF THE MACON PLATEAU CULTURE:

By AD 1150, the town on the Macon Plateau was no longer a thriving center of Mississippian culture. The people may have migrated elsewhere or have been assimilated by the people who originally inhabited the area. After this time, Mississippian culture thrived at places like Etowah in Northern Georgia, Moundville in Alabama, and Spiro, Oklahoma. By AD 1350, a late Mississippian town which archaeologists call "Lamar" (after an early landowner) was thriving about 2-1/2 miles down the Ocmulgee River from the Macon Plateau. Two earthen mounds were built at the site, one encircled by a unique spiral ramp, the only one of its kind still known to exist in this country. A widespread late Mississippian Southeastern culture was named for this site which is also protected as a separate unit of the Ocmulgee National Monument. .

Source: http://www.nps.gov/ocmu/Bulletins.htm#Mississippian

HOW WELL DID YOU UNDERSTAND THIS SELECTION?

1. Describe the nature of the mounds at Ocmulgee National Monument.

2. Compare the athletic contests of our day with those played at Ocmulgee a thousand years ago.

From the Atlantic coast of Florida to the tundra of Alaska, Native Americans demonstrated their ingenuity by adapting to a wide variety of natural conditions. In spite of the harsh, dry conditions of the Southwest, a vibrant Native American culture flourished. The structural remains of the Anasazi culture are now preserved by the National Park Service in places like Chaco Canyon, New Mexico.

As the Mississippian Culture flourished in the center of the North American continent, the natives of the Southwest were developing a unique, urban culture of their own. The Anasazi ancestors of the modern Pueblo Indians inhabited a vast area in present day New Mexico, Arizona, Utah and Colorado. Chaco Canyon in northern New Mexico was one center of Anasazi life one thousand years ago. The following description of the Chaco Canyon Anasazi is taken from the web page of Chaco Canyon National Historic Park.

The Anasazi ruins of Chaco are the tangible remains of a culture that flourished in the canyon from A.D. 900 through A.D. 1150. There are 13 major ruins in the canyon, and over 3,500 sites have been recorded within the park boundaries. Out of the 3,500 sites, approximately half are above ground, either as masonry structures or rock art in the cliff faces. The major ruins consist of multi-roomed and multi-stored structures, some of which cover several acres and contain as many as 800 rooms. The most famous of these is Pueblo Bonito. With its finely detailed masonry, elegantly battered walls and overall imposing massiveness, it is difficult to believe that this finely engineered structure was built without the use of power tools, beasts of burden, or the wheel.

Today the ruins look very similar to what they did within a few hundred years of abandonment. None of the structures in the park have been completely reconstructed, although it has been necessary to maintain and stabilize them since excavation. For example, when the great kiva of Casa Rinconada was excavated, it was in very poor condition and a great deal of repair work was done to restore its well-built appearance. Yet, it still is not a complete structure. The other large sites in the central canyon have also been excavated and extensive maintenance has been done on them. Other sites have been excavated and covered over again. All of the major ruins have had some stabilization above ground, but care has been taken not to alter the appearance of the walls as they were found.

Chaco Canyon, for all its wild beauty, seems an unlikely place for a major center of ancestral Puebloan culture to take root and flourish. This is high desert country, with long winters, short growing seasons, and marginal rainfall. Yet, a thousand years ago, this valley was a center of community life, commerce, and ceremony. People built monumental masonry buildings that were connected to other communities by a wide-ranging network of "roads." In architecture, complexity of community life, social organization, and regional integration, the master builders of Chaco Canyon attained a unique cultural expression.

The cultural flowering of the Chacoan people began in the mid-800s and lasted over three hundred years. We can see it clearly in the grand scale of the architecture. Using masonry techniques unique for their time, they constructed massive stone buildings ("great houses") of multiple stories containing hundreds of rooms much larger than any they had previously built. The buildings were planned from the start, in contrast to the usual practice of adding rooms to existing structures as needed. Construction on some of these buildings spanned decades and even centuries. Although each is unique, all great houses share architectural features that make them recognizable as "Chacoan."

During the middle and late 800s, the great houses of Pueblo Bonito, Una Vida, and Penasco Blanco were constructed, followed by Hungo Pavi, Chetro Ketl, Pueblo Alto, and others. These structures were often oriented to solar, lunar, and cardinal directions. Lines of sight between the great houses allowed communication. Sophisticated astronomical markers, communication features, water control devices, and formal earthen mounds surrounded them. The buildings were placed within a landscape surrounded by sacred mountains, mesas, and shrines that still have deep spiritual meaning for American Indian descendants.

By 1050, Chaco was well on the way to becoming the political, economic, and ceremonial center of the San Juan Basin. Its sphere of influence was extensive. Dozens of great houses in Chaco Canyon were connected by roads to over 150 great houses built throughout the region. Current thought is that the great houses were not traditional farming villages occupied by large populations. They may instead have been impressive examples of "public architecture" that were used only periodically during times of ceremony, commerce, and trading when temporary populations arrived in the canyon for these events.

Why the need for social complexity and integration on such a large scale? Chaco was the hub of an extensive trading network. Turquoise was processed into beads, ornaments, and jewelry at Chaco, and traded throughout the Southwest and northern Mexico for parrots, macaws, copper bells, and other precious commodities. Chaco may have been a distribution center for food and resources in response to the region's highly variable climate and growing populations. Ceremonies may have brought "pilgrims" to Chaco along a ritually used road system that connected Chaco to distant communities and to the sacred landscape. We may never fully understand the Chaco story.

After prevailing for 300 years, Chaco Canyon declined as a regional center during the middle 1100s, when new construction ceased. Chacoan influence continued at Aztec Ruins and other centers to the north, south, and west into the late 1100s and 1200s. In time, the people shifted away from Chacoan ways, migrated to new areas, reorganized their world, and eventually interacted with foreign cultures. Their descendants are the modern Southwest Indians. Many Southwest Indian people today look upon Chaco as an important stop along their clans' sacred migration paths—a spiritual place to be honored and respected.

Source: http://www.nps.gov/chcu/history.htm.

HOW WELL DID YOU UNDERSTAND THIS SELECTION?

1. Compare the ruins of Chaco Canyon with the Mississippian people along the banks of the Ocmulgee River.

2. How did the environment of the American Southwest help shape the lifestyle of the people of Chaco Canyon?

EUROPEANS REACT TO THE CULTURES THEY ENCOUNTERED IN NORTH AMERICA

The sixteenth century witnessed the onset of the conquest of North America by European powers. In many respects, that conquest represented a clash of cultures. Europeans encountered and confronted a great variety of Native American communities, and they reacted to them based upon their preconceived notions of civil conduct.

We are all prisoners of culture. Marston Bates noted: "The outstanding peculiarity of man is the great control of custom, of culture, over behavior."[1] Small wonder that we are forced to judge people from other cultures by our own cultural standards. Western Civilization, in its twentieth-century form, prides itself on toleration. It has become, in effect, intolerant of intolerance.

How then, can we accept the observations of sixteenth-century Europeans as they met, interacted with, and sometimes conquered the Indian peoples of North America? Western Civilization, in its sixteenth-century form, did not pride itself on toleration. Sectarian violence typified the century as Protestant battled Catholic and all Christians on the Continent were forced to confront a mighty invasion by the Islamic Turks.

Historians had tended to be critical of sixteenth-century Europeans because they did not accept or fully appreciate North American cultures. William Graves reported that, "Ethnocentric European pride prejudiced his perceptions of other people. The 'uncivilized' Red man . . . was a 'barbarian' and a 'savage' both terms implying a moral judgement of culture and cultural status."[2] Gary B. Nash and James Axtell believe that European reaction to Indian cultures was somewhat more complex. Nash put forth the notion that Europeans quickly developed "a split image of the natives of North America." One stereotype portrayed Indians as noble and "gentle people." The other image "cast him as a savage, hostile, beastlike animal."[3] In the case of the English, James Axtell has implied that practical matters dictated which image would triumph. The Indians "were noble as well as ignoble, depending on English needs and circumstances."[4] Robert F. Berkhofer urges students of history to reject all European evaluations of Native Americans. "Whether evaluated as noble or ignoble, whether seen as exotic or degraded, the Indian as an image was always alien to the white."[5]

A closer examination of the chronicles written during the sixteenth century reveal that Europeans made a great variety of observations about the natives of North America. They found things to admire and to scorn as they attempted to evaluate these newfound peoples. Europeans of the Early Modern Period were certainly limited by their own cultural values but, within that context, many of their observations were astute, accurate, and, at times, sympathetic. Europeans who actually spent time in America during the sixteenth century tended to judge various Indian cultures on their own merits rather than lumping all native groups together. In a real sense, their perceptions of Indian life are no more distorted than those generally prevalent today.

This essay will consider the way in which Europeans reacted to a variety of native social customs. In particular, it will consider reports about the religions of North America, native dress, sexuality, courage and honesty. In addition to these societal manifestations, European assessments of the physical appearance, prowess, capacity for love and intellectual ability have also been noted.

Due to the importance of religion in the lives of sixteenth-century Europeans, the Caucasian invaders paid extraordinary attention to the religious practices of the North Americans. Gary Nash noted that, "religion was the organizing principle of life," for Europeans during this period.[6] In a real sense, this was also true for the Indians they encountered.

Some of the religious practices found in North America were particularly offensive to Europeans. It should come as little surprise to anyone that many Europeans believed that Indian peoples worshipped idols, false gods or even the devil. "Reports that Amerindians had no religion were bad enough; worse were those that claimed they were devil-worshippers."[7]

Sixteenth-century Christians truly believed that Satan was an active force in the world. As Don Juan de Onate marched into New Mexico in 1599, he attributed discontent among his own soldiers to the devil, "who must greatly resent the big loss he is to suffer through the conversion of these provinces."[8] Indeed, the forces of the devil seemed to be particularly strong in the New World.

As the Spanish conquistadors moved from the Caribbean islands to the mainland of North America, evidence of "idol worship" was readily apparent. The men who accompanied Juan de Grijalva were much impressed by the Mayan temples of the Yucatan. Gonzalo Fernandez de Oviedo reported that, "inside there were certain cemis (devils) or idols which those Indians adored, as they are all idolators."[9] As Cortez moved through Mexico, he frequently took the time to combat idolatry. On more than one occasion he ordered his men "to break up the idols and roll them down the steps." In place of the pagan idols he would erect "a very fair alter, on which we placed the image of Our Lady."[10] Bishop Diego de Landa painfully noted that even after the natives of the Yucatan were introduced to Christianity, "they were perverted by their priests and chiefs to return to their idolatry."[11]

As the Spaniards moved northward from Mexico later in the century, they continued to be distressed by additional evidence of idolatry among other native peoples. While in Florida, Alvar Nunez Cabeza de Vaca reported that native burial practices in that region appeared "to be a kind of idolatry."[12] John Ortiz, a Spanish captive liberated by Hernan de Soto, told members of de Soto's party that the Indians of Vcita were "worshippers of the devil" and that "he speaketh with them and telleth them that he is a thirst, and willeth them to sacrifice unto him."[13] Pedro de Castaneda observed that the Tahus of northwestern Mexico "worship idols and make presents to the devil of their goods and riches, consisting of cloth and turquoises."[14] A member of the de Sosa Expedition into New Mexico referred to the kiva at the pueblo of San Ildefonso as a "mosque where, on some days of the year, they meet to perform idolatries, because it contains many idols."[15]

Accusations of idolatry were not unique to the Spanish explorers and missionaries. The English and French adventurers made similar observations. When Sir Francis Drake visited California, he and his men "groaned in spirit to see the power of Sathan so farre prevaile in seducing these so harmlesse soules."[16] Arthur Barlowe maintained that the idol worshipped by the Indians on the coast of North Carolina was "nothing else but a mere illusion of the devil."[17] When the Indians of the St. Lawrence River Valley told Jacques Cartier's Frenchmen about Cudruaigni, a native deity, they responded by telling the natives that Cudruaigni, "is a divell and an evill spirit."[18]

Not all Europeans were willing to classify North Americans as devil-worshippers. "It was even conceded that they believed in immortality of the soul, and that not all the supernatural beings they believed in could be classified as devils."[19] Hernando de Alarcon discovered that the Indians of the lower Colorado River Valley had no real conception of divine beings, but they "venerated the sun above all thing."[20] Hernando do Alvarado believed that the inhabitants of Taos Pueblo in New Mexico" worship the sun and water."[21] Coronado believed that all of the Pueblo Indians worshipped water "because they say that it makes the maize grow and sustains their life"[22] French settler Nicolas Le Challeux went so far as to state that the natives of northern Florida, "are not without some idea of Divinity."[23]

Astute observers of Indian religions could not help but to notice strange parallels between Christian and native beliefs and ceremonies. Bishop de Landa was puzzled by the fact that the Mayans of the Yucatan practiced baptism, confessed their sins, and burned incense before their gods.[24] In addition, the Mayans also went on pilgrimage to holy places. "They held Cozumel and the well at Chichen Itza in as great veneration as we have in our pilgrimages to Jerusalem in Rome; they visit them to offer gifts...and when they did not visit they sent offerings."...[25] Bishop de Landa went so far as to speculate that "all the in habitants of the Indies must be of Jewish descent."[26]

Roanoke colonist Thomas Hariot was aware that the Indians of coastal North Carolina shared similar religious sentiments with the Anglican settlers. "Some religion they have alreadie, which although it be farre from the truth, yet beying as it is, there is hope it may bee the easier and sooner reformed." Hariot was smart enough to realize that the Eastern Woodland Indians were practicing a form of urmonotheism. Although they recognized numerous supernatural entities, they had "one onely chiefe and great God, which hath bene from all eternitie." They also believed in the immortality of the soul and in the "perpetuall bliss" of a heaven. Hariot believed that the natives showed an "earnest desire" to learn more about the religion of the English.[27]

Bartolome de Las Casas believed that the Indians of Mexico were, by their very nature, religious beings. He wrote that, "these people of New Spain were the most religious that there have ever been among the natives who had no knowledge of the true God."[28] Indeed, de Las Casas asserted that Indians generally were "very apt to receive our Religion, which when they have but once tasted, they are carryed on with a very ardent and zealous desire to make a further progress in it."[29]

Evidence that some Indian peoples practiced human sacrifice, cannibalism and mortification of the flesh had a strong negative impact upon Europeans. Sinteenth-century Europeans were not squeamish people. Brutal massacres were frequently committed by Spanish, French and English soldiers, often in the name of religion. Yet prohibitions against blood sacrifices were deeply rooted in Christian tradition. Historian Olive Dickason believes that the "ritual aspects of cannibalism were missed at first."[30] In actuality, it was probably the ritual aspects of cannibalism that so horrified the European invaders.

One discovers a mixture of disgust and fascination as European chroniclers recorded descriptions of human sacrifice. Fernandez de Oviedo reported that when the members of the Grijalva Expedition discovered a temple contained decapitated heads, "they were shocked, as they at once suspected what it was." A local inhabitant told them that the heads and hearts of the victims were offered to the pagan god. In addition to this "the flesh from the arms, the calves of the legs and the thighs" were hacked off and eaten by the participants of the ceremony.[31] Indians on the east coast of Mexico also cut their ears and offered their own blood in a "ceremony to appease the devil."[32] Bernal Diaz confirmed Fernandez de Oviedo's opinion that Grijalva's men were genuinely appalled by the Mexican practice of the blood sacrifice. When native priests attempted to honor the Spaniards by burning incense over them, the Spaniards refused to let them. "We were all too upset by the sight of those two dead boys (whose hearts were sacrificed), and too indignant at their cruelty."[33] Cortez firmly told Aztec officials at San Juan de Ulua "that our great Emperor's purpose in sending us to their lands was to abolish human sacrifices and other evil rites."[34] Bishop de Landa recorded his disgust by stating that in times of distress the Mayans, "forgetful of all natural piety and all law of reason they made sacrifices of human beings as easily as they did birds."[35] John Ortiz told a member of de Soto's party that certain tribes in Florida, "are wont to offer up unto him (the Devil) the lives and blood of their Indians, or of any other people they can come by."[36]

Although the Europeans were adamant in their condemnation of the blood sacrifice, they were clearly intrigued by it. Bernal Diaz wrote detailed descriptions of the manner which the Aztecs and their Mexican neighbors performed their ceremonies. The following passage is typical of his accounts.

> I have already described the manner of their sacrifices. They strike open the wretched Indian's chest with flint knives and hastily tear out the palpitating heart which, with the blood, they present to idols in whose name they have performed the sacrifice. Then they cut off the arms, thighs, and head, eating the arms and thighs at their ceremonial banquets. The head they hang upon a beam, and the body of the sacrificed man is not eaten but given to beasts of prey.[37]

Bishop de Landa gave a graphic account of the manner in which the Indians of the Yucatan would piece holes through their penises in order to collect blood to offer to an idol.[38] Such accounts were clearly designed to titillate the psyche of the European reader.

Occasionally Europeans would record instances of cannibalism for its own sake. Hernando de Alarcon noted that the natives of the lower Colorado River Valley would make war in order to eat the fallen bodies of their enemies.[39] Pedro de Castaneda wrote that the Acaxes of northwestern Mexico, "all eat human flesh, and he who has the most human bones and skulls hung up around his house is most feared and respected." However, few sixteenth-century chroniclers believed that cannibalism was generally practice by Indians throughout North America. It is also important to note that Europeans showed little interest in the subject when it was devoid of religious significance.

European chroniclers expressed a keen interest in native clothing or lack of it. Clothing was essential to Europeans because "dress indicated rank and authority." Olive Dickason has asserted that nudity was associated "with lack of social order."[41] Most Europeans who visited North America did comment on the "nakedness" of the native populations. Castaneda wrote that Baja California was "inhabited by brutish, bestial, naked people who eat their own offal."[42] When John Ortiz, a Spaniard, was discovered in Florida living among the natives, he "was naked" like his Indian companions.[43] Cabeza de Vaca pointed out that the people who lived on the coast of Texas all "go naked" except for the "damsels" who "dress themselves in deer-skin."[44] Bishop de Landa was certain that the Indians had carved the reliefs on the ancient Mayan temples because the "stone figures of men" were "unclothed but with the middle covered by certain long fillets."[45]

Explorers from Northern Europe were even more conscious of nudity than were the Iberians. Arthur Barlowe was little impressed by the flimsy arrows of Roanoke natives but felt they were "sufficient enough to kill a naked man."[46] When Drake reached California, he bestowed upon the natives "necessary things to cover their nakednesse; withall signifying unto them we were no Gods, but men, and had neede of such things to cover our owne shame."[47]

Jacques Cartier reported that the "wilde" men he met in Canada "goe altogether naked saving their privities."[48] He noted that along the banks of the St. Lawrence River" the inhabitants of the countrey cloth themselves with the skinnes of certain wilde beasts, but very miserably."[49] Rene Goulaine de Laudonniere was very upset when he found Christians living among the Indians of northern Florida. He "gave them clothes, and ordered their hair to be cut."[50]

Not all Europeans were critical of native dress. Hernando de Alarcon was both amazed and amused by the manner in which Indians of the Colorado River Valley adorned themselves.

> Some wore masks of the same color, shaped like their faces. On their heads they wore a deerskin about two spans in size, worn like a helmet, and on it a small crest with some feathers....They have their noses pierced, and from them hung some pendants, while others wore shells. They have their ears pierced with many holes in which they place beads and shells.[51]

The gentleman of Elvas reported that the natives of Toalli, in what is now the southeastern part of the United States, were well dressed. The women wore long mantles made of inner bark and grass" with their right arme out, like unto the Egyptians." The men also wore a mantle over their shoulders "and have their secrets hid with a Deeres skin, made like a linen breech, which was wont be used in Spaine."[52] The chronicler of the de Sosa Expedition was very impressed by the dress of the people of Pecos Pueblo in New Mexico.[53] Father Fray Francisco del Spiritu Sancto reported that the people of New Mexico were "white like the Spaniards and very well dressed."[54]

If Europeans were rarely impressed by Indian dress, they generally found the physical appearance of the North Americans to be pleasing. Barlowe referred to the Indians on the coast of North Carolina as "very handsome and goodly people."[55] Le Challeux described the Indians of Florida as being "straight and well proportioned, of a somewhat ruddy color."[56] Fellow Frenchman le Moyne noted that local chieftan, Saturiba, came to their settlement "with seven or eight hundred handsome, strong, and well-built men."[57] Alarcon had little good to say about the natives of the lower Colorado, but he did report that they "were large and well formed, without being fat."[58] De Landa wrote the Mayans of the Yucatan" are people of good physique, tall, robust and of great strength."[59] Coronado found the women of Quivira "comely, with faces more like Moorish than Indian women."[60] Giovanni da Verrazano, the gentleman of Elvas and Cabeza de Vaca, also praised the beauty and physical appearance of various Indian groups.[61]

Commentators who did not find Indians universally attractive would sometimes overcome their prejudice and acknowledge the beauty of individual Indians. Bernal Diaz remarked that the daughter of a Mexican chieftain "was very beautiful, for the Indian."[62] Diaz was very impressed with Montezuma, the great Aztec leader.

> The great Montezuma was about forty years old, of good height, well proportioned, spare and slight, and not very dark, though of the usual Indian complexion. He did not wear his hair long but just over his ears and he had a short black beard, well-shaped and thin. His face was rather long and cheerful, he had fine eyes, and in his appearance and manner could express geniality or, when necessary, a serious composure.[63]

Many Europeans were in awe of the strength and physical prowess of some Native American groups. Vincente de Zaldibar Mendoza reported that Plains Indians "grow up healthy, strong, and brave."[64] Fletcher revealed that the natives of California displayed extraordinary strength and swiftness.[65] Cabeza de Vaca took a page from Tacitus when he wrote that the people on the Texas coast "see and hear better, and have keener senses than any other in the world. They are great in hunger, thirst, and cold, as if they were made for the endurance of these more than other men, by habit and nature."[66] Cartier noted that the Indians of Canada were "more able to resist cold then savage beasts."[67] Only Father de Las Casas dissented. The Spanish priest believed that Indians generally "are most delicate and tender, enjoying such a feeble constitution of body as does not permit them to endure labour."[68]

The mating habits of the natives of North America drew more than a little attention from European chroniclers. The Spanish seem to have been particularly interested in commenting on Indian sexuality. Marital fidelity and female chastity drew praise from Europeans. Evidence of homosexuality, prostitution, and incest were vigorously condemned.

In one of his most bitter tirades against the American Indians, Gonzalo Fernandez de Oviedo stated that, their "marriages are not a sacrament but a sacrilege. They are idolatrous, libidinous, and commit sodomy. Their chief desire is to eat, drink, and worship heathen idols and commit bestial obscenities."[69] Fernandez de Oviedo actually believed that because the Indians practiced the "dreadful sin of sodomy," God punished them and "they have been forgotten by His mercy for so many centuries."[70]

Bernal Diaz was shocked when he entered a Mayan temple on the Isla Mujeres and saw "many idols of baked clay, some with demons' faces, some with women's, and others equally ugly which seemed to represent Indians committing sodomy with one another." He noted that Cortez admonished the Cempoalo Indians of central Mexico to "give up sodomy, for they had boys dressed as women who practised that accursed vice for profit." One of the reasons that Diaz held Montezuma in high esteem was that the Aztec leader "was quite free from sodomy."[71]

Alarcon and Cabeza de Vaca both made reference to transvestites who lived among the natives of the southwestern portion the present-day United States. Cabeza de Vaca noted that while among a group of Indians in Texas, "I witnessed a diabolical practice; a man living with another, one of those who are emasculate and impotent."[72] Alarcon was amazed when an Indian in the Colorado River Valley showed him "a son of his dressed as a woman and used as such."[73] Bishop de Landa hinted at what he saw as the effeminate characteristics of Mayan males, but he stopped short of accusing them of homosexual behavior.[74]

Pedro de Castaneda wrote more than any other European chronicler about the sex lives of the American Indian. As he marched with Coronado from central Mexico to the Rio Grande Valley, he studied the native groups along the way with a keen eye for sexual perversion. He was particularly harsh on the Indians of Culiacan province in Mexico. Among the people of Petlatan there was much sodomy. Among the Tahus "there are men dressed like women who marry other men and serve as their wives." The Tahus also held a great celebration during which the local chiefs dance naked around a consecrated woman, adorning her with fine jewelry, "and then the chiefs go in one by one to lie with her, and all others who wish, follow them." The Pacaxes were even worse. They committed sodomy and "have many wives, even when these are sisters." Castaneda considered the Pima of southern Arizona to be "great sodomites" and he criticized the people of Baja California for coupling "like animals, the female openly getting down on all fours." It must be noted, however, the Castaneda did not accuse all Indians of perversion. He had praise for the inhabitants of Tiguex Pueblo because "Sodomy is not found among them."[75]

In addition to homosexuality, other North American mating customs were frowned upon by Europeans. Alarcon discovered that a class of prostitutes "who lived apart from the married women" existed among the natives of the Colorado River Valley.[76] Cartier was disgusted by the fact that unmarried women among the natives of Canada were housed "in a common place, as harlots free for every man that will have to doe with them, untill such time as they find a match."[77] Bishop de Landa listed divorce and public orgies among the vices of the Mayans.[78] Cabeza de Vaca reported that the natives of Texas had rather loose marriage bonds until a child was born. Husbands "who have children remain with their wives and never abandon them."[79]

The Europeans readily bestowed praise on Indian mating customs when they conformed to Christian standards. Bishop de Landa gave credit to Mayan women for their chastity.[80] Le Challeux wrote that the Indians of Florida "keep their marriage bond with all rigor."[81] Cabeza de Vaca found that usually in Texas a man had but one wife. However, physicians were allowed to "have two or three wives, among whom exist the greatest friendship and harmony."[82] Among the Mariames of Texas, daughters were often killed at birth out of fear that they might grow up to have sexual relations with a relative or with a tribal enemy.[83] Cabeza de Vaca did not criticize this practice, for dishonor was a greater sin than murder to a sixteenth-century Spaniard. Alarcon liked the marriage rules among the Indians of the Colorado because they closely conformed to the marriage principles common in Europe. Incest was strictly forbidden. Women were expected to be virgins before marriage. If a woman "had relations with men before she married, her husband abandoned her and moved to another nation." If a man committed adultery, he was executed.[84]

Sixteenth-century Europeans were aggressive and a militant ethic dominated their mind-set. They admired bravery, valor, and ferocity. They loathed the cowardly, the passive and the lethargic. There were, of course, a few exceptional individuals who recognized the discrepancy between the message of the Christian gospels and the violent spirit of the age. However, most chose to ignore the notion that the meek would inherit the earth. It was the fighter who won praise from most Europeans.

It seems almost ironic that the Spaniards most admired Indian nations that fiercely resisted their armies. Fernandez de Oviedo displayed little sympathy for Indians, but he complimented the "very splendid people" of southeast Mexico who launched war canoes "with the determination to attack the ships of the (Spanish) fleet."[85] Bernal Diaz praised the warriors of Tabasco who met Cortez's army "face to face, fighting most valiantly and persistently." Even when the Indians of Mexico gave way in battle they "kept their ranks and fought well for a considerable time." Diaz actually believed that poor leadership on the part of Indian captains saved Cortez's army during an especially fierce encounter fought on September 5, 1519.[86] A Portuguese soldier in de Soto's army reported that the Indians of Florida were "so warlike and so nimble, that they care not a whit for any footemen." At Manilla, the inhabitants "fought with such courage, that many times they drove our men out of the towne."[87] The chronicler of the do Sosa Expedition into New Mexico was astonished by the bravery of the defenders of Pecos Pueblo.

> Although the Indians saw how much we were hurting them, they did not give way. And in spite of all this, there were none who left their houses or passages, but rather each one managed to defend what was in his care without fleeing-a thing not to be believed, that uncivilized people should be so clever.[88]

Even though Bishop de Landa believed the Spanish conquest of the Yucatan was in the best interest of all concerned, he did state that "the Indians were right in defending their liberty and trusting to the valor of their chiefs."[89] Cabeza de Vaca noted that the Indians of Texas "have as much strategy for protecting themselves against enemies as they could have were they reared in Italy in continual feuds."[90]

There were a few Europeans who believed the North Americans to be cowardly. Ralph Lane showed contempt for the military prowess of the Indians of North Carolina when he asserted that ten armed Englishmen "would be a match for a hundred of their best men."[91] Thomas Hariot was not very impressed by Indian warfare. He noted that set battles were rare and that surprise attacks and ambushes were common.[92]

Bartolome de Las Casas approached the question of bravery from a different perspective than most of his contemporaries. True to his Christian convictions, he felt that a passive nature was preferable to an aggressive nature. He saw the Indians of Mexico and Central America as God's finest children because they were "patient, meek and peaceful, and who, laying all contentions and tumultous thoughts aside, live without any hatred or desire of revenge."[93]

A few Europeans recognized that Indian peoples were capable of love as well as bravery. Cabeza de Vaca believed that the natives of Malhado on the coast of Texas "love their offspring the most of any in the world and treat them with the greatest mildness."[94] Father de Las Casas wrote that the Mayans of the Yucatan loved their children "as dearly as the apple of their eyes."[95]

The chroniclers were divided in their opinion as to the honesty of the North American peoples they encountered. Arthur Barlowe noted that Granganimeo, the brother of an Indian king on the Atlantic coast, always kept his promises.[96] Castaneda felt that the nomadic Indians of the southern Plains were "faithful friends."[97] Marcos de Niza reported in 1539 that "he had never caught the Indians in a lie."[98] Subsequent events may have altered his viewpoint.

Other Europeans were more cautious in evaluating the North Americans. Fletcher believed that the people of California were "without guile or treachery." However, the members of the Drake Expedition "thought it no wisdome too farre to trust them."[99] Cabeza de Vaca was generally positive in his evaluation of Indian character but he did criticize the Yguazes for being great liars, thieves and drunkards.[100]

Many visitors from the Old World had no trust in the native inhabitants of the New World. The Spaniards who accompanied Cortez to Tenochtitlan, the Aztec capital, warned their leader "that the hearts of men are very fickle, especially among the Indians."[101] Ralph Lane reported that when the Indians of Roanoke Island believed that an armed band led by Lane had been defeated by a tribe on the mainland, they began to treat the English "with contempt, and also to blaspheme against our God."[102] Jacques Cartier felt the French must not trust Indians of Canada "for all their faire ceremonies and signs of joy."[103] Two Spaniards warned Frenchman Rene Goulaine de Laudonniere "not to put any faith in" the Indians of Florida "since they invariably behaved most amiably when they are plotting some treachery and were by nature utter traitors and deceivers."[104]

As with everything else, the European writers and explorers failed to agree on the mental capacity of the North Americans. Most found the natives they encountered to be very intelligent. The English settlers of Roanoke certainly came to respect the intellectual abilities of the Woodland Indians. Thomas Hariot wrote that "they seeme very ingenious" and "they shewe excellencie of wit."[105] The paintings of John White "reveal a genuine appreciation of the Indians' ability to control their environment through their methods of hunting and agriculture, their family and communal life, and other aspects of their culture."[106] Even the critical Ralph Lane was forced to admit that Indian King Menatonon "is, for a savage, unusually grave and wise."[107] Castaneda readily conceded that the Hopi of Tusayan "were very intelligent people."[108] Although Cartier believed the people of the St. Lawrence River Valley were savages, he acknowledged that it was easy to "make them learne what one would."[109]

Of course a few Europeans were blind to the evidence of Indian ingenuity. Juan Gines de Sepulveda could "scarcely find traces of humanity" among the Indians of the Yucatan. He asserted that they "not only lack culture but do not even know how to write," and they kept, "no records of their history except certain obscure and vague reminiscences of some things put down in certain pictures."[110] Bishop de Landa recognized that the Mayans of the Yucatan were literate and had their own science. However, de Landa ordered that Mayan books be destroyed because "they contained nothing but superstitious and falsehoods of the devil."[111]

Some Europeans showed little respect for the medical knowledge of the Indians. When the Indians of Texas explained their method of casting out infirmity to Cabeza de Vaca, he laughed at them and told them "it was folly." Later, however, he did come to recognize that some Indian cures were surprisingly effective.[112] Hariot believed that Indian physicians were charlatans who hid their ignorance with hocus-pocus.[113]

What probably impressed European visitors to North America more than anything else were the architectural achievements of the Indians of the Yucatan, Mexico and the Rio Grande River Valley of New Mexico. The Indians of these regions were among the greatest builders on earth. Bishop de Landa wrote that in the Yucatan there were "many edifices of great beauty. "More important, he acknowledged that these magnificent structures were "not the work of other peoples, but of the Indians themselves."[114] As Bernal Diaz marched with Cortez into the heart of the Aztec Empire he was awestruck. "These great towns and cues and buildings rising from the water, all made of stone, seemed like an enchanted vision from the tale of Amadis." When the Spaniards compared the great market in Tenochtitlan to those in Constantinople, Rome and other European cities, they concluded that "they had never seen a market so well laid out, so large, so orderly, and so full of people."[115]

As the Spanish conquistadors pushed northward into New Mexico, they were impressed by the Pueblo cultures. The Pueblo Indians did not achieve the wealth and splendor of the Indians of central Mexico. In that sense, the Spanish were disappointed. By the same token, the Spaniards could not help but to notice that Pueblo villages looked remarkably like towns in southern Europe. Gary B. Nash observed that "Pueblo society on the eve of Spanish arrival was not radically different from peasant communities in most of the Euro-Asian world."[116] Coronado was so impressed by the towns of New Mexico that he could not believe the Indians had the ability "to build these houses in the way in which they are built."[117] Juan de Onate reported back to Spain that the Pueblo Indians "live very much the same as we do, in houses with two and three terraces, each an estado and a half high."[118] A member of the de Sosa expedition felt the irrigation system of New Mexico was so sophisticated that it was "a thing (which would) not (be) believed if we had not seen it with our own eyes." He also commented that the earthenware of Pecos Pueblo was "very elegant."[119]

It is clear that the Europeans who wrote the chronicles of the sixteenth century did not see the American Indian as a one dimensional figure. They judged Indian nations by European standards, but they recognize both positive and negative features within various native cultures. Europeans were critical of North Americans who practiced idol worship, human sacrifice and cannibalism, but some did recognize similarities between Christianity and Indian religions. Many Europeans were distressed by the lack of clothing found among many North Americas groups, yet most felt that the Indians were physically attractive and displayed remarkable physical prowess. Cultures which tolerated homosexuality and/or promiscuity were vigorously condemned by Europeans, but native peoples who practiced monogamy or who valued female chastity were applauded. Some North Americans were viewed as brave and honest while others were given little credit for literacy (even in the Yucatan), some Europeans were impressed by the ability of the natives to control their environment.

The sixteenth-century European visitor to North America tended not to issue general condemnations of Indians as a people. By the same token, Father de Las Casas was exceptional in characterizing the Indians as savage innocents. The "good Indian" was typified by the peasant farmer of New Mexico. Castaneda reported that among the Zuni of Cibola "there is no drunkenness . . . nor sodomy or sacrifices, neither do they eat human flesh nor steal, but they are usually at work."[120] The Pueblo Indians gained the admiration of the Spanish because they shared many of the same values. The same was true of any North American Indian group encountered by Europeans during this early stage of interaction.

Source: Thomas D. Matijasic, "Reflected Values: Sixteenth-Century Europeans View The Indians of North America," *American Indian Culture and Research Journal*, 11:2 (1987), pp. 31-50.

HOW WELL DID YOU UNDERSTAND THIS SELECTION?

1. In judging Native Americans, what aspects of their culture did Europeans tend to emphasize?

2. Did Europeans view all Native Americans the same or did they view some as being superior to others?

3. Do you consider yourself to be ethnocentric? If so, why?

SELF TEST:

MULTIPLE CHOICE: Circle the correct response. The correct answers are given at the end.

1. The term " Paleo-Indians" refers to
   a. the town dwelling Native-Americans of Central America
   b. the nomadic hunters and gathers who first inhabited the Americas
   c. people who pretended to be Native Americans but were not
   d. the farming cultures of the Midwest

2. The Aztecs of central Mexico can be characterized as
   a. passive and ignorant
   b. impoverished and primitive
   c. aggressive and rigidly stratified
   d. democratic and egalitarian

3. The two pre-Columbian farming cultures that built mounds throughout the Ohio River Valley are referred to as
    a. the Mayans and the Inca
    b. the Pueblo people
    c. the Adena and Hopewell cultures
    d. the Iroquois Confederation

4. The great Iroquois leader Deganawida
    a. united five tribes into a confederacy in order to control violence and warfare
    b. built the great city of Teotihuacan
    c. ordered the building of the Great Serpent Mound in Ohio
    d. designed the first teepee for greater mobility

5. These were among the crops cultivated by Native Americans:
    a. wheat, barley, and rye
    b. rice, millet, and oranges
    c. maize (corn), beans, squash, and peppers
    d. bread fruit and limes

6. Among the luxury goods Europeans obtained through trade with Asians were
    a. silver and hunting hawks
    b. heroin and tobacco
    c. lumber and grain
    d. silk and spices

7. The growth of capitalism helped to
    a. restore the religious unity of Europe
    b. unite merchants and monarchs to create greater stability
    c. foster feudal wars and decentralized government
    d. prevent long distance trading

8. The effect of the Protestant Reformation was to
    a. shatter the religious unity of Western Europe and reduce the power of the papacy
    b. restore the power of the papacy in most of Europe
    c. destroy the power of the Turkish sultan
    d. organize military crusades to recapture Jerusalem

9. Medieval Scandinavian literature indicates that
    a. the Japanese were the first to sail around the world
    b. the Vikings explored the coast of North America long before Columbus
    c. Columbus was from Norway
    d. Native Americans sailed to Ireland during the Middle Ages

10. Christopher Columbus can be described as
    a. the first European to visit the Americas
    b. a man of little courage or vision
    c. the first man to sail around the world
    d. a European navigator searching for a short water route to Asia

Answers:
1-b; 2-d; 3-c; 4-a; 5-c; 6-d; 7-b; 8-a; 9-b; 10-d.

ESSAYS:

1. Consider the life and accomplishments of Christopher Columbus. Was he a hero, a villain or something in between? Justify your answer.

2. Discuss the system of imperial rule established by the Spanish during their first century of colonization. What was the encomienda system? What was the hacienda system?

3. What was the Columbian Exchange? What region of the world benefited the most from the development of the Atlantic trade network?

OPTIONAL ACTIVITIES: (Use your knowledge **and** imagination.)

1. Locate a pre-Columbian Native American site in your area. Visit the site and write down your impressions.

2. Divide your class into two groups. Each group will organize its own community. Each group will choose a leader, develop an economy, draw the houses that exist within their community, and write down their mating habits. When each group has completed the creation of their community, invite a member of the other community to visit your community. At the same time, sent one of your members to the other group for a visit. Allow the visitors to contrast their communities with the communities they are visiting.

WEB SITE LISTINGS:

Ocmulgee National Monument, Georgia - Chronology of Amerindian archeology in the southwest U.S.
   http://www.nps.gov/ocmu/History.htm

Chaco Culture National Historical Park
   http://www.nps.gov/chcu/history.htm

The Columbus Navigation Homepage
   http://www1.minn.net/~keithp/

The European Voyages of Exploration
   http://www.acs.ucalgary.ca/HIST/tutor/eurvoya/columbus.html

Internet Medieval Sourcebook
   http://www.fordham.edu/halsall/sbook.html

The History of the Mayans
   http://www.brownpride.com/history/mayans.html

L'Anse aux Meadows Archeological Site
   http://parkscanada.pch.gc.ca/unesco/MEAD/Mead_e.htm

Vikings in America
   http://www.pitt.edu/~dash/vinland.html

Cahokia Mounds State Historic Site
   http://medicine.wustl.edu/~mckinney/cahokia/cahokia.html

Hopewell Culture National Historic Park
   http://www.nps.gov/hocu/

Chapter Two

COLONIZATION

The creation of English colonies along the coast of North America during the seventeenth century would be stimulated by a variety of motives. The transformation of English agriculture from a manorial system of open-field grain farming to commercial wool production created a surplus of unskilled peasant labor. Religious conflict between Catholics, Anglicans, Puritans, and other Protestant dissenters created a desire for safe havens from persecution. A desire for profits and secure markets would also promote the cause of colonization as new capitalist institutions emerged in England.

England's first attempt to create a colony in North America failed. Sir Walter Raleigh's English settlers quickly alienated the local natives with their constant demands for food. When a second party of settlers was sent to Roanoke Island in 1587, they disappeared without a trace.

In 1607, the Virginia Company of London would finance an expedition that built the settlement of Jamestown on the shores of the James River in modern Virginia. For more than a decade, Jamestown would struggle to survive amid disease, hostile Native Americans, and internal dissent. However, the Virginians would find salvation in the cultivation of tobacco for export to England.

As Virginians began to successfully develop their new cash crop, they would develop a system of servile labor to work their plantations. The English settlers would first turn to the use of indentured servants and later utilize increasing numbers of African slaves to cultivate their crops. Slavery would develop slowly in Virginia, with the first African arrivals being treated as indentured servants. By 1640 black servants were being treated differently than white servants, and in 1661, the Virginia legislature began to institutionalize slavery based on race.

Virginia would soon share the Chesapeake watershed with the colony of Maryland. Created as a religious refuge for English Catholics, the proprietary Calvert family attempted to recreate the feudal society of medieval Britain. The migration of Virginia Puritans to Maryland and the hostility of the Virginia colonial government caused internal conflict within the colony. By the end of the seventeenth century, Protestant settlers so dominated Maryland's colonial government that they passed laws forbidding the open practice of Catholicism within the colony.

The struggle between the Stuart kings and Calvinistic Puritans would dominate the political life of England for much of the seventeenth century. As the titular head of the Church of England, King James I, and later his son, Charles I, would attempt to enforce conformity to the official church of their realm. Their efforts would lead first to a mass migration of Puritans to New England and later to a civil war within England itself.

As early as 1608, Separatists (Pilgrims) would flee to Holland to avoid persecution by the government. Finding Dutch culture foreign to their English sensibilities, they would migrate to America and found the Plymouth colony. Under the inspired leadership of William Bradford, the Pilgrims would survive in the harsh climate of New England but they would not prosper.

A decade after the Pilgrims founded Plymouth, a mass migration of English Puritans to Massachusetts Bay would begin. The Puritan exodus was stimulated by the attempt of King Charles I to introduce greater ceremony into the services of the Anglican Church. Charles also dissolved Parliament and attempted to rule by royal decree.

John Winthrop, the first governor of the colony, led the well-organized colonization of Puritan Massachusetts. The purpose of the migration was to create a perfect Puritan community that would serve as a model for the reformation of English society. The colonial government enforced the Calvinistic teachings of the Puritan church, and little dissent was tolerated. The Puritans of New England also showed little regard for Native Americans, forcing them to concede land whenever English settlers needed it.

Unable to accept the intolerance of Puritan Massachusetts, Roger Williams founded the colony of Rhode Island based upon the notion that church and state should be separate. Williams tolerated a wide variety of denominations within his colony, even if he found them to be personally repugnate. Williams also sought the friendship of Native Americans, gaining him the scorn of many New Englanders.

While Anglicans and Puritans struggled for supremacy in England, a new group of non-conformists would appear to challenge the doctrines of both groups. Known as the Friends or Quakers, the disciples of George Fox would profess a potent blend of social equality and pacifism. In an effort to rid himself of a personal debt and rid England of Quakers, King Charles II would grant William Penn, Jr. a proprietary colony called Pennsylvania, where English Quakers could settle. The abundance of good land and the Quaker practice of religious toleration would soon make Pennsylvania a haven for a number of European ethnic and religious groups.

Greater diversity was added to British North America when the English conquered the Dutch settlements in New York and New Jersey. James, the Duke of York, had little sympathy for representative government, but his departure from the English throne in 1688 would pave the way for a representative assembly in New York.

The Caribbean would influence English colonization of the subtropical regions of South Carolina and Georgia. Many of the early settlers of South Carolina were sugar planters from Barbados. They were well acquainted with slave labor. When South Carolina proved unsuitable for sugar cultivation, the settlers turned to rice as a cash crop. By the end of the seventeenth century, African slaves outnumbered European settlers.

Georgia was founded as a military buffer zone between South Carolina and Spanish Florida. Founder James Oglethorpe attempted to forbid slavery and alcohol within his colony. He also envisioned Georgia as a haven for English debtors. Unfortunately, early Georgians failed to adhere to Oglethorpe's high moral standards.

By the end of the seventeenth century, the English were firmly in control of most of the Atlantic coast of North America. Though many of the initial settlers were social or religious outcasts, they did transplant the English language, culture, and traditions to the New World.

IDENTIFICATION: Briefly describe each term

Sir Walter Raleigh

Roanoke Island

John White

Melungeons

Enclosure

Church of England (Anglican)

Puritan Revolution (English Civil War)

The Glorious Revolution

Mercantilism

Balance of Power

Henry VIII

Virginia Company of London

Jamestown

John Smith

Powhatan

John Rolfe

Tobacco

Indentured servants

House of Burgesses

Royal African Company

Sir William Berkeley

Nathaniel Bacon

Cecilius Calvert, Lord Baltimore

Act of Toleration (1649)

Separatists (Pilgrims)

Mayflower Compact

William Bradford

Puritans

King Charles I (1625-1649)

John Winthrop

General Court

Anne Hutchinson

Roger Williams

Pequot War (1637)

King Phillip (Wamsutta)

Calvinists

Fundamental Orders of Connecticut

Quakers (Friends)

Margaret Fell

George Fox

William Penn

King Charles II (1660-1685)

James, the Duke of York

Iroquois Confederacy

Barbados planters

James Oglethorpe

THINK ABOUT:

1. Had the Protestant Reformation not shattered the religious unity of Europe, the English colonization of the Atlantic coast would have taken a different course. How did religion influence that colonization process?

2. Many groups fled to the English colonies to escape religious persecution. Once established in America, which groups were willing to extend religious toleration to others? Which were not?

===

"OF THE NATURE AND MANNERS OF THE PEOPLE" THE ENGLISH ENCOUNTERED ON ROANOKE ISLAND, By Thomas Hariot

===

The first attempt by the English to plant a permanent settlement on the North American continent occurred on Roanoke Island in 1585. Much of what we know of this first English venture comes from the writings of Oxford scholar Thomas Hariot. He wrote in great detail about the environment and the people of coastal North Carolina.

Of the nature and manners of the people

It resteth I speake a word or two of the naturall inhabitants, their natures and maners, leaving large discourse thereof untill time more convenient hereafter: nowe onely so farresoorth, as that you may know, how that they in respect of troubling our inhabiting and planting, are not to be feared; but that they shall have cause both to feare and love us, that shall inhabite with them.

They are a people clothed with loose mantles made of Deere skins, & aprons of the same rounde about their middles; all els naked; of such a difference of statures only as wee in England; having no edge tooles or weapons of yron or steeele to offend us withall, neither know they how to make any: those weapons y they have, are onlie bowes made of Witch hazel, & arrowes of reeds; flat edged truncheons also of wood about a yard long, neither have they any thing to defed theselves but targets made of barks; and some armours made of stickes wickered together with thread.

Their townes are but small, & neere the sea coast but few, some containing but 10 or 12 houses: some 20 the greatest that we have seene have bene but of 30 houses: if they be walled it is only done with barks of trees made fast to stakes, or els with poles onely fixed upright and close one by another.

31

Their houses are made of small poles made fast at the tops in rounde forme after the maner as is used in many arbories in our gardens of England, in most townes covered with barkes, and in some with artificiall mattes made of long rushes; from the tops of the houses downe to the ground. The length of them is commonly double to the breadth, in some places they are but 12 and 16 yardes long, and in other some wee have seene of foure and twentie.

In some places of the countrey one onely towne belongeth to the government of a *Wiroans* or chiefe Lorde; in other some two or three, in some sixe, eight, & more; the greatest *Wiroans* that yet we had dealing with had but eighteene townes in his government, and able to make not above seven or eight hundred fighting men at the most: The language of every government is different from any other, and the farther they are distant the greater is the difference.

Their maner of warres amongst themselves is either by sudden surprising one an other most comonly about the dawning of the day, or moone light; or els by ambushes, or some suttle devises: Set battels are very rare, except it fall out where there are many trees, where eyther part may have some hope of defence, after the deliverie of every arrow, in leaping behind some or other.

If there fall out any warres between us & them, what their fight is likely to bee, we having advantages against them so many maner of waies, as by our discipline, our strange weapons and devises els; especially by ordinance; great and small, it may be easily imagined; by the experience we have had in some places, the turning up of their heeles against us in running away was their best defence.

In respect of us they are a people poore, and for want of skill and judgement in the knowledge and use of our things, doe esteeme our trifles before thinges of greater value: Notwithstanding in their proper manner considering the want of such meanes as we have, they seeme very ingenious; For although they have no such tooles, nor any such craftes, sciences and artes as wee; yet in those thinges they doe, they shewe excellencie of wit. And by howe much they upon due consideration shall finde our manner of knowledges and craftes to exceede theirs in perfection, and speed for doing or execution, by so much the more is it probable that they shoulde desire our friendships & love, and have the greater respect for pleasing and obeying us. Whereby may bee hoped if meanes of good government bee used, that they may in short time be brought to civilitie, and the imbracing of true religion.

Some religion they have alreadie, which although it be farre from the truth, yet beyng as it is, there is hope it may bee the easier and sooner reformed.

They beleeve that there are many Gods which they call *Montoac*, but of different sortes and degrees; one onely chiefe and great God, which hath bene from all eternitie. Who as they affirme when hee purposed to make the worlde, made first other goddes of a principall order to bee as meanes and instruments to bee used in the creation and government to follow; and after the Sunne, Moone, and Starres, as pettie goddes and the instruments of the other order more prinicpall. First they say were made waters, out of which by the gods was made all diversitie of creatures that are visible or invisible.

For mankind they say a woman was made first, which by the woorking of one of the goddes; conceived and brought foorth children: And in such sort they say they had their beginning.

But how manie yeeres or ages have passed since, they say they can make no relatio, having no letters nor other such meanes as we to keepe recordes of the particularities of times past, but onelie tradition from father to sonne.

They thinke that all the gods are of humane shape, & therfore they represent them by images in the formes of men, which they call *Kewasowok* one alone is called *Kewas*; Them they place in houses appropriate or temples which they call *Machicomuck*; Where they woorship, praie, sing, and make manie times offerings unto them. In some *Machicomuck* we have seene but on *Kewas*, in some two, and in other some three; The common sort thinke them to be also gods.

They beleeve also the immoralitie of the soule, that after this life as soone as the soule is departed from the bodie according to the workes it hath done, it is eyther carried to heaven the habitacle of gods, there to enjoy perpetuall blisse and happinesse, or els to a great pitte or hole, which they thinke to bee in the furthest partes of their part of the worlde towarde the sunne set, there to burne continually: the place they call *Popogusso*.

For the confirmation of this opinion, they tolde mee two stories of two men that had been lately dead and reunited againe, the one happened but few yeres before our comming into the countrey of a wicked man which having beene dead and buried, the next day the earth of the grave beeing seene to move, was taken up againe; Who made declaration where his soule had beene, that is to saie very neere entring into *Popogusso*, had not one of the gods saved him & gave him leave to returne againe, and teach his friends what the should doe to avoid that terrible place of torment.

The other happened in the same yeere wee were there, but in a towne that was threescore miles from us, and it was tolde mee for straunge newes that one beeing dead, buried and taken up againe as the first, shewed that although his bodie had lien dead in the grave, yet his soule was alive, and had travailed farre in a long broade waie, on both sides whereof grewe most delicate and pleasaunt trees, bearing more rare and exellent fruites then ever hee had seene before or was able to expresse, and at length came to most brave and faire houses, neere which hee met his father, that had beene dead before, who gave him great charge to goe backe againe and shew his friendes what good they were to doe to enjoy the pleasures of that place, which when he had done he should after come againe.

What subtilty soever be in the *Wiroances* and Priestes, this opionion worketh so much in manie of the common and simple sort of people that it maketh them have great respect to their Governours, and also great care what they do, to avoid torment after death, and to enjoy blisse; although notwithstanding there is punishment ordained for malefactours, as stealers, whoremoongers, and other sortes of wicked doers; some punished with death, some with forfeitures, some with beating, according to the greatnes of the factes.

And this is the summe of their religio, which I learned by having special familiarity with some of their priestes. Wherein they were not so sure grounded, nor gave such credite to their traditions and stories but through conversing with us they were brought into great doubts of their owne, and no small admiration of ours, with earnest desire in many, to learne more than we had meanes for want of perfect utterance in their language to expresse.

Most thinges they sawe with us, as Mathematicall instruments, sea compasses, the vertue of the loadstone in drawing yron, a perspective glasse whereby was shewed manie strange fightes, burning glasses, wildefire woorkes, gunnes, bookes, writing and reading, spring clocks that seeme to goe of themselves, and manie other thinges that wee had, were so straunge unto them, and so farre exceeded their capacities to comprehend the reason and meanes how they should be made and done, that they thought they were rather the works of gods then of men, or at the leastwise they had bin given and taught us of the gods. Which made manie of them to have such opinion of us, as that if they knew not the trueth of god and religion already, it was rather to be had from us, whom God so specially loved then from a people that were so simple, as they found themselves to be in comparison of us. Whereupon greater credite was given unto that we spake of concerning such matters.

Source: *A Brief and True Report of the New Found Land of Virginia*, by Thomas Hariot (London, 1588).

HOW WELL DID YOU UNDERSTAND THIS SELECTION?

1. Why did Thomas Hariot describe the natives of Roanoke Island as being poor?

2. Discuss the religion of the Native Americans on Roanoke Island as described by Thomas Hariot.

"POWHATAN INDIAN LIFEWAYS" by Lee Cotton, Park Ranger, Colonial National Historical Park

As John Smith and his fellow Englishmen paddled ashore on the coast of Virginia in 1607, they ventured into the territory of a mighty ruler. The great Powhatan controlled many villages in the Tidewater, and he was less than pleased by the arrival of these European invaders. Though the English felt superior to Powhatan and his people, they were forced to recognize the power of his empire.

When the English began exploring and, later, colonizing North America, they were both aware of and fascinated by the native people they encountered. Fortunately for students of history, some of these explorers and settlers chose to commit their observations to paper. Although archeology and oral traditions play a role in our appreciation of the largely-vanished culture of the Powhatan Indians in Virginia, it is the accounts of such Englishmen as John Smith, William Strachey, Robert Beverley, and George Percy which provide the detail of the everyday life of these people.

Even thought the English viewed the Powhatan Indian culture as savage and primitive, we can still utilize the facts and details presented by one group of people commenting on and describing another. Since the English found the Powhatans so different from themselves, they took great pains at recording those differences for the education of their contemporaries.

The 104 Englishmen who landed at Jamestown on May 13, 1607 chose that settlement site partially because no one else was presently occupying the small peninsula, an unhealthy, highly defensible area. This lack of inhabitants was hardly the case for most of Tidewater Virginia, as the English were soon to discover. Although it is difficult to estimate, modern historians number the native population of 1607 Tidewater Virginia at 13,000 to 14,000. Powhatan settlements were concentrated along the rivers, which provided both food and transportation; the folk who inhabited them spoke a now-extinct form of Algonquian, a language which was common with many native peoples from present-day New York south to Florida.

The undisputed ruler of Tidewater Virginia was Wahunsonacock, usually referred to by this title as "Powhatan." John Smith describes Powhatan as *"a tall well proportioned man, with a sower look, his head somewhat gray, his beard so thinne, that it seemeth none at all, his age* (as of 1608) *neare sixtie, of a very able and hardy body to endure any labour."*

Powhatan had inherited six tribes located not far from present-day Richmond. By 1607, he had added considerably to his domain which, at its peak, numbered over 30 tribes. Each tribe was governed by a werowance, a chief who owed allegiance and tribute Powhatan. Although Powhatan maintained residences amongst all the tribes, his usual dwelling-place was a Werowocomoco, on the north side of the York River.

In addition to his councilors, whom he kept about him always, Powhatan also had an extensive family. Because of the large amounts of tribute collected (estimated by one settler as eight parts out of ten of all that his people produced) Powhatan could support over a hundred wives and the resulting offspring, the most famous of whom was Matoaka, better known by her nickname "Pocahontas."

Powhatan's people lived in villages, which could number as many as one hundred homes. Some villages were protected by wooden palisades; each house boasted an extensive and carefully-tended garden, in which was sown such staples as corn, beans, peas, squash, pumpkin, sunflowers and maypops (passionflower). Tobacco, primarily used for ceremonial purposes, was grown apart from the rest of the crops.

Although the gardens were an important food source, the Powhatans' diet was far more extensive. John Smith remarked that for the bulk of the year, Powhatans relied on other sources of food. The waterways afforded a rich diet of fish and shellfish and the woods yielded nuts, fruits and berries. Since the dog was the only animal domesticated by the Powhatans, hunting was an important way to supplement the diet, and was a task relegated to the men of the tribe. At a very young age, a boy was taught the use of the bow. Rather than a recreational activity for the wealthy, as hunting was perceived by the English, Powhatans considered it a very serious business, an important way of securing food and clothing.

The hard work of Powhatan women was more often remarked upon by the English. Whether she was gathering wood, making pottery, preparing food, dressing hides, caring for the garden or making clothing, a Powhatan woman was seldom at rest.

Some of the most detailed descriptions of Powhatan people concerns their appearance. According to John Smith, the native Virginians were "Generally tall and straight," an observation confirmed by archeological analysis, which estimates that the average Powhatan stood at about six feet. William Strachey, another 17th-centruy author, recorded that Powhatans were "Generally of a cullour brown or rather tawny."

Costume varied according to sex, age and status. The most common article of apparel for men was a breech-clout of skin worn between the thighs. According to Smith, "The common sort have scarce to cover their nakedness but with grasse, the leaves of trees, or such like… The better sort use large mantels of deare skins not much different from the Irish mantels." A man of high status might wear a shirt-like garment made of fringed deerskin or a mantle of turkey feathers. The hair was shaven from the right side of the head (to reduce the risk of entanglement in the hunter's bowstring); the hair on the other side of the head was allowed to grow long and often pulled into a knot and decorated with everything from shells to the dead hand of an enemy. Men used body paint in preparation for war or games.

Werowances (chiefs) wore fine clothes and many ornaments of pearl, rare shell beads and copper, the precious metal of the Powhatans. George Percy described the headdress of one werowance: "a crown of deares haire colloured red, in fashion of a rose fasted about his knot of haire, and a great plate of copper on the other side of his head; with two long feathers in fashion of a pair of horns placed in the midst of his Crowne."

In his History and Present State of Virginia (1705), colonist Robert Beverley opined that Powhatan Indian "women are generally beautiful, possessing an uncommon delicacy of shape and features." The skirt was the ubiquitous garment for women; those of higher-status swathed themselves in fringed deerskin. The hair of a married woman was worn long and plaited in the back; a young girl had her head on the front and sides shaven close, with the rest of the hair growing long and braided down the back.

George Strachey remarked at length on the use of tattooed decorations by the Powhatan Indian women, commenting that they "have their armes, breasts, thighes, shoulders, and faces, cuningly ymbrodered with divers workes, for pouncing and searing their skyns with a kind of instrument heated in the fier. They figure therein flowers and fruits of sondry lively kinds, as also snakes, serpents."

Although early interaction between the English and Powhatans was sometimes violent and exploitive on both sides, leaders of both peoples realized the mutual benefit which could be derived from peaceful relations. Powhatan craved the trade goods brought by the English, which would give him increased status, make his peoples' lives easier and also help him to expand his empire to the west. The English needed food, allies and knowledgeable guides to help them locate raw materials, precious metals and the much-sought trade route to the Far East. The marriage of Powhatan's favorite daughter Pocahontas to settler John Rolfe in 1614 ensured a few peaceful years between the Powhatans and the English.

This brief time of peace ended in 1617 with the death of Pocahontas during a trip to England and, the next year, of her father. Opitchapan, Powhatan's brother, served briefly as chief, and then retired in favor of Opechancanough, the powerful and aggressive werowance whose land centered around present-day West Point. Opechancanough resented the English, and, although Powhatan had been assured the Jamestown settlement was merely a temporary one, the new chief saw all too clearly that the English were in Virginia to stay. Thanks to the introduction of a successful strain of tobacco by John Rolfe, the colonists had a way to achieve a profit and, consequently, the need for greater and greater tracts of land on which to grow their crop.

On March 22, 1622, Opechancanough's carefully-orchestrated plan to dismay and perhaps even rout his enemy was executed by his warriors throughout the small English settlements in Virginia. Although some areas, including Jamestown, escaped unscathed, within a few hours as many as 400 English settlers had lost their lives and the colony had received a near-fatal blow.

The surviving settlers' reaction to the Powhatan uprising was retaliation, and the English, better armed and organized than the Powhatans, set to with a vengeance. The Virginia Company instructed the settlers to wage a total war against the Powhatan people, doing whatever it took to subdue them utterly. For over a decade, the English killed men and women, captured children and systematically razed villages, seizing or destroying crops.

After the uprising, the colonists recovered and expanded their territory, even as the Powhatan empire declined both in power and population. Even so, in 1644, Opechancanough rallied his small forces to make a final attempt at routing the English from his people's land. The attack, launched on April 17, 1644, resulted in the death of hundreds of colonists, but, like the attempt made 22 years earlier, did not achieve its objective. The English captured Opechancanough, by then an old and feeble man, and brought him to Jamestown, where he was shot in the back by a soldier against orders.

As in 1622, the English retaliated. Finally, in 1646 and 1647, treaties were made with Opechancanough's successor which severely restricted the Powhatan people's territory and confined them to small reservations. Tribute was to be offered to the English king of "Twenty beaver skins att the going away of geese yearely." The Powhatan's land was further reduced in a treaty of 1677.

By 1669, the population of Powhatan Indians in Tidewater Virginia had dropped to about 1,800 and by 1722, many of the tribes comprising the empire of Chief Powhatan were reported extinct. Several tribes lost their reservations and some opted to blend into the colonial scene as best they could. By the beginning of the 20th century, only the Pamunkey and Mattaponi peoples retained their reservations.

Today, the Pamunkey and Mattaponi reservations, located near West Point, have endured as two of the oldest in the United States. Many Virginia Indians were encouraged by those tribes' example of courage and determination, and, in the early 20th century, began to reorganize their tribes. Crafts, dances, oral tradition and other almost-forgotten aspects of the Powhatan Indian culture were shared with other Virginians. In 1983, the Virginia Council on Indians was established, consisting of nine tribal representatives and three at-large members. In the same session of the General Assembly, six tribes were officially recognized; by 1990, two more tribes were given official status. Today, the Virginia Indian community is a strong one which takes pride in its heritage and responsibility for teaching others about its unique culture, which impacts on the life of every American today.

Bibliography
  Egloff, Keith and Deborah Woodward. *First People: The Early Indians of Virginia.* Charlottesville: The University Press of Virginia, 1992.
  McCary, Ben C. *Indians in Seventeenth-Century Virginia.* Charlottesville: The University Press of Virginia. 1957.
  Rountree, Helen C. *The Powhatan Indians of Virginia.* Norman: University of Oklahoma Press, 1989.

Source: http://www.nps.gov/colo/Jthanout/Indianlife.html

HOW WELL DID YOU UNDERSTAND THIS SELECTION?

1.   What did the English record regarding their observations of Native American women and their role within the Powhatan Confederation?

2.   Discuss the causes and consequences of Opechancanough's wars against the English colonists.

"SOME ACCOUNT OF THE PROVINCE OF PENNSYLVANIA" by William Penn, Jr.

In 1681, English King Charles II granted William Penn, Jr. a charter for the colony of Pennsylvania. Penn, a devote Quaker, hoped to create a social environment based upon the principles of peace and toleration inherent in the beliefs of his denomination. Hoping to appeal to people weary of religious strife and government oppression, Penn wrote the following tract outlining the advantages of his colony.

Since (by the good providence of God) a country in America is fallen to my lot, I thought it not less my duty than my honest interest to give some public notice of it to the world, that those of our own, or other nations, that are inclined to transport themselves or families beyond the seas, may find another country added to their choice; that if they shall happen to like the *places, conditions* and *constitutions* (so far as the present infancy of things will allow us any prospect), they may, if they please, fix with me in the *province* hereafter described. But before I come to treat of my particular concernment, I shall take leave to say something of the benefit of *plantations* or *colonies* in general, to obviate a common objection.

Colonies, then, are the seeds of nations begun and nourished by the care of wise and populous Countries, as conceiving them best for the increase of human stock, and beneficial for commerce.

Some of the wisest men in history have justly taken their fame from this design and service. We read the reputation given on this account to *Moses*, *Joshua* and *Caleb* in Scripture records; . . . Nor is the *Roman* account wanting of instances to the credit of that people . . . [who] not only reduced, but moralized the manners of the nations they Subjected, so that they may have been rather said to conquer their barbarity than them.

Nor did any of these ever dream it was the way of decreasing their people or wealth. For the cause of the decay of any of those states or empires was not their plantations, but their luxury *and corruption of manners*. For when they grew to neglect their ancient discipline that maintained and rewarded virtue and industry, and addicted themselves to *pleasure* and *effeminacy*, they debased their spirits and debauched their morals, from whence ruin did never fail to follow to any people. With justice, therefore, I deny the vulgar opinion against *plantations, that they weaken* England. They have manifestly enriched and so strengthened her, which I briefly evidenced thus:

1st. Those that go into a foreign *plantation*, their industry there is worth more than if they stayed at home, the product of their labor being in commodities of a superior nature to those of this country. For instance, what is an improved acre in *Jamaica* or *Barbados* worth to an improved acre in England? We know it is three times the value, and the product of it comes for England, and is usually paid for in *English growth* and *manufacture*. . . .

2dly. More being produced and imported than we can spend here, we export it to other countries in *Europe*, which brings in money or the growth of those countries, which is the same thing. And this is [to] the advantage of the English merchants and seamen.

3dly. Such as could not only not *marry* here, but hardly live and allow themselves clothes, do marry there, and bestow thrice more in all necessaries and conveniences (and not a little in ornamental things, too) for themselves, their wives, and children, both as to apparel and household Stuff, which coming out of *England, I say it is impossible that England should not be a considerable gainer.*

4thly. But let it be considered *that the plantations employ many hundreds of shipping and many thousands of seamen*, which must be in diverse respects an advantage to England, being an island, and by nature fitted for navigation above any country in *Europe*. . . .

I. Something of the Place. . . .

II. The Constitutions.

For the Constitution of the country, the patent shows, first, that the people and governor have a legislative power, so that no law can be made, nor money raised, but by the people's consent.

2dly. That the rights and freedoms of *England (the best and largest in* Europe) shall be in force there.

3dly. That making no law against allegiance (*which should we, it were by the law of* England, *void of itself that moment*) we may enact what laws we please for the good prosperity and security of the said province.

4thly. That so soon as any are engaged with me, we shall begin a *scheme* or draft together such as shall give ample testimony of my sincere inclinations to encourage planters, and settle a free, just and industrious colony there.

III. The Conditions.

My conditions will relate to three sorts of people: 1st, those that will *buy*; 2dly, those that take up land upon *rent*; 3dly, servants. To the first, the shares I sell shall be certain as to number of acres; that is to say, every one shall contain five thousand acres, free from any *Indian* encumbrance, the price f100, and for the quitrent but one *English* shilling or the value of it yearly for a hundred acres; and the said quitrent not to begin to be paid till *1684*. To the second sort, that take up land upon rent, they shall have liberty so to do, paying yearly *one penny* pre acre, not exceeding two hundred acres. To the third sort, to wit, *servants* that are carried over, fifty acres shall be allowed to the master for every head, and fifty acres to every servant when their time is expired. . . .

IV. These persons that Providence seems to have most fitted for plantations are,

1ˢᵗ. Industrious *husbandmen* and *day laborers*, that are able (with extreme labor) to maintain their families and portion their children.

2dly. Laborious *handicrafts*, especially *carpenters, masons, smiths, weavers, tailors, tanners, shoemakers, shipwrights*, etc., where they may be spared or are low in the world. And as they shall want no encouragement, so their labor is worth more there than here, and there provision cheaper.

3dly. A plantation seems a fit place for those *ingenious spirits* that being low in the world, are much clogged and oppressed about a livelihood. For the means of subsisting being easy there, they may have time and opportunity to gratify their inclinations, and thereby improve science and help nurseries of people.

4thly. A fourth sort of men to whom a *plantation* would be proper, takes in those that are *younger brothers* of small inheritances; yet because they would live in sight of their kindred in some proportion to their quality, and can't do it without a labor that looks like *farming*, their condition is too strait for them; and if married, their children are too numerous for the estate, and are frequently bred up to no trades, but are a kind of *hangers on or retainers to the elder brothers' table and charity*; which is a mischief, as in itself to be lamented, so here to be remedied. For land they have for next to nothing, which with moderate labor produces plenty of all things necessary for life and such an increase as by traffic may supply them with all conveniences.

Lastly, there are another sort of persons, not only fit for but necessary in *plantations*, and that is, *men of universal spirits* that have an eye to the good of posterity, and that both understand and delight to promote good discipline and just government among a plain and well intending people. Such persons may find *room in colonies for their good counsel and contrivance*, who are shut out from being much use or service to great nations under settled customs. These men deserve much esteem, and would be hearkened to. Doubtless it was this (*as I observed before*) that put some of the famous *Greeks* and *Romans* upon transplanting and regulating colonies of people in diverse parts of the world, whose names, for giving so great proof of their wisdom, virtue, labor and constancy, are with justice honorably delivered down by story to the praise of our own times; though the world, after all its higher pretenses of religion, barbarously errs from their excellent example.

Source: William Penn, "Some Account of the Province of Pennsylvania ..." (London, 1681).

HOW WELL DID YOU UNDERSTAND THIS SELECTION?

1. In Penn's view, how did colonies benefit the mother country?

2. What type of people did Penn hope to attract to his colony?

"THE INDISPENSABLE ROLE OF WOMEN IN VIRGINIA" by Sandy Groves, Park Ranger, Colonial National Historical Park

Historians have long neglected the role of women in the formation of colonial communities. Though the first English colonists in Virginia were exclusively male, they were soon joined by English women. By 1620, significant numbers of English women began to arrive in the colony, helping to assure its success.

"...the plantation can never florish till families be planted and the respect of wives and children fix the people on the soil."

Sir Edwin Sandys, Treasurer
Virginia Company of London, 1620

THE LURE OF VIRGINIA: GOD, GLORY, AND GOLD. These were the forces that lured the first English settlers in 1606 to the new and untamed wilderness of Virginia. They carried with them the Church of England and the hopes to convert the Native Americans to Protestant Christianity. They wanted to establish an English hold on the New World and exploit its resources for use in the mother country. Some desired to find its fabled gold and riches and others longed to discover a northwest passage to the treasures of the Orient.

INITIAL LACK OF WOMEN: The settlers were directed by the Virginia Company of London, a joint-stock commercial organization. The company's charter provided the rights of trade, exploration and settlement in Virginia. The first settlers that established Jamestown in 1607 were all male. Although some, like historian, Alf J. Mapp Jr. believe that "...it was thought that women had no place in the grim and often grisly business of subduing a continent..." the omission of women in the first group of settlers may simply mean that they were not, as yet, necessary.

REASONS BEHIND DELAY: The company's first priority in Virginia was possibly to build an outpost, explore and determine the best use of Virginia's resources for commercial profits. The exclusion of women in the first venture supports the possibility that it was an exploratory expedition rather than a colonizing effort. According to historian Philip A. Bruce, it is possible that had colonization not been required to achieve their commercial goals, the company might have delayed sending permanent settlers for a number of years.

ESTABLISHING PERMANENCY: Once the commercial resources were discovered, the company's revenues would continue only if the outpost became permanent. For Jamestown to survive, many unstable conditions had to be overcome.

1. A clash of cultures existed between the Englishmen and the Native Americans with whom they soon found the need to trade as well as to Christianize.

2. Settlers were unprepared for the rugged frontier life in a wilderness.

3. Many settlers intended to remain in Virginia only long enough to make their fortune and then return home to England.

WOMEN'S INDISPENSABLE ROLE: Providing the stability needed for Jamestown's survival was the indispensable role played by Virginia women. Their initial arrival in 1608 and throughout the next few years contributed greatly to Jamestown's ultimate success. Lord Bacon, a member of His Majesty's Council for Virginia, stated about 1620 that "When a plantation grows to strength, then it is time to plant with women as well as with men; that the plantation may spread into generations, and not be ever pieced from without."

CONTRIBUTIONS OF EARLY VIRGINIA WOMEN: The first woman to foster stability in Jamestown was not an English woman but a native Virginian. **Pocahontas**, the daughter of Chief Powhatan, was among the first Native Americans to bring food to the early settlers. She was eventually educated and baptized in the English Religion and in 1614 married settler John Rolfe. This early Virginia woman helped create the "Peace of Pocahontas," which for several years, appeased the clash between the two cultures.

One of the first English women to arrive and help provide a home life in the rugged Virginia wilderness was young **Anne Burras**. Anne was the personal maid of Mistress Forrest who came to Jamestown in 1608 to join her husband. Although the fate of Mistress Forrest remains uncertain, that of Anne Burras is well known. Her marriage to carpenter John Laydon three months after her arrival became the first Jamestown wedding. While Jamestown fought to become a permanent settlement, Anne and John began a struggle to raise a family of four daughters in the new Virginia wilderness. Certainly, Anne and her family began the stabilization process which would eventually spur the colony's growth.

Another young woman, **Temperance Flowerdew**, arrived with 400 ill-fated settlers in the fall of 1609. The following winter, dubbed the "Starving Time," saw over 80 percent of Jamestown succumb to sickness, disease and starvation. Temperance survived this season of hardship but soon returned to England. By 1619, Temperance returned to Jamestown with her new husband, Governor George Yeardley. After his death in 1627, she married Governor Francis West and remained in Virginia until her death in 1628. Her many years in Virginia as a wife and mother helped fill the gap in Jamestown's early family life.

In July 1619, settlers were granted acres of land dependent on the time and situation of their arrival. This was the beginning of private property for Virginia men. These men, however, asked that land also be allotted for their wives who were just as deserving "…because that in a newe plantation it is not knowen whether man or woman be the most necessary."

The Virginia Company of London seemed to agree that women were indeed quite necessary. They hoped to anchor their discontented bachelors to the soil of Virginia by using women as a stabilizing factor. They ordered in 1619 that "…a fit hundredth might be sent of women, maids young and uncorrupt, to make wives to the inhabitants and by that means to make the men there more settled and less movable…" Ninety arrived in 1620 and the company records reported in May of 1622 that, "57 young maids have been sent to make wives for the planters, divers of which were well married before the coming away of the ships."

Jamestown would not have survived as a permanent settlement without the daring women who were willing to leave behind their English homes and face the challenges of a strange new land. These women created a sense of stability in the untamed wilderness of Virginia. They helped the settlers see Virginia not just as a temporary place for profit or adventure, but as a country in which to forge a new home.

Bibliography

Billings, Waren. *The Old dominion in the 17ᵗʰ Century;* Brown, Alexander. *The Genesis of the U.S.;* Bruse, Philip. *History of Virginia Colonial Period 1607-1763;* Ibid., *Social Life of Virginia in the 17ᵗʰ Century;* Jester, Annie. *Domestic Life in Virginia in the 17ᵗʰ Century;* Lebsock, Suzanne. *A Share of Honour: Virginia Women 1600-1945;* Mapp, Alf Jr.. *The Virginia Experiment: 1607-1781* Morton, Richard. *Colonial Virginia;* Phillips, Leon. *First Lady of America, Pocahontas;* Spruill, Julia. *Women's Life and Work in the Southern Colonies;* Tate, Thad and Ammerman, David. *The Chesapeake in the 17ᵗʰ Century: Essays on Anglo-American Society;* Turman, Nora. *George Yeardley;* Virginia Company. *Records of the Virginia Company, I & II*

Source: http://www.nps.gov/colo/Jthanout/Women.html

HOW WELL DID YOU UNDERSTAND THIS SELECTION?

1. Who were the first known English women to settle at Jamestown and what were their stations in life?

2. Why did the Virginia Company of London promote the migration of women to Jamestown after 1619?

Modern students of the period often view the Puritans of New England as stoic and determined settlers. Apparently at least one was willing to record his disappointment in his new home. The author of the following poem demonstrates that Puritans were fully capable of displaying humor and discontent.

New England's annoyances[1] you that would know them,
Pray ponder these verses which briefly do show them.
The place where we live is a wilderness wood,
Where grass is much wanting that's fruitful and good.

From the end of November till three months are gone,
The ground is all frozen as hard as a stone.
Our mountains and hills and our valleys below
Being commonly covered with ice and with snow.
And when the northwest wind with violence blows,
Then every man pulls his cap over his nose:
But if any's so hardy and will it withstand,
He forfeits a finger, a foot, or a hand.

But when the spring opens, we then take the hoe
And make the ground ready to plant and to sow;
Our corn being planted and seed being sown,
The worms destroy much before it has grown.

And while it is growing some spoil there is made
By birds and by squirrels that pluck up the blade.
And when it is come to full corn in the ear,
It is often destroyed by racoon and by deer.

And now our apparel begins to grow thin,
And wool is much wanted to card and to spin.
If we get a garment to cover without,
Our other ingarments are clout upon clout.[2]

Our clothes we brought with us are apt to be torn,
They need to be clouted before they are worn.
But clouting our garments doth injure us nothing:
Clouts double are warmer then single whole clothing.

If fresh meat be wanting to fill up our dish,
We have carrots and pumpkins and turnips and fish;
And if there's a mind for a delicate dish,
We haste to the clam banks and take that we wish.

Stead of pottage and puddings and custards and pies,
Our turnips and parsnips are common supplies.
We have pumpkins at morning and pumpkins at noon,
If it was not for pumpkins, we should be undone.
(If barley be wanting to make into malt,
We must be contented and think it no fault;
For we can make liquor to sweeten our lips
Of pumpkins and parsnips and walnut tree chips.)

And of our green cornstalks we make our best beer,
We put in it barrels to drink all the year.
Yet I am as healthy, I verily think,
Who make the spring water my commonest drink.

Our money's soon counted, for we have just none,
All that we brought with us is wasted and gone.
We buy and sell nothing but upon exchange,
Which makes all our dealings uncertain and strange.

And we have a cov-nant one with another
Which makes a division 'twixt brother and brother:
For some are rejected and others made saints,
Of those that are equal in virtues and wants.

For such like annoyances we've many mad fellows
Find fault with our apples before they are mellow,
And they are for England, they will not stay here,
But meet with a lion in shunning a bear.

Now while such are going, let others be coming,
Whilst liquor is boiling, it must have a scumming.
And I will not blame them, for birds of a feather
Are choosing their fellows by flocking together.

But you whom the Lord intends hither to bring
Forsake not the honey for fear of a sting:
But bring both a quiet and contented mind,
And all needful blessings you surely shall find.

Source: Anonymous, "New England's Annoyances," *Laughter in the Wilderness: Early American Humor to 1783*, edited by W. Howland Kenney (Kent, Ohio: Kent State Press, 1976), pp.34-36.

HOW WELL DID YOU UNDERSTAND THIS SELECTION?

1. Explain the hardships suffered by New England farmers as expressed in this poem?

2. Does the author of this poem fit the stereotype of the stoic New England Puritan?

Another facet of life in the new land was the aspect of slavery. Indentured servants in the South could not keep up with the demand for labor and were difficult to control. The falling price of tobacco forced planters to look for a more economical source of labor. The status of the first slaves arriving in 1619 was not completely defined. As the use of slaves continued to grow, the government in Virginia attempted to define the institution of slavery and identify how it was different from servitude. The following is from the Virginia Statues at Large.

December 1662 - 14th Charles II, 2;170, Act XII.
WHEREAS some doubts have arisen whether children got by any Englishman upon a negro woman should be slave or ffree, *Be it therefore enacted and declared by this present grand assembly,* that all children borne in this country shalbe held in bond or free according to the condition of the mother, *And* that if any christian shall commit ffornication with a negro man or woman, hee or shee so offending shall pay double the ffines imposed by the former act.

September 1667 - 19th Charles II, ACT III 2:260.
WHEREAS some doubts have risen whether children that are slaves by birth, and by the charity and piety of their owners made pertakers of the blessed sacrament of baptisme, should by vertue of their baptisme be made free. *It is enacted and declared by this grand assembly, and the authority thereof,* that the conferring of baptisme doth not alter the condition of the person as to his bondage or freedome; that diverse masters, ffreed from this doublt, may more carefully endevor the propagation of christianity by permitting children, though slaves, or those of growth if capable to be admitted to that sacrament.

June 1680 - 32nd Charles II, Act X, 2:481
WHERAS the frequent meeting of considerable numbers of negro slaves under pretence of feasts and burialls is judged of dangerous consequence; for prevention whereof for the future, *Bee it enacted by the kings most excellent majesties by and with the consent of the generall assembly, and it is hereby enacted by the authority aforesaid,* that from and after the publication of this law, it shall not be laefull for any negroe or other slave to carry or arme hemselfe with any club, staffe, gunn, sword or any other weapon of defence or offence, not to goe or depart from of his masters ground without a certificate from his master, mistris or overseer, and such permission not be be granted but on perticuler and necessary occasions; and every negroe or slave so offending not haveing a certificate as aforesaid shalbe sent to the next constable, who is hereby enjoyned and required to give the said negroe twenty lashes on his bare back well layd on, and soe sent home to his said master, mistris or overseer. *And it is further enacted by the authority aforesaid* that if any negroe or other slave shall presume or lift up his hand in opposition against any christian, shall for every such offense, upon due proofe made thereof by the oath of the party before a magistrate, have and receive thirty lashed on his bare back well laid on. *And it is hereby further enacted by the authority aforesaid* that if any negroe or other slave shall absent himself form his masters service and lye hid and luking in obscure places, comitting injuries to the inhabitants, and shall resist any person or persons that shalby any lawful authority by imployed to apprehend and take the saod negroe, that then in case of such resistance, it shalbe lawful for such person or persons to kill the said negroe, or slave soe lying out and resisting, and that this law be once every six months published at the respective county courts and parish churches within this colony.

VII. *And also be it enacted, by the authority aforesaid, and it is hereby enacted,* That all masters and owners of servants, shall find and provide for their servants, wholesome and competent diet, clothing, and lodging, by the discretion of the county court; and shall not, at any time, give immoderate correction; neither shall, at any time, whip a christian white servant nakerd, without an order from a justice of the peace;

XI. And for a further christian care and usuage of all christian servants, *Be it also enacted by the authority aforesaid, and it is hereby enacted,* That no negroes, mulattos, or Indians, although christians, of Jew of Moors, Mahometans, or other infifels, shall, at any time, purchase any christian servant, not any other, except of their own complexion, or such as are declared slaves by this act; shall, notwithstanding, purchase any christian white servant, the said servant shall, *ipso facto*, become free and acuqit from any service then due, and shall be so held, deemed, and taken; And if any person, having such christian servant, shall intermarry with any such negro, mulatto, or Indian, Jew, Moor, Mahametan, or other infidel, every christian white servant of every such person so intermarrying, shall *ipso facto*, became free and acquit from any service then due to such master or mistress so intermarrying, as aforesaid.

XIX. And for a further prevention of that abominable mixture and spurious issue, which hereafter may increase in this her majesty's colony and dominion, as well by English, and other white men and women intermarrying with negros or mulattos, as by their unlawful coition with them. *Be it enacted, by the authority aforesaid, and it is hereby enacted*, That whatsoever English, or other white man or woman, being free, shall intemarry with a negro or mulatto man or woman, bond or free, shall, by judgement of the county court, be committed to prison, and there remain, during the space of six months, without bail or mainprize; and shall forfeit and pay ten pounds current money of Virginia, to the use of the parish, as aforesaid.

XXI. And because poor people may not be destitute of emploiement, upon suspicion of being servants, and servants also kept form running away, *Be it enacted, by the authority aforesaid, and it is hereby enacted*, That every servant, when his or her time of service shall be expired, shall repair to the court of the county where he or she served the last of his or her time, and from there, upon sufficient testimony, have his or her freedom entered; and a certificate thereof from the clerk of the said court, shall be sufficient to suthorise any person to entertain or hire such servant, without any danger of this law.

XXXII. *And also be it enacted, by the authority aforesaid, and it is hereby enacted*, That no master, mistress, or overseer of a family, shall knowingly permit any slave, not belonging to him or her, to be and remain upon his or her plantation, above four hours at any one time, without the leave of such slave's master, mistress, or overseer, on penalty of one hundred and fifty pounds of tobacco to the informer; cognizab; e by a justice of the peace of the country wherein such offence shall be committed.

XXXIV. And if any slave resist his master, or owner, or other person, by his or her order, correcting such slave, and shall happen to be killed in such correction, it shall not be accounted felony; but the master, owner, and every such person so giving correction, shall be free and acquit of all punishment for the same, as if such accident had never happened: And also, if any negro, mulatto, or Indian, bond or free, shall at any time, lift his or her hand, in opposition against any christian, not being negro, mulatto, or Indian, he or she so offending, shall, for every such offence, proved by the oath of the party, reeive on his or her bare back, thirty lashes, well laid on; cognizable by a justice of the peace for that county wherein such ofence shall be committed.

XXXVI. *And also it is enacted and declared*, That baptism of slaves doth not exempt them from bondage; and that all children shall be bond or free, according to the condition of their mothers, and the particular directions of this act.

XXXVII. And whereas, many times, slaves run away and lie out, hid and lurking in swamps, woods, and other obscure places, killing hogs, and committing other injuries to the inhabitants of this her majesty's colony and dominion, *Be it therefore enacted, by the authority aforesaid, and it is hereby enacted*, That in all such cases, upon intelligence given of any slaves laying out, as aforesaid, any two justices (*Quorum unus*) of the peace of the county wherein such slave is supposed to lurk or do mischief, shall be and are impowered and required to isssue proclamation against all such slaves, reciting their names, and owners names, if they are known...And in case any slave, against whom proclamation hath been thus issued, and once published at any church or chapel aforesaid, stay out, and do not immediately return home, it shall be lawful for any person or persons whatsoever, to kill and destroy such slaves by such ways and means as he, she, or they shall think fit, without accusation or impeachment of any crime for the same: And if any slave, that hath run away and lain out as aforesaid, shall be apprehended by the sheriff, or any other person, upon the application of the owner of the said slave, it shall and may be lawful for the county court, to order such punishment to the said slave, either my dismembring, or any other way, not touching his life, as they in their discretion shall think fit, for the reclaiming any such incorrigible slave, and terrifying others from the like practices.

XXXVIII. *Provided always, and it is further enacted*, That for every slave killed, in pursuance of this act, be put to death by law, the master or owner of such slave shall be paid by the public:

XXXIX. And to the end the true value of every slave killed, or put to death, as aforesaid, may be the better known; and by that means, the assembly the better enable to make a suitable allowance thereupon, *Be it enacted*, That upon application of the master or owner of any such slave, to the court appointed for the proof of public claims, the said court shall value the slave in money, and the clerk of the court shall return a certificate thereof to the assembly, with the rest of the public claims.

Source: Virginia Slavery Statues

HOW WELL DID YOU UNDERSTAND THIS SELECTION?

1. What laws provide evidence of problems with runaways and slaves?

2. How did the laws treat intermarriage between white and black?

3. What were some differences in the treatment of servants compared to the treatment of slaves?

4. How were the deaths of slaves treated, both in terms of punishment for those who killed them and in terms of reimbursement to the owner for the loss of the slave?

"THE TRYAL OF BRIDGET BISHOP, ALIAS OLIVER, AT THE COURT OF OYER AND TERMINER, HELD AT SALEM, JUNE 2, 1692."

Cotton Mather can be characterized as one of the best minds of colonial Massachusetts. Yet this minister and scholar firmly believed in witchcraft, and he was convinced that those convicted during the Salem trial in 1692 were truly guilty. In order to justify the executions, he published accounts of the trials and noted the evidence used against the convicted witches.

I. She was Indicted for Bewitching of several Persons in the Neighbourhood, the Indictment being drawn up, according to the *Form* in such Cases usual. And pleading, *Not Guilty*, there were brought in several persons, who had long undergone many kinds of Miseries, which were preternaturally inflicted, and generally ascribed unto an *horrible Witchcraft*. There was little occasion to prove the *Witchcraft*, it being evident and notorious to all beholders.

Now to fix the *Witchcraft* on the Prisoner at the Bar, the first thing used, was the Testimony of the *Bewitched*; whereof several testifi'd, That the *Shape* of the Prisoner did oftentimes very grievously Pinch them, Choak them, Bite them, and Afflict them; urging them to write their Names in a *Book*, which the said Spectre called, *Ours*. One of them did further testifie, that it was the *Shape* of this Prisoner, with another, which one day took her from her Wheel, and carrying her to the Riverside, threatned there to Drown her, if she did not Sign to the *Book* mentioned: which yet she refused. Others of them did also testifie, that the said *Shape* did in her Threats brag to them that she had been the Death of sundry Persons, then by her named; that she had *Ridden* a Man then likewise named. Another testifi'd, the Apparition of *Ghosts* unto the Spectre of *Bishop*, crying out, *You Murdered us!* About the Truth whereof, there was in the Matter of Fact but too much suspicion.

II. It was testifi'd, That at the Examination of the Prisoner before the Magistrates, the Bewitched were extreamly tortured. If she did but cast her Eyes on them, they were presently struck down; and this in such a manner as there could be no Collusion in the Business. But upon the Touch of her Hand upon them, when they lay in their Swoons, they would immediately Revive; and not upon the Touch of any ones else. Moreover, Upon some Special Actions of her Body, as the shaking of her Head, or the turning of her Eyes, they presently and painfully fell into the like postures. And many of the like Accidents now fell out, while she was at the Bar. One at the same time testifying, That she said, *She could not be troubled to see the afflicted thus tormented.*

III. There was Testimony likewise brought in, that a Man striking once at the place, where a bewitched person said, the *Shape* of this *Bishop* stood, the bewitched cried out, *That he had tore her Coat*, in the place then particularly specifi'd; and the Woman's Coat was found to be Torn in that very place.

IV. One *Deliverance Hobbs*, who had confessed her being a Witch, was now tormented by the Spectres, for her Confession. And she now testif'd, That this *Bishop* tempted her to Sign the *Book* again, and to deny what she had confess'd. She affirm'd, That it was the Shape of this Prisoner, which whipped her with Iron Rods, to compel her thereunto. And she affirmed, that this *Bishop* was at a General Meeting of the Witches, in a Field at *Salem*-Village, and there partook of a Diabolical Sacrament in Bread and Wine then administred.

V. To render it further unquestionable, that the Prisoner at the Bar, was the Person truly charged in THIS *Witchcraft*, there were produced many Evidences of OTHER *Witchcrafts*, by her perpetrated. For Instance, *John Cook* testifi'd, That about five or six Years ago, one Morning, about Sun-Rise, he was in his Chamber assaulted by the *Shape* of this Prisoner: which look'd on him, grinn'd at him, and very much hurt him with a Blow on the side of the Head: and that on the same day, about Noon, the same *Shape* walked in the Room where he was, and an Apple strangely flew out of his Hand, into the Lap of his Mother, six or eight Foot from him.

VI. *Samuel Gray* testifi'd, That about fourteen Years ago, he wak'd on a Night, and saw the Room where he lay full of Light; and that he then saw plainly a Woman between the Cradle, and the Bed-side, which look'd upon him. He rose, and it vanished; tho' he found the Doors all fast. Looking out at the Entry-door, he saw the same Woman, in the same Garb again; and said, *In God's Name, what do you come for?* He went to Bed, and had the same Woman again assaulting him. The Child in the Cradle gave a great Screech, and the Woman disappeared. It was long before the Child could be quieted; and tho' it were a very likely thriving Child, yet from this time it pined away, and, after divers Months, died in a sad Condition. He knew not *Bishop*, nor her Name; but when he saw here after this, he knew by her Countenance, and Apparel, and all Circumstances, that it was the Apparition of this *Bishop*, which had thus troubled him.

VII. *John Bly* and his Wife testifi'd, That he bought a Sow of *Edward Bishop*, the Husband of the Prisoner; and was to pay the Price agreed, unto another person. This Prisoner being angry that she was thus hindred from fingring the Mony, quarrell'd with *Bly*. Soon after which, the Sow was taken with strange Fits; Jumping, Leaping, and Knocking her Head against the Fence; she seem'd Blind and Deaf, and would neither Eat nor be Suck'd. Whereupon a Neighbour said, she believed the Creature was *Over-looked*; and sundry other Circumstances concurred, which made the Deponents believe that *Bishop* had bewitched it.

VIII. *Richard Coman* testifi'd, That eight Years ago, as he lay awake in his Bed, with a Light burning in the Room, he was annoy'd with the Apparition of this *Bishop*, and of two more that were strangers to him, who came and oppressed him so, that he could neither stir himself, nor wake any one else, and that he was the Night after, molested again in the like manner; the said *Bishop*, taking him by the Throat, and pulling him almost out of the Bed. His Kinsman offered for this cause to lodge with him; and that Night, as they were awake, discoursing together, this *Coman* was once more visited by the Guests which had formerly been so troublesom; his Kinsman being at the same time struck speechless, and unable to move Hand or Foot. He had laid his Sword by him, which these unhappy

Spectres did strive much to wrest from him; only he held too fast for them. He then grew able to call the People of his House; but altho' they heard him, yet they had not power to speak or stir; until at last, one of the People crying out, *What's the matter?* The Spectres all vanished.

IX. *Samual Shattock* testify'd, That in the Year, 1680, this *Bridget Bishop*, often came to his House upon such frivolous and foolish Errands, that they suspected she came indeed with a purpose of mischief. Presently, where-upon, his eldest Child, which was of as promising Health and Sense, as any Child of its Age, began to droop exceedingly; and the oftner that *Bishop* came to the House, the worse grew the Child. As the Child would be standing at the Door, he would be thrown and bruised against the Stones, by an invisible Hand, and in like sort knock his Face against the sides of the House, and bruise it after a miserable manner. Afterwards this *Bishop* would bring him things to Dye, whereof he could not imagin any use; and when she paid him a piece of Mony, the Purse and Mony were unaccountably conveyed out of a lock'd Box, and never seen any more. The Child was immediately, hereupon, taken with terrible Fits, whereof his Friends thought he would have dyed: Indeed he did almost nothing but Cry and Sleep for several Months together; and at length his Understanding was utterly taken away. Among other Symptoms of an Inchantment upon him, one was, That there was a Board in the Garden, whereon he would walk; and all the Invitations in the World could never fetch him off. About 17 or 18 years after, there came a Stranger to *Shattock's* House, who seeing the Child, said, *This poor Child is Bewitched; and you have a Neighbour living not far off, who is a Witch.* He added, *Your Neighbour has had a falling out with your Wife; and she said, in her Heart, your Wife is a proud Woman, and she would bring down her Pride in this Child.* He then remembred, that *Bishop* had parted from his Wife in muttering and menacing Terms, a little before the Child was taken Ill. The abovesaid Stranger would needs carry the bewitched Boy with him, to *Bishop's* House, on pretence of buying a pot of Cyder. The Woman entertained him in furious manner; and flew also upon the Boy, scratching his Face till the Blood came; and saying, *Thou Rogue, what dost thou bring this Fellow here to plague me?* Now it seems the Man had said, before he went, That he would fetch Blood of *her.* Ever after the Boy was follow'd with grievous Fits, which the Doctors themselves generally ascribed unto *Witchcraft*; and wherein he would be thrown still into the *Fire* or the *Water*, if he were not constantly look'd after; and it was verily believed that *Bishop* was the cause of it.

X. *John Louder* testify'd, That upon some little Controversy with *Bishop* about her Fowls, going well to Bed, he did awake in the Night by Moonlight, and did see clearly the likeness of this Woman grievously oppressing him; in which miserable condition she held him, unable to help himself, till near Day. He told *Bishop* of this; but she deny'd it, and threatned him very much. Quickly after this, being at home on a Lords day, with the doors shut about him, he saw a black Pig approach him; at which, he going to kick, it vanished away. Immediately after, sitting down, he saw a black Thing jump in at the Window, and come and stand before him. The Body was like that of a Monkey, the Feet like a Cocks, but the Face much like a Mans. He being so extreamly affrighted, that he could not speak; this Monster spoke to him, and said, *I am a Messenger sent unto you, for I understand that you are in some Trouble of Mind, and if you will be ruled by me, you shall want for nothing in this World.* Whereupon he endeavoured to clap his Hands upon it; but he could feel no substance; and it jumped out of the Window again; but immediately came in by the Porch, tho' the Doors were shut, and said, *You had better take my Counsel!* He then struck at it with a Stick, but struck only the Ground-sel, and broke the Stick: The Arm with which he struck was presently Disenabled, and it vanished away. He presently went out at the Back-door, and spied this *Bishop*, in her Orchard, going toward her House; but he had not power to set one foot forward unto her. Whereupon, returning into the House, he was immediately accosted by the Monster he had seen before; which Goblin was now going to fly at him; whereat he cry'd out, *The whole Armour of God be between me and you!* So it sprang back, and flew over the Apple-tree; shaking many Apples off the Tree, in its flying over. At its leap, it flung Dirt with its Feet against the Stomack of the Man; whereon he was then struck Dumb, and so continued for three Days together. Upon the producing of this Testimony, *Bishop* deny'd that she knew this Deponent: Yet their two Orchards joined; and they had often had their little Quarrels for some years together.

XI. *William Stacy* testify'd, That receiving Mony of this *Bishop*, for work done by him; he was gone but a matter of three Rods from her, and looking for his Mony, found it unaccountably gone from him. Some time after, *Bishop* asked him, whether her Father would grind her Grist for her? He demanded why? She reply'd, *Because Folks count me a Witch.* He answered, *No question but he will grind it for you.* Being then gone about six Rods from her, with a small Load in his Cart, suddenly the Off-wheel stump'd, and sunk down into an hole, upon plain Ground; so that the Deponent was forced to get help for the recovering of the Wheel: But stepping back to look for the hole, which might give him this Disaster, there was none at all to be found. Some time after, he was waked in the Night; but it seem'd as light as day; and he perfectly saw the shape of this *Bishop* in the Room, troubling of him; but upon her going out, all was dark again. He charg'd *Bishop* afterwards with it, and she deny'd it not; but was very angry. Quickly after, this Deponent having been threatned by *Bishop*, as he was in a dark Night going to the Barn, he was very suddenly taken or lifted from the Ground, and thrown against a Stone-wall: After that, he was again hoisted up and thrown down a Bank, at the end of his House. After this again, passing by this *Bishop*, his Horse with a small Load, striving to draw, all his Gears flew to pieces, and the Cart fell down; and this Deponent going then to lift a Bag of Corn, of about two Bushels, could not budge it with all his Might.

Many other Pranks of this *Bishop's* this Deponent was ready to testify. He also testify'd, That he verily believ'd, the said *Bishop* was the Instrument of his Daughter *Priscilla's* Death; of which suspicion, pregnant Reasons were assigned.

XII. To crown all, *John Bly* and *William Bly* testify'd, That being employ'd by *Bridget Bishop*, to help to take down the Cellar-wall of the old House wherein she formerly lived, they did in holes of the said old Wall, find several *Poppets*, made up of Rags and Hogs-bristles, with headless Pins in them, the Points being outward; whereof she could give no Account unto the Court, that was reasonable or tolerable.

XIII. One thing that made against the Prisoner was, her being evidently convicted of *gross Lying* in the Court, several times, while she was making her Plea; but besides this, a Jury of Women found a preternatural Teat upon her Body: But upon a second search, within 3 or 4 hours, there was no such thing to be seen. There was also an Account of other People whom this Woman had Afflicted; and there might have been many more, if they had been enquired for; but there was no need of them.

XIV. There was one very strange thing more, with which the Court was newly entertained. As this Woman was under a Guard, passing by the great and spacious Meeting-house of *Salem*, she gave a look towards the House: And immediately a *Demon* invisibly entring the Meeting-house, tore down a part of it; so that tho' there was no Person to be seen there, yet the People, at the noise, running in, found a Board, which was strongly fastned with several Nails, transported unto another quarter of the House.

Source: Cotton Mather, *The Wonders of the Invisible World: Being an Account of the Tryals of Several Witches, Lately Executed in New-England* (London: John Dunton, 1693)

HOW WELL DID YOU UNDERSTAND THIS SELECTION?

1. What was the nature of the evidence used to convict Bridget Bishop of practicing witchcraft?

2. What symptom did the "bewitched victims" of Bishop exhibit?

"FORT MOSE: FORTRESS OF FREEDOM" by Robbi Burgi

The first Africans to arrive in Virginia were probably treated more like indentured servants than slaves. Yet by the 1640s, the status of African servants had deteriorated and many were being treated as slaves. As new English colonies were being founded along the east coast of North America, black servants were increasingly treated as hereditary slaves. Some refused to accept this status and rebelled against a system of oppression that not only condemned them to a life of servitude, but also bound their children to a lowly position in colonial society. The Spanish colony of Florida offered hope to runaway slaves from the English colonies.

St. Augustine is located on that fine line just between Northeast Florida and Central East Florida. Founded by Spanish explorer Don Pedro Mendez Aviles in 1565, the Oldest City in America is known for its world-class golf facilities, 43 miles of pristine beach and unique historical charm. What is less well-known, however, is that just a few miles up the coast from St. Augustine, nestled in a seascape of low-lying tidal marshes inhabited by armies of small, brown sand crabs, lies one of America's most important National Historic Landmarks.

Fort Mose (pronounced Moh-SAY) was the first legally sanctioned free black community in what is now the United States. Established in 1738 by Spanish Florida's Governor Manuel Montiano, Fort Mose provided refuge for more than 100 African fugitives fleeing South Carolina to Spanish colonial territory. As Spanish Florida's first line of defense against the British colonies, Mose represents a unique testimonial to the courageous African Americans who risked their lives in the long struggle to achieve freedom. Yet for more than 175 years, the remains of the fort and its nearby colony, Gracia Real de Santa Teresa de Mose, lay buried from history on a small island in the marsh north of St. Augustine. However, thanks to a combination of efforts by archaeologists, historians, and legislators, a long lost and little-known chapter of America's colonial past has recently been recovered.

Because of Mose's unusual origins and political and military significance, the Spanish documented its history with considerable care. Records show that the first group of fugitives arriving in Fort Mose in 1687 included eight men, two women, and a nursing child. In the following years, word of the Spanish policy of giving religious sanctuary to escaped slaves spread rapidly among the black population in the Carolinas and Georgia, and the number of escapees steadily increased. By 1738, more than 100 Africans had reached St. Augustine, prompting the Spanish government to establish Fort Mose and the nearby community of Gracia Real de Santa Teresa de Mose. Thirty-eight households of men, women, and children lived at Mose, learning the language and customs of the English, Indians, and Spanish.

Located just two miles north of St. Augustine, Mose was the Spanish colony's first line of defense against English attack. A free black militia was formed in 1738, headed by Francisco Menendez, an escaped slave who had achieved the rank of captain in the St. Augustine militia. The original fort was a small, twenty-meter-square enclosure, containing a watchtower, a well, and a guardhouse. With three walls made of earth, stakes, and cactus, the fort was surrounded by a shallow moat and rested on a tidal creek to the east. Residents of Mose came from diverse cultures in the Caribbean and West Africa, and their skilled labor, technology, art, music, ideas and traditions served as valuable resources to the Spanish residents of nearby St. Augustine.

Source: *Florida History & the Arts Magazine*, Winter 2001 issue. Reprinted with permission of Florida Department of State, Division of Historical Resources. For further information, call 1.800.847.7278 or visit www.flheritage.com."

HOW WELL DID YOU UNDERSTAND THIS SELECTION?

1. Why do you believe that the Spanish were willing to grant refuge to escaped slaves from the English colonies?

2. Why does the author believe that the site of Fort Mose is one of the most important National Historic Landmarks in the country?

SELF TEST:

MULTIPLE CHOICE: Circle the correct response. The correct answers are given at the end.

1. The Puritans were so named because they wanted to purify
   a. Parliament
   b. the Catholic Church
   c. the British monarchy
   d. the Church of England

2. John Smith was able to get all of the Jamestown settlers to work by instituting a policy of
   a. giving them land of their own
   b. paying them wages
   c. allowing them to work when they wanted to
   d. "no work, no eat."

3. In the context of Puritan religious beliefs, the concept of predestination asserts that
   a. good deeds get you into heaven
   b. after death, you will be reborn as another person
   c. God has predetermined whether you are going to heaven or hell
   d. you are saved by faith alone.

4. Separatists founded and controlled the colony of
   a. Massachusetts Bay
   b. Virginia
   c. Maryland
   d. Plymouth

5. Indentured servants
   a. sold their labor for a fixed period of time in exchange for passage to America
   b. were slaves for life
   c. were always treated well by their masters
   d. would usually return to England upon completing their term of service.

6. The enclosure movement in England
   a. prevented many from migrating to America
   b. made more land available to small farmers
   c. displaced large numbers of tenant farmers from the land
   d. had little effect upon colonization.

7. The first African servants in Virginia
   a. were considered to be slaves
   b. were immediately granted their freedom
   c. were treated much like indentured servants
   d. joined with Native Americans in a war against the English.

8. Lord Baltimore hoped to develop his colony of Maryland as a religious sanctuary for
   a. Separatists
   b. Catholics
   c. Puritans
   d. Quakers

9. The Quakers stressed
    a. predestination
    b. abstinence from sex
    c. equality and pacifism
    d. the need for wealth in order to get to heaven.

10. The Hudson River Valley of present day New York was first colonized by
    a. the French
    b. the Spanish
    c. the English
    d. the Dutch

Answers:
1-d; 2-d; 3-c; 4-d; 5-a; 6-c; 7-c; 8-b; 9-c; 10-d.

ESSAYS:

1. Compare the early settlement of Virginia with the settlement of Massachusetts Bay.

2. How did the Quaker colony of Pennsylvania differ from her colonial neighbors?

3. Who was Anne Hutchinson and why was she seen as a threat to good order in Massachusetts Bay?

OPTIONAL ACTIVITIES: (Use your knowledge **and** imagination.)

1. Divide the class into landowners, indentured servants, and African slaves. Each member of the class will then write a personal narrative about their life based upon their assigned status.

2. Hold a witchcraft trial. Choose four members of the class to act as judges. Divide the remaining students into accusers, accused, friends of the accused, and friends of the accusers. Allow the defendants time to organize their defense and gather character witnesses. Allow the accusers time to gather evidence against the person or persons they have accused of being a witch. The judges will ultimately determine guilt or innocence, and they will be responsible for sentencing.

WEB SITE LISTINGS:

Colonial National Historical Park
    http://www.nps.gov/colo/Jthanout
Roger Williams National Memorial
    http://www.nps.gov/rowi/
Fort Raleigh National Historic Site
    http://www.nps.gov/fora/
Plymouth. Its History and People
    http://pilgrims.net/plymouth/history/#compact
Pennsylvania State History: The Quaker Province, 1681-1776
    http://www.state.pa.us/PA_Exec/Historical_Museum/quaker.htm
Chronology on the History of Slavery and Racism
    http://innercity.org/holt/slavechron.html
Black History Museum
    http://www.afroam.org/history/history.html

Chapter Three

COLONIAL SOCIETY

Life in the American colonies was formulated by many factors. The colonists brought with them their languages, customs, political thoughts, religious beliefs, and perceptions on many topics. Once they arrived in the colonies, however, these systems were tempered by the reality of life in the new land.

One of the first challenges the colonists faced was how to deal with those people already living on the land that made up the "New World." The arrival of the white man had (to say the least) a profound impact on the natives living on the land. Large numbers died due to exposure to European diseases and a lack of any natural immunities. The natives' social, religious, and political systems underwent tremendous change as they struggled to deal with the new situation they found thrust upon them.

The Spanish were the first to encounter the natives and interact with them. The conquistadors—sent by the Spanish King to the New World for reasons of gold, glory, and God—were involved in many atrocities against the natives in order to conquer them. The subject of who actually owned the land was one that the Spanish also considered, as well as the circumstances that would justify their taking it over. A Spanish scholar, Francisco de Vitoria, gave several lectures at the University of Salamanca, which became the basis for Spanish laws in dealing with the native peoples found in the New World.

Within the colonies of North America, the predominant feeling was that the land was there for those who would make the best use out of it. To the whites, this meant farming. The natives encountered by the English and others in North America were primarily hunter-gatherers. As a result, they were not as strong in number as those encountered by the Spanish nor concentrated in large population centers. Instead, they lived, for the most part, in small, scattered impermanent settlements.

At Jamestown, founded by the Virginia Company of London, a joint-stock company of investors in 1607, the initial interactions between whites and the natives under Chief Powhatan were peaceful. This was aided by the fact that the chief's daughter, Pocahontas, had married one of the colonists, John Rolf. Upon Powhatan's death, however, his brother, Chief Opechancanough, could not maintain the peace following growing English encroachment on Powhatan land. What resulted was an Indian uprising against the inhabitants of Jamestown in 1622, which killed 347 people. The natives had quickly learned that progress for the White settlers meant continued encroachment on their lands and a resulting negative impact on their lives.

In the 1750s, the English and French prepared for a showdown over control of the Ohio River Valley. The English needed this area to expand inland from the coast. The French needed it in order to maintain their control of the interior Mississippi River Valley. On the eve of the French and Indian War, native tribes were asked by both the French and the English to join their respective sides in the upcoming battles. The natives discussed choosing between the two white groups. Many of their leaders recognized that it was a no win situation for their people.

Among the groups displacing Native Americans in New England were the Pilgrims and Puritans. Their life centered mainly around their religious beliefs. Most had come from England to practice their own form of religion. Laws passed by the government, therefore, were used to enforce their perception of God's laws. As a result, there was no separation between church and state.

For those colonists who settled in the South, religion was not as important as the profit that could be made from such staple agricultural crops as tobacco. The rise of labor intensive crops, however, created the need for large numbers of workers. Indentured servants could not keep up with the demand for labor and were, moreover, hard to control. The falling price of tobacco forced planters to look for a more economical source of labor. The status of the first slaves who arrived in 1619 was not initially defined. As the use of slaves continued to grow, however, the government in Virginia tried to formally define the institution of slavery and determine how it was different from servitude. Although slavery might have begun for economic reasons, race became a powerful molder of this "peculiar institution" in the South.

The climate of the South gave rise to large plantations of tobacco, rice, cotton, and indigo. It also gave rise to diseases such as malaria. Unlike the climate of the New England colonies, the southern climate was detrimental to the colonists' health. Compared to their New England counterparts, Southerners lost about ten years of life. As a result, their family life experiences were different. Southern families tended to be "blended" ones where the mother and father of a household were not necessarily (both) the biological parents of their children. Another impact of this higher death rate was a tendency for women in the South to have more say in their personal affairs, as they might not have a husband around to direct them.

Opportunities for women, however, were limited with their roles restricted to mostly domestic duties and, in the case of the upper classes, cultural enhancement. There were, however, exceptions to these in all areas and classes. Due to the length of time it took for travel and necessary absences on the part of spouses or fathers, many women achieved a greater economic role than might be thought proper for women of their time.

There are generalities to be made among all groups and classes for colonial times, but keep in mind there were exceptions to every rule. Not all women were powerless, all men powerful, all whites supreme, and all African Americans illiterate slaves. By making such generalities, we often forget the many notable exceptions.

We must also remember that in trying to deal with the challenges presented to them in this new land, colonial men and women nonetheless still had the same day-to-day routines, customs, and life experiences (in good times and bad) as did those in the old world. In trying to keep a common thread with the old, they often passed laws to maintain their customs and beliefs. These laws, however, also reflected the unique problems of their new home. Many of the laws and events in the following chapter occurred at the early stages of colonial development. They have, however, become the foundation and fabric of American life right into the twenty-first century.

IDENTIFICATION: Briefly describe each term.

Gold, Glory and God

Conquistadors

Natural immunities

Hunter-gatherers

Jamestown

Impermanent settlements

Virginia Company of London

Joint-stock company

Headright System

Chief Powhatan

Pocahontas

John Rolfe

Chief Opechancanough

Mississippi River Valley

Ohio River Valley

French and Indian War

Indentured servants

Slaves

Newport, Rhode Island

Southern Climate

Blended Families

Staple crops

Peculiar Institution

Labor intensive crops

New England Climate

Navigation Acts

Quakers

Pilgrims

Puritans

Heterogeneous Population

THINK ABOUT:

1. How might the level of civilization of the native peoples impact the manner in which the white settlers treated them? Why didn't the Spanish develop a reservation system in the areas where they settled? Why did the English do so?

2. How did religious freedom play a part in the growth of the various colonies?

3. What were some of the factors that helped to mold the English system of slavery in the colonies?

FRANCISCO DE VITORIA'S PRINCIPLES

One of the first challenges the colonists faced was how to deal with the people already living on the land when they arrived. The Spanish were the first to encounter the natives and interact with them. As has been often noted, the Spanish participated in many atrocities against the natives in order to conquer them. But the subject of who owned the land was one that the Spanish also considered, as well as situations that would warrant them taking it over. A Spanish scholar, Francisco de Vitoria, presented a series of lectures at the University of Salamanca, which became the basis for Spanish laws in dealing with those natives encountered in the New World. This reading is a summary of de Vitoria's lectures, given at the University in 1532.

1. Since unbelief does not preclude ownership of property, the Indians are not precluded from owning property, and they are therefore the true owners of the New World, as they were before the advent of the Spaniards.
2. The Emperor is not the lord of the whole world, and, even if he were, he would not therefore be entitled to seize the provinces of the Indians, to put down their lords, to raise up new ones, and to levy taxes.
3. Neither is the Pope the civil or temporal lord of the whole world. He has no secular power except in so far as it subserves things spiritual. He can have no power over the dominions of unbelievers and therefore cannot give such dominions to secular princes. A refusal on the part of the aborigines to recognize the power of the Pope cannot therefore be regarded as a reason for making war upon them and seizing their goods. If the Christian religion had been expounded to the Indians with never so much sufficiency of proof, and they still refused to accept it, this would not render it lawful to make war upon them and despoil then of their possessions.

4. The Spaniards, on the other hand, have the right to go to the lands of the Indians, dwell there and carry on trade, so long as they do no harm, and they may not be prevented by the Indians from so doing. If the Spaniards have diligently informed the Indians that they have not come to interfere in any way with the peace and welfare of the Indians, and if the Indians still show hostility toward them and attempt to destroy them, then, and only then, will it be lawful to make war upon the Indians. In the event of war the Indians may be despoiled of their goods and reduced to slavery, because in the law of nations whatever we take from the enemy becomes ours at once, and so true is this, that men may be brought into slavery to us.

5. The Christians have the right to preach the Gospel among the barbarians. The Pope had the right to entrust the conversion of the Indians to the Spaniards alone, and to forbid all other nations to preach or trade among them, if the propagation of the Faith would thus be furthered. If the Indians do not hinder the preaching of the Gospel they may not be subjected by war, whether they accept it or not.

HOW WELL DID YOU UNDERSTAND THIS SELECTION?

1. Who do the Spanish feel the land belongs to and why?

2. What events would give the Spanish the right to take the land?

3. How do the Spanish use religion as a reason to conquer?

LESSONS OF THE MASSACRE AT JAMESTOWN

Within the colonies of North America, the feeling was that the land was there for those who would make the best use out of it. At Jamestown, the initial interaction between whites and the natives under Chief Powhatan was peaceful. This was aided by the fact that the chief's daughter, Pocahontas, had married one of the colonists, John Rolf. However, upon Powhatan's death, his brother, Chief Opechancanough, could not maintain the peace amid growing English encroachment on the Powhatan land. What resulted was an Indian uprising against the inhabitants of Jamestown in 1622, which killed 347 people. What follows is a response to that event by the officials of the Virginia Company of London, written in 1622.

Thus have you seen the particulars of this massacre, wherein treachery and cruelty have done their worst to us, or rather to themselves; for whose understanding is so shallow, as not to perceive that this must needs be for the good of the plantation after, and the loss of this blood to make the body more healthful, as by these reasons may be manifest.

First, because betraying innocence never rests unpunished.

Secondly, because our hands, which before were tied with gentleness and fair usage, are now set at liberty by the treacherous violence of the savages, not untying the knot, but cutting it. So that we, who hitherto have had possession of no more ground than their waste, and our purchase at a valuable consideration to their contentment gained, may now, by right of war and law of nations, invade the country, and destroy them who sought to destroy us. Whereby we shall enjoy their cultivated places, possessing the fruits of others' labors. Now their cleared grounds in all their villages (which are situated in the fruitfulest places in the land) shall be inhabited by us, whereas heretofore the grubbing of woods was the greatest of labor.

Thirdly, because those commodities which the Indians enjoyed as much or rather more than we, shall now also be entirely possessed by us. The deer and other beasts will be in safety, and infinitely increase, which heretofore not only in the general hunting of the King, but by each particular Indian were destroyed at all times of the year, without any difference of male, dame or young.

There will be also a great increase of wild turkeys, and other weighty fowl, for the Indians never put difference of destroying the hen, but kill them whether in season or not, whether in breeding time, or sitting on their eggs, or having new hatched, it is all one to them.

Fourthly, because the way of conquering them is much more easy than civilizing them by fair means, for they are a rude, barbarous, and naked people, scattered in small companies, which are helps to victory, but hindrance to civility. Besides that, a conquest may be of many and at once; but civility is in particular and slow, the effect of long time, and great industry. Moreover, victory of them may be gained in many ways; by force, by surprise, by famine in burning the corn, by destroying and burning their boats, canoes and houses, by breaking their fishing wares, by assailing them in their huntings, whereby they get the greatest part of their sustenance in winter, by pursuing and chasing them with our horses and bloodhounds to draw and after them, and mastiffs to tear them.

HOW WELL DID YOU UNDERSTAND THIS SELECTION?

1. How are the whites going to take advantage of this massacre?

2. Why is it easier to conquer the natives than to civilize them?

3. Why are the natives considered uncivilized?

"THE SALEM WITCH TRIALS OF 1692" AND "FREQUENTLY ASKED QUESTIONS ABOUT THE SALEM WITCH TRIALS" by Alison D'Amario, Director of Education, Salem Witch Museum

As the Puritan experiment began to crumble in New England, social anxieties expressed themselves in the form of a witchcraft hysteria. Belief in witches and witchcraft was common in the world of the seventeenth century. Yet the witchcraft trials that took place in Salem, Massachusetts in 1692 have long gripped the popular imagination.

The Salem Witch Trials of 1692

In January of 1692, the daughter and niece of Reverend Samuel Parris of Salem Village became ill. When they failed to improve, the village doctor, William Griggs, was called in. His diagnosis of bewitchment put into motion the forces that would ultimately result in the death by hanging of nineteen men and women. In addition, one man was crushed to death; seventeen others died in prison, and the lives of many were irrevocably changed.

To understand the events of the Salem witch trials, it is necessary to examine the times in which accusations of witchcraft occurred. There were the ordinary stresses of 17th-century life in Massachusetts Bay Colony. A strong belief in the devil, factions among Salem Village fanatics and rivalry with nearby Salem Town, a recent small pox epidemic and the threat of attack by warring tribes created a fertile ground for fear and suspicion. Soon prisons were filled with more than 150 men and women from towns surrounding Salem. Their names had been "cried out" by tormented young girls as the cause of their pain. All would await trial for a crime punishable by death in 17th-century New England, the practice of witchcraft.

In June of 1692, the special Court of Oyer (to hear) and Terminer (to decide) sat in Salem to hear the cases of witchcraft. Presided over by Chief Justice William Stoughton, the court was made up of magistrates and jurors. The first to be tried was Bridget Bishop of Salem who was found guilty and was hanged on June 10. Thirteen women and five men from all stations of life followed her to the gallows on three successive hanging days before the court was disbanded by Governor William Phipps in October of that year. The Superior Court of Judicature, formed to replace the "witchcraft" court, did not allow spectral evidence. This belief in the power of the accused to use their invisible shapes or spectres to torture their victims had sealed the fates of those tried by the Court of Oyer and Terminer. The new court released those awaiting trial and pardoned those awaiting execution. In effect, the Salem witch trials were over.

As years passed, apologies were offered, and restitution was made to the victims' families. Historians and sociologists have examined this most complex episode in our history so that we may understand the issues of that time and apply our understanding to our own society. The parallels between the Salem witch trials and more modern examples of "witch hunting" like the McCarthy hearings of the 1950s, are remarkable.

FAQs About the Salem Witch Trials

1. How was the practice of witchcraft viewed in 17th century New England?
Under British law, the basis for Massachusetts Bay Colony legal structure in the 17th century, those who were accused of consorting with the devil were considered felons, having committed a crime against their government. The punishment for such a crime was hanging.

2. What was the difference between the "afflicted" and the "accused"?
The "afflicted" were those supposedly "possessed" and "tormented"; it was they who accused or "cried out" the names of those who were supposedly possessing them.

3. What caused the girls' behavior?
This is a complex question. There are many theories to explain the "fits" of the young girls who accused so many of practicing witchcraft. Among the theories are adolescent hysteria and ergot poisoning; however, there is no definite answer.

4. What role did Tituba play in the Salem witch trials?

Tituba, an Arawak or Carib Indian from Barbados, was Reverend Samuel Parris' slave. Her documented role in the witch trials includes arrest and confession of witchcraft on March 1, 1692. Her influence on the afflicted girls' behavior is unclear.

5. Were only women accused of practicing witchcraft?

Actually, men were accused as well. Five men were convicted and hanged, and one man, Giles Corey, was pressed to death for refusing to cooperate with the court.

6. Who was executed during the Salem witch trials?

With the exception of Giles Corey, who was pressed to death, the following were hanged:

> Bridget Bishop
> George Burroughs
> Martha Carrier
> Martha Corey
> Mary Easty
> Sarah Good
> Elizabeth Howe
> George Jacobs, Sr.
> Susannah Martin
> Rebecca Nurse
> Alice Parker
> Mary Parker
> John Proctor
> Ann Pudeator
> Wilmott Redd
> Margaret Scott
> Samuel Wardwell
> Sarah Wildes
> John Willard

7. Where are the victims buried?

This question remains unanswered. Because of the nature of their alleged crime, victims were not allowed to be buried in consecrated ground. Tradition has it that families came to Gallows Hill to claim their relatives and buried their bodies privately. A memorial honoring the victims of the witch trials was built in Salem in 1992.

8. How long did the witch trials era last?

The witch trials era lasted less than a year. The first arrests were made on March 1, 1692 and the final hanging day was September 22, 1692. The Court of Oyer and Terminer was dissolved in October of 1692.

9. What was the aftermath of the trials?

Jurors and magistrates apologized; restitution was made to the victims' families and a Day of Fasting and Remembrance was instituted. Little is known of the lives of the afflicted girls. Tituba is believed to have been sold and taken out of the Salem Village area. The 300th anniversary of the trials served as an opportunity to bring a sense of reconciliation and an appreciation of the lessons of that time.

10. What are contemporary perceptions of witchcraft?

It is widely understood that witchcraft is a pantheistic religion that includes reverence for nature, belief in the rights of others and pride in one's own spirituality. Practitioners of witchcraft focus on the good and positive in life and in the spirit and entirely reject any connection with the devil. Their beliefs go back to ancient times, long before the advent of Christianity; therefore no ties exist between them and the Christian embodiment of evil. Witchcraft has been confused in the popular mind with pointy black hats, green faces and broomsticks. This is a misrepresentation that witches are anxious to dispel.

Source: Salem Witch Museum Education – Salem Massachusetts.
http://www.salemwitchmuseum.com/learn2.html

HOW WELL DID YOU UNDERSTAND THIS SELECTION?

1. Under British law, who could be considered a witch?

2. How many people were executed as a result of the Salem witchcraft hysteria?

3. Where were the witches buried?

TREATY NEGOTIATIONS BETWEEN CANASSATEGO AND GEORGE THOMAS, 1742

The natives quickly learned that progress for the whites meant continued encroachment on their lands and a resulting negative impact on their lives. In 1742, during a treaty renewal negotiation, the following exchange between Canassatego and George Thomas highlights the difference between the two cultures, a difference that was never able to be resolved.

Canassatego: We received from the Proprietors Yesterday, some Goods in consideration of our Release of the Lands on the West-side of Sasquehannah. It is true, we have the full Quantity according to Agreement; but if the Proprietor had been here himself, we think, in Regard to our numbers and Poverty, he would have made an Addition to them. If the Goods were only to be divided amongst the Indians present, a single Person would have but a small Portion; but if you considered what Numbers are left behind, equally entitled with us to a Share, there will be extremely little. We therefore desire, if you have the Keys to the Proprietor's Chest, you will open it, and take out a little more for us.

We know our Lands are now becoming more valuable: The white People think we do not know their value; but we are sensible that the Land is everlasting, and the few Goods we receive for it are soon worn out and gone...Besides, we are not well used with respect to the Lands still unsold by us. Your People daily settle on these Lands and spoil our Hunting. We must insist on your removing them...

It is customary with us to make a Present of Skins, whenever we renew our Treaties. We are ashamed to offer our Brethren so few, but your Horses and Cows have eat the Grass our Deer used to feed on. This has made them scare, and will, we hope, plead in Excuse for our not bringing a larger Quantity. If we could have spared more, we would have given more; but we are really poor; and desire you'll not consider the Quantity, but few as they are, accept them in Testimony of our Regard.

George Thomas: In answer to what you say about the Proprietaries. They are all absent, and have taken the Keys to their Chest with them; so that we cannot, on their Behalf, enlarge the Quantity of Goods: Were they here they might perhaps, be more generous; but we cannot be liberal for them. The Government will, however, take your Request into Consideration...

It is very true, that Lands are of late become more valuable; but what raises their Value? It is not entirely owning to the Industry and Labour used by the white People, in their Cultivation and Improvement? Had not they come amongst you, these Lands would have been of no Use to you, any further than to maintain every Thing; but you know very well, that they cost a great deal of Money and the Value of Land is no more than it is worth in Money.

HOW WELL DID YOU UNDERSTAND THIS SELECTION?

1. How do the Indians say the impact of whites hurt them?

2. What do they ask the whites to do?

3. According to George Thomas, who makes the land valuable and why? As a result, who has the right to the land?

THE CHOICE BETWEEN THE ENGLISH OR THE FRENCH

On the eve of the French and Indian War, many native tribes were asked by the French and the English to join their side in the upcoming battles. The natives discussed choosing sides between the two white groups. What follows is a speech made by Sconondoa, an Oneida elder, as to what he recommends to the Iroquois Confederacy.

My children, none among all the Iroquois here have lived as long as Sconondoa and no more than two or three even half as long. Yet, surely among you there must be some who remember what we are and who we are and what we once had. Are there none here who remember when the cry "The Iroquois are coming!" was alone enough to make the hearts of the bravest warriors of other tribes fail within their breasts? Are there none here who remember when this land was all ours and that though other tribes were round before us; are their none here who remember that from the green sea to the east and the blue sea to the south, the land of always-winter in the north and the land of always-summer in the west, they feared us?

But then came the men in their boats and they brought us gifts. They asked for just a little land and we foolishly gave it to them. Then, when they asked us for more land and we would not give it to them, they asked us to sell it to them and because they had goods that were new and powerful to us, we sold them some. Then they asked us for more land and when we would not give it or sell it, they took it from us and we talked and talked and always it was we who gave in and signed a new treaty and took gifts for what was taken, but the gifts were cheap and worthless and lasted but a day, while the land lasts forever.

My children, raise your heads! Open your eyes! Can you not see that it makes no difference whether these white men are of the French or the English or any other of the peoples from across the sea? All of them threaten our very existence. All of them! When they came here they had nothing. Now, like a great disease they have spread all over the east until for twelve days' walk from the sea there is no room for an Indian to stay and he is made unwelcome. Yet this was not long ago Indian land. How has it gone? As these white men have stained the east and the north with their presence, so now they extend themselves to the west, and the northwest and the southwest, forcing all Indians to take sides for them or against them, whether they are French of English, but in such a game the Indian cannot win.

HOW WELL DID YOU UNDERSTAND THIS SELECTION?

1. What mistakes did the Indians make in their dealings with whites according to Sconondoa?

2. What was the effect of the treaties made with whites on the native population?

3. What does Sconondoa say the natives should do and why?

THE ENFORCEMENT OF GOD'S LAW

The Puritans came to England to practice their religion and keep their community as free from sin as possible. As a result, many of the laws passed had a basis in Scripture. The goal was to have government serve as an enforcer of religious beliefs. The following are laws passed by the colony of Massachusetts.

TO OUR BELOVED BRETHERN AND NEIGHBOURS the inhabitants of the Massachusetts, the Governour, Assistants and Deputies assembled in the generall Court of that Jurisdiction with grace and peace in our Lord Jesus Christ.
By order of the Generall Court.
INCREASE NOWEL SECR.

CAPTIAL LAWES
If any man after legal conviction shal HAVE OR WORSHIP any other God, but the LORD GOD: he shall be put to death. Exod.22. 20 Deut, 13 6. & 10. Deut. 17. 2. 6.

2. If any man or woman be a WITCH, that is, hath or consulteth, with a familiar spirit, they shall be put to death. Exod. 22. 18 Levit. 20 27. Deut. 18. 10. 11.

3. If any person with this Jurisdiction whether Christian or Pagan shall wittingly and willingly presume to BLAS-PHEME the holy name of God, Father, Son or Holy-Ghost, with direct, expresse, presumptous, or high-handed blasphemy, either by wilfull or obstinate denying the true God, or his Creation, or Government of the world: or

shall curse God in like manner, or reproach the holy Religion of God as if it were but a politick device to keep ignorant men in awe; or shal utter any other kinde of Blasphemy of the like nature & degree they shall be put to death. Levit.24,15,16.

5. If any person slayeth another suddenly in his ANGER, or Cruelty of passion, he shall be put to death. Levit.24.17. Numb. 35. 20. 21.

9. If any person commit ADULTERIE with a married, or espoused wife; the Adulterer & Adulteresse shal surely be put to death. Lev. 20. 19. & 18. 20. Deu. 22. 23. 27.

10. If any man STEALETH A MAN, of Man-kinde, he shall surely be put to death. Exodus 21. 16.

12. If any man shall CONSPIRE, and attempt any Invasion, Insurrection, or publick Rebellion against our Common-Wealth...and persidiously attempt the Alteration and Subversion of our frame of Politie, or Government fundamentally he shall be put to death. Numb. 16. 2 Sam. 3. 2 Sam. 18. 2 Sam. 20.

14. If a man have a stubborn or REBELLIOUS SON, of sufficient years & undestanding (viz) sisteen years of age, which will not obey the voice of his Father, or the voice of his Mother, and that when they have chastened him will not harken unto them... such a son shal be put to death.

Bond-slavery.
It is ordered by this Court and authorities therof, that there shall never by any bond-slavery, villenage or captivities amongst us; unlesse it be lawful captives, taken in just warrs, and such strangers as willingly sell themselves, or are solde to us; and such shall have libertyes and christian usuages which the law of God established in Israell concerning such persons doth morally require, provided, this exempts none from servitude who shall be judged thereto by Authoritie.

Gaming.
Upon complaint of great disorder by the use of the game called Suffle-board, in houses of comon entertainment, whereby much pretious times is spent unfruitfuly and much wast of wine and ber occasioned, it is therefore ordered and enacted by the Authoritie of this Court; That no person shall henceforth use the said game of Shuffle-board in any such house.

Idlenes.
It is ordered by this Court and Authorities thereof, that no person, Householder or other shall spend his time idely or unproffitably under pain of such punishment as the Court of Assistants of County Court shall think meet to inflict.

Jesuits.
It is ordered and enacted by Authorities of this Court, That no Jesuit or spiritual or ecclesiastical person (as they are termed) ordained by the authoritie of the Pope, or Sea of Rome shall henceforth at any time repair to, or come to this Jurisdiction.

Masters, Servants, and Labourers
3. It is also ordered that when any servants shall run from their masters, or any other inhabitants shall privily goe away with suspicion of ill intentions it shall be lawful...to presse men and boats or pinnaces at the publick charge to pursue such person by Sea or Land and bring them back by force of Arms.

6. It is ordered, and by this Court declared, that if any servant shall flee from the tyrannie and crueltie of his, or her Master to the house of any Freeman of the same town, they shall be there protected and susteined til due order be taken for their relief.

8. And that if any man smite out the eye, or tooth of his man-servant, or maid-servant; or   otherwise maim, or much disfigure the (unless it be by meer casualtie) he shall let them goe free from his service, and shall allow such farther recompence as the Court shall adjudg him.

9. And all servants that have served diligently and faithfully to the benefit of their Masters seven years shall not be sent away emptie: and if any have been unfaithfull, negligent, or unprofitable in their service, nothwithstanding the good usage of their Masters, they shall not be dismissed till they have made satisfaction according to the judgement of Authoritie.

Strangers.
It is ordered by this Court and the Authoritie therof; that no Town or person shal receive any stranger resorting hither with intent to reside in this Jurisdiction, nor shall allow any Lot of Habitation to any, or entertain any such above three weeks...

Tobacco.
...That no man shall take any tobacco within twenty poles of any house, or so neer as may indanger the same, or neer any Barn, corn, or hay-cock as may occasion the fyring thereof...Nor shall any take tobacco in any Inne or common Victualing-house, except in a private room there, so as neither the Master of said house nor any other Guests there shall take offence therat, which if any doe, then such person shall forthwith forbear...

HOW WELL DID YOU UNDERSTAND THIS SELECTION?

1.   What were the laws calling for Capital punishment based upon?

2.   How are these laws different from the rules regarding servants and masters in the Virginia Statutes?

3.   What would be the motivation for each of the laws regarding Idleness, Jesuits and Strangers?

Often, society has defined certain roles for women, and colonial America was no exception. However, there were many women who did not fill the role expected of them by society. Some were forced, due to circumstances beyond their control, to take over a husband's business or to run one of their own. The reality of many women's lives often tended not to be the ideal that society wanted or expected, as the following readings demonstrate.

A diary entry of Judge Sewell of Massachusetts

1703-04... Took 24s on my pocket, and gave my Wife the rest of my cash L4. 3-8 and tel her she shall now keep the Cash; if I want I wil borrow of her. She has a better faculty than I at managing Affairs; I will assist her; and will endeavor to live upon my salary; will see ehat it will doe

Source: Carl Holliday. *Woman's Life in Colonial Days* (New York: The Cornhill Publishing Company, 1922) p. 133.

A letter to Eliza Pinckney of South Carolina to her father.

I wrote you in former letters we had a fine crop of Indigo Seed upon the ground and since informed you the frost took it before it was dry. I picked out the best of it and had it planted but there is not more than a hundred bushes of it come up, which proves the more unlucky as you have sent a man to make it.

To a friend she writes of how she spend her day.

In genl I rise at five o'clock in the morning, read till seven - then take a walk in the garden or fields, see that the Servants are at their respective business, then to breakfast. The first hour after breakfast is spent in musick, the next is constantly employed in recolecting something I have learned...such as french and shorthand. After that I devote the rest of the time till I dress for dinner, to our little Polly, and too black girls, who I teach to read...The first hour after dinner, as...after breakfast, at musick, the rest of the afternoon in needlwork till candle light, and from that time to bed time to read or write...Thursday, the whole day except to the necessary affairs of the family take up, is spent in writing, either on the business of the plantations or on letters to my friends...

Source: Carl Holliday. *Woman's Life in Colonial Days* (New York: The Cornhill Publishing Company, 1922) pp. 295-296.

Thomas Jefferson's letter of advice to his daughter concerning how she spend her day.

Dear Patsy: - With respect to the distribution of your time, the following is what I should approve:
From 8 to 10, practice music
From 10 to 1, dance one day and draw another
From 1 to 2, draw on the day you dance, and write a letter on the next day.
From 3 to 4, read French
From 5 until bedtime, read English, write, etc.
Informe me what books you read, what tunes you learn, and inclose me your best copy of every lesson in drawing...Take care that you never spell a word wrong...It produces great praise to a lady to spell well...

Source: Carl Holliday. *Woman's Life in Colonial Days* (New York: The Cornhill Publishing Company, 1922) p. 74.

A letter from Benjamin Franklin concerning a printer's wife who took charge of her husband's business after his death.

I mention this affair chiefly for the sake of recommening that branch of education for our young females as likely to be of more use to them and their children in case of widowhood than either music of dancing, by preserving them from losses by imposition of crafty men, and enabling them to continue perhaps a profitable mercantile house with establish'd correspondence, till a son is grown up fit to undertake and go on with it.

Source: Carl Holliday. *Woman's Life in Colonial Days* (New York: The Cornhill Publishing Company, 1922) p. 74.

A poem by Ann Bradstreet, one of the first women poets in America

If ever two were one, then surely we;
If ever man were loved by wife, then thee
If ever wife was happy in a man
Compare with me, ye women, if you can
I prize thy love more than whole than whole mines of gold,
Or all the riches that the East doth hold,
My love is such that rivers cannot quench,
Nor aught but love from thee give recompense.
My love is such I can no way repay;
The heavens reward thee manifold, I pray,
Then while we live in love let's persevere,
That when we live no more we may live ever.

Source: Carl Holliday. *Woman's Life in Colonial Days* (New York: The Cornhill Publishing Company, 1922) p 99.

HOW WELL DID YOU UNDERSTAND THIS SELECTION?

1. What was the role that society wanted these women to have?

2. What are the different views of women as seen in these articles?

3. How did these colonial women view their role?

The following quotes are by Benjamin Franklin:

By heaven we understand a state of happines infinite in degree, and endless in duration.

Any fool can criticise, condem and complain, and most fools do.

I haven't failed, I've found 10,000 ways that don't work.

There was never a good war or a bad peace.

Whatever is begun in anger ends in shame.

Beware of little expenses; a small leak will sink a great ship.

No nation was ever ruined by trade.

Either write something worth reading or do something worth writing.

Read much, but not many books.

Most fools think they are only ignorant.

He's a fool that cannot conceal his wisdom.

We are all born ignorant, but one must work hard to remain stupid.

Dost thou love life? Then do not squander time, for that's the stuff life is made of.

Those that love deeply never grow old; they may die of old age, but they die young.

Poverty often deprives a man of all spirit and virtue. It is hard for an empty bag to stand upright.

Don't throw stones at your neighbors', if you own windows are glass.

Three may keep a secret if two of them are dead.

To the discontented man no chair is easy.

Never leave that till to-morrow which you can do to-day.

Fish and visitors smell after three days.

The absent are never without fault. Nor the present without excuse.

All mankind is divided into three classes; those that are immovable, those that are movable, and those that move.

HOW WELL DID YOU UNDERSTAND THIS SELECTION?

1. What are several basic themes that run through these quotes?

2. What generalizations can you make about colonial society from these?

NEWS ACCOUNTS FROM WENHAM, MASSACHUSETTS

The people who came to the colonies faced — and endured — many hardships. Once a settlement was established, there were often threats from Native Americans who would not accept white encroachment on their land. Notwithstanding the challenges of life in the new land, the colonists also experienced the same daily routines, trials, tribulations, and good times that people of their time experienced in Europe. The following excerpts are taken from the Wenham, Massachusetts newspapers.

1643: "Enon shall be called Wenham. Wenham is granted to be a town and hath liberty to send a deputy.

1643: It is voted that no inhabitant may introduce any one into the town without consent under the penalty of five shillings per week, every week that such person remains within the limits of the town.

1644: A bounty of 20 shillings is offered to every man who should kill a wolf.

1646: William Fiske keeper of the ordinary is licensed "to sell wine and strong water."

December 22, 1646: John Fairfield, eminent inhabitant of Wenham dies today, leaving wife Elizabeth and two sons, Walter and Benjamin.

1650: John Gown is fined for selling a gun to an Indian.

October, 1652: Citing extravagance, Thomas Fiske's wife was recently fined 10 shillings and court costs for wearing and for flaunting a "tiffany."

1659: The following inhabitants are imposed rates to support the Rev. Mr. Newman; Phineas Fiske, Mr. Gott, Austin Kilham, Henry Kimball, Richard Kimball, Richard Hutton, Robert Gowen, James Moulton, Sr., John Dodge, John Fiske, Damiel Kilham, John Gooland, John Powling, John Abby, Mark Batchelder, Richard Goldsmith, James Moulton, Jr., Alexander Moxey, William Gore, Edward Waldron, Henry Haggett, John Kilham, John Batchelder, Abner Ordway, Thomas White, Richard Coy, Thomas Fisk.

May 18, 1673: Richard Goldsmith dies today of lightning strike while sitting on Rev. Newmans's front porch engaged in conversation. His dog, sitting beneath the chair was also killed.

Nov. 30, 1675: Mark Batchelder, Caleb Kimball killed in the bloody Narragausett Battle; Thomas Abby and John Fiske were among those wounded.

March 5, 1700: Thomas Goodwin, a lad of about 14, was killed by "being catcht by the whell of a saw-mill & so killed, att John Leeches."

1713: Capt. Willaim Rogers has been appointed schoolmaster, succeeding Capt. Thomas Fiske. He is the second person to have enjoyed the high military dignity of captain in "ye trainband."

1737: "Throat distemper" has claimed about twenty lives in Wenham, including all five children of John Gott, and all four children of Richard Dodge.

1742: Hon. William Fairfield, a highly respected citizen of Wenham dies today. We are reminded of an anecdote concerning him: Setting out to attend a session of the Legislature, he became so absorbed in thinking of the business at hand that he actually reached Boston, bridle in hand before discovering that he had left his horse at home.

HOW WELL DID YOU UNDERSTAND THIS SELECTION?

1. What do these excerpts tell you about the reality of life in colonial America?

2. What are some real fears that Americans had at this time?

3. How were ministers supported in the community?

The people of Deerfield, Massachusetts lived in an area that was more beset with violence between the Native Americans and settlers than was the case in Wenham, Massachusetts. The following are news items from Deerfield, Massachusetts.

1669: Samuel Hinsdale breaks first ground and completes home. Sampson Frary becomes the second settler. Other early settlers include Francis Barnard, Philip Barsham, William Bartholomew, Joshua Carter, Samuel Daniels, John Farrington, Zecheriah Field, Frary Samson, Joseph Gillett, Samuel Harrington, Robert Hinsdale, Quintus Stockwell, Nathaniel Sutleff, William Smead, James Tuffts, Daniel Weld, Richard Weller and Rev. Samuel Mather.

1674: Moses Craft is licensed to keep an ordinary tavern here.

September 18, 1675: John Allen, husband of Mary Hannum, and son Samuel the emigrant, was among those killed recently in the tragic battle of "Bloody Brook." Captain Thomas Lathrop also lost his life. Other of Deerfield who lost their lives include John Barnard, John Hinsdale, Jonathan Plympton and Philip Barsham.

1677: John Plympton taken captive by the Indians, tortured and burned at the stake. He was married to Jane Dummer by whom he had 13 children.

1687: Joseph Barnard, with the consent of the town, is appointed town clerk.

June 6, 1693: Tragedy has struck the homes of Thomas Broughton and Widow Hepzibah Wells. Broughton, his wife and three children were tomahawked and scalped. Widow Wells, staying with a sick child nearby, had left her four children at home. Mary, Sarah and Hepzibah were all tomahawked and scalped. Daniel, asleep in the chamber, slept through the whole horrid mess. Mrs. Wells who rushed to the aid of her children suffered the same fate as her three daughters.

1698: King William's War and the earlier Indian attacks have left the town impoverished. Fields are neglected, fences broken down, provisions exhausted, clothing nearly worn out and the children almost naked.

1699. Joseph Barnard, son of Francis, mortally wounded at Indian Bridge by a party of Indians in ambush.

Feb. 1703-04: A force of 200 French and Indians, led by Captain Hertell de Rouville, sacked Deerfield, murdering men, women and children alike. 54 in all were killed, almost all buried in a common grave. Twelve captives were taken, about eight murdered, with about twelve perishing on the march to Canada.

1704: Thomas French, son of John Northampton, his wife and six children captured and taken into captivity. His wife and one child were killed on the march.

1706: John Sheldon, who on snow-shoes tracked through the wilderness to Canada to recover his for children and friends held in captivity, has returned with one daughter, and several others. His second wife, Elizabeth Pratt of Hartford, Conn., and one child were killed in 1704.

HOW WELL DID YOU UNDERSTAND THIS SELECTION?

1. How is life in Deerfield different from life in Wenham?

2. What aspects of colonial life might have been excluded? Why?

3. Why might these people have risked living where they did?

SELF TEST:

MULTIPLE CHOICE: Circle the correct response. The correct answers are given at the end.

1. The natives encountered by the Spanish
    a. were hunter-gatherers.
    b. lived in large, populated areas.
    c. were the same level of development as those encountered by the English.
    d. were unaffected by disease.

2. The English felt that they had claim to the land over the Native Americans because
    a. they farmed it.
    b. they had legal claim to it.
    c. the Pope had decreed the land theirs.
    d. the joint-stock companies bought it.

3. Jamestown found it profitable to grow
    a. corn.
    b. cotton.
    c. tobacco.
    d. rice.

4. In the 1750s the English and French went to war over
    a. the Mississippi River Valley.
    b. control of the fur trade.
    c. the Ohio River Valley.
    d. trying to put down Indian uprisings.

5. Most of New England's profits came from
    a. tobacco.
    b. shipping.
    c. grains.
    d. fruits.

6. Puritan government demonstrated
    a. separation of church and state.
    b. religious freedom.
    c. religious toleration.
    d. the state enforcing Puritan religion laws.

7. Life in New England, compared to the southern colonies, tended to be
    a. shorter but less stable.
    b. shorter but more stable.
    c. longer and more stable.
    d. longer and less stable.

8. English colonists in the South turned to slavery because
    a. of the falling price of tobacco.
    b. indentured servants were too troublesome.
    c. slaves were more economical.
    d. all of the above.

9. The Middle Colonies thrived because
   a. of their fertile soil.
   b. their religious conformity.
   c. the tight control of the Navigation Acts.
   d. their homogeneous population.

10. One unique factor of American colonial society was
   a. upward social-economic mobility for all.
   b. upward social-economic mobility for white males.
   c. religious freedom for all.
   d. little economic discrimination towards women.

Answers:
   1-b; 2-a; 3-c; 4-c; 5-b; 6-d; 7-c; 8-d; 9-a; 10-b.

ESSAYS:

1. Describe what factors influenced the evolution of the colonies into three distinct regions: New England, Middle and Southern.

2. What factors helped cause the evolution of slavery in the colonies?

OPTIONAL ACTIVITIES: (Use your knowledge **and** imagination.)

1. You are a Native American. In two or three pages, write down what would be an oral history describing your first contact with the whites over the course of a year and how it affects your life.

2. As a person living in an American colony, write a series of letters to a relative back in England describing your life. Include in your letters what influences, if any, are different in the colony than in England.

WEB SITE LISTINGS:

Colonial Life and Laws
   http://www.fordham.edu/halsall/mod/modsbook07.html
Hubsite for Colonial People and Documents, managed by Kendall Simmons, Government Documents Library, University of Kansas
   http://www.ukans.edu/carrie/docs
The National Women's History Project's List of History Website Links
   http://www.nwhp.org/tlp/links/links.html
Laws Regarding Slavery
   http://ccwf.cc.utexas.edu/~russell/hal/docs/virginiaslaverystatues.htm
Excerpts from Slave Narratives, edited by Steven Mintz, University of Houston
   http://vi.uh.edu/pages/mintz/primary.htm
University of Virginia Library
   http://www.lib.virginia.edu
Avalon Project by Yale University: Documents in Law, History and Diplomacy
   http://www.yale.edu/lawweb/avalon/avalon.htm
Salem Witch Museum
   http://www.salemwitchmuseum.com/learn2.html

Chapter Four

TOWARD REVOLUTION

America during the eighteenth century was a place that was growing and expanding in many different ways. One example of growth and development in the colonies was seen in the context of its religious theories. There had been a feeling on the part of many in the colonies that people had become apathetic about religion. In the 1730s, Rev. Jonathan Edwards (a Congregational minister in Northampton, Massachusetts) began preaching a series of sermons that presented God in a vengeful way. In his sermons, he reminded his listeners that they could be neither smug nor rational about salvation. This emotional religious revival was made even more well known by the preaching of Rev. George Whitefield, an English minister who came to America in the 1740s and spoke to thousands of people at huge prayer meetings. This religious movement eventually became known as the Great Awakening and was a unique experience shared by most Americans, regardless of social class or the section of the country in which they lived.

In contrast, the movement known as the Enlightenment left many intellectuals with the belief that reason led to the path of God, not revelation. Many men, including Benjamin Franklin, Thomas Jefferson and Thomas Paine, identified themselves as Deists, believing in a rational God whose existence could be seen in the natural order of the Universe. Deism denied the authority of the Bible and the divinity of Jesus Christ.

Another facet of growth in colonial America was an increasing political awareness, not only of individual rights within each colony but also of individuals' rights as Americans (as opposed to colonials under British rule). This was demonstrated in 1735 in the trial of John Zenger. Zenger, a printer, was accused of seditious libel against an officer of the crown, the Governor of New York. At his trial, his lawyer, Andrew Hamilton, stated that what Zenger said was true and not libelous. The jury found him not guilty and thereby helped establish the idea of freedom of the press.

The French and Indian War brought a change in British colonial policy. Before the war, most government regulation came in the form of external trade legislation, as evidenced by the Navigation Acts. These acts were designed to limit foreign competition and to keep colonial trade between the colonies and England.

After the French and Indian War, the British government launched a series of new revenue acts. These laws went beyond the trade regulation of the Navigation Acts and included such legislation as the Sugar Act in 1764. The purpose of the laws was now no longer the regulation of trade in and of itself, but rather to use trade as a means of increasing revenue to the British government, to be used for the protection of the colonies and to defray the debt incurred in fighting the French and Indian War.

Colonial reaction to the Sugar Act was both negative and immediate and gave rise to such actions as non-importation of English products. These opposition efforts eventually caused a lowering of the tax. Colonials felt strongly that the right to tax remained with their own colonial legislative bodies, and not with Parliament.

Parliament, however, was not to be stopped in its efforts to raise revenue through the taxation of its American colonies. In 1765, it passed the Stamp Act, a law taxing all colonial legal and business documents including licenses, almanacs, newspapers, pamphlets, and playing cards. The outcry of opposition was loud and immediate. American colonials feared this new form of taxation, one that had nothing to do with trade but was rather a tax on internal goods within the colonies.

A Stamp Act Congress was called for and, in 1765, met in New York where its members confirmed their loyalty to the English Crown but asserted their belief that only their own legislative assemblies could legally tax them. The uproar in the colonies made it almost impossible to enforce the Stamp Act, and it was eventually repealed by Parliament in 1766.

While repealing the Stamp Act, however, Parliament at the same time passed the Declaratory Act. This law was aimed at clarifying the authority of Parliament to tax the colonies "in all cases whatsoever" and attempted to resolve the issue over which legislative body, the colonial legislatures or Parliament, had the right to impose taxes on the colonists.

Against this background, Parliament tried its hand yet again in taxing the colonies. In 1767, the Townsend Acts were passed. These laws returned to the idea of taxing external goods (paper, paint, lead, glass, and tea) coming into the country. Once again there was an uproar and the resulting colonial non-importation of British goods put such a strain on British merchants that Parliament was pressured into repealing the duties in 1770. The repeal applied to all goods with the exception of tea, as a reminder to the colonies that Parliament did, indeed, have the right to tax them.

In the midst of all of this, the East India Tea Company was approaching bankruptcy, and Parliament moved to save it. To do so, Parliament passed the Tea Act, which, in essence, gave the East India Tea Company a monopoly on all tea sold in the colonies.

A loud public outcry was once again heard, focusing on the same unresolved question of who had the right to tax the colonies. Colonial opposition against the landing of the tea lead to the Boston Tea Party, where a group of Americans disguised as Indians boarded a ship in Boston Harbor and dumped its cargo of tea into the water in order to prevent it from being sold.

In response to this, Parliament passed a series of acts known in the American colonies as the Intolerable Acts. These laws, designed to punish Boston and the colony of Massachusetts, instead galvanized the other colonies to support Massachusetts and coalesced their own feelings against the Crown.

By May 1775, open rebellion became a reality, with first blood being shed in Lexington and Concord in April. Still, the members of the Congress were hesitant to break the long-standing ties that bound them to Britain. Even after appointing George Washington as the commander of the American Continental Army, it was difficult to take the giant leap to independence.

What brought most Americans to take that momentous jump was a pamphlet published in January 1776 by Thomas Paine entitled *Common Sense*. In his article, Paine did not spare any words — independence is a must; revolution a necessity. Its wide circulation made most Americans, even the many who were unable to read, aware of the reasons for independence.

IDENTIFICATION: Briefly describe each term

Briefly describe each term

Jonathan Edwards

George Whitefield

The Great Awakening

New Lights

Old Lights

Deism

Zenger Trial

Alexander Hamilton

Seditious Libel

Salutary Neglect

Navigation Acts

Raw Materials

Finished Products

Revenue Acts

Sugar Act

Stamp Act

External tax

Internal tax

Non-importation

Self-taxation

Stamp Act Congress

Declaratory Act

Townshend Acts

East India Tea Company

Tea Act

Committees of Correspondence

Samuel Adams

Boston Tea Party

Sons of Liberty

Coercive Acts

Continental Congress

Suffolk Resolves

Boycott

Lexington and Concord

Thomas Paine

Common Sense

Second Continental Congress

Richard Henry Lee

Thomas Jefferson

Declaration of Independence

THINK ABOUT:

1. How might new religious theories and ideas questioning traditional religious authority lead to the questioning of established political authority?

2. What was the question that the colonies and the British government could never agree on? What was the basis of each side's view?

SINNERS IN THE HANDS OF AN ANGRY GOD by Jonathan Edwards (1735)

The following is a sermon given by Jonathan Edwards in 1735. In this sermon, he reminded the listener that God was a God of wrath and that Hell would be a reality for many if they refused to change. He warned people that they were dependent upon the mercy of God and that such mercy could be gained only by a repentance of their sins and their acceptance of Jesus Christ. Sermons like this were typical of those of the Great Awakening.

Their foot shall slide in due time - Deut.xxxii.35

...The observation from the words that I would now insist upon is this. "There is nothing that keeps wicked men at any one moment out of hell, but the mere pleasure of God." By the mere pleasure of God, I mean his sovereign pleasure, his arbitrary will, restrained by no obligation, hindered by no manner of difficulty, any more than if nothing else but God's mere will had in the least degree, or in any respect whatsoever, any hand in the preservation of wicked men one moment...

...Unconverted men walk over the pit of hell on a rotten covering, and there are innumerable places in this covering so weak that they will not bear their weight, and these places are not seen...

8. Natural men's prudence and care to preserve their own lives, or the care of others to preserve them, do not secure them a moment. To this, divine providence and universal experience do also bear testimony. There is clear evidence that men's own wisdom is no security to them from death; that if it were otherwise we should see some difference between the wise and politic men of the world, and others, with regard to their liableness to early and unexpected death; but how is it in fact? Eccles.ii.16 "How dieth the wise man? even as the fool."

9. All wicked men's pains and contrivance which they use to escape hell, while they continue to reject Christ, and so remain wicked men, do not secure them from hell one moment. Almost every natural man that hears of hell, flatters himself that he shall escape it; he depends upon himself for his own security; he flatters himself in what he has done, in what he is now doing, or what he intends to do. Every one lays out matters in his own mind how he shall avoid damnation, and flatters himself that he contrives well for himself, and that his schemes will not fail...

...But the foolish children of men miserably delude themselves in their own schemes, and in confidence in their own strength and wisdom; they trust to nothing but a shadow...

...So that, whatever some have imagined and pretended about promises made to natural men's earnest seeking and knocking, it is plain and manifest, that whatever pains a natural man takes in religion, whatever prayers he makes, till he believes in Christ, God is under no manner of obligation to keep him a moment from eternal destruction.

So that, thus it is that natural men are held in the hand of God, over the pit of hell; they have deserved the fiery pit, and are already sentenced to it; ...In short, they have no refuge, nothing to take hold of, all that preserves them every moment is the mere arbitrary will, and uncovenanted, unobliged forbearance of an incensed God.

APPLICATION

The use of this awful subject may be for awakening unconverted person in this congregation. This that you have heard is the case of every one of you that are out of Christ. That world of misery, that lake of burning brimstone, is extended abroad under you. There is the dreadful pit of the glowing flames of the wrath of God; there is hell's wide gaping mouth open; and you have nothing to stand upon, nor any thing to take hold of, there is nothing between you and hell but the air; it is only the power and mere pleasure of God that hold you up...

...The God that holds you over the pit of hell, much as one holds a spider, or some loathsome insect over the fire, abhors you, and is dreadfully provoked; his wrath towards you burns like fire; he looks upon you as worthy of nothing else, but to be cast into the fire...

...How dreadful is the state of those that are daily and hourly in danger of this great wrath and infinite misery! But this is the dismal case of every soul in this congregation that has not been born again, however moral and strict, sober and religious, they may otherwise be...There is reason to think, that there are many in this congregation now hearing this discourse, that will actually be the subjects of this very misery to all eternity. We know not who they are, or in what seats they sit, or what thoughts they now have. It may be they are now at ease, and hear all promising themselves that they shall escape...And it would be a wonder, if some that are now present should not be in hell in a very short time, even before this year is out. And it would be no wonder if some persons, that now sit here, in some seats of this meeting-house, in health, quiet and secure, should be there before to-morrow morning....

...And now you have an extraordinary opportunity, a day wherein Christ has thrown the door of mercy wide open, and stands in calling and crying with a loud voice to poor sinners; a day wherein many are flocking to him and pressing into the kingdom of God. Many are daily coming from the east, west, north and south; many that were very lately in the same miserable condition that you are in, are now in a happy state, with their hearts filled with love to him who has loved them, and washed them from their sins in his own blood, and rejoicing in hope of the glory of God. How awful is it to be left behind at such a day! To see so many other feasting, while you are pining and perishing! To see so many rejoicing and singing for joy of heart, while you have cause to mourn for sorrow of heart, and howl for vexation of spirit!...

...Therefore, let every one that is out of Christ, now awake and fly from the wrath to come. The wrath of Almighty God is now undoubtedly hanging over a great part of this congregation: Let every one fly out of Sodom: "Haste and escape for your lives, look not behind you escape to the mountain, lest you be consumed."

HOW WELL DID YOU UNDERSTAND THIS SELECTION?

1. How does Edwards say that man must reach salvation?

2. How does man delude himself?

3. How does Edwards portray God in this sermon?

OF THE RELIGION OF DEISM COMPARED WITH THE CHRISTIAN RELIGION
by Thomas Paine

Those people who called themselves Deists took a more liberal view of religion. Such people believed that God was essentially a heavenly "engineer" who got the Universe up and running and left the rest in the hands of men. In the following reading, Thomas Paine attempts to compare Deism and Christianity.

Every person, of whatever religious denomination he may be, is a DEIST in the first article of his Creed. Deism from the Latin word Deus, God, is the belief of a God, and this belief is the first article of every man's creed...

...But when the divine gift of reason begins to expand itself in the mind and calls man to reflection, he then reads and contemplates God and His works, and not in the books, pretending to be revelation. The creation is the Bible of the true believer in God. Everything in this vast volume inspires him with sublime ideas of the Creator. The little and paltry, and often obscene, tales of the Bible sink into wretchedness when put in comparison with this mighty work.

The Deist needs none of those tricks and shows called miracles to confirm his faith, for what can be a greater miracle than the creation itself, and his own existence?

There is a happiness in Deism, when rightly understood, that is not to be found in any other system of religion. All other systems have something in them that either shock our reason, or are repugnant to it, and man, if he thinks at all, must stifle his reason in order to force himself to believe them.

But in Deism our reason and our belief become happily united. The wonderful structure of the universe, and everything we behold in the system of creation, prove to us, far better than books can do, the existence of a God, and at the same time proclaim His attributes.

It is by the exercise of our reason that we are enabled to contemplate God is His works, and imitate Him in His ways, When we see His care and goodness extend over all His creatures, it teaches us our duty toward each other, while it calls forth our gratitude to Him. It is by forgetting God in His works, and running after the books of pretended revelation, that man had wandered from the straight path of duty and happiness, and become by turns the victim of doubt and the dupe of delusion.

...The truth of the first article is proved by God Himself, and is universal; for the creation is of itself demonstration of the existence of a Creator. But the second article, that of God's begetting a son, is not proved in like manner, and stands on no other authority than that of a tale...

The evidence upon this article bears no comparison with evidence upon the first article, and therefore is not entitled to the same credit, and ought not to be made an article in a creed, because the evidence of it is defective, and what evidence there is, is doubtful and suspicious. We do not believe the first article in the authority of books, whether called Bibles or Korans, nor yet on the visionary authority of dreams, but on the authority of God's own visible works in the creation...

When we see a watch, we have as positive evidence of the existence of a watchmaker, as if we saw him; and in like manner the creation is evidence to our reason and our senses of the existence of a Creator. But there is nothing in the works of God that is evidence that he begot a son, nor anything in the system of creation that corroborates such an ides, and therefore, we are not authorized in believing it...

...But this is not all. The second article of the Christian creed having brought the son of Mary into the world...the next article goes on to account for his being begotten, which was, that when he grew a man he should be put to death, to expiate, they say, the sin that Adam brought into the world by eating an apple or some kind of forbidden fruit.

But though this is the creed of the church of Rome, from whence the Protestants borrowed it, it is a creed which that Church has manufactured of itself, for it is not contained in nor derived from, the book called the New Testament.

The four books called the Evangelists, Matthew, Mark, Luke and John, which give, or pretend to give, the birth, sayings, life, preaching, and death of Jesus Christ, make no mention of what is called the fall of man; nor is the name of Adam to be found in any of those books, which it certainly would be if the writers of them believed that Jesus was begotten, born, and died for the purpose of redeeming mankind from the sin which Adam had brought into the world. Jesus never speaks of Adam himself, or the garden of Eden, nor of what is called the fall of man.

But the Church of Rome having set up its new religion, which it called Christianity, invented the creed which it named the Apostle's Creed, in which it calls Jesus the only son of God, conceived by the Holy Ghost, and born of the Virgin Mary; things of which it is impossible that man or women can have any idea, and consequently no belief but in words; and for which there is no authority but the idle story of Joseph's dream in the first chapter of Matthew, which any designing impostor or foolish fanatic might make...

...As priestcraft was always the enemy of knowledge, because priestcraft supports itself by keeping people in delusion and ignorance, it was consistent with its policy to make the acquisition of knowledge a real sin...

The belief of the redemption of Jesus Christ is altogether an invention of the Church of Rome, not the doctrine of the New Testament. What writers of the New Testament attempted to prove by the the story of Jesus is the resurrection of the same body from the grave, which was the belief of the Pharisees, in opposition to the Sadducees (a sect of Jews) who denied it.

...The dogma of redemption is the fable of priestcraft invented since the time the New Testament was compiled, and the agreeable delusion of it suited with the depravity of immoral livers. When men are taught to ascribe all their crimes and vices to the temptations of the devil, and to believe that Jesus, by his death, rubs all off, and pays their passage to heaven gratis, they become as careless in moral as a spendthrift would be of money, were he told that his father had engaged to pay off all his scores.

It is a doctrine not only dangerous to morals in this world, but to our happiness in the next world, because it holds out such a cheap, easy, and lazy way of getting to heaven, as had a tendency to induce men to hug the delusion of it to their own injury.

But there are times when men have serious thoughts, and it is such times, when they begin to think, that they begin to doubt the truth of the Christian religion; and well they may, for it is too fanciful and too full of conjecture, inconsistency, improbability and irrationality, to afford consolation to the thoughtful man. His reason revolts against his creed. He sees that none of its articles are proved, or can be proved.

He may believe that such a person as is called Jesus (for Christ was not his name) was born and grew to be a man, because it is no more than a natural and probable case, but who is to prove he is the son of God, that he was begotten by the Holy Ghost? Of these things there can be no proof; and that which admits not of proof, and is against the laws of probability and the order of nature, which God Himself has established, is not an object for belief. God has not given man reason to embarrass him, but to prevent his being imposed upon...

...When an article in a creed does not admit proof nor of probability, the salvo is to call it revelation; but this is only putting one difficulty in the place of another, for it is as impossible to prove a thing to be revelation as it is to prove that Mary was gotten with child by the Holy Ghost.

Here it is that the religion of Deism is superior to the Christian Religion. It is free from all those invents and torturing articles that shock or reason or injure our humanity, and with which the Christian religion abounds, Its creed is pure, and sublimely simple. It believes in God, and there it rests.

It honors reason as the choicest gift of God to man, the faculty by which he in enable to contemplate the power; wisdom and goodness of the Creator displayed in the creation; and reposing itself on His protection, both here and hereafter, is avoids all presumptuous beliefs, and rejects, as the fabulous inventions of men, all books pretending to revelation.

HOW WELL DID YOU UNDERSTAND THIS SELECTION?

1. What proves the existence of God to Deists?

2. What does Paine see as a dangerous doctrine?

3. What does Paine see as the best gift of God to man? Why?

4. How would Jonathan Edwards respond to what Paine has to say?

THE POEMS OF PHILLIS WHEATLEY

Phillis Wheatley was brought to America as a slave while still a child. She was eventually sold to a man in Boston where she was taught by his wife to read and write. Phillis soon mastered English as well as Greek and Latin. She traveled to England with their son and, while there, published her first book in 1773 entitled "Poems on Various subjects, Religion and Moral." Phillis became free upon the death of Mr. and Mrs. Wheatley. She was the first African-American poet and, as the following poems demonstrate, wrote about a wide variety of topics, including slavery.

ON THE DEATH OF THE REV. MR. GEORGE WHITEFIELD, 1770

Hail, happy faint, on thine immortal throne,
Poffeft of glory, life, and blifs unknown,
We hear no more the mufic of thy tongue,
The wonted auditories ceafe to throng,
Thy fermons in unequall'd accents flow'd,
And ev'ry bofom with devotion glow'd;
Thou didft in ftains of eloquence refin'd
Inflame the heart, and captivate the mind.
Unhappy we the fetting fun deplore,
So glorious once, but ah! if fhines no more.

Behold the prophet in his tow'ring flight!
He leaves the earth for heav'n's unmeafur'd
        height,
And worlds unknown receive him from our fight.
There Whitefield wings with rapid courfe his way,
And fails to Zion through vast feas of day.
Thy pray'rs, great faint, and thine inceffant cries
Have pierc'd the bofom of thy native fkies.

Thou moon haft feen, and all the ftars of light,
How he had wreftled with his God by night.
He pray'd that grace in ev'ry heart might dwell,
He long'd to fee America excel;
He charg'd its youth that ev'ry grace divine
Should with full luftre in the conduct fine;

The greateft gift that ev'n a God can give,
He freely offer'd to the num'rous throng,
That on his lips with lift'ning lpeafure hung.

"Take him, ye wretched, for your only good,
"Take him ye ftarving finners, for your food;
"Ye thirfty, come to this life-giving ftream,
"Ye preachers, take him for your joyful theme;
"Take him my dear Americans, he faid,
"Be your complaints on his kind bofom laid:
"Take him, ye Africans, he longs for you,
"Impartial Savior is his title due:
"Wafh'd in the fountain of redeeming blood,
"You fhall be fons, and kings and priefts to God."

Great Countefs*, we Americans revere
Thy name, and mingle in the grief fincere;
New England deeply feels, the Orphans mourn,
Their more than father will no more return.

But, though affefted by the hand of death,
Whitefield no more exerts his lab'ring breath,
Yet let us view him in th' eternal fkies,
Let ev'ry heart to this bright vifion rife;
While the tomb fafe retains its facred truth,
Till life divine re-animats his duft.

* The Countefs of Huntingdon, to whom Mr. Whitefield was Chaplin.

HOW WELL DID YOU UNDERSTAND THIS SELECTION?

1. According to the poem, what were some of Whitefield's attributes?

2. Who does Wheatley say will be affected by Whitefield's death?

TO HIS EXCELLENCY GENERAL WASHINGTON

Celestial choir! enthron'd in realms of light,
Columbia's scenes of glorious toils I write.
While freedom's cause her anxious breast alarms,
She flashes dreadful in refulgent arms.
See mother earth her offspring's fate bemoan,
And nations gaze at scenes before unknown!
See the bright beams of heaven's revolving light
Involved in sorrows and veil of night!

The goddess comes, she move divinely fair,
Olive and laurel bind her golden hair;
Wherever shines this native of the skies,
Unnumber'd charms and recent graces rise.

Muse! bow propitious while my pen relates
How pour her armies through a thousand gates,
As when Eolus heaven's fair face deforms,
Enwrapp'd in tempest and a night of storms;
Astonish'd ocean feels the wild uproar,
The refluent surges beat the sounding shore;
Or thick as leaves in Autumn's golden reign,
Such, and so many, moves the warrior's train.
In bright array they seek the work of war,
Where high unfurl'd the ensign waves in air.
Shall I to Washington their praise recite?
Enough thou know'st them in fields of fight.
Thee, first in peace and honours, - we demand
The grace and glory of thy martial band.
Fam'd for thy valour, for thy virutes more,
Hear every tongue they guardian aid implore!

One century scarce perform'd its destined round,
When Gallic powers Columbia's fury found;
And so may you, whoever dares disgrace
The land of freedom's heaven-defended race!
Fix'd are the eyes of nations on the scales,
For in their hopes Columbia's arm prevails.
Anon Britannia droops the pensive head,
While round increase the rising hills of dead.
Ah! cruel blaindness to Columbia's state!
Lament thy thirst of boundless power too late.

Proceed, great chief, with virtue on thy side,
Thy ev'ry action let the goddess guide,
A crown, a mansion, and a throne that shine,
With gold infading, WASHINTON! be thine.

Source: *Providence*, October 26, 1775

HOW WELL DID YOU UNDERSTAND THIS SELECTION?

1. What are the qualities that the author sees in Washington?

2. Who does the author infer is on Washington's side?

ANDREW HAMILTON'S ARGUMENTS IN DEFENSE OF JOHN PETER ZENGER

John Peter Zenger was jailed and put on trial for seditious libel by the British royal governor of New York. In his newspaper, Zenger had attacked the opinions and actions of the Royal Governor, William Cosby. It was considered libelous to attack any official of the Crown. At his trial, the jury heard evidence that what Zenger had printed was true and, therefore, should not be considered as libelous. The jury found him innocent of the charge. Their decision helped to establish the foundation in American legal thought of freedom of the press.

The high things that are said in favor of rulers, and of their dignities, and upon the side of power, will not be able to stop people's mouths when they feel themselves oppressed, I mean in a free government.

There is heresy in law, as well as in religion, and both have changed very much; and we well know that it is not two centuries ago that a man would have been burnt as a heretic, for owning such opinions in matters of religion, as are publicly wrote and printed at this day. They were fallible men, it seems, and we take the liberty not only to differ from them in religious opinion, but to condemn them and their opinions too...In New-York, a man may make free with his God, but he must take special care what he says of his governor.

Who, that is the least aquainted with history of law, can be ignorant of the specious pretences, which have often been made use of by men in power, to introduce arbitrary rule, and destroy the liberties of a free people...it is a duty which all good men owe to their country, to guard against the unhappy influences of ill men when intrusted with power, and especially against their creatures and dependents, who, as they are generally more necessitous, are surely more covetous and cruel.

Men who injure and oppress the people under their administration provoke them to cry out and complain; and then make that very complaint the foundation for new oppressions and prosecutions...

...The question before the Court and you, gentlemen of the jury, is not of small nor private concern, it is not the cause of a poor printer, nor of New-York alone, which you are not trying. No! it may in its consequence, affect every freeman that lives under a British government in America. It is the best cause. It is the cause of liberty...of exposing and opposing arbitrary power (in these parts of the world at least) by speaking and writing truth.

HOW WELL DID YOU UNDERSTAND THIS SELECTION?

1. What arguments does Hamilton make in defense of Zenger?

2. What does Hamilton say is the duty of all good men?

3. What is really on trial according to Hamilton?

4. What is its significance to American history?

The Stamp Act Crisis caused Massachusetts to call for a meeting of the colonies to protest the Stamp Act. Nine colonial delegates met in New York in October 1765. The delegates passed a declaration to be sent to the King, which asserted their loyalty but also expressed their concerns at the same time.

The members of this Congress, sincerely devoted, with the warmest sentiments of affection and duty to his majesty's person and government, inviolably attached to the present happy establishment of the Protestant succession, and with minds deeply impressed by a sense of the present and impending misfortunes of the British colonies on the continent; having considered, as maturely as time will permit, the circumstances of the said colonies, esteem it our indispensable duty, to make the following declarations of our humble opinion, respecting the most essential rights and liberties of the colonists, and of the grievances under which they labour, by reason of several late acts of parliament.

1. That his majesty's subjects in these colonies, owe the same allegiance to the crown of Great Britain, that is owning from his subjects born within the realm, and all due subordination to that august body the parliament of Great Britain.

2. That his majesty's liege subjects in these colonies, are entitled to all the inherent rights and liberties of his natural born subjects, within the kingdom of Great Britain.

3. That it is inseparably essential to the freedom of a people, and the undoubted right of Englishmen, that no taxes be imposed on them, but with their own consent, given personally, or by their representatives.

4. That the people of these colonies are not, and from their local circumstances cannot be, represented in the House of Commons in Great Britain.

5. That the only representatives of the people of these colonies, are persons chosen therein by themselves, and that no taxes ever have been, or can be constitutionally imposed on them, but by their respective legislature.

6. That all supplies to the crown being free gifts of the people, it is unreasonable and inconsistent with the principles and spirit of the British constitution, for the people of Great Britain to grant his majesty the property of the colonists.

7. That trial by jury, is the inherent and invaluable right of every British subject in these colonies.

8. That the late act of parliament, entitled, an act for granting and applying certain stamp duties, and other duties, in the British colonies and plantations in America, by imposing taxes on the inhabitants of these colonies, and the said act, and several other acts, by extending the jurisdiction of the courts of admiralty beyond its ancient limits, have a manifest tendency to subvert the rights and liberties of the colonists.

9. That the duties imposed by several late acts of parliament, from the peculiar circumstances of these colonies, will be extremely burdensome and grievous; and from the scarcity of specie, the payment of them absolutely impracticable.

10. That as the profits of the trade of these colonies ultimately center in Great Britain, to pay for the manufactures which they are obliged to take from thence, they eventually contribute very largely to all supplies granted there to the crown.

11. That the restrictions imposed by several late acts of parliament on the trade of these colonies, will render them unable to purchase the manufactures of Great Britain.

12. That the increase, prosperity, and happiness of these colonies, depend on the full and free enjoyments of their rights and liberties, and an intercourse with Great Britain mutually affectionate and advantageous.

13. That it is the right of the British subjects in these colonies, to petition the king, or either house of parliament.

Lastly, That it is the indispensable duty of these colonies, to the best of sovereigns, to the mother country, and to themselves, to endeavor by a loyal and dutiful address to his majesty, and humble applications to both houses of parliament, to procure the repeal of the act for granting and applying certain stamp duties, of all clauses of any other acts of parliament, whereby the jurisdiction of the admiralty is extended as aforesaid, and of the other late acts for the restriction of American commerce.

HOW WELL DID YOU UNDERSTAND THIS SELECTION?

1. What rights do the colonists claim they have?

2. How do they say that Parliament has violated those rights?

3. What do they want Parliament to do?

Thomas Paine came to the United States in 1774, and quickly became involved in the cause for independence. His pamphlet, "Common Sense," was published in January 1776 and was an immediate success. The pamphlet helped to turn the tide towards a formal break with England.

In the following pages I offer nothing more than simple facts, plain arguments, and common sense: and have no other preliminaries to settle with the reader, than that he will divest himself of prejudice and prepossession, and suffer his reason and his feelings to determine for themselves: that he will put on, or rather that he will not put off, the true character of a man, and generously enlarge his views beyond the present day...

..I have heard it aserted by some, that as America has flourished under her former connection with Great Britain, the same connection is necessary towards her future happiness, and will always have the same effect. Nothing can be more fallacious than this kind of argument. We may as well assert that because a child has thrived upon milk, that it is never to have meat, or that the first twenty years of our lives is to become a precedent for the next twenty. But even this is admitting more than is true; for I answer roundly that America would have flourished as much and probably much more, had no European power taken any notice of her. The commerce by which she hath enriched herself are the necessaries of life, and will always have a market while eating is the custom of Europe.

But she has protected us, say some. That she hath engrossed us us true, and defended the Continent at our expense as well as her own, is admitted; and she would have defended Turkey form the same motive, viz. for the sake of trade and dominion.

Alas! we have been long led away by ancient prejudies and made large sacrifices to superinstitution. We have boasted the protection of Great Britain, without considering, that her motive was interest not attachment; and that she did not protect us from our enemies on our account: but from her enemies on her account, from those who had no quarrel with us on any other account, and who will always be our enemies on the same account. Let Britain waive her pretensions to the Continent, or the Continent throw off the dependence and we should be at peace with France and Spain, were they at war with Britain. The miseries of Hanover last war ought to warn us against connections...

...But Britain is the parent country, say some. Then the more shame upon her conduct. Even brutes do not devour their young, nor savages make war upon their own families. Wherefore, the assertion, if true, turns to her reproach; but it happens not to be true, or only partly so, and the phrase parent or mother country hath been jesuitically adopted by the King and his parasites, with low papistical design of gaining an unfair bias on the credulous weakness of our minds. Europe, and not England, is the parent country of America. This new World hath been the asylum for the persecuted lovers of civil and religious liberty from every part of Europe. Hither have they fled, not from the tender embraces of the mother, but from the cruelty of the monster; and it is do far true of England, but from the same tyranny which drove the first emigrants from home, pursues their decendents still...

...I challenge the warmest advocate for reconciliation to show a single advantage that this continent can reap by being connected with Great Britain. I repeat the challenge; not a single advantage is derived. Our corn will fetch its price in any market in Europe, and our imported goods must be paid for buy them where we will.

But the injuries and disadvantages which we sustain by that connection, are without number; and our duty to mankind at large, as well as to ourselves, instruct us to renounce the alliance: because, any submission to, or dependence on, great Britain, tends directly to involve this Continent in European wars and quarrels, and set us at variance with nations who would otherwise seek out friendship, and against whom we have neither anger nor complaint. As Europe is our market for trade, we ought to form no partial connection with any part of it. It is the true interest of America to steer clear of European contentions which she never can do, while, by her dependence on Britain, she is made the make-weight in the scale of British politics.

Europe is too thickly planted with Kingdoms to be long at peace, and whenever a war breaks out between England and any foreign power, the trade of America goes to ruin because of her connections with Britain. The next war may not turn out like the last, and should not, the advocates for reconciliation now will be wishing for separation then, because neutrality in that case would be a safer convoy than a man of war. Every thing that is right or reasonable pleads for separation. The blood of the slain, the weeping voice of nature cries, 'TIS TIME TO PART. Even the distance at which the Almighty hath placed England and America is a strong and natural proof that the authority of the one over the other, was never the design of Heaven. The time likewise at which the Continent was discovered, adds weight to the argument, and the manner which it was peopled, encrease the force of it. The Reformation was preceded by the discovery of America: As if the Almighty graciously, meant to open a sanctuary to the persecuted in future years, when home should afford neither friendship nor safety...

..Men of passive tempers look somewhat lightly over the offences of Great Britain, and, still hoping for the best, are apt to call out, Come, come, we shall be friends again for all this.

But examine the passions and feelings of mankind: bring the doctrine or reconciliation to the touchstone of nature, and then tell me whether you can herafter love, honor, and faithfuly serve the power that hath carried fire and sword into your land? If cannot do all these, then are you only deceiving yourselves, and by your delay bringing ruin upon posterity. Your future connection with Britain, whom you can neither love nor honor, will be forced and unnatural, and being formed only on the plan of present convenience, will in a little time fall into a relapse more wretched than the first. But if you say, you can still pass the violations over, then I ask, hath your house been burnt? Hath your property been destroyed before your face? Are you wife and children destitute of a bed to lie on, or bread to live on? Have you lost a parent or child by their hands, and yourself the ruined and wretched survivor? If you have not, then are you not a judge of those who have. But if you have, and can still shake hands with the murderers, then are you unworthy the name of husband, father, friend or lover, and whatever may be your rank or title in life, you have the heart of a coward, and the spirit of a sycophant...

...Small islands not capable of protecting themsleves are the proper objects for government to take under their care; but there is something absurd, in supposing a Continent to be perpetually governed by an island. In no instance hath nature made the satellite larger than its primary planet; and as England and America, with respect to each other, reverse the common order of nature, it is evident that they belong to different systems. England to Europe; America to itself...

...No man was a warmer wisher for a reconciliation than myself, before the fatal nineteenth of April, 1775, but the moment the event of that day was made known, I rejected the hardened, sullen-tempered Paraoh of England for ever; and disdain the wretch, that with the pretended title of FATHER OF HIS PEOPLE can unfeelingly hear of their slaughter, and composedly sleep with their blood upon his soul...

..But the most powerful of all arguments is, that nothing but independence, i.e. a Continental form of government, can keep the peace of the Continent and preserve it inviolate from civil wars. I dread the event of a reconciliation with Britain now, as it is more than probable that it will be followed by a revolt some where or other, the consequences of which may be far more fatal than all the malice of Britain...

...I have heard men say, many of whom I believe spoke without thinking, that they dreaded an independence, fearing that it would produce civil wars: It is but seldom that our first thoughts are truly correct, and that is the case here; for there is ten times more to dread from a patched up connection than from independence. I make the sufferer's case my own, and I protest, that were I driven from house and home, my property destroyed, and my circumstances ruined, that as a man, sensible of injuries, I could never relish the doctrine of reconciliation, or consider myself bound thereby...

...Ye that tell us of harmony and reconciliation, can ye restore to us the time that is past? Can ye give to prostitution its former innocence? neither can ye reconcile Britain and America. The last cord now is broken, the people of England are presenting addresses against us. There are injuries which nature cannot forgive; she would cease to be nature if she did...

...O! ye that love mankind! Ye that dare oppose not only the tyranny but the tyrant, stand forth! Every spot of the old world is overrun with oppression. Freedom hath been hunted round the Globe. Asia and Africa have long expelled her. Europe regards her like a stranger, and England hath given her warning to depart. O! receive the fugitive, and prepare in time an asylum for mankind.

HOW WELL DID YOU UNDERSTAND THIS SELECTION?

1. What arguments does Paine give as to why America should separate with England?

2. How had our relationship with England hurt America?

3. What does he see as a future role for the new country?

4. Why was this so influential?

SELF TEST:

MULTIPLE CHOICE: Circle the correct response. The correct answers are given at the end.

1. The primary reason for the population growth in the American colonies was
   a. immigration.
   b. natural reproduction.
   c. the introduction of slaves.
   . d. the subjugation of native tribes.

2. The Great Awakening
   a. helped to break down sectional boundaries.
   b. was a highly intellectual experience.
   c. was based on man's reason.
   d. was limited only to the west.

3. The trial of John Zenger
    a. established the idea of religious freedom.
    b. established the idea of unifying the colonies.
    c. established the idea of trial by jury.
    d. established the idea of freedom of the press.

4. The Navigation Acts
    a. concerned themselves with freedom on the sea.
    b. concerned themselves with trade between England and Europe.
    c. were designed to regulate trade between the colonies and England.
    d. were designed to standardize the rules of shipping.

5. The aftermath of the French and Indian War
    a. saw England relaxing its control of the colonies.
    b. saw England tighten its control of the colonies.
    c. saw England fight another war with France over Canada.
    d. saw France increase its share of the fur trade.

6. The Stamp Act
    a. was well received by the Americans.
    b. was the first attempt at internal taxation.
    c. was successful in what it hoped to accomplish.
    d. was the first attempt at external taxation.

7. Why did Parliament repeal most of the Townsend Acts?
    a. because non-importation of British goods hurt British merchants.
    b. because the King felt Parliament had overstepped its authority.
    c. because they were declared illegal by the British Courts.
    d. because the need for them no longer existed.

8. The Coercive or Intolerable Acts
    a. were designed to punish the French agitators in Canada.
    b. were designed to punish Philadelphia for hosting the Continental Congress.
    c. were designed to punish Boston and Massachusetts for The Boston Tea Party.
    d. were designed to punish the British soldiers for not doing their job.

9. "Common Sense"
    a. called for reconciliation with England.
    b. called for revolution.
    c. called for a cooling-off period between England and the American colonies.
    d. was circulated secretly to avoid British spies.

10. The colonies and England were never able to solve the issue of
    a. who had the right to tax the colonies.
    b. the role of the king in the colonies.
    c. the role of Royal Governors.
    d. who controlled trade.

Answers:
        1-b; 2-a; 3-d; 4-c; 5-b; 6-b; 7-a; 8-c; 9-b; 10-a;

ESSAYS:

1.   Explain how religious and political events in colonial America might have helped encourage the colonies to revolt against Britain?

2.   Based on the readings here of Thomas Paine, would he have supported the principles behind the Constitution? Explain your answer.

OPTIONAL ACTIVITIES: (Use your knowledge **and** imagination when appropriate.)

1.   You are in a religious debate with Jonathan Edwards over the way to find salvation. You are a Deist. What would your position be? What would Edward's position be?

2.   Imagine that you are a leader in colonial America. What would you propose the colonies do instead of revolting against England?

3.   You are a member in Parliament. The debate is over what should be done with the American colonies after the French and Indian War. What would you recommend?

WEB SITE LISTINGS:

Hubsite for Pre-Revolutionary Period People and Documents, managed by Kendall Simmons, Government Documents Library, U. of Kansas
>   http://www.ukans.edu/carrie/docs/amdocs_index.html

The Writings of Jonathan Edwards
>   http://membersaol.com/jonathanedw/sinners.htm

The Religion of Deism and Writings of Thomas Paine
>   http://www.deism.com/paine.htm

Documents Concerning the Stamp Act and other Pre-Revolutionary Documents
>   http://www.usconstitution.net

Yale University's Avalon Project Dealing With Documents of the Time Period
>   http://www.yale.edu/lawweb/avalon/avalon.htm

The University of Virginia
>   http://www.lib.virginia.edu

Chapter Five

A NEW NATION IS CREATED

Once the colonies in America declared their independence, they then had to accomplish several things simultaneously. First, they had to organize some type of formal government to rule and conduct the new nation's business. In addition, they also had to wage a victorious war in order to guarantee the survival of their new country.

The colonies (now states) had previously been advised to adopt their own state constitutions. There was, however, no framework in place for a political system that would unite all of the states. The Second Continental Congress conducted the affairs of the United States and eventually drafted a framework for governmental operation known as the Articles of Confederation. This document was sent to states for ratification in 1777 and was finally ratified in 1781.

The Articles of Confederation reflected the old fears of the colonies. Since they had been afraid of an all-powerful king in the past, the new confederation had no executive branch. Likewise, there was no national court system, with the role of the judiciary being left up to the states. The sole governmental body was a one-house Congress. Within its body, each state held one vote. Important decisions required nine out of thirteen states. To change the Articles required a unanimous vote of the states. Fearing an office-holding elite, the members of the Congress would serve a total of six years, three years on and three years off.

The Revolutionary War did not go well in the beginning for the Americans. The army endured a series of retreats from the British in the opening months of the war. December 1776 saw the Revolutionary Army's strength erode from approximately twenty thousand members to only a few hundred. The cause for independence needed a victory to rally the American people to its side. General George Washington provided that victory on December 26, 1776. In a bold move, he and his army crossed the Delaware River and surprised Hessian soldiers hired by the English and stationed at Trenton, New Jersey. Only a few days later, on January 3, 1777, this victory was followed by another. This time Washington defeated British General Cornwallis, forcing a retreat and freeing most of New Jersey from British control. Other victories followed, including the Battle of Saratoga (in which British General Burgoyne was forced to surrender five thousand men to the American army) and the Battle of Yorktown, the final major conflict of the war where General Cornwallis surrendered on October 24, 1781. Although it took some time for all fighting powers to come to an agreement, the Treaty of Paris, signed on September 3, 1783, officially recognized the independence of the United States.

The Articles of Confederation had helped to win the war, but they now presented problems. The confederation that had been created under the Articles was really just a loose alliance of states. This situation tended to create chaos and confusion. For instance, each state claimed sovereign power and, as such, could levy import and export duties and even coin its own money. Congress did not have the power to control this chaos. In fact, it had very little control over the states.

An event in Massachusetts, known as Shays' Rebellion, highlighted the problems of the confederacy. From August 1786 to February 1787, the farmers in that state (led by Daniel Shays, a veteran of the Revolutionary War) tried to close down the courts in order to protest the taking of farms due to bankruptcy. Shays and his followers tried to seize the government's arsenal at Springfield, Massachusetts. The government under the Articles was unable to put down the rebellion. The merchants and other propertied classes within the state finally hired a military force to end it.

This event frightened many people of the upper classes who feared economic chaos. It helped give volume to the rising voice of those concerned that the Articles of Confederation could not protect their interests. They felt a stronger central government was needed. Eventually, a call was heard for a national convention to be held in Philadelphia to deal with the problems of the Articles of Confederation.

The delegates who were sent to Philadelphia in May 1787 to revise and correct the problems of the Articles became the Constitutional Convention. Once the meeting began, the delegates attending decided that the best way to revise the Articles was to replace them altogether. They kept their deliberations secret throughout the long, hot summer of 1787, and in September of that year came up with a document that was much different than the Articles of Confederation it intended to replace.

This new document was made possible by several compromises. The Great Compromise created a two-house legislature, with the lower house's representation based on population and the upper house made up of two representatives per state.

With the framework of the new Congress set up, the Convention had to decide how the members would actually be selected. It was finally determined that members of the lower house would be chosen by the voters while those of the upper house would be elected by state legislatures.

Unlike the government established under the Articles, there would be a chief executive, chosen by an "electoral college." The government that evolved was, in fact, a blend of democratic (the House of Representatives), aristocratic (the Senate) and monarchic (the President) principles.

Another compromise dealt with the issue of slavery. The South wanted its slaves counted for representation purposes; the North for taxation purposes. However, for the Southerners to count a slave as a person would be admitting to a racial equality that would never do. A formula was worked out where each slave would be counted as three-fifths (3/5s) of a white man.

Another compromise concerning slavery allowed commerce bills to be passed by a simple majority. The South relented on this to the North while the North, in return, agreed to not stop the importation of slaves for twenty years. Northern delegates further allowed the South its wish to require that the Senate ratify treaties.

The Constitution made the United States a nation. The federal government was stronger than, and had more control over, the states. Equally important, the Constitution allowed for change. The amendment process allowed the document the ability to change with the times, tempers, and values of the people it governed.

IDENTIFICATION: Briefly describe each term

Second Continental Congress

Articles of Confederation

Battle of Trenton

Battle of Saratoga

French Intervention

Yorktown

Treaty of Paris

Loyalists

Northwest Ordinance of 1785

Northwest Ordinance of 1787

Shays Rebellion

Annapolis Convention

Constitutional Convention

The Great Compromise

Three-fifths Compromise

Federal government

States rights

Amendment process

Federalists

Anti-Federalists

Bill of Rights

THINK ABOUT:

1.   What were some of the forces at work that allowed the Americans to win the Revolutionary War?

2.   Could the Continental Congress, instead of the Articles of Confederation, have adopted the Constitution? Why or why not?

3.   What problems in the Articles of Confederation were corrected by the Constitution?

Throughout the Revolutionary War, American women had to take care of their families and business affairs while their husbands were away fighting or involved in the governmental functions of the new country. In addition to tending to many new responsibilities and duties, many of these women had to face being on or near the front lines during the war.

Abigail Adams suffered through many long absences of her husband, John. While he was a member of Congress in Philadelphia, her letters to him told of the war effort in the area near Boston where she was living. They also included her own observations on people and thoughts about the events of her time. The first few letters begin prior to the formal break with England in the Declaration of Independence. In them, Abigail Adams writes of the hardships experienced by the people in Boston due to the Coercive Acts passed by the British in retaliation for the Boston Tea Party.

Sunday, 18 June, 1775...

The day,—perhaps the decisive day,—is come, on which the fate of America depends. My bursting heart must vent at my pen. I have just heard, that our dear friend, Dr. Warren, is no more, but fell gloriously fighting for his country; saying, better to die honorably in the field, than ignominiously hang upon the gallows. Great is our loss. He has distinguished himself in every engagement, by his courage and fortitude, by animating the soldiers, and leading them on by his own example. A particular account of these dreadful, but I hope glorious days will be transmitted you, no doubt, in the exactest manner.

"The race is not to the swift, not the battle to the strong; but the God of Israel is he, that giveth strength and power unto his people. Trust in him at all times, ye people, pour out your hearts before him; God is a refuge for us." Charlestown is laid in ashes. The battle began upon our intrenchments upon Bunker's Hill, Saturday morning about three o'clock, and has not ceased yet, and it is now three o'clock Sabbath afternoon.

It is expected they will come out over the Neck to-night, and a dreadful battle must ensue. Almighty God, cover the heads of our countrymen, and be a shield to our dear friends! How many have fallen, we know not. The constant roar of the cannon is so distressing, that cannot eat, drink, or sleep. May we be supported and sustained in the dreadful conflict. I shall tarry here till till it is thought unsafe by my friends, and then I have secured myself a retreat at your brother's, who has kindly offered me part of his house. I cannot compose myself to write any further at present. I will add more as I hear further...

...16 July, 1775...

...As to intelligence from Boston, it is but seldom we are able to collect any thing that may be relied on; and to report the vague, flying rumors, would be endless. I heard yesterday, by one Mr. Roulstone, a goldsmith, who got out in a fishing schooner, that their distress increased upon them fast. Their beef is all spent; their malt and cider all gone. All the fresh provisions they can procure, they are obliged to give to the sick and wounded. Thirteen of our men who were in jail, and were wounded at the battle of Charlestown, were dead. No man dared now be seen talking to his friend in the street. They were obliged to be within, every evening, at ten o'clock, according to martial law; nor could any inhabitant walk any street in town after that time without a pass from Gage. He has order all the molasses to be distilled up into rum for the soldiers; taken away all licenses, and given out others, obliging to a forfeiture of ten pounds, if any rum is sold without written orders from the general...

As to the situation of the camps, our men are in general healthy, much more so at Roxbury than at Cambridge, and the camp is in vastly better order. General Thomas has the character of an excellent officer. His merit has certainly been overlooked, as modest merit generally is. I hear General Washington is much pleased with his conduct.

Every article here in the West India way is very scarce and dear. In six weeks we shall not be able to purchase any article of the kind. I wish you would let Bass get me one pound of pepper, and two yards of black calamanco for shoes. I cannot wear leather, if I go barefoot. Bass may make a fine profit if he lays in stock for himself. You can hardly imagine how much we want many common small articles, which are not manufactured amongst ourselves; but we will have them in time; not one pin to be purchased for love or money. I wish you could convey me a thousand by any friend travelling this way. It is very provoking to have such a plenty so near us, but Tantalus-like, not be able to touch. I should have been glad to have laid in a small stock of the West India articles, but cannot get one copper; no one person thinks of paying any thing, and I do not choose to run in debt.

We have not yet been so much distressed for grain. Every thing at present looks blooming. O that peace would once more extend her olive branch...

...12 November, 1775

The intelligence you will receive before this reaches you, will, I should think, make a plain path, though a dangerous one, for you. I could not join to-day, in the petitions of our worthy pastor, for a reconciliation between our no longer parent state, by tyrant state, and these colonies. Let us separate; they are unworthy to be our brethren. Let us renounce them; and, instead of supplications as formerly, for their prosperity and happiness, let us beseech the Almighty to blast their counsels, and bring to nought all their devices...

Saturday Evening, 2 March, 1776...

...I heartily wish every Tory was extirpated form America; they are continually, by secret means, undermining and injuring our cause.

I am charmed with the sentiments of "Common Sense," and wonder how an honest heart, one who wishes the welfare of his country and the happiness of posterity, can hesitate one moment at adopting them. I want to know how these sentiments are received in Congress. I dare to say there would be no difficulty in procuring a vote and instructions from all the Assemblies in New England for Independency. I most sincerely wish, that now, in the lucky moment, it might be done.

I have been kept in a continual state of anxiety and expectation, ever since you left me. It has been said "to-morrow" and "to-morrow" for this month, but when the dreadful to-morrow will be, I know not. But Hark! The house this instant shakes with the roar of cannon. I have been to the door and find it is a cannonade from our army. Orders, I find, are come for all remaining militia to repair to the lines Monday night by twelve o'clock. No sleep for me to-night. And if I cannot, who have no guilt upon my soul with regard to this cause, how shall the miserable wretches, who have been the procurers of this dreadful scene, and those who are to be the actors, lie down with the load of guilt upon their souls?

Sunday Evening, 3 March

I went to bed after twelve, but got no rest; the cannon continued firing, and my heart beat pace with them all night. We have had a pretty quiet day, but what to-morrow will bring forth, god only knows.

Monday evening

Tolerably quiet. To-day the militia have all mustered, with three days' provision, and are all marched by three o'clock this afternoon, though their notice was no longer ago than eight o'clock, Saturday. And now we have scarcely a man, but our regular guards, either in Weymouth, Hingham, Braintree, or Milton, and the militia from the more remote towns are called in as seacoast guards. Can you form to yourself an idea of our sensations?

I have just returned from Penn's Hill, where I have been sitting to hear the amazing roar of cannon, and from whence I could see every shell which was thrown. The sound, I think, is one of the grandest in nature, and is of the true species of the sublime. 'Tis now an incessant roar; but O! the fatal ideas, which are connected with the sound! How many of our dear countrymen must fall!

Tuesday Morning

I went to bed about twelve, and rose again a little after one. I could no more sleep than if I had been in the engagement; the rattling of the windows, the jar of the house, the continual roar of twenty-four pounders, and the bursting of shells, give us such ideas, and realize a scene to us of which we could form scarcely any conception. About six, this morning, there was quiet. I rejoiced in a few hours' calm. I hear we got possession of Dorchester hill last night; four thousand men upon it to-day; lost but one man. The ships are all drawn round the town. To-night we shall realize a more terrible scene still. I sometimes think I cannot stand it. I wish myself with you, out of hearing, as I cannot assist them. I hope to give you joy of Boston, even if it is in ruins, before I send you this away. I am too much agitated to write as I ought, and languid for want of rest.

HOW WELL DID YOU UNDERSTAND THIS SELECTION?

1. What are the conditions in Boston and the surrounding areas due to the Coercive Acts?

2. How are the Americans dealing with the situation?

3. What do these readings tell you about what colonial women's life was like during the war?

"THE GAME IS PRETTY NEAR UP"

The following letter was sent by George Washington to his brother, Augustine Washington, December 18, 1776, at a low point in the American War for Independence.

Owing to the number of letters I write, the recollection of any particular one is destroyed, but I think my last to you was by Colonel Woodford, from Hackinsac. Since that time, and a little before, our affairs have taken an adverse turn, but not more than was to be expected from the unfortunate measures, which have been adopted for the establishment of our army...

...We are in a very disaffected part of the Province; and, between you and me, I think out affairs are in a very bad situation; not so much from apprehension of General Howe's army, as from the defection of New York, Jerseys, and Pennsylvania...

I have no doubt but that General Howe will still make an attempt upon Philadelphia this winter. I see nothing to oppose him a fortnight hence, as the time of all the troops, except those of Virginia reduced (almost to nothing,) and Smallwood's regiment of Maryland, equally as bad, will expire in less than that time. In a word, my dear Sir, if every nerve is not strained to recruit the new army with all possible expedition, I think the game is pretty near up, owing, in great measure, to the insidious arts of the enemy, and disaffection on the colonies before mentioned, but principally to the accursed policy of short enlistment's, and placing too great a dependence on the militia, the evil consequences of which were foretold fifteen months ago, with a spirit almost Prophetic...

HOW WELL DID YOU UNDERSTAND THIS SELECTION?

1. What does Washington see as problems in the army?

2. What does Washington allude to as to the loyalty of the people in the area where he is?

3. What does the army need at this point?

THE CRISIS PAPERS—NUMBER 1 By Thomas Paine

---

*The **Crisis Papers** were a series of essays written by Thomas Paine from 1776 to 1783 covering a variety of current topics of the times. In this, his first paper, his goal is to rally the Americans to fight for their new country. This paper (written just a few days after Washington's letter) expresses the same concerns yet is optimistic.*

December 23, 1776

These are the times that try men's souls. The summer soldier and the sunshine patriot will in this crisis, shrink from the service of his country; but he that stands it NOW, deserves the love and thanks of man and woman. Tyranny, like hell, is not easily conquered; yet we have this consolation with us, that the harder the conflict, the more glorious the triumph. What we obtain too cheap, we esteem too lightly; 'tis dearness only that gives everything its value. Heaven knows how to put a proper price upon its goods; and it would be strange indeed, if so celestial an article as FREEDOM should not be highly rated. Britain, with an army to enforce her tyranny, has declared that she has a right (*not only to* TAX) but "to BIND *us in* ALL CASES WHATSOEVER," and if being *bound in that manner*, is not slavery, then is there not such a thing as slavery upon earth. Even the expression is impious, for so unlimited a power can belong only to God.

Whether the independence of the continent was declared too soon, or delayed too long, I will not now enter into as an argument; my own simple opinion is, that had it been eight months earlier, it would have been much better. We did not make a proper use of last winter, neither could we, while we were still in a dependent state. However, the fault, if it were one, was all our own; we have none to blame but ourselves. But no great deal is lost yet; all that Howe had been doing for this month past, is rather ravage than a conquest, which the spirit of the Jerseys a year ago would have quickly repulsed, and which time and a little resolution will soon recover.

I have as little superstition in me as any man living, but my secret opinion have ever been, and still is, that God Almighty will not give up a people to military destruction, or leave then unsupportedly to perish, who have so earnestly and so repeatedly sought to avoid the calamities of war, by every decent method which wisdom could invent. Neither have I so much infidel in me, as to suppose that he has relinquished the government of the world, and given us up to the care of devils; and as I do not, I cannot see on what grounds the king of Britain can look up to heaven for help against us: a common murderer, a highwayman, or a house-breaker, has as good a pretense as he.

...I shall not now attempt to give all the particulars of our retreat to the Delaware; suffice for the present to say, that both officers and men, though greatly harasses and fatigued, without rest, covering, or provision, the inevitable consequences of a long retreat, bore it with a manly and martial spirit. All their wishes centred in one, which was, that the country would turn out and help them to drive the enemy back...

...I shall conclude this paper with some miscellaneous remarks on the state of our affairs; and shall begin with asking the following question: Why is it that the enemy have left the New-England provinces, and made these middle ones the seat of war? The answer is easy: New-England is not infested with tories and we are. I have been tender is raising the cry against these men, and I used numberless arguments to show them their danger, but it will not do to sacrifice a world either to their folly or their baseness. The period is now arrived, in which either they or we must change our sentiments, or one or both must fall. And what is a tory? Good God! what is he? I should not be afraid to go with a hundred whigs against a thousand tories, were they to attempt to get into arms. Every tory is a coward; for servile, slavish, self-interested fear is the foundations of toryism; and a man under such influence, though he may be cruel, never can be brave...

...Quitting this class of men, I turn with the warm ardor of a friend to those who have nobly stood, and are yet determined to stand the matter out; I call not upon a few, but upon all; not on *this* state or *that* state, but on *every* state; up and help us; lay your shoulders to the wheel; better have too much force than too little, when so great an object is at stake. Let it be told to the future world, that in the depth of winter, when nothing but hope and virtue could survive, that the city and the country, alarmed at one common danger, came forth to meet and repulse it. Say not that thousands are gone, turn out your tens of thousands; throw not the burden of the day upon Providence, but "*show your faith by your works,*" that God may bless you. It matters not where you live, or what rank of life you hold, the evil or the blessing will reach you all. The far and the near, the home counties and the back, the rich and the poor, will suffer or rejoice alike...

...I thank God that I fear not. I see not real cause for fear. I know our situation well and can see the way out of it. While our army was collected, Howe dared not risk a battle; and it is no credit to him that he decamped from the White Plains, and waited a mean opportunity to ravage at the defenseless Jerseys; but it is a great credit to us, that, with a handful of men, we sustained an orderly retreat for near an hundred miles, brought off our ammunition, all our field pieces, the greatest part of our stores, and had four rivers to pass. None can say that our retreat was precipitate, for we were near three weeks in performing it, that the country might have time to come in. Twice we marched back to meet the enemy, and remained out till dark. The sign of fear was not seen in our camp, and had not some of the cowardly and disaffected inhabitants spread false alarms through the country, the Jerseys had never been ravaged. Once more we are again collected and collecting, our new army at both ends of the continents is recruiting fast, and we shall be able to open the next campaign with sixty thousand men, well armed and clothed. This is our situation, and who will may know it. By perseverance and fortitude we have the prospect of a glorious issue; by cowardice and submission, the sad choice of a variety of evils - a ravaged country- a depopulated city-habitations without safety, and slavery without hope- our homes turned into barracks and bawdy-houses for Hessians, and a future race to provide for, whose fathers we shall doubt of. Look on the picture and weep over it! and if there yet remains one thoughtless wretch who believes it not, let him suffer it unlamented.

HOW WELL DID YOU UNDERSTAND THIS SELECTION?

1. What does Paine think should have been done sooner? Why?

2. Why does Paine think the Americans will win the war?

3. What does he call on Americans to do? What does he say to convince them?

BATTALIONS OF NEGROES

One question that the Americans had to answer in the Revolutionary War was whether they should use slaves to help in the fight. At first, many Americans were against this idea. Some were against it because of the racial issues involved. Others were against it because it seemed hypocritical to seek their own freedom while enslaving others. What follows is a letter written by Alexander Hamilton (who at the time was aide-de-camp to George Washington) to John Jay.

Hamilton was a student at Kings College (later named Columbia) when the Revolutionary War broke out. He became Washington's aide-de-camp in the war. After the war, Hamilton was a strong supporter of the Constitution and served as the first Secretary of the Treasury in Washington's administration.

Head-quarters, March 14th, 1779

Dear Sir,

Colonel Laurens, who will have the honour of delivering you this letter, is on his way to South Carolina, on a project which I think, in the present situation of affairs there, is a very good one, and deserves every kind of support and encouragement. This is to raise two, three, or four battalions of negroes, with the assistance of the government of that State, by contributions from the owners, in proportion to the number they possess. If you should think proper to enter upon the subject with him, he will give you a detail of this plan. He wishes to have it recommended by Congress to the State; and as an inducement, that they would engage to take those battalions into continental pay.

It appears to me that an expedient of this kind, in the present state of southern affairs, is the most rational that can be adopted, and promises very important advantages. Indeed, I hardly see how a sufficient force can be collected in that quarter without it; and the enemy's operations there are growing infinitely serious and formidable. I have not the least doubt that the negroes will make very excellent soldiers with the proper management; and I will venture to pronounce that they cannot be put into better hands than those of Mr. Laurens. He has all the zeal, intelligence, enterprise, and every other qualification necessary to succeed in such an undertaking. It is a maxim with some great military judges, that with sensible officers, soldiers can hardly be too stupid; and, on this principle, it is thought that the Russians would make the best troops in the world, if they were under other officers than their own. The King of Prussia is among the number who maintain this doctrine, and has a very emphatical saying on the occasion, which I do not exactly recollect. I mention this, because I hear it frequently objected to the scheme of imbodying negroes, that they are too stupid to make soldiers. This is so far from appearing to me a valid objection, that I think their want of cultivation (for their natural faculties are probably as good as ours,) joined to that habit of subordination, which they acquire from a life of servitude, will make them sooner become soldiers than our white inhabitants. Let officers be men of sense and sentiment, and the nearer the soldiers approach to machines, perhaps the better.

I foresee that this project will have to combat much opposition from prejudice and self-interest. The contempt we have been taught to entertain for the blacks, makes us fancy many things that are founded neither in reason nor experience; and an unwillingness to part with property of so valuable a kind, will furnish a thousand arguments to show the impracticability, or pernicious tendency, of a scheme which requires such a sacrifice. But it should be considered, that if we do not make use of them in this way, the enemy will probably will; and that the best way to counteract the temptations they will hold out, will be to offer them ourselves. An essential part of the plan is to give them their freedom with their muskets. This will secure their fidelity, animate their courage, and, I believe, will have good influence upon those who remain, by opening a door to their emancipation. This circumstance, I confess, has no small weight in inducing me to wish the success of the project; for the dictates of humanity and true policy equally interest me in favour of this unfortunate class of men.

With the truest respect and esteem,

I am, sir your most obedient servant,
Alex. Hamilton

HOW WELL DID YOU UNDERSTAND THIS SELECTION?

1. What reasons does Hamilton give as to why black soldiers should be used now?

2. Why does Hamilton feel that "Negroes" will make better soldiers than whites?

3. Why does Hamilton feel that the blacks should be freed upon enlistment?

As the Revolutionary War was raging, Congress drafted and sent to the states the Articles of Confederation for their approval as the form of government of the new nation. The Articles were agreed to by Congress on November 15, 1777 and finally ratified on March 1, 1781.

Preamble

To all whom these Presents shall come, we the undersigned Delegates of the States affixed to our names send greetings. Whereas the Delegates of the United States of America in Congress assembled did on the fifteenth day of November in the Year of our Lord One Thousand Seven Hundred and Seventy Seven, and in the Second Year of the Independence of America agree to certain articles of Confederation and perpetual Union between the States of New Hampshire, Massachusetts bay, Rhode Island and Providence Plantations, Connecticut, New York, New Jersey, Pennsylvania, Delaware, Maryland, Virginia, North Carolina, South Carolina, and Georgia in the Words following, viz. "Articles of Confederation and and perpetual Union between the States of New Hampshire, Massachusetts bay, Rhode Island and Providence Plantations, Connecticut, New York, New Jersey, Pennsylvania, Delaware, Maryland, Virginia, North Carolina, South Carolina and Georgia.

Article I. The Style of this confederacy shall be "The United States of America."

Article II. Each state retains its sovereignty, freedom, and independence, and every power, jurisdiction and right, which is not by this Confederation expressly delegated to the United States, in Congress assembled.

Article III. The said States hereby severally enter into a firm league of friendship with each other, for their common defence, the security of their liberties, and their mutual and general welfare, binding themselves to assist each other, against all force offered to, or attacks made upon them, or any of them, on account of religion, sovereignty, trade or any other pretence whatever.

Article IV. The better to secure and perpetuate mutual friendship and intercourse among the people of the different States in this Union, the free inhabitants of each of these States, paupers, vagabonds, and fugitives from justice excepted, shall be entitled to all privileges and immunities if free citizens in the several States; and the people of each state shall have free ingress and regress to and from any other State, and shall enjoy therein all the privileges of trade and commerce, subject to the same duties, impositions and restrictions as the inhabitants thereof respectively, provided that such restriction shall not extend so fare as to prevent the removal of property imported into any states, to any other state of which the Owner is an inhabitant; provided also that no imposition, duties or restriction shall be laid by any states, on the property of the United States, or either of them.

If any person guilty of or charged with treason, felony, or other high misdemeanor in any state, shall flee from justice, and be found in any of the United States, he shall upon the demand of the governor or executive power of the state from which he fled, be delivered up and removed to the State having jurisdiction of his offence.

Full faith and credit shall be given in each of these States to the records, acts and judicial proceedings of the courts and magistrates of every other state.

Article V. For the more convenient management of the general interests of the United States, delegates shall be annually appointed in such manner as the legislature of each state shall direct, to meet in Congress on the first Monday in November, in every year, with a power reserved to each state, to recall its delegates, or any of them, at any time within the year, and to send others in their stead, for the remainder of the year.

No states shall be represented in Congress by less than two, nor by more than seven Members; and no person shall be capable of being for more than three years in any term of six years; nor shall any person, being a delegate, be capable of holding any office under the United States, for which he, or another for his benefit receives any salary, fees or emolument of any kind.

Each state shall maintain its own delegates in a meeting of the States, and while they act as members of the committee of the States.

In determining questions in the United States, in Congress assembled, each State shall have one vote.

Freedom of speech and debate in Congress shall not be impeached or questioned in any Court, or place out of Congress, and the members of Congress shall be protected in their persons from arrests and imprisonments, during their time of going to and from, and attendance on Congress, except for treason, felony, or breach of the peace.

Article VI. No state without the Consent of the United States in Congress assembled, shall send any embassy to, receive any embassy from, or enter into any conference, agreement, or alliance or treaty with any king, prince or state; nor shall any person holding any office of profit or trust under the United States, or any of them, accept of any present, emolument, office or title of any kind whatever form any king, prince or foreign state; nor shall the United states in Congress assembled, or any of them, grant any title of nobility.

No two or more States shall enter into any treaty, confederation, or alliance whatever between them, without the consent of the United States in Congress assembled, specifying accurately the purposes for which the same is to be entered into, and how long it shall continue.

No state shall lay any imposts or duties, which may interfere with any stipulations in treaties, entered into by the United States in Congress assembled, with any king, prince or state, in pursuance of any treaties already proposed by Congress, to the courts of France and Spain.

No vessels of war shall be kept up in time of peace by any State, except such number only, as shall be deemed necessary by the United States in congress assembled, for the defence of such State or its trade; nor shall any body of forces be kept up by any State, in time of peace, except such number only, as in the judgment of the United States in Congress assembled, shall be deemed requisite to garrison the forts necessary for the defence of the State; but ever State shall always keep a well regulated and disciplined militia, sufficiently armed and accoutered, and shall provide and constantly have ready for use in public stores, a due number of field pieces and tents, and a proper quantity of arms, ammunition and camp equipage.

No state shall engage in war without the consent of the United States in Congress assembled, unless such state be actually invaded by enemies, or shall have received certain advice of a resolution being formed by some nation of Indians to invade such State, and the danger is so imminent as not to admit of a delay, till the United States in Congress assembled can be consulted; nor shall any state grant commissions to any ships or vessels of war, nor letters of marque or reprisal, except to be after a declaration of war by the United States in Congress assembled, and then only against the kingdom or State and the subjects thereof, against which war had been so declared, and under such regulations as shall be established by the United States in Congress assembled, unless such state be infested by pirates, in which case vessels of war my be fitted our for that occasion, and kept so long as the danger shall continue, or until the United States in Congress assembled shall determine otherwise...

...Article VIII. All charges or war, and all other expenses that shall be incurred for the common defence or general welfare, and allowed by the United States in Congress assembled, shall be defrayed out of a common treasury, which shall be supplied by the several States, in proportion to the value of all land within each state, granted to or surveyed for any person, as such land and the buildings and improvements thereon shall be estimated according to such mode as the United States in Congress assembled, shall from time to time direct and appoint. The taxes for paying that proportion shall be laid and levied by the authority and direction of the legislatures of the several States within the time agreed upon by the United States in Congress assembled.

Article IX. The United States in Congress assembled, shall have the sole and exclusive right and power of determining on peace and war, except in the cases mentioned in the sixth article- of sending and receiving ambassadors- entering into treaties and alliances, provided that no treaty of commerce shall be made whereby the legislative power of the respective States shall be restrained from imposing such imposts and duties on foreigners, as their own people are subjected to, or from prohibiting the exportation or importation of any species of goods or commodities what- soever...

....The United States in Congress assembled shall also have the sole and exclusive right and power of regulating the alloy and value of coin struck by their own authority, or by that of the respective States - fixing the standard of weights and measures throughout the United states. - regulating the trade and managing all affairs with the Indians, not members of any of the States, provided that the legislative rights of any state within its own limits be not infringed or violated - establishing and regulating post offices from one State to another; throughout all the United States...

...The United States in Congress assembled shall also be the last resort on appeal in all disputes and differences now subsisting or that hereafter may arise between two or more States concerning boundary, jurisdiction or any other cause whatever;...

...Article XI. Canada acceding to this Confederation, and joining in the measures of the United States, shall be admitted into, and entitled to all the advantages of this Union; but no other colony shall be admitted into the same, unless such admission be agreed to by the nine States.

...Article XII. Every State shall abide by the determinations of the United States in Congress assembled, on all questions which by this Confederation are submitted to them. And the Articles of this Confederation shall be inviolably observed by every state, and the union shall be perpetual; nor shall any alteration at any time hereafter be made in any of them; unless such alteration be agreed to in a Congress of the United States, and afterwards confirmed by the legislatures of every State.

HOW WELL DID YOU UNDERSTAND THIS SELECTION?

1. Who appoints the delegates to the Congress?

2. Who taxes the states their share of what they owe the confederation? What might be some problems with this?

3. Which branch of the government seems to hold the most power, the states or the confederation? What is your evidence for this?

The Constitutional Convention was originally called in order to revise the Articles of Confederation. However, the delegates found it easier to create a new government, hopefully without the problems encountered under the Articles, and replace the Articles with it. The delegates met in Philadelphia from May to September 1787. It was agreed that they would meet and conduct their work in secrecy until a completed document could be presented to the country. James Madison, who is often called the Father of the Constitution, took notes of the proceedings.

In this reading, we can follow the debate of the delegates as to how the framework of the new government would be drawn up. In the debates, we can see the delegates' concerns and reasonings behind the final document that would become the Constitution.

5/30 Mr. RANDOLPH moved, on the suggestion of Mr. G. MORRIS, that the three following [propositions be considered]:

1. That a union of the States merely federal will not accomplish the objects proposed by the articles of Confederation, namely, common defence, security of liberty and general welfare.

2. That no treaty or treaties among the whole or part of the States, as individual sovereignties, would be sufficient.

3. That a national government ought to be established, consisting of a supreme Legislative, Executive and Judiciary"

5/31 Mr. BUTLER apprehended that the taking so many powers out of the hands of the States as was proposed, tended to destroy all that balance and security of interest among the states which was necessary to preserve...

6/2...Mr. DICKINSON: The happiness of this country, in his opinion, required considerable powers to be left in the hands of the States.

6/2 Mr. MASON: Some mode of displacing an unfit magistrate is rendered indispensable by the fallibility of those who choose, as well as by the corruptibility of the man chosen. He opposed decidedly the making the Executive the mere creature of the Legislature, as a violation of the fundamental principle of good government.

Mr. DICKINSON: the Legislative, Executive and Judiciary departments ought to be made as independent as possible...One source of stability is the double branch of the Legislature. The division of the country into distinct States formed the other principle source of stability. This division ought therefore to be maintained, and considerable powers to be left with the States. This was the ground of his consolation for the future fate of his country. Without this, and in case of consolidation of the States into one great republic, we might read its fate in the history of smaller ones.

6/12 Mr. RANDOLPH was for the term of seven years. The democratic licentiousness of the State Legislatures proved the necessity of a firm Senate. The object of this second branch is to control the democratic branch of the National Legislature. If it not be a firm body, the other branch, being more numerous, and coming immediately from the people will overwhelm it...A firmness and independence may be more necessary, also, in this branch, as it ought to guard the Constitution against encroachments of the Executive, who will be apt to form combinations with the demagogues of the popular branch.

6/20 Col. MASON [speaking of only having one branch of the legislature]: Is it to be thought that the people of America, so watchful over their interests, so jealous of their liberties, will give up their all, will surrender both the sword and the purse, to the same body, —and that, too, not chosen immediately by themselves? They never will. They never ought.

6/25 Mr. MASON: It has been agreed on all hands that an efficient government is necessary; that, to render it such, it ought to have the faculty of self-defence; that to render its different branches effectual, each of them ought to have the same power of self-defence...He only wondered that there should be any disagreement about the necessity of allowing the State Governments the same self-defence. If they are to be preserved, as he conceived to be essential, they certainly ought to have this power; and the only mode left of giving it to them was by allowing them to appoint the second branch of the National Legislature.

6/26 Mr. MADISON: In order to judge of the form to be given this institution [the senate], it will be proper to take a view of the ends to be served by it. These were,—first, to protect the people against their rulers, secondly, to protect the people against the transient impressions into which they themselves might be led...An obvious precaution against this danger would be, to divide the trust between different bodies of men, who might watch and check each other...In all civilized countries the people fall into different classes, having a real or supposed difference of interests. There will be creditors and debtors; farmers, merchants, and manufacturers...We cannot, however, be regarded, even at this time, as one homogeneous mass, in which everything that affects a part will affect in the same manner a whole. In framing a system which we wish to last for ages, we should not lose sight of the changes which ages will produce... No agrarian attempts have yet been made in this country; but symptoms of a levelling spirit, as we have understood, have sufficiently appeared in a certain quarter, to give notice of the future danger...Among other means, by the establishment of a body, in the government, sufficiently respectable for its wisdom and virtue to aid, on such emergencies, the preponderance of justice, by throwing its weight to that scale, Such being the objects of the second branch in the proposed Government, he thought a considerable duration ought to be given to it.

6/30 Mr. MADISON: He admitted that every peculiar interest, whether in any class of citizens, or any description of States, ought to be secured as far as possible...he contended that the States were divided into different interest, not by their difference of size, but other circumstances, the most material of which resulted partly from climate, but principally from the effects of their having or not having slaves. These two causes concurred in forming the great division of interests in the United States. It did not lie between the large and small States. It lay between the Northern and Southern; and if any defensive power were necessary, it ought to be mutually given to these two interests. He was so strongly impressed with this important truth, that he had been casting about in his mind for some expedient that would answer the purpose. The one which had occurred was, that, instead of proportioning the votes of the States in both branches, to their respective numbers of inhabitants, computing the slave in the ration of five to three, they should be represented in one branch according to the number of free inhabitants only; and in the other according to the whole number, counting the slaves as free. By this arrangement the Southern scale would have the advantage in one House, and the Northern in the other...

7/2 Mr. GOUVERNEUR MORRIS: The mode of appointing the second branch tended, he was sure, to defeat the object of it. What is this object? To check the precipitation, changeableness, and excesses of the first branch. ...Abilities and virtue are equally necessary in both branches. Something more, then, is now wanted... In the first place, the checking branch must have a personal interest in checking the other branch, One interest must be opposes to another interest...In the second place, it must have great personal property; it must have the aristocratic spirit; it must love to lord it through pride...In the third place it should be independent...The aristocratic body should be as independent, and as firm, as the democratic...To make it independent, it should be for life...The rich will strive to establish their dominion and enslave the rest. They always did. They always will. The proper security against them is to form them into a separate interest. The two forces will them control each other...By thus combining, and setting apart, the aristocratic interest, the popular interest will be combined against it. There will be a mutual check and mutual security. In the fourth place an independence for life, involves the necessary permanency. If we change our measures nobody will trust us, —and how avoid a change in measures, but by avoiding a change of men?...He was also against paying the Senators. They will pay themselves, if they can. If they cannot, they will be rich and can do without it. Of such the second branch ought to consist; and none but such can compose it, if they are not to be paid. He contended that the Executive should appoint the Senate, and fill up vacancies...A Senate for life will be a noble bait. Without such captivating prospects, the popular leaders will oppose and defeat the plan. A firm government alone an protect our liberties...The only security against encroachments, will be a select and sagacious body of men, instituted to watch against them on all sides.

7/10 Mr. GERRY: The larger the number [of representatives], the less danger of their being corrupt. The people are accustomed to and fond of, a numerous representation; and will consider their rights as better secured by it

7/17 Mr. GOUVERNEUR MORRIS: If the Executive be chosen by the national Legislature he will not be independent of it; and if not independent, usurpation and tyranny on the part of the Legislature will be the consequence.

7/17 Mr. MADISON: If it be essential to the preservation of liberty that the Legislative, Executive, and Judiciary powers be separate. it is essential to a maintenance to the separation, that they should be independent of each other...

7/21 Mr. MADISON: If a constitutional discrimination of the departments on paper were a sufficient security to each against encroachment of the others, all further provisions would indeed be superfluous. But experience had taught us a distrust of the security; and that it is necessary to introduce such a balance of powers and interests as will guarantee the provisions on paper. Instead, therefore, of contenting ourselves with laying down the theory in the Constitution, that each department ought to be separate and distinct, it was proposed to add a defensive power to each, which should maintain the theory in practice.

7/24 MR. GOUVERNEUR MORRIS: It is the most difficult to all, rightly to balance the Executive. Make him too weak: the Legislature will usurp his power, Make him too strong: he will usurp on the Legislature.

HOW WELL DID YOU UNDERSTAND THIS SELECTION?

1. Where does Mr. Dickinson feel that power should be left?

2. What does Mr. Randolph see as the role of the Senate?

3. Where do you find the rationale for the amendment process in the Constitution?

4. What does Mr. Gouverneur Morris propose for the makeup of the Senate members?

Several of the issues that the delegates of the Constitutional Convention had to deal with were over slavery. How were the slaves to be counted in terms of representation? Should there be a duty on slaves brought into the country as a result of the slave trade? As the members of the convention debated this, southern representatives sought to protect their rights, recognizing that they constituted a minority within the framework of the new government.

6/6 Mr. MADISON: He differed form the member from Connecticut, (Mr. SHERMAN,) in thinking the objects mentioned to be all the principled ones that required a national government. Those were certainly important and necessary objects; but he combined with them the necessity of providing more effectually for the security of private rights and the steady dispensation of justice. Interferences with these wee evils which had, more perhaps than anything else, produced this convention...We have seen the mere distinction of color made, in the most enlightened period of time, a ground of the most oppressive dominion ever exercised by man over man. What has been the source of those unjust laws complained of among ourselves? Has it not been the real or supposed interest of the major number?...The lesson we are to draw form the whole is, that where a majority are united by a common sentiment, and have an opportunity, the rights of the minor party become insecure. In a republican government, the majority, if united, have always an opportunity. The only remedy is, to enlarge the sphere, and thereby divide the community into so great a number of interests and parties, that, in the first place, a majority will not be likely, at the same moment, to have a common interest separate form that of the whole, or of the minority; and in the second place, that in case they should have such an interest, they may not be so apt to unite in pursuit of it. It was incumbent on us, then, to try this remedy, and, with that view, to frame a republican system on such a scale, and in such form, as will control all evils which have been experienced.

6/30 Mr. MADISON: He admitted that every peculiar interest, whether in any class of citizens, or any description of States, ought to be secured as far as possible...he contended that the States were divided into different interest, not by their difference of size, but other circumstances, the most material of which resulted partly from climate, but principally from the effects of their having or not having slaves. These two causes concurred in forming the great division of interests in the United States. It did not lie between the large and small States. It lay between the Northern and Southern; and if any defensive power were necessary, it ought to be mutually given to these two interests. He was so strongly impressed with this important truth, that he had been casting about in his mind for some expedient that would answer the purpose. The one which had occurred was, that, instead of proportioning the votes of the States in both branches, to their respective numbers of inhabitants, computing the slave in the ration of five to three, they should be represented in one branch according to the number of free inhabitants only; and in the other according to the whole number, counting the slaves as free. By this arrangement the Southern scale would have the advantage in one House, and the Northern in the other...

7/9 Mr. PATTERSON: He could regard Negro slaves in no light but as property. They are no free agents, have no personal liberty, no faculty of acquiring property, but on the contrary are themselves property, and like other property entirely at the will of the master. Has a man in Virginia a number of votes in proportions to the number of his slaves? and if negroes are not represented in the States to which they belong, why should they be represented in the General Government. What is the true principle of representation? It is an expedient by which an assembly of certain individuals, chosen by the people, is substituted in place of the inconvenient meeting of the people themselves. If such a meeting of the people was actually to take place, would the slaves vote? They would not. Why then should they be represented? He was so against such an indirect encouragement of the slave trade; observing that Congress, in their Act relating to the eighth Article of Confederation, has been ashamed to use the term "slaves" and had substituted a description.

7/11 Mr. BUTLER insisted that the labor of a slave in South Carolina was as productive and valuable, as that of a freeman in Massachusetts; that as wealth was the great means of defence and utility to the nation, they were equally valuable to it with freemen; and that consequently an equal representation ought to be made for them in a government which was instituted principally for the protection of property, and was itself to be supported by property.

Mr. MASON could not agree to the motion, notwithstanding it was favourable to Virginia, because he thought it unjust.

7/11 Mr. WILLIAMSON reminded Mr. GORHAM that if the Southern States contended for the inferiority of blacks to whites when taxation was in view, the Eastern States, on the same occasion, contended for their equality. He did not, however, either then or now, concur in either extreme, but approved of the ration of three-fifths.

7/11 Mr. KING, being much opposed to fixing numbers as the rule of representation, was particularly so on the account on the blacks. He thought the admission of them along with whites at all, would excite great discontent among the States having no slaves.

7/11 Mr. GOUVERNEUR MORRIS was compelled to declare himself reduced to the dilemma of doing injustice to the Southern States, or to human nature; and he must therefore do it to the former. For he could never agree to give such encouragement to the slave trade, as would be given by allowing them a representation for their Negroes; and he did not believe those States would ever confederate in terms that would deprive them of that trade.

7/12 Mr. DAVIE said it was high time to now speak out. He saw that it was meant by some gentlemen to deprive the Southern States of any share of representation for their blacks. He was sure that North Carolina would never confederate on any terms that did not rate them at least three-fifths. If the Eastern States meant, therefore, to exclude then altogether, the business was at an end.

7/12 General PINCKNEY desired that..property in slaves should not be exposed to danger, under a government instituted for the protection of property.

7/12 Mr. PINCKNEY moved to amend Mr. RANDOLPH'S motion, so as to make "blacks equal to the whites in the ration of representation." This he urges was nothing more than justice. The blacks are the laborers, the peasants, of the southern States. They are as productive of pecuniary resources as those of the Northern States. They add equally to the wealth, and, considering money as the sinew of war, to the strength, of the nation. It will also be politic with regard to the Northern States, as taxation is to keep pace with representation.

7/13 Mr. BUTLER: The security the Southern States want is that their negroes may not be taken from them, which some gentlemen within or without doors have a very good mind to do.

7/14 Mr. MADISON: It seems now to be pretty well understood that the real difference of interests lay, not between the large and the small, but between the Northern and Southern States. The institution of slavery, and its consequences, formed the line of discrimination.

7/23 Mr. GERRY moved, that the proceedings of the Convention for the establishment of a National Government (except the part relating to the Executive) be referred to a Committee to prepare and report a Constitution conformable thereto.

General PINCKNEY reminded the Convention, that if the Committee should fail to insert some security to the Southern States against the emancipation of slaves, and taxes on imports, he should be bound by duty to his States to vote against the report.

8/8 Mr. KING: The admission of slaves was a most grating circumstance on his mind, and he believed would be so to a great part of the people of America.

8/8 Mr. SHERMAN regarded the slave trade as iniquitous

8/8 Mr. GOUVERNEUR MORRIS: He never would concur in upholding domestic slavery. It was a nefarious institution. It was the curse of Heaven on the States where it prevailed...Upon what principle is it that the slaves shall be computed in the representation? Are they men? Then make them citizens, and let them vote. Are they property? Why, then is no other property included? The houses in this city (Philadelphia) are worth more than all the wretched slaves who cover the rice swamps of South Carolina. The admission of slave into the representation, when fairly explained, comes to this, that the inhabitant of Georgia and South Carolina who goes to the coast of Africa, and, defiance of the most sacred laws of humanity, tears away his fellow creatures form their dearest connections, and damns them to the most cruel bondage, shall have more votes in a government instituted for protection of the rights of mankind, than the citizen of Pennsylvania or New Jersey, who views with a laudable horror so nefarious a practice...And what is the proposed compensation to the Northern States, for a sacrifice of every principle of right, of every impulse of humanity? They are to bind themselves to march their militia for the defence of the Southern States, for their defense against those very slaves of whom they complain. They must supply vessels and seamen, in case of foreign attack. The Legislature will have infinite power to tax them by excises, and duties on imports; both of which will fall heavier on them than on their Southern inhabitants; for the Bohea tea used by a Northern freeman will pay more tax than the whole consumption of the miserable slave, which consists of nothing more than his physical subsistence and the rag that covers his nakedness. On the other side the Southern States are not to be restrained from importing fresh supplies of wretched Africans, at once to increase the danger of attack, and the difficulty of defence; nay, they are to be encouraged to it, by an assurance of having their votes in the National Government increased in proportion; and are, at the same time, to have their exports and their slaves exempt from all contributions for the public service.

8/21 Mr. L. MARTIN proposed to vary Article 7, Section 4, so as to allow a prohibition or tax on the importation of slaves. In the first place, as five slaves are to be counted as three freemen, the apportionment of Representatives, such a clause would leave encouragement to this traffic. In the second place, slaves weakened on part of the union, which the other parts were bound to protect; the privilege of importing them was therefore unreasonable. And in the third place, it was inconsistent with the principles of the Revolution, and dishonourable to the American character, to have such a feature in the Constitution.

Mr. RUTLEDGE ...The true question at present is, whether the Southern States shall or shall not be parties to the Union. If the Northern States consult their interest, they will not oppose the increase of slaves, which will increase the commodities of which they will become the carriers.

Mr. ELLSWORTH was for leaving the clause as it stands, Let every State import what it pleases. The morality or wisdom of slavery are considerations belonging to the States themselves. What enriches a part enriches the whole, and the States are the best judges of their particular interest. The old Confederation had not meddled with this point; and he did not see any greater necessity for bringing it within the policy of the new one.

Mr. PINCKNEY: South Carolina can never receive the plan if it prohibits the slave trade. In every proposed extension of the powers of Congress, that State has expressly and watchfully excepted that of meddling with the importation of negroes...

8/22 Article 7, Section 4, was resumed.

Mr. SHERMAN was for leaving the clause as it stands. He disapproved of the slave trade; yet as the States were now possessed the right to import slaves, as the public good did not require it to be taken from them, and as it was expedient to have as few objections as possible to the proposed scheme of government, he thought it best to leave the matter as we find it. He observed that the abolition of slavery seemed to be going on in the United States, and the good sense of the several States would probably by degrees complete it. He urged on the Convention the necessity of despatching its business.

8/22 Col. MASON This infernal traffic originated in the avarice of British merchants. The British Government constantly checked the attempts of Virginia to put a stop to it.

8/22 Col. MASON: Every master of slaves is born a petty tyrant. They bring the judgment of Heaven, on a country. As nations cannot be rewarded or punished in the next world, they must be in this. By an inevitable chain of causes and effects, Providence punishes nation sins by national calamities. He lamented that some of our Eastern brethren had, from a lust of gain, embarked in this nefarious traffic. As the States being in possession of the right to import, this was the case with many other rights, now to be properly given up. He held it essential in every point of view, that the General government should have power to prevent the increase of slavery.

8/22 Mr. PINCKNEY: If the Southern States were let alone, they will probably of themselves stop importations. He would himself, as a citizen of South Carolina, vote for it. An attempt to take away the right, as proposed, will produce serious objections to the Constitution, which he wished to see adopted.

8/22 General PINCKNEY: He contended that the importation of slaves would be for the interest of the whole Union. The more slaves the more produce to employ the carrying trade, the more consumption also; and the more of this the more revenue for the common treasury.

8/22 Mr. BALDWIN: If left to herself, she may probably put a stop to the evil.

8/22 Mr. GERRY thought we had nothing to do with the conduct of the States as to slaves, but ought to be careful not to give any sanction to it. 8/22 Mr. DICKINSON considered it as inadmissible, on every principle of honor and safety, that the importation of slaves should be authorized to the States by the Constitution.

8/22 Mr. SHERMAN: he was opposed to a tax on slaves imported, as making the matter worse, because it implied they were property. He acknowledged that if the power of prohibiting the importation should be given to the General Government, that it would be exercised. He thought it would be its duty to exercise the power.

8/25 General PINCKNEY moved to strike our the words, "the year eighteen hundred," as the year limiting the importation of slaves; and to insert the words, "the year eighteen hundred and eight."

Mr. GORHAM seconded the motion.

Mr. MADISON: Twenty years will produce all the mischief that can be apprehended from the liberty to import slaves. So long a term will be more dishonourable to the American character, than to say nothing about the Constitution.

On the motion, which passed in the affirmative, —New Hampshire, Massachusetts, Connecticut, Maryland, North Carolina, South Carolina Georgia, aye —7, New Jersey, Pennsylvania, Delaware, Virginia, no—4.

Mr. GOUVERNEUR MORRIS was for making the clause read, at once, "the importation of slaves into North Carolina, South Carolina, and Georgia, shall not be prohibited, &c."... He wished it to be known, also, that this part of the Constitution was a compliance with those States. If the change of language, however, should be objected to, by the members from those States, he should not urge it.
Colonel MASON was not against using the term "slaves," but against naming North Carolina, South Carolina, and Georgia, lest it should give offence to the people of those States.

Mr. WILLIAMSON said, that both in opinion and practice he was against slavery; but thought it more in favor of humanity, from a view of all circumstances, to let in South Carolina, and Georgia on those terms, than to exclude them from the Union.

Mr. GOUVERNEUR MORRIS withdrew his motion.

The first part of the Report was then agreed to, amended as follows: "The migration or importation of such person as the several States now existing shall think proper to admit, shall not be prohibited by the Legislature prior to the year 1808."

New Hampshire, Massachusetts, Connecticut, Maryland, North Carolina. South Carolina, Georgia, aye—7, New jersey, Pennsylvania, Delaware, Virginia, no —4.

Mr. BALDWIN, in order to restrain and more explicitly define, "the average duty" moved to strike out of the second part the words, "average of the duties laid on imports," and insert "common impost on articles not enumerated;" which was agreed to, nem.con.

Mr. SHERMAN was against this second part, as acknowledging men to be property, by taxing them as such under the character of slaves.

Mr. KING and Mr. LANGDON considered this as the price of the first part.

General PINCKNEY admitted that it was so.

Colonel MORRIS: Not to tax, will be the equivalent to a bounty on, the importation of slaves.
Mr. GORHAM thought Mr. SHERMAN should consider the duty, not as implying that slaves are property, but as a discouragement to the importation of them.

Mr. MADISON thought it wrong to admit in the Constitution the idea that there could be property in men. The reason of duties did not hold, as slaves are not, like merchandise consumed, &c.

It was finally agreed, nem.con., to make the clause read: "but a tax or duty may be imposed on such importation, not exceeding ten dollars for each person;" and then the second part, as amended, was agreed to.

9/15 Article 4, Sect. 2, (the third paragraph) the term "legally" was struck out; and the words, "under the laws thereof," inserted after the word "State," in compliance with the wish of some who thought the term legal equivocal, and favoring the idea that slavery was legal in a moral view.

HOW WELL DID YOU UNDERSTAND THIS SELECTION?

1. Why does Mr. Madison say we must listen to the minority's interests?

2. What are some of the arguments against counting slaves for representation? Arguments for representation?

3. Why did the northern states accept the three-fifths compromise on the counting of slaves?

4. What compromise did the members come up with in regard to slave importation?

SELF TEST:

MULTIPLE CHOICE: Circle the correct response. The correct answers are given at the end.

1. The first framework adopted for the government in the United States was
    a. the Constitution.
    b. the Articles of Confederation.
    c. the Albany Plan of Union.
    d. the Declaration of Independence.

2. Washington reinvigorated the American war effort when
    a. he attacked the British at New York.
    b. he was victorious in defeating the British in Boston.
    c. he defeated the Hessian soldiers in Trenton.
    d. he pledged his own property and money for the war effort.

3. The French entered into a formal alliance with the United States when
    a. Washington was victorious at Trenton.
    b. it became clear that Britain would lose the war.
    c. Spain came to our aid.
    d. after the British defeat at Saratoga.

4. One of the reasons that America was able to win the Revolutionary War was
    a. Britain became involved in other wars in Europe.
    b. France helped to supply us with money, troops and a fleet.
    c. Washington's ability as a military leader.
    d. all of the above.

5. The Treaty of Paris which ended the Revolutionary War
    a. set the boundaries of the United States.
    b. guaranteed that Canada would be independent too.
    c. gave the United States control of Florida.
    d. had the United States give up fishing rights off the coast of Canada.

6. One of the problems under the Articles of Confederation was
   a. Congress was too powerful.
   b. the states had too little power.
   c. Congress had too little power.
   d. Congress was too corrupt.

7. The Constitutional Convention
   a. revised the Articles of Confederation.
   b. was a continuation of the Second Continental Congress.
   c. held public meetings to let the people know what they were planning to do.
   d. replaced the Articles of Confederation with the Constitution.

8. The Great Compromise involved
   a. the creation of a chief executive.
   b. the creation of a federal judiciary.
   c. the creation of a two-house legislature and its membership.
   d. the taxing to slaves.

9. The Three-Fifths Compromise was concerned with
   a. the counting of a slave as three-fifths a free man.
   b. the counting of duties on slave imports.
   c. the counting of tariffs in the southern states.
   d. the counting of electoral votes.

10. To appease those that were against the Constitution for what it lacked
    a. a second Constitutional Convention was called.
    b. the ability to change the Constitution by amendments was added.
    c. the Convention made immediate changes.
    d. the Bill of Rights was added.

Answers: 1-b; 2-c; 3-d; 4-d; 5-a; 6-c; 7-d; 8-c; 9-a; 10-d.

ESSAYS:

1. What events could have led to a British victory in the American Revolution?

2. Could the United States have evolved into the country that it is if the Articles of Confederation had never been changed?

OPTIONAL ACTIVITIES: (Use your knowledge **and** imagination)

1. You are a soldier in Washington's army at the end of November 1776. Write a letter to your family at home describing the mood of the army.

2. You are a woman left behind to take care of family and business matters during the war. Write a letter to a relative and describe what problems you are encountering.

3 What other ways might you suggest to correct the problems of the Articles of Confederation?

4. You are a delegate at the Constitutional Convention. What would you propose to do over the issue of slavery? What is the reason for your choice?

WEB SITE LISTINGS:

The Men Who Signed the Declaration of Independence
http://www.rebelswithavision.com

The First Ladies of the United States
http://www.firstladies.org/Flbib2.htm

Spies of the American Revolution
http://www.si.umich.edu/spies/letter.htm

The Articles of Confederation
http://www.usconstitution.net

The Declaration of Independence
http://www.usconstitution.net

The Debate Over the Constitution
http://www.usconstitution.net

Yale University Documents on the Revolution
http://www.yale.edu/lawweb/avalon/avalon.htm

Revolutionary Documents from Internet Modern History Sourcebook, Fordham University
http://www.fordham.edu/halsall/mod/modsbook12.html

The University of Virginia Library
http://www.lib.virginia.edu

H-Net hubsite on The American Revolution
http://www.revolution.h-net.msu.edu

Women and Their Role in the American Revolution
http://www.nwhp.org/tlp/links/links.html

Chapter Six

THE EARLY REPUBLIC

The new Constitution of 1787 provided a skeletal framework for a federated, national government. The citizens of the republic, working through their elected representatives, would face the difficult task of applying "flesh and blood" to that skeletal framework. The Constitution of 1787 would become a living document through the human interpretation and application of its various provisions.

The political tempo of the early republic would be set during the presidency of George Washington (1789-1797). Secretary of State Thomas Jefferson and Secretary of the Treasury Alexander Hamilton would dominate Washington's cabinet. Jefferson favored a "strict construction" of the new U.S. Constitution in order to limit the power of the federal government. Hamilton advocated a "loose construction" of the Constitution in order to promote a more powerful central government. Early debate in Congress would focus on a series of proposals introduced by Hamilton that were designed to strengthen the nation's economy while enhancing the powers of the federal government. Politicians associated with Thomas Jefferson and James Madison feared Hamilton's proposals would harm the economic interests of yeoman farms, threaten individual liberties, and challenge the power of state governments. This division would lead to the creation of America's first two-party system.

European wars between Britain and France helped to crystalize the differences between Hamiltonian Federalists and Jeffersonian Democratic-Republicans. Responsive to the needs of business interests, the Federalists were generally willing to conciliate the British while taking a much firmer stand against violations of American honor by France. The Jeffersonian Republicans were far more sympathetic to France. During the term of Federalist President John Adams, the United States would fight an undeclared naval war with France. Following Thomas Jefferson's elevation to the presidency in 1801, the United States would successfully negotiate the purchase of the vast Louisiana Territory from France and enact economic sanctions designed to counter the harassment of American ships by the British navy.

The seizure of American cargo and sailors by the British navy combined with the fear generated by a Native American cultural revival in the Old Northwest would lead to war between Britain and the United States in June 1812. Although the war would end in a stalemate, it would have important consequences for the United Sates. The Native American cultural revival was crushed, and Native Americans east of the Mississippi were no longer able to resist the military power of the U.S. government. The anti-war posture of the Federalist Party during the War of 1812 would discredit its leaders and doom that party to irrelevance when the war ended on honorable terms. Our ability to fight the British would convince Spain to concede Florida to the United States in exchange for a clearly defined border between the United States and the northern provinces of New Spain.

During the Era of Good Feeling (1817-1824), one party rule by the Democratic-Republicans would reorient the national government by adopting many of the old Federalist economic policies. The Panic of 1819 and the depression that followed, would force a re-examination of those policies, especially with regard to the tariff and the national bank. New political factions began to emerge by 1824, grouped around the strong personalities of Andrew Jackson, John Quincy Adams, and Henry Clay. Following the 1824 presidential election, the partisans of Andrew Jackson would do all in their power to obstruct the proposals of President John Quincy Adams and his Secretary of State Henry Clay.

By the 1820s, Americans had proven the viability of their young republic. Yet the issue of slavery would haunt Americans as settlers moved beyond the Mississippi River into the Louisiana Territory. When Missouri applied for admission into the Union, a northern Congressman proposed that she enact a program of gradual emancipation. The proposal set-off bitter debate in Congress, which ended with a face-saving compromise.

During the entire period of the early republic, most Americans lived in rural areas, their lives dominated by agriculture. The pace of life was slow, dictated by nature rather than the clock. The availability of formal education was limited but community gatherings, enlivened by alcohol, provided entertainment. Life expectancy was short, and adult women were particularly vulnerable to infections following childbirth.

Much was accomplished during the period from 1789 to 1827. The Washington Administration stabilized the financial affairs of the federal government. The electoral college was perfected, enabling the United States to accomplish a peaceful transfer of power from one political party to another. The size of the nation was doubled by the Louisiana Purchase. The military power of the Native Americans who lived east of the Mississippi River was permanently broken. The United States also survived conflicts with both France and Britain. Yet the controversy over the expansion of slavery into the western territories would continue to haunt the nation for another thirty years.

IDENTIFICATION: Briefly describe each term.

Tenskwatawa (the Prophet)

George Washington

James Madison

Bill of Rights

Alexander Hamilton

Thomas Jefferson

Bank of the United States

Report on Manufacturers

Whiskey Rebellion

Federalist Party

Democratic-Republican Party

Citizen Edmund Genet

Jay's Treaty

The Pinckney Treaty

Aaron Burr

XYZ Affair

Alien and Sedition Acts

John Adams

Naturalization Act

Virginia and Kentucky Resolutions

John Marshall

Marbury v. Madison

Samuel Chase

Louisiana Purchase

Sacajawea

Lewis and Clark Expedition

"broken voyage"

Impressment

U.S.S. Chesapeake

The Embargo

Macon's Bill Number Two

War Hawks

Tecumseh

William Hull

Oliver Hazard Perry

Battle of Horseshoe Bend (1814)

Battle of New Orleans (1815)

Treaty of Ghent (1814)

Hartford Convention (1814)

Henry Clay

American System

Panic of 1819

Missouri Compromise

Adams-Otis Treaty

Monroe Doctrine

"the Corrupt Bargain"

"child bed" fever

THINK ABOUT:

1. Think of our government today. Does it reflect Hamilton's interpretation of the Constitution or Jefferson's interpretation of that document?

2. If you were alive in 1795, would you have given your support to the Democratic-Republican Party or to the Federalist Party? How did you make your decision?

THE PROCLAMATION OF NEUTRALITY (1793), By the President of the United States

---

As President Washington began his second term in office, the wars of the French Revolution engulfed the continent of Europe. France was allied to the United States against Britain during the War for Independence. In 1793, she called upon the United States to join in her war against Britain and her allies. President Washington believed that the United States had little to gain and much to lose by joining in the conflict. In response to the crisis, he declared American neutrality.

Whereas it appears that a state of war exists between Austria, Prussia, Sardinia, Great Britain, and the United Netherlands, of the one part, and France on the other; and the duty and interest of the United States require, that they should with sincerity and good faith adopt and pursue a conduct friendly and impartial toward the belligerant Powers;

I have therefore thought fit by these presents to declare the disposition of the United States to observe the conduct aforesaid toward those Powers respectfully; and to exhort and warn the citizens of the United States carefully to avoid all acts and proceedings whatsoever, which may in any manner tend to contravene such disposition.

And I do hereby also make known, that whatsoever of the citizens of the United States shall render himself liable to punishment or forfeiture under the law of nations, by committing, aiding, or abetting hostilities against any of the said Powers, or by carrying to any of them those articles which are deemed contraband by the modern usage of nations, will not receive the protection of the United States, against such punishment or forfeiture; and further, that I have given instructions to those officers, to whom it belongs, to cause prosecutions to be instituted against all persons, who shall, within the cognizance of the courts of the United States, violate the law of nations, with respect to the Powers at war, or any of them.

In testimony whereof, I have caused the seal of the United States of America to be affixed to these presents, and signed the same with my hand. Done at the city of Philadelphia, the twenty—second day of April, one thousand seven hundred and ninety—three, and of the Independence of the United States of America the seventeenth.

GEORGE WASHINGTON, April 22, 1793

Source: Prepared by Gerald Murphy (The Cleveland Free—Net – aa300)
Distributed by the Cybercasting Services Division of the National Public Telecomputing Network (NPTN)
http://www.msstate.edu/Archives/History/USA/early_republic/proclamation-of-neutrality

HOW WELL DID YOU UNDERSTAND THIS SELECTION?

1. Did Washington's proclamation offer protection to U.S. citizens who attempted to aid a nation at war?

2. Why would Washington issue such a proclamation?

With the ratification of the U.S. Constitution of 1787, the federal government was to begin anew. Hoping to take advantage of that circumstance, free blacks from Charleston, South Carolina would petition their legislature for basic civil rights denied them under state law.

To the Honorable David Ramsay Esquire President and to the rest of the Honorable New Members of the Senate of the State of South Carolina The Memorial of Thomas Cole Bricklayer P. B. Mathews and Mathew Webb Butchers on behalf of themselves & others Free-Men of Colour.

Humbly Sheweth

That in the Enumeration of Free Citizens by the Constitution of the United States for the purpose of Representation of the Southern States in Congress Your Memorialists have been considered under that description as part of the citizens of this State. Although by the Fourteenth and Twenty-Ninth clauses in an Act of Assembly made in the Year 1740 and intitled an Act for the better Ordering and Governing Negroes and other slaves in this Province commonly called The Negro Act now in force Your Memorialists are deprived of the Rights and Privileges of Citizens by not having it in their power to give Testimony on Oath in prosecutions on behalf of the State from which cause many Culprits have escaped the punishment due to their atrocious Crimes, nor can they give their Testimony in recovering Debts due to them, or in establishing Agreements made by them within the meaning of the Statutes of Frauds and Perjuries in force in this State except in cases where Persons of Colour are concerned, whereby they are subject to great Losses and repeated Injuries without any means of redress.

That by the said clauses in the said Act, they are debarred of the Rights of Free Citizens by being subject to a Trial without the benefit of a jury and subject to Prosecution by Testimony of Slaves without Oath by which they are placed on the same footing.

Your Memorialists show that they have at all times since the Independence of the United States contributed and do now contribute to the support of the government by cheerfully paying their Taxes proportionable to their Property with others who have been during such period, and now are in full enjoyment of the Rights and Immunities of Citizens Inhabitants of a Free Independent State.

That as your Memorialists have been and are considered as Free-Citizens of this State they hope to be treated as such, they are ready and willing to take and subscribe to such oath of Allegiance to the States as shall be prescribed by this Honorable House, and are also willing to take upon them any duty for the preservations of the Peace in the City or any other occasion if called on.

Your Memorialists do not presume to hope that they shall be put on an equal footing with the Free white Citizens of the State in general they only humbly solicit such indulgence as the Wisdom and Humanity of this Honorable House shall dictate in their favor by repealing the clauses the act aforementioned, and substituting such a clause as will effectually Redress the grievances which your Memorialists humbly submit in this their Memorial but under such restrictions as to your Honorable House shall seem proper.

May it therefore please your Honors to take your Memorialists case into tender consideration, and make such Acts or insert such clauses for the purpose of relieving your Memorialists from the unremitted grievance they now Labour under as in your Wisdom shall seem meet.

And as in duty bound your Memorialists will ever pray.

Source: "A Memorial to the South Carolina Senate," Records of the General Assembly, Petitions, 1791, No. 181, South Carolina Department of Archives and History, as reproduced.   http://www.pbs.org/wgbh/aia/part 2/2h7ot.html

HOW WELL DID YOU UNDERSTAND THIS SELECTION?

1. What basic rights were these "Free-Men of Colour" requesting?

2. Why did free blacks in Charleston feel that they had a right to a redress of their grievances?

THE TREATY OF GREENVILLE

Following the demoralizing defeat of the Native American coalition at Fallen Timbers in 1794, the Washington Administration would force a major land cession upon the tribes of the Old Northwest. The Treaty of Greenville would lead to the impoverishment of large numbers of Native Americans and prepare the way for the great cultural revival led by Tenskwatawa and Tecumseh.

TREATY OF GREENVILLE
WYANDOTS, DELAWARES, ETC.
(concluded August 3, 1795)

A treaty of peace between the United States of America, and the tribes of Indians called the Wyandots, Delawares, Shawanees, Ottawas, Chippewas, Pattawatimas, Miamis, Eel Rivers, Weas, Kickapoos, Piankesaws, and Kaskaskias

To put an end to a destructive war, to settle all controversies, and to restore harmony and friendly intercourse between the said United States and Indian tribes, Anthony Wayne, major general commanding the army of the United States, and sole commissioner for the good purposes above mentioned, and the said tribes of Indians, by their sachems, chiefs, and warriors, met together at Greenville, the head quarters of the said army, have agreed on the following articles, which, when ratified by the President, with the advice and consent of the Senate of the United States, shall be binding on them and the said Indian tribes.

Art. 1: Henceforth all hostilities shall cease; peace is hereby established, and shall be perpetual; and a friendly intercourse shall take place between the said United States and Indian tribes.

Art. 2: All prisoners shall, on both sides, be restored. The Indians, prisoners to the United States, shall be immediately set at liberty. The people of the United States, still remaining prisoners among the Indians, shall be delivered up in ninety days from the date hereof, to the general or commanding officer at Greenville, fort Wayne, or fort Defiance; and ten chiefs of the said tribes shall remain at Greenville as hostages, until the delivery of the prisoners shall be effected.

Art. 3: The general boundary line between the lands often United States and the lands of the said Indian tribes, shall begin at the mouth of Cayahoga river, and run thence up the same to the portage, between that and the Tuscarawas branch of the Muskingum, thence down that branch to the crossing place above fort Lawrence, thence westerly to a fork of that branch of the Great Miami river, running into the Ohio, at or near which fork stood Loromie's store, and where commences the portage between the Miami of the Ohio, and St. Mary's river, which is a branch of the Miami which runs into lake Erie; thence a westerly course to fort Recovery, which stands on a branch of the Wabash; thence southwesterly in a direct line to the Ohio, so as to intersect that river opposite the mouth of Kentucke or Cuttawa river. And in consideration of the peace now established; of the goods formerly received from the United States; of those now to be delivered; and of the yearly delivery of goods now stipulated to be made hereafter; and to indemnify the United States for the injuries and expenses they have sustained during the war, and the said Indian tribes do hereby cede and relinquish forever, all their claims to the lands lying eastwardly and southwardly of the general boundary line now described: and these lands, or any part of them, shall never hereafter be made a cause or pretence, on the part of the said tribes, or any of them, of war or injury to the United States, or any of the people thereof.

And for the same considerations, and as an evidence of the returning friendship of the said Indian tribes, or their confidence in the United States, and desire to provide for their accommodations, and for that convenient intercourse which will be beneficial to both parties, the said Indian tribes do also cede to the United States the following pieces of land, to wit: 1) One piece of land six miles square, at or near Loromie's store, before mentioned. 2) One piece two miles square, at the head of the navigable water or landing, on the St. Mary's river, near Girty's town. 3) One piece six miles square, at the head of the navigable water of the Auglaize river. 4) One piece six miles square, at the confluence of the Auglaize and Miami rivers, where fort Defiance now stands. 5) One piece six miles square, at or near the confluence of the rivers St. Mary's and St. Joseph's, where fort Wayne now stands, or near it. 6) One piece two miles square, on the Wabash river, at the end of the portage from the Miami of the lake, and about eight miles westward from fort Wayne. 7) One piece six miles square, at the Ouatanon, or Old Wea towns, on the Wabash river. 8) One piece twelve miles square, at the British fort on the Miami of the lake, at he foot of the rapids. 9) One piece six miles square, at the mouth of the said river, where it empties into the lake. 10) One piece six miles square, upon Sandusky lake, where a fort formerly stood. 11) One piece two miles square, at the lower rapids of Sandusky river. 12) The post of Detroit, and all the land to the north, the west and the south of it, of which the Indian title has been extinguished by gifts or grants to the French or English governments: and so much more land to be annexed to the district of Detroit, as shall be comprehended between the river Rosine, on the south, lake St. Clair on the north, and a line, the general course whereof shall be six miles distant from the west end of lake Erie and Detroit river. 13) The post of Michilimackinac, and all the land on the island on which that post stands, and the mail land adjacent, of which the Indian title has been extinguished by gifts or grants to the French or English governments; and a piece of land on the main to the north of the island, to measure six miles, on lake Huron, or the strait between lakes Huron and Michigan, and to extend three miles back from the water of the lake or strait; and also, the Island De Bois Blanc, being an extra and voluntary gift of the Chippewa nation. 14) One piece of land six miles square, at the mouth of Chikago river, emptying into the southwest end of lake Michigan, where a fort formerly stood. 15) One piece twelve miles square, at or near the mouth of the Illinois river, emptying into the Mississippi. 16) One piece six miles square, the old Piorias fort and village near the south end of the Illinois lake, on said Illinois river. And whenever the United States shall think proper to survey and mark the boundaries of the lands hereby ceded to them, they shall give timely notice thereof to the said tribes of Indians, that they may appoint some of their wise chiefs to attend and see that the lines are run according to the terms of this treaty.

And the said Indian tribes will allow to the people of the United States a free passage by land and by water, as one and the other shall be found convenient, through their country, along the chain of posts hereinbefore mentioned; that is to say, from the commencement of the portage aforesaid, at or near Loromie's store, thence along said portage to the St. Mary's, and down the same to fort Wayne, and then down the Miami, to lake Erie; again, from the commencement of the portage aforesaid, to Sandusky river, and down the same to Sandusky bay and lake Erie, and from Sandusky to the post which shall be taken at or near the foot of the Rapids of the Miami of the lake; and from thence to Detroit. Again, from the mouth of Chikago, to the commencement of the portage, between that river and the Illinois, and down the Illinois river to the Mississippi; also, from fort Wayne, along the portage aforesaid, which leads to the Wabash, and then down the Wabash to the Ohio. And the said Indian tribes will also allow to the people of the United States, the free use of the harbors and mouths of rivers along the lakes adjoining the Indian lands, for sheltering vessels and boats, and liberty to land their cargoes where necessary for their safety.

Art. 4: In consideration of the peace now established, and of the cessions and relinquishments of lands made in the preceding article by the said tribes of Indians, and to manifest the liberality of the United States, as the great means of rendering strong and perpetual, the United States relinquish their claims to all other Indian lands northward of the river Ohio, eastward of the Mississippi, and westward and southward of the Great Lakes and the waters, uniting them, according to the boundary line agreed on by the United States and the King of Great Britain, in the treaty of peace made between them in the year 1783. But from this relinquishment by the United States, the following tracts of land are explicitly excepted:

1st. The tract on one hundred and fifty thousand acres near the rapids of the river Ohio, which has been assigned to General Clark, for the use of himself and his warriors.

2nd. The post of St. Vincennes, on the River Wabash, and the lands of adjacent, of which the Indian title has been extinguished.

3rd. The lands at all other places in possession of the French people and other white settlers among then, of which the Indian title has been extinguished. as mentioned in the 3d article; and

4th. The post of fort Massac towards the mouth of the Ohio. To which several parcels of land so excepted, the said tribes relinquish all the title and claim which they or any of them may have.

And for the same considerations and with the same views as above mentioned, the United States now deliver to the said Indian tribes a quantity of goods to the value of twenty thousand dollars, the receipt whereof they do hereby acknowledge; and henceforward every year, forever, the United States will deliver, at some convenient place northward of the river Ohio, like useful goods, suited to the circumstances of the Indians, of the value of nine thousand five hundred dollars; reckoning that value at the first cost of the goods in the city or place in the United States where they shall be procured. The tribes to which those goods are to be annually delivered, and proportions in which they are to be delivered, are the following:

1st. To the Wyandots, the amount of one thousand dollars.

2nd. To the Delawares, the amount of one thousand dollars.

3rd. To the Shawanees, the amount of one thousand dollars.

4rd. To the Miamis, the amount of one thousand dollars.

5th. To the Ottawas, the amount of one thousand dollars.

6th. To the Chippewas, the amount of one thousand dollars.

7th. To the Pattawatimas, the amount of one thousand dollars, and

8th. To the Kickapoo, Wea, Eel River, Piankeshaw, and Kaskaskia tribes, the amount of five hundred dollars each.

Provided, that if either of the said tribes shall hereafter, at an annual delivery of their share of the goods aforesaid, desire that a part of their annuity should be furnished in domestic animals, implements of husbandry, and other utensils convenient for them, and in compensation to useful artificers who may reside with or near them, and be employed for their benefit, the same shall, at the subsequent annual deliveries, be furnished accordingly.

Art. 5: To prevent any misunderstanding about the Indian lands relinquished by the United States in the fourth article, it is now explicitly declared, that the meaning of that relinquishment is this: the Indian tribes who have a right to those lands, are quietly to enjoy them, hunting, planting and dwelling thereon, so long as they please, without any molestation from the United States; but when those tribes, or any of them, shall be disposed to sell their lands, or any part of them, they are to be sold only to the United States; and until such sale, the United States will protect all the said Indian tribes in the quiet enjoyment of their lands against all citizens of the United States, and against all other white persons who intrude upon the same. And the said Indian tribes again acknowledge themselves to be under the protection of the said United States, and no other power whatever.

Art. 6: If any citizen of the United States, or any other white person or persons, shall presume to settle upon the lands now relinquished by the United States, such citizen or other person shall be out of the protection of the United States; and the Indian tribe, on whose land the settlement shall be made, may drive off the settler, or punish him in such manner as they shall think fit; and because such settlements, made without the consent of the United States, will be injurious to them as well as to the Indians, the United States shall be at liberty to break them up, and remove and punish the settlers as they shall think proper, and so effect that protection of the Indian lands herein before stipulated.

Art. 7: The said tribes of Indians, parties to this treaty, shall be at liberty to hunt within the territory and lands which they have now ceded to the United States, without hindrance or molestation, so long as they demean themselves peaceably, and offer no injury to the people of the United States.

Art. 8: Trade shall be opened with the said Indian tribes; and they do hereby respectively engage to afford protection to such persons, with their property, as shall be duly licensed to reside among them for the purpose of trade; and to their agents and servants; but no person shall be permitted to reside at any of their towns or hunting camps, as a trader, who is not furnished with a license for that purpose, under the hand and seal of the superintendent of the department northwest of the Ohio, or such other person as the President of the United States shall authorize to grant such licenses; to the end, that the said Indians may not be imposed on in their trade. And if any licensed trader shall abuse his privilege by unfair dealing, upon complaint and proof thereof, his license shall be taken from him, and he shall be further punished according to the laws of the United States. And if any person shall intrude himself as a trader, without such license, the said Indians shall take and bring him before the superintendent, or his deputy, to be dealt with according to law. And to prevent impositions by forged licenses, the said Indians shall, at least once a year, give information to the superintendent, or his deputies, on the names of the traders residing among them.

Art. 9: Lest the firm peace and friendship now established, should be interrupted by the misconduct of individuals, the United States, and the said Indian tribes agree, that for injuries done by individuals on either side, no private revenge or retaliation shall take place; but instead thereof, complaint shall be made by the party injured, to the other: but the said Indian tribes or any of them, to the President of the United States, or the superintendent by him appointed; and by the superintendent or other person appointed by the President, to the principal chiefs of the said Indian tribes, or of the tribe to which the offender belongs; and such prudent measures shall then be taken as shall be necessary to preserve the said peace and friendship unbroken, until the legislature (or great council) of the United States, shall make other equitable provision in the case, to the satisfaction of both parties. Should any Indian tribes meditate a war against the United States, or either of them, and the same shall come to the knowledge of the before mentioned tribes, or either of them, they do hereby engage to give immediate notice thereof to the general, or officer commanding the troops of the United Sates, at the nearest post.

> *See, in relation to this licensed trade, the "first explanatory article" of the treaty of
> amity, commerce, and navigations, between the United States and Great Britain, of the
> 19th of November, 1974.

And should any tribe, with hostile intentions against the United States, or either of them, attempt to pass through their country, they will endeavor to prevent the same, and in like manner give information of such attempt, to the general, or officer commanding, as soon as possible, that all causes of mistrust and suspicion may be avoided between them and the United States. In like manner, the United States shall give notice to the said Indian tribes of any harm that may be meditated against them, or either of them, that shall come to their knowledge; and do all in their power to hinder and prevent the same, that the friendship between them may be uninterrupted.

Art. 10: All other treaties heretofore made between the United States, and the said Indian tribes, or any of them, since the treaty of 1783, between the United States and Great Britain, that come within the preview of this treaty, shall henceforth cease and become void.

In testimony whereof, the said Anthony Wayne, and the sachems and war chiefs of the before mentioned nations and tribes of Indians, have hereunto set their hands and affixed their seals.

Done at Greenville, in the territory of the United States northwest of the river Ohio, on the third day of August, on thousand seven hundred and ninety five.

Source: Prepared by Nancy Troutman (The Cleveland Free-Net - aa 345). Distributed by the Cybercasting Services
Division of the National Public Telecomputing Network (NPTN)
http://www.msstate.edu/Archives/History/USA/early-republic/treaty-of-greenville

HOW WELL DID YOU UNDERSTAND THIS SELECTION?

1. Who negotiated the treaty for the U.S. government?

2. What did the Native Americans receive from the U.S. government in exchange for their land?

The inauguration of Thomas Jefferson brought about the first peaceful transfer of power from one political party to another under our present Constitution. Jefferson correctly noted in his inaugural address that, "the right of election by the people," was, "a mild and safe corrective of abuses which are lopped by the sword of revolution where peaceful remedies are unprovided...." Jefferson hoped to reorient the federal government during his presidency so that it would conform to his narrow interpretation of the Constitution. He eloquently stated his principles of government in the following address.

Called upon to undertake the duties of the first executive office of our country, I avail myself of the presence of that portion of my fellow citizens which is here assembled to express my grateful thanks for the favor with which they have been pleased to look toward me, to declare a sincere consciousness that the task is above my talents, and that I approach it with those anxious and awful presentiments which the greatness of the charge and the weakness of my powers so justly inspire. A rising nation, spread over a wide and fruitful land, traversing all the seas with the rich productions of their industry, engaged in commerce with nations who feel power and forget right, advancing rapidly to destinies beyond the reach of mortal eye, when I contemplate these transcendent objects, and see the honor, the happiness, and the hopes of this beloved country committed to the issue, and the auspices of this day, I shrink from the contemplation, and humble myself before the magnitude of the undertaking. Utterly, indeed, should I despair did not the presence of many who I see here remind me that in the other high authorities provided by our Constitution I shall find resources of wisdom, of virtue, and of zeal on which to rely under all difficulties. To you, then, gentlemen, who are charged with the sovereign functions of legislation, and to those associate with you, I look with encouragement for that guidance and support which may enable us to steer with safety the vessel in which we are all embarked amidst the conflicting elements of a troubled world.

During the contest of opinion through which we have passed the animation of discussions and of exertions has sometimes worn an aspect which might impose on strangers unused to think freely and to speak and to write what they think; but this being now decided by the voice of the nation, announced according to the rules of the Constitution, all will of course arrange themselves under the will of the law, and unite in common efforts for the common good. All, too, will bear in mind this sacred principle, that though the will of the majority is in all cases to prevail, that will to be rightful must be reasonable; that the minority possesses their equal rights, which equal law must protect, and to violate would be oppression. Let us, then, fellow citizens, unite with one heart and one mind. Let us restore to social intercourse that harmony and affection without which liberty and even life itself are but dreary things. And let us reflect that, having banished from our land that religious intolerance under which mankind so long bled and suffered, we have yet gained little if we countenance a political intolerance as despotic, as wicked, and capable of as bitter and bloody persecutions. During the throes and convulsions of the ancient world, during the agonizing spasms of infuriated man, seeking through blood and slaughter his long lost liberty, it was not wonderful that the agitation of the billows should reach even this distant and peaceful shore; that this should be more felt and feared by some and less by others, and should divide opinions as to measures of safety. But every difference of opinion is not a difference of principle. We have called by different names brethren of the same principle. We are all republicans, we are all federalists. If there be any among us who would wish to dissolve the Union or to change its republican form, let them stand undisturbed as monuments of the safety with which error of opinion may be tolerated where reason is left free to combat it. I know, indeed, that some honest men fear that a republican government can not be strong, that this Government is not strong enough; but would the honest patriot, in the full tide of successful experiment, abandon a government which has so far kept us free and firm on the theoretic and visionary fear that this Government, the world's best hope, may by possibility want energy to preserve itself? I trust not. I believe this, on the contrary, the strongest Government on earth. I believe it the only one where every man, at the call of the law, would fly to the standard of the law, and would meet invasions of the public order as his own personal concern. Sometimes it is said that man cannot be trusted with the government of himself. Can he, then, be trusted with the government of others? Or have we found angels in the forms of kings to govern him? Let history answer this question.

Let us, then, with courage and confidence pursue our own Federal and Republican principles, our attachment to union and representative government. Kindly separated by nature and a wide ocean from the exterminating havoc of one quarter of the globe; too high-minded to endure the degradations of the others; possessing a chosen country, with room enough for our descendants to the thousandth and thousandth generation; entertaining a due sense of our equal right to the use of our own faculties, to the acquisitions of our own industry, to honor and confidence from our fellow citizens, resulting not from birth, but from our actions and their sense of them; enlightened by a benign religion, professed, indeed, and practiced in various forms, yet all of them inculcating honesty, truth, temperance, gratitude, and the love of man; acknowledging and adoring an overruling Providence, which by all its dispensations proves that it delights in the happiness of man here and his greater happiness hereafter, with all these blessings, what more is necessary to make us a happy and a prosperous people? Still one thing more, fellow citizens, a wise and frugal Government, which shall restrain men from injuring one another, shall leave them otherwise free to regulate their own pursuits of industry and improvement, and shall not take from the mouth of labor the bread it has earned. This is the sum of good government, and this is necessary to close the circle of our felicities.

About to enter, fellow citizens, on the exercise of duties which comprehend everything dear and valuable to you, it is proper you should understand what I deem the essential principles of our Government, and consequently those which ought to shape its Administration. I will compress them within the narrowest compass they will bear, stating the general principle, but not all its limitations. Equal and exact justice to all men, of whatever state or persuasion, religious or political; peace, commerce, and honest friendship with all nations, entangling alliances with none; the support of the State governments in all their rights, as the most competent administrations for our domestic concerns and the surest bulwarks against anti-republican tendencies; the presentation of the General Government in its whole constitutional vigor, as the sheet anchor of our peace at home and safety abroad; a jealous care of the right of election by the people, a mild and safe corrective of abuses which are lopped by the sword of revolution where peaceable remedies are unprovided; absolute acquiescence in the decisions of the majority, the vital principle of republics, from which is no appeal but to force, the vital principle and immediate parent of despotism; a well disciplined militia, our best reliance in peace and for the first moments of war, till regulars may relieve them; the supremacy of the civil over the military authority; economy in the public expense, that labor may be lightly burdened; the honest payment of our debts and sacred preservation of the public faith; encouragement of agriculture, and of commerce as its handmaid; the diffusion of information and arraignment of all abuses at the bar of the public reason; freedom of religion; freedom of the press, and freedom of person under the protection of the habeas corpus, and trial by juries impartially selected. These principles form the bright constellation which has gone before us and guided our steps through an age of revolution and reformation. The wisdom of our sages and blood of our heroes have been devoted to their attainment. They should be the creed of our political faith, the text of civic instruction, the touchstone by which to try the services of those we trust; and should we wander from them in moments of error or of alarm, let us hasten to retrace our steps and to regain the road which alone leads to peace, liberty, and safety.

I repair, then, fellow citizens, to the post you have assigned me. With experience enough in subordinate offices to have seen the difficulties of this the greatest of all, I have learnt to expect that it will rarely fall to the lot of imperfect man to retire from this station with the reputation and the favor which bring him into it. Without pretensions to that high confidence you reposed in our first and greatest revolutionary character, whose preeminent services had entitled him to the first place in his country's love and destined for him the fairest page in the volume of faithful history, I ask so much confidence only as may give firmness and effect to the legal administration of your affairs. I shall often go wrong through defect of judgment. When right, I shall often be thought wrong by those whose positions will not command a view of the whole ground. I ask your indulgence for my own errors, which will never be intentional, and your support against the errors of others, who may condemn what they would not if seen in all its parts. The approbation implied by your suffrage is a great consolation to me for the past, and my future solicitude will be to retain the good opinion of those who have bestowed it in advance, to conciliate that of others by doing them all the good in my power, and to be instrumental to the happiness and freedom of all.

Relying, then, on the patronage of your good will, I advance with obedience to the work, ready to retire from it whenever you become sensible how much better choice it is in your power to make. And may that Infinite Power which rules the destinies of the universe lead our councils to what is best, and give them a favorable issue for your peace and prosperity.

Source: Prepared by Nancy Troutman (The Cleveland Free-Net - aa345). Distributed by the Cybercasting Services
    Division of the National Public Telecomputing Network (NPTN)
    http://www.msstate.edu/Archives/History/USA/early_republic/jefferson-inaugural

HOW WELL DID YOU UNDERSTAND THIS SELECTION?

1. What do you think Jefferson meant when he promised the citizens of the United States a "wise and frugal Government"?

2. What did Jefferson view as the principle duties of the federal government?

KNIFE RIVER INDIAN VILLAGES: The People

*In May 1804, William Clark and Meriwether Lewis would begin to lead their **Corps of Discovery** up the waters of the Missouri River. The famed Lewis and Clark expedition was commissioned by President Thomas Jefferson to explore the northern portion of the Louisiana Territory and to report on the nature of its environment and on the people who inhabited the region. The **Corps** would eventually make its way across the Rocky Mountains to the Pacific Ocean. They would not return from their adventure until September 1806.*

In October 1804, Lewis and Clark reach the Mandan villages at the confluence of the Knife and Missouri Rivers. They would spend the winter among the Mandan and learn a great deal about their culture. The sites of these villages are preserved today by the National Park Service as a part of Knife River Indian Village National Historical Site.

For centuries the Upper Missouri River Valley was a lifeline winding through a harsh land, drawing Northern Plains Indians to its wooded banks and rich soil. Earthlodge people, like the nomadic tribes, hunted bison and other game but were essentially a farming people living in villages along the Missouri and its tributaries. At the time of their contact with Europeans, these communities were the culmination of 700 years of settlement in the area. Traditional oral histories link the ancestors of the Mandan and Hidatsa tribes living on the Knife River with tribal groups east of the Missouri River. Migrating for several hundred years along waterways, they eventually settled along the Upper Missouri. One Mandan story tells of the group's creation along the river. Coming into conflict with other tribes, the Mandans moved northward to the Heart River and adopted an architecture characterized by round earthlodges.

The Hidatsas were originally divided into three distinct sub-tribes. The Awatixa were created on the Missouri River, according to their traditions. Awaxawi and Hidatsa-Proper stories place them along streams to the east. The Hidatsas moved farther north to the mouth of the Knife, settling Awatixa Xi'e Village (Lower Hidatsa Site) around 1525 and Hidatsa Village (Big Hidatsa Site) around 1600. They were never as sedentary as the Mandans, but did borrow from them, learning corn horticulture and adopting some of their pottery patterns. Intermarriage and trade helped cement relations, and eventually the two cultures became almost indistinguishable. With the Arikaras to the south, they formed an economic force that dominated the region.

After contact with Europeans in the early 18th century, the villages began to draw a growing number of traders. Tragically, the prosperity that followed was accompanied by an enemy the Indians could not fight: European disease. When smallpox raged the tribes in 1781, the Mandans fled upriver, nearer Hidatsa Village. The people from Awatixa Xi'e abandoned their village, returning to the area in 1796 to build Awatixa Village (Sakakawea Site). The weakened tribes were now easier targets for Sioux raiders, who burned Awatixa village in 1834. After another epidemic in 1837 almost destroyed the Mandans, the villages broke up. Their movements for the next few years are obscure. In 1845, the Mandans and Hidatsas founded Like-A-Fishook village upriver, where they were joined in 1862 by the Arikaras. The tribes were forced in 1885 to abandon their village and make their final move onto the Fort Berthold Reservation. Today the tribes, now called the Three Affiliated Tribes, continue to practice their traditional ways.

Village Life

The Mandan, Hidatsa, and Arikara tribes shared a culture superbly adapted to the conditions of the upper Missouri valley. Their summer villages, located on natural terraces above the river, were ordered communities as large as 120 lodges. These spacious structures sheltered families of 10 to 30 people from the region's extreme temperatures. The villages were strategically located for defense, often on a narrow bluff with water on two sides and a palisade on the third. In winter the inhabitants moved into smaller lodges along the bottom lands, where trees provided firewood and protection from the cold wind.

In this society, men lived in the household of their wives, bringing only their clothes, horses, and weapons. Women built, owned, and maintained the lodges and owned the gardens, gardening tools, food, dogs, and colts. Related lodge families made up clans, whose members were forbidden to marry inside the group. Cutting across village boundaries, a clan expected its members to help and guide each other. Clans were competitive, especially regarding success in war, but it was the age-grade societies, transcending village and clan, that were looked to for personal prestige. Young men purchased membership in the lowest society at 12 or 13, progressing to higher and more expensive levels as they reached the proper age. Besides serving as warrior bands, each group was responsible for a social function: policing the village, scouting, or planning the hunt. Most importantly, the societies were a means of social control, setting standards of behavior and transmitting tribal lore and custom.

The roles of the sexes were strictly defined. Men spent their time seeking spiritual knowledge or hunting and horse raiding, difficult and dangerous but relatively infrequent undertakings. Women performed virtually all of the regular work: gardening, preparing food, maintaining the lodges, and, until the tribes obtained horses, carrying burdens. The lives of these people were not totally devoted to subsistence, however. They made time for play, such as the hoop and spear game. Honored storytellers passed on oral traditions and moral lessons, focusing on traditional tribal values of respect, humility, and strength. The open area in the center of each Mandan village was often given over to dancing and ritual, which bonded the members of the tribe and reaffirmed their place in the world.

The Village Economy

Agriculture was the economic foundation of the Knife River people, who harvested much of their food from rich floodplain gardens. The land was controlled by women-the size of a family's plot was determine by the number of women who could work it-and passed through the female line. They raised squash, pumpkin, beans, sunflowers, and, most importantly, tough, quick-maturing varieties of corn that thrived in the meager rainfall and short growing season. Summer's first corn was celebrated in the Green Corn ceremony. Berries, roots, and fish supplemented their diet. Upland hunting provided buffalo meat, hides, bones, and sinew.

These proficient farmers traded their surplus produce to nomadic tribes for buffalo hides, deer skins, dried meat, and other items in short supply. At the junction of major trade routes, they became middlemen, dealing in goods from a vast network: obsidian from Wyoming, copper from the Great Lakes, shells from the Gulf of Mexico and the Pacific Northwest, and, after the 17th century, guns, horses, and metal items. High quality flint quarried locally found its way to tribes over a large part of the continent through this trade system.

The Battle and the Hunt

In this warrior culture, raiding and hunting were the chief occupations of the men. When conflict was imminent, a war chief assumed leadership of the village. Tangible results—horses and loot—often came from the raids, which were really stages on which warriors could prove themselves. Hunting parties were planned in much the same fashion, with a respected hunter choosing participants and planning the event, prowess in battle and hunt led to status in the village, both individually and for the societies and clans. Ambitious young men would risk leading a party-highly rewarding if successful, ruinous to a reputation if not. The primary weapon was the bow and arrow, along with clubs, tomahawks, lances, shields, and knives. Even more prestigious than wounding or killing an enemy was "counting coup"—touching him in battle. But ambition did not spur every action: The warriors often had to defend the village against raids by other tribes. When the men prevailed in battle or hunt, the women would celebrate with dance and song throughout the village.

Spirit and Ritual

Spirits guided the events of the material world, and from an early age, tribal members (usually male) sought their help. Fasting in a sacred place, a boy hoped to be visited by a spirit, often in animal form, who would give him "power" and guide him through life. The nature of the vision that he reported to elders determine his role within the tribe. If directed by his vision, he would as a young man make a greater sacrifice to the spirits, spilling his blood in the Okipa ceremony. The Okipa was the most important of a number of ceremonies performed by Mandan clans and age-grade societies to ensure crops, successful hunts, and victory in battle. Ceremonies could be conducted only by those with "medicine", which was obtained by purchasing from a fellow clan or society member one of the bundles of sacred objects associated with tribal mythology. With bundle ownership came responsibility for knowledge of the songs, stories, prayers, and rituals necessary for spiritual communication. Certain bundle owners were looked upon as respected leaders of the tribe.

Reading the Past

The story of Knife River is still being written. Long-held theories have been revised by recent archeological research. From 1976 to 1983, Dr. Stanley Ahler of the University of North Dakota directed excavations in the park. Piecing together the story from the remains of earthlodges, 150,000 pottery shards, and 8,400 stone tools, Dr. Ahler now believes that the Hidatsa arrived in the area earlier (around 1300) than had been thought. Evidence from some 50 sites constitutes an unbroken record of 500 years of human inhabitation. Even this period represents a fraction of the time that humans have lived here. Research at Knife River and nearby sites documents 11,000 years of human activity. The earliest known people in the region during the Paleo-Indian period (10,600-6000 BC) were nomads who hunted now-extinct large game. Archaic (6,000 BC - AD1) people, also nomadic, lived by hunting and gathering. The earliest artifacts found at Knife River date from this period. Signs of semi-sedentary living and rudimentary agriculture occur in the Woodland period (1000 BC-AD 1000). Permanent earthlodge villages and a horticultural economy characterize the Plains Village Period (AD 1000-1885), of which the Knife River sites represent the final and most sophisticated phase.

Source: The National Park Service, "Knife River Indian Villages: The People."
        http://www.nps.gov/knri/people.htm

HOW WELL DID YOU UNDERSTAND THIS SELECTION?

1. Discuss the role of women in Mandan society?

2. What was the Okipa?

3. What great tragedy befell the Mandan and Hidatsas in the late 18th and early 19th centuries?

The early republic was a time when the new United States proved the strength and stability of republican institutions. Unfortunately, many people were excluded from direct participation in government and were denied the freedom claimed by the white majority. In the South, millions of Africans and African Americans dreamed of freedom from bondage. Some, like Gabriel Prosser, acted in the hope that their dream would become a reality.

In 1776, the year of America's independence as a county, a slave child named Gabriel was born to the family owned by Thomas Henry Prosser of the Brookfield Plantation in Henrico County.

As an adult, Gabriel Prosser would herald the cause of independence for himself and for all slaves. It was a cause for which he was willing to take the most extreme measures.

Regarded as a "fellow of courage and intellect above his rank and life" by both blacks and whites, Gabriel was a commanding figure. Dark-skinned, he stood 6 feet, 2 or 3 inches tall. He had lost two front teeth and his head was scarred.

Unlike the vast majority of slaves, Gabriel had been educated in his youth. He became a blacksmith, a skill that gave him access to life beyond the plantation.

Following the American Revolution, slave laws were relaxed and skilled slaves were often hired out. Many slaves also got half of Saturday and all of Sunday off. The artisans could use that time to earn some money of their own — after paying a portion to their masters.

But the market was no more free than the slaves themselves.

White merchants controlled the flow of raw goods into and out of the city, and they could pressure the skilled slaves to lower their prices by simply choking off the stream of materials. The masters, meanwhile, still got their share off the top.

This repressive system was fertile ground for the idea of revolt among the slaves. The firebrands among them were emboldened by accounts of a bloody slave uprising in Haiti in 1791. In 1800, Gabriel and several other slaves plotted their own revolution.

It was to be an apocalypse for the slave masters. Gabriel and his co-conspirators planned to marshal the forces of up to 10,000 blacks, who would take Richmond in an armed insurrection and kill every white, save the French, the Methodists, the Quakers and the poor.

The plan called for a three-pronged assault on the city on the night of Aug. 30. Gov. James Monroe would be captured and held while other slaves, poor whites and Indians joined the fighters.

But Gabriel's Insurrection was put down just as it got started.

Two slaves who lived on the Henrico plantation of Meadow Farm betrayed the plot to the plantation's owner, Mosby Sheppard. Sheppard immediately informed the governor, who called out the militia. On Aug. 30 torrential rains washed away roads and bridges, limiting the movement of the rebellious slaves. About 30 slaves were captured and executed.

Gabriel, however, eluded the militia and escaped down the Chickahominy River. Monroe put a $300 reward on his head, and on Sept. 24, Gabriel was captured aboard a ship in Norfolk. On Oct. 10, 1800 at Richmond's gallows at 15th and Broad streets, Gabriel Prosser was hanged. He was 24 years old.

Gabriel's bid for freedom only tightened the grip of slavery. In the aftermath of the insurrection, slave laws were toughened not only in Virginia but also in other states, North and South.

In Virginia, abolition societies were driven underground. Travel was restricted. Free blacks who didn't leave the state within six months risked re-enslavement.

For slaves, the dream of freedom did not die, but the reality was still more than half a century away.

Sources: *Gabriel's Rebellion*, The Virginia Slave Conspiracies of 1800 and 1802 by Douglas R. Egerton; *Many Thousand Gone* by Virginia Hamilton; Meadow Farm Museum; Virginia Historical Society
Teresa Lemons Coleman, "Gabriel Prosser," *Richmond Times-Dispatch* (Richmond, VA: Richmond Newspapers Inc., 1997) reprinted with the expressed permission of the Richmond Times-Dispatch.

HOW WELL DID YOU UNDERSTAND THIS SELECTION?

1. How did Gabriel Prosser differ from most slaves?

2. How did Gabriel's rebellion influence the slave system of the South?

DISCRIMINATION IN OHIO DURING THE EARLY REPUBLIC
By Thomas D. Matijasic

When discussing African Americans in the early republic, most scholars focus on the condition of slaves in the southern states. However, tens of thousands of free blacks lived in the North, and they were subjected to a considerable amount of humiliation. Discrimination was widespread throughout the North and was especially harsh in the Midwest.

During the winter of 1816-1817, the American Colonization Society (A.S.C.) was formed to promote the voluntary deportation of American blacks to West Africa. With the aid of the United States government, land was purchased on the African coast and the colony of Liberia was established. Due to meager funds and organizational difficulties within the American Colonizations Society, Liberia grew slowly.

In an effort to stimulate renewed interest in the colonization cause, the leadership of the A.C.S. began to emphasize the creation of permanent local support groups. In 1824, the Board of Managers passed a resolution recommending, "the formation, as soon as practicable, of an auxiliary Society in the principal City of each State in the Union and the establishment of Societies subordinate to these in each county or town of the several states."(1) American Colonization Society Secretary Ralph R. Gurley eagerly sought to implement the Board's suggestion.

Between 1825 and 1833, Gurley sent out dozens of A.C.S. agents to bring the colonization message to every county in the North and Upper South. Particular attention was paid to activating auxiliary societies in the states of the Old Northwest. The American Colonization Society missionaries found a ready audience for the message in Ohio due to the peculiar racial attitudes held by the residents of the Buckeye State.

In most northern states, during the first half of the nineteenth century, blacks were free but far from equal. "Legal and extralegal discrimination restricted northern Negroes in virtually every phase of existence. Where laws were lacking or ineffectual, public opinion provided its own remedies."(2) Widespread laws directed against blacks throughout the "free" states reveal the fact that many, perhaps most, northern whites had little sympathy for their black countrymen. Some were undoubtedly revolted by the excesses of the slave system, but they were unwilling to accept large numbers of blacks within their social environment. The black population was generally viewed as a problem to be handled, a disease to be cured.

The idea developed that blacks were, in some way, a degraded form of humanity. "From all parts of the Union there came declarations concerning the degraded and degrading conditions of the free Negro. The opinion was not sectional; it was national."(3) White Americans were shocked by the disproportionate number of free blacks that were imprisoned throughout the free states. (4) They took this as evidence that Blacks were unable to compete in an open society and, therefore, took to crime. At least one historian has suggested that white fears were based upon the economic threat posed by free black labor. "Every report of their weakness of degradation seemed welcome... Very often the intensity of the hatred was due not to their idleness but to their industry and competition with white labor."(5) Whatever the cause, anti-black prejudice throughout the North was real and many state legislatures passed laws to discourage the immigration of Negroes.

There is ample evidence to indicate that large numbers of Ohioans would have preferred that the state be preserved as a haven for the Caucasian. From the beginning, blacks were treated as second class citizens by the state government of Ohio.

> To any one reading the Constitution of 1802, it is clear that the framers intended the negro to occupy the same relation to the Government that the Indian or unnaturalized foreigner did. They were permitted to live in the state and the protection of the laws was offered them, but in the government of the state they had no part. Civic duties were not to be demanded of them nor any of the distinctive privileges of a citizen to be allowed them. (6)

In short, Ohio's first Constitutional Convention refused to grant black men the franchise and restricted access to elective office to white men. (7)

The legal position of blacks in the Buckeye State continued to deteriorate during the first decade of the nineteenth century. In 1804 the Ohio General Assembly passed legislation requiring all blacks who entered the state to be able to provide proof of their status as free men. All resident blacks were required to register with their county clerk in order to protect them from undue harassment. A stiff fine was levied against anyone who employed a black, who could not produce evidence of his free status. In 1807 the legislature required blacks entering the state to post a bond of $500 as security against their future conduct. A statute was also passed forbidding a black to testify against a white man in court. (8)

One of the most crippling disadvantages Ohio blacks were forced to suffer was a general lack of educational opportunities. Education has long been recognized by Americans as a primary means of social advancement. Certainly the founding fathers wanted to encourage education on the frontier by stipulating in the Ordinance of 1785 that one section of land be set aside in each township for the benefit of public education. In observing Ohio's pioneers, traveler D. Griffths reported, "If but half a dozen families settle in a new township, they build themselves a school-house in the center."(9) Black children, however, did not profit from the educational enthusiasm of white Ohioans. Historian Frank Quillin reported that prior to 1848, Ohio law failed to provide educational opportunities for black children, and little was done at the local level to compensate for the lack of action by the state government. (10)

It is generally agreed that the discriminatory laws passed by the Ohio General Assembly failed to discourage black immigrants from entering the state. It has been estimated that Ohio's black population increased by as much as 102 percent during the 1820's. (11) This rapid increase in the size of the Negro population caused anxiety in the white community and led to a heightening of racial tension. In particular, many Ohioans were concerned that the Buckeye State was being used as a dumping ground for the unwanted slaves and free blacks of Kentucky and Virginia. One of the state's newspapers went so far as to call them, "worse than drones to society". (12) In 1819 an Ohioan visiting Richmond, Virginia was informed that hundreds of liberated slaves were being marched to Ohio. Shortly thereafter, he expressed his feelings about the subject to a Chillicothe newspaper editor:

> Ohio will suffer seriously from the iniquitous policy pursued by the States of Virginian and Kent., in driving all their free negroes upon us. The people of Ohio are bound in justice to themselves to adopt some measure. Many people here are of the opinion that we may be compelled to introduce slavery in Ohio in self-defense, and they appear to be gratified that we are suffering many of the evils attending it, without (as they call it) any of the benefits. (13)

William Graham, a Presbyterian minister from Chillicothe, was similarly dismayed at the influx of blacks into the sate. He believed that whites throughout Ohio shared his concern.

> In most of the towns in Ohio there are a number of free Blacks who with few exceptions are little less than a nuisance and their numbers are every year increasing by immigration as well as other causes. All of the whites would willingly do something to free themselves from this evil.(14)

Robert S. Hall of Georgetown, Ohio felt that his new black neighbors were engaged in widespread pilfering and "entertained hostile intentions against the whites." (15)

Much has been made of the fact that large numbers of Southern born whites settled in the southern counties of Ohio. Certainly many of these families brought their anti-Negro prejudices with them when they crossed the Ohio River. However, the widespread antipathy toward blacks evident in Ohio, and existence of discrimination against African-Americans in many northeastern states indicates that other groups of whites within the state were not immune to prejudice. Charles Wilson noted, "that the Middle States Scotch-Irish lined up, with the Southerners of their racial type,. . in supporting legislation to discourage colored immigration into Ohio. (16) A friend of Charles Hammond reported that "the antipathy between the Irish and our race of Blacks is as strong as that between the Cat and the Curd." (17)

By the mid-1820's, the question of what to do about the growing number of free blacks was becoming a major political issue. State Representative Anthony Walke of Ross County reported to the Ohio House that although they (free Blacks) are nominally free, that freedom confers only the privilege of being more idle and vicious than slaves. In an appeal to the self evident, Walke asserted that, "This is obvious to every man who witnesses its effects in our towns and villages and turns his attentions to the relative proportion of crime between the colored and white population of the state." (18) In 1832 a legislative committee of the Ohio General Assembly accepted Walke's conclusions. (19) Walke also introduced a resolution, "to prevent the settlement of free people of colour in this state who are not citizens of another state, by such penalties, disqualifications and disabilities as they may deem best calculated to effect the object." (20) In his 1827 message to the Ohio legislature, Governor Allen Trimble devoted considerable attention to the increase in Ohio's black population. Realizing the emotional impact of the issue, he reported, "Their rapid increase has already given serious alarm to many of our citizens." Trimble further implied that it might soon "be necessary for us (in self defense) to adopt some measure to counteract the policy of slave states which tends to throw from themselves upon us, the whole mass of their free colored population." (21)

White fears were particularly acute in Cincinnati, where large numbers of free blacks congregated in hopes of finding employment amidst the bustling economy of the Queen City. By 1829 blacks composed about one percent of the city's total population. (22) White residents of Cincinnati were probably correct in assuming that unless some action were taken, the number of blacks living in the city would continue to grow at a fast pace for "fugitive slaves found Cincinnati's ghetto, known as 'little Africa,' a safe refuge from their masters."(23) In Cincinnati, just as in other towns throughout the state, Caucasians tended to identify Negroes with the existence of a seamy underworld of corruption. Richard C. Wade, in his study of the Afro-American community of Cincinnati, indicated that this image was not totally unfounded. "In fact, underneath Negro life in Cincinnati lay an ugly layer of vice, crime, and violence."(24) and that all black residents suffered heavily from job discrimination and lack of educational opportunities. Unable to make an honest living, many blacks were forced to survive any way they could. Few whites, however, were willing to consider the larger picture. Instead, they called for an immediate program to rid the city of its black "problem."

In 1829 Cincinnati officials, responding to public pressure, threatened to enforce the Black Laws of 1807. Those blacks unable to produce evidence of freedom or post the $500 bond were required to leave the city within thirty days. "The local Negro population promptly obtained a time extension, sent a delegation to Canada to find suitable location for resettlement, and petitioned the legislature for repeal of those obnoxious Black Laws."(25) The tactical delay maneuvers of black leaders soon aroused the ire of local ruffians which resulted in three days of racial rioting in the black section of the city. By the end of the year, over 1,000 blacks left Cincinnati for friendlier parts. (26)

While large numbers of white Ohioans disliked and distrusted blacks, this does not mean that they were in any way pro-slavery. Charles J. Wilson accurately summarized the basic premises necessary for understanding the attitude of Ohioans with regard to issues relating to blacks. He wrote:

> The first of these is that there was at no time in the history of the state any preponderant pro-slavery sentiment in Ohio; and the second is that the ultimate disagreement in the state over the negro question was not a struggle waged by pro-slavery against anti-slavery forces as such. It was a clash between one element instilled with the humanitarian spirit in the apotheosis of its idealism and another group which was grimly determined to prevent the admission of negroes into the state. . . (27)

Slavery was, of course, prohibited in the territory north of the Ohio River by the Northwest Ordinance of 1787. Ohio's founding fathers continued this prohibition against slavery at the Ohio Constitutional Convention of 1802. There is, however, some evidence that a few blacks were held in bondage within the state as late as 1830 and that a black man was actually sold in Ohio in 1813. (28) Be that as it may, the vast majority of Ohioans were thoroughly dedicated to the principle of a fee labor economy, and they regarded slavery as harmful to the national welfare.

Discussion of the Missouri question brought forward the vigorous antislavery sentiments of Ohioans in 1820. Most Ohioans appear to have favored a strict anti-extension stand. *The Supporter* reprinted an article from a New Jersey newspaper which predicted that unless something was done to put the slave system on the road to extinction, Southerners "may see rising into view, conspiracies, insurrections, massacres, servile war and mutual extermination." More important, the editorial went on the predict that within 115 years, the black population throughout the country would exceed forty million. When this mass of humanity struck for freedom, it would "effect a universal explosion, and produce tremendous calamities."(29) The Ohio General Assembly also voiced its opinion of the issue. In January 1820, the Ohio Senate approved a resolution "instructing our members in Congress to oppose the admission into the Union of any new state, the constitution of which tolerates slavery." The State House of Representatives urged Ohio's Congressional delegation to oppose "the extension of slavery, and the introduction of it into any of the territories of the U. States or states to be formed," but it recommended that "the territories now holding slaves [be allowed] to retain them."(30) Senator Ben Ruggles presented the resolutions to the U.S. Senate, where they were read and promptly laid on the table. (31) There is even evidence to indicated that Henry Clay gained no gratitude from his Ohio supporters for his role in constructing the Missouri Compromise. Ohio Congressman John Sloane of Wooster wrote Clay in October 1822, that having "seen gentlemen from all parts of the Eastern section" of the state, he was "happy to hear from them that you continue to stand high in public estimation as a presidential candidate, & were it not [for] the recollection of the Missouri questions, there would scarcely be a dissenting voice."(32)

The admission of Missouri to the union as a slave state and the establishment of a line dividing the remainder of the Louisiana Territory into free and slave sections did not end discussion of the slavery issue in Ohio. On December 11,1823, one term Assemblyman Henry Steece of Adams County, introduced a forceful resolution into the legislature suggesting that Congress and the state "adopt some measures to emancipate all the slaves in the United States, by purchasing them of their masters, and colonizing them in some place, to be agreed upon by the different Christian powers of Europe." Steece also recommended that "a direct tax be levied on the people of the United States for the purpose." State Representative Henry Bacon of Montegomery County raised objections to the Steece Resolution because he felt the government could not afford to undertake the expense of such a program. However,

John Goodenow of Jefferson County and James Kilbourne of Franklin County, defended the proposal and it was referred to a select committee. (33) On January 1, 1824, the select committee of the Ohio House of Representatives reported favorably on the Steece Resolution and suggested that the national government "shall provide that children of persons now held in slavery, born after the passage of such law, shall be free at the age of 21 years, and recognizing the principle, that the evil of slavery is a national one," that all of the states should contribute to the cost of "removing it."(34) After minor alterations both houses approved the resolution. In February 1824, Congressman Wright of Ohio, presented the resolution to the Congress of the United States (35) and copies were distributed by Governor Jeremiah Morrow to state legislatures throughout the Union. Within two years, the state legislatures of Delaware, Connecticut, Illinois, and Indiana passed resolutions concurring with the Ohio antislavery resolve.

Unfortunately, the deep South looked far less favorably upon the Steece Resolution. The Mississippi legislature replied with a sharp rebuke of the Ohio General Assembly. The Mississippians contended that "the right of property in Slaves, is as sacred and inviolate as that of any other species of personal property whatever." Recognizing that slavery was, indeed, an evil "circumstances over which we could have no control have rendered it inevitable and place it without the pale of legislative authority." Any form of emancipation, they felt would violate "the constitutional rights of our citizens."(36) South Carolina referred to it as "a very strange and ill advised communication."(37) However, these objections did not move the Ohio legislature to apologize for its stand.

The antislavery resolutions passed by the Ohio General Assembly undoubtedly helped alert the leadership of the American Colonization Society to the potential for organizing state and local auxiliaries in the West. Colonization rested upon a dual set of convictions. The first was, of course, that slavery was wrong and should be discontinued. The second was that blacks should be excluded from white society. Both of these principles had widespread appeal in Ohio during the 1820's and, therefore, attracted the state's established political leaders to the banner of colonizaiton. When the agents of the American Colonization Society arrived in the Buckeye State, they found a ready audience for their message.

Source: Thomas D. Matijasic, "The Foundations of Colonization: The Peculiar Nature of Race Relations in Ohio During the Early Anite-Bellum Period," Queen City Heritage, 49:4, 1991, pp. 23-41.

HOW WELL DID YOU UNDERSTAND THIS SELECTION?

1. What forms of legal discrimination did African Americans face in Ohio during the early 19th century?

2. Did most white Ohioans favor an extension of slavery into new territories? What evidence can you site to explain your answer?

PRESIDENT JAMES MADISON'S WAR MESSAGE TO CONGRESS

In June 1812, the United States declared war on Great Britain. The United States was particularly offended by the harassment of American commercial vessels by the British navy. The United States attempted to resolve the problem through economic coercion, but when that failed, President Madison heeded the cries of the War Hawks in Congress and asked for a declaration of war.

British cruisers have been in the continued practice of violating the American flag on the great highway of nations, and of seizing and carrying off persons sailing under it, not in the exercise of a belligerent right founded on the law of nations against an enemy, but on a municipal prerogative over British subjects. British jurisdiction is thus extended to neutral vessels in a situation where no laws can operate but the law of nations and the laws of the country to which the vessels belong, and a self-redress is assumed which, if British subjects were wrongfully detained and alone concerned, is that substitutions of force for a resort to the responsible sovereign which falls within the definition of war. Could the seizure of British subjects in such cases be regarded as within the exercise of a belligerent right, the acknowledged laws of war, which forbid an article of captured property to be adjudged without a regular investigation before a competent tribunal, would imperiously demand the fairest trial where the sacred rights of persons were at issue. In place of such a trial these rights are subjected to the will of every petty commander.

British cruisers have been in the practice also of violating the rights and the peace of our coasts. They hover over and harass our entering and departing commerce. To the most insulting pretensions they have added the most lawless proceedings in our very harbors, and have wantonly split American blood within the sanctuary of our territorial jurisdiction. . .

Not content with these occasional expedients for laying waste our neutral trade, the cabinet of Britain resorted at length to the sweeping system of blockades, under the name of orders in council, which has been molded and managed as might best suit its political views, its commercial jealousies, or the avidity of British cruisers. . .

In reviewing the conduct of Great Britain toward the United States our attention is necessarily drawn to the warfare just renewed by the savages on one of our extensive frontiers—a warfare which is known to spare neither age nor sex and to be distinguished by featured peculiarly shocking to humanity. It is difficult to account for the activity and combinations which have for some time been developing themselves among tribes in constant intercourse with British traders and garrisons without connecting their hostility with that influence and without recollecting the authenticated examples of such interpositions heretofore furnished by the officers and agents of that Government. Our moderation and conciliation have had no other effect than to encourage perseverance and to enlarge pretensions. We behold our seafaring citizens still the daily victims of lawless violence, committed on the great common and highway of nations, even within sight of the country which owes them protection. We behold our vessels, freighted with the products of our soil and industry, or returning with the honest proceeds of them, wrested from their lawful destinations, confiscated by prize courts no longer the organs of public law but the instruments of arbitrary edicts, and their unfortunate crews dispersed and lost, or forced or inveigled in British ports into British fleets, whilst arguments are employed in support of these aggressions which have no foundation but in a principle equally supporting a claim to regulate our external commerce in all cases whatsoever.

We behold, in fine, on the side of Great Britain a state of war against the United States, and on the side of the United States a state of peace toward Great Britain.

Whether the United States shall continue passive under these progressive usurpations and these accumulating wrongs, or, opposing force to force in defense of their national rights, shall commit a just cause into the hands of the Almighty Disposer of Events, avoiding all connections which might entangle it in the contest or views of other powers, and preserving a constant readiness to concur in an honorable reestablishment of peace and friendship, is a solemn question which the Constitution wisely confides to the legislative department of the Government. In recommending it to their early deliberations I am happy in the assurance that the decision will be worthy [of] the enlightened and patriotic councils of a virtuous, a free, and a powerful nation.

Source: "To The Senate and House of Representatives of the United States, June 1,1812," in James D. Richardson, A Compilation of the Message and Papers of the Presidents, 1789-1908 (Washington: Bureau of National Literature and Art, 1909), Vol. 1, pages 500-505 as reproduced by http://www.geocities.com/CollegePark/Campus/6925/doc_madison.htm

HOW WELL DID YOU UNDERSTAND THIS SELECTION?

1. What reasons did President Madison give for advocating war with Britain in 1812?

2. How did President Madison describe Native Americans and their methods of warfare?

THE BATTLE OF NEW ORLEANS (January 8, 1815)

The War of 1812 was essentially a stalemate. After two and a half years of inconclusive fighting, both Britain and the United States wanted to end the struggle. On Christmas Eve 1814, diplomats representing the belligerent nations signed the Treaty of Ghent ending the war. Unfortunately, news of the treaty did not reach the United States for several weeks. The battle of New Orleans, the single greatest American victory of the war, was actually fought after the war was over.

General Andrew Jackson's stunning victory over crack British troops at Chalmette planation on January 8, 1815, was the greatest American land victory of the War of 1812. Commonly called the Battle of New Orleans—the last battle of the last war ever fought between England and the United States—it preserved America's claim to the Louisiana Purchase, prompted a wave of migration and settlement along the Mississippi River, and restored American pride and unity. It also made Jackson a national hero.

The War of 1812 was fought to vindicate U.S. maritime rights, secure the western frontier from British provocation of the Indians, and pave the way for the annexation of Canada. It was pursued half-heartedly by both sides, and with little success for either. Also, battling Napoleon's armies in Europe, England could spare few troops to fight in the United States and did little more than help to defend Canada. American victories were few and mostly at sea. When England defeated Napoleon in the spring of 1814, the character of the American war changed dramatically. Thousands of battle-tested British soldiers sailed for the United States, and invasion thrusts were planned via Lake Champlain, the Chesapeake Bay, and, later, the Gulf coast.

The first thrust ended when Commander Thomas MacDonough defeated the British fleet in the Battle of Lake Champlain in September 1814. The second was turned back about the same time at Fort McHenry, the main defense of Baltimore, but not before the British had burned the White House and the Capitol at Washington. The third began in late December when 36-year-old British Major General Sir Edward M. Pakenham led 10,000 troops overland from Lake Borgne to attack New Orleans. The capture of this important port was Britain's main hope for exacting a favorable peace settlement from the Americans. By controlling the mouth of the Mississippi River, England could seriously threaten the economic well-being of the entire Mississippi Valley and hamper U.S. westward expansion.

Defending New Orleans were about 5,000 militia and volunteer soldiers (including a contingent of Jean Lafitte's Baratarians) under 47-year-old Major General Andrew Jackson. On December 23, when Pakenham's troops were within nine miles of the city, Jackson halted their advance in a fierce night attack that caught the British off guard. The Americans then withdrew behind the banks of the Rodriguez Canal.

The Rodriguez Canal formed the boundary between the Chalmette and Macarty planations and marked the most narrow strip of dry land between the Mississippi River and an impassable cypress swamp. The stubbled sugar cane fields provided an excellent field of fire for American artillery and small arms. Jackson's men widened and deepened the canal and partially filled it with water. Behind it they built a mud rampart shoulder-high and thick enough to withstand a cannon shot. Then they waited for the British to attack. Pakenham tried to dislodge the Americans on December 28 with an infantry attack and again on January 1 with artillery fire. When these efforts failed, he knew he must either withdraw, risking the demoralization of his men and an American attack, or assault Jackson's line, trusting to good leadership and the general superiority of the British soldier. Instinctively, he chose to attack.

On January 8, 1815, Pakenham sent 5,400 soldiers head on against the American positions. The withering fire from Jackson's artillery and small arms tore through their ranks with devastating effect. Gen. Samuel Gibbs' brigade came under tremendous fire from Gen. John Coffee's Tennesseans holding the American left flank near the swamp, and many of the British officers, including Gibbs, were killed. Gen. John Keane, attempting to come to Gibb's aid, ordered the 93rd Highlanders to march diagonally across the field from near the river. This movement exposed the regiment to a raking fire from the American line that inflicted frightful casualties, including Keane himself. Pakenham rode forward to rally his men for another attack and was mortally wounded. Col. Robert Rennie's British units nearest the river actually gained the top of the mud rampart before being repulsed.

The Battle of New Orleans lasted less than two hours, with the major fighting confined to about 30 minutes. British casualties exceeded 2,000; the Americans reported only 13. On January 18 the British retreated to Lake Borgne, ending the Louisiana campaign and ensuring the United States of a bright future for the lower Mississippi Valley.

Source: The National Park Service, "Chalmette Battlefield and National Cemetery."
http://www.nps.gov/jela/Chalmette%20Battlefield.htm

HOW WELL DID YOU UNDERSTAND THIS SELECTION?

1. What did the British hope to accomplish with the capture of New Orleans?

2. Who won the battle of New Orleans? Why did they emerge victorious?

SELF TEST:

MULTIPLE CHOICE: Circle the correct response. The correct answers are given at the end.

1. Alexander Hamilton's economic proposals included a plan to
    a. provide relief for the poor.
    b. fund the debt in bonds at face value.
    c. repudiate the national debt inherited from the confederation government.
    d. force the states to take over payment of the national debt.

2. Thomas Jefferson objected to plans to create a national bank because
    a. he believed such a plan was unconstitutional.
    b. he favored private initiative.
    c. he felt it would compete against his own bank.
    d. he favored using the Bank of England.

3. The visit of French diplomat Edmund Genet
    a. helped improve relations between France and the United States
    b. led to the resignation of Thomas Jefferson as Secretary of State
    c. led to war between France and the United States
    d. led to the resignation of Alexander Hamilton as Secretary of the Treasury

4. The Sedition Act was designed to
    a. promote freedom of speech
    b. gain the presidency for Aaron Burr
    c. establish a permanent separation between church and state
    d. stifle political opposition

5. Thomas Jefferson's greatest achievement as president was
    a. gaining respect for our neutral trading rights.
    b. achieving a permanent peace with the Native Americans of the Old Northwest.
    c. gaining the admission of Missouri into the Union as a free state.
    d. the purchase of the Louisiana Territory.

6. The greatest diplomatic challenge faced by President Jefferson was
    a. the XYZ Affair.
    b. the Spanish seizure of Florida.
    c. the failure of Congress to enact an income tax.
    d. the harassment of American ships by the British navy.

7. The Treaty of Ghent, which ended the War of 1812,
    a. provided for a massive exchange of territory.
    b. ended the war on honorable terms for both countries involved.
    c. forced Britain to concede Canada to the U.S.
    d. allowed the U.S. to annex parts of Canada.

8. During the Era of Good Feeling (1817-1824),
    a. the Democratic-Republican Party would rule without significant opposition.
    b. the United States functioned without a national bank.
    c. the nation was economically prosperous at all times.
    d. slavery was gradually ended in the border states.

9. The issue of slavery in the Louisiana Territory was temporarily settled with the
   a. Dred Scott decision.
   b. Mexican Cession.
   c. Treaty of Ghent.
   d. Missouri Compromise.

10. Throughout the early republic, most Americans
    a. lived in poverty and squalor.
    b. lived in cities and worked in factories.
    c. lived in rural communities and farmed.
    d. were well educated and lived into old age.

Answers: 1-b; 2-a; 3-b; 4-d; 5-d; 6-d; 7-b; 8-a; 9-d; 10-c.

ESSAYS:

1. Contrast Alexander Hamilton and Thomas Jefferson. Why did they clash?

2. In his "Farewell Address," President George Washington warned against becoming involved in the affairs of European nations. Yet, during the years of the early republic, European nations involved themselves in American affairs. Could the presidents who followed Washington as chief executive of the nation have followed Washington's advice?

3. How did one-party rule during the Era of Good Feeling actually lead to a modification of Democratic-Republican policies and principles?

OPTIONAL ACTIVITIES:

1. You are Thomas Jefferson. Allow members of the class to ask questions about your political principles, your programs, and your personal life. Defend yourself as best you can.

2. You are Tecumseh. Write a three-page paper appealing for tribal unity and resistance in the face of pressure by the U.S. government to sell tribal lands.

3. Compare the Alien and Sedition Acts passed by the Federalist dominated Congress in 1798 with the recently passed Patriot Act. How are they similar? How are they different?

WEB SITE LISTINGS:

Don Mabry's Archival Sources of U.S. History during the Early Republic
   http://www.geocities.com/Athens/Forum/9061/USA/early/early.html
The Knife River Indian Village of North Dakota
   http://www.nps.gov/knri/lodge/lodge_0.htm
War of 1812 Index
   http://www.multieducator.com/1812/
Military History of the War of 1812 (1812-1814)
   http://www.cfcsc.dnd.ca/links/milhist/1812.html
Monticello - The Home of Thomas Jefferson
   http://www.monticello.org/
Website of the PBS Documentary on Thomas Jefferson by Ken Burns
   http://www.pbs.org/jefferson/
   http://www.jmu.edu/madison/hamilton.htm

Chapter Seven

CLAIMING THE COMMONS:
Constructing an American Identity

The defeat of President Adams in his bid for re-election in 1828 showed a new trend in politics. Along with the changes in state and local government structures came a change in how American citizens viewed their role. Rather than expecting the descendents of their Founding Fathers to watch over the nation in a disinterested fashion, Americans began to demand that the problems they were experiencing at the local level be taken directly to the federal level. This new belief in a personal interest in government activities fueled the longlasting charisma of a western, homespun, and heroic officer like Andrew Jackson. With the solid organization of two new national parties, Whigs and Democrats, Americans began in large numbers to parade, eat, drink, fight, and vote for their chosen political parties.

Frequent elections meant frequent attempts at persuading the huge numbers of voters to cast their votes for a certain candidate. During the antebellum decades, the new forms of appealing to a mass electorate included public "treats" (usually in the form of whiskey), public celebrations (such as parades and barbecues or levees), and long-winded rhetorical works (both in live performances and in pamphlet form). The most popular orators or pamphleteers were those who could, at length, express themselves with overblown prose, clever word tricks, and thinly disguised racist or sexual innuendo. At the same time concerned citizens formed conventions on almost every politicized issue of the day: women's rights, unionism, public schools, slave uprisings, abolitionism, colonization, nativism and expatriation, prostitution, temperance, sabbitarianism, and poor relief. These conventions would send letters to their representatives or declare their resolutions in the newspapers. During this era in our nation's history, the United States changed from a republic to a democracy.

The two-term presidency of Andrew Jackson serves as a case study in how the two national political parties clarified this new sense of accountability to the American citizenry. From the implementation of his "Spoils System" to the Bank War, Andrew Jackson's presidential actions emphasized the Democratic Party's effort to restrict the role of government, especially to curb the activities of legislatures bent on supporting the nascent industrial and transportation revolutions. Using the presidential veto, Jackson wielded a heavy fist against congressional efforts, often going directly to the people in open letters or speeches to explain his veto as a protection of the interests of the "Common Man."

The U.S. as a whole tripled its population in the antebellum period. With the opening up of public lands, the Western states began to increase in population to rival those states in the Northeast. While the lure of cheap public land and high profitability of cotton production caused a bubble of speculation, the upward economic trend of the 1830s was followed by a sharp decline with the Panic of 1837. Even the personal power of "Old Hickory" could not shake the feeling that there needed to be a stronger governmental oversight of the volatile economy in the 1840s. The Hayne-Webster debates in Congress exemplified the passions and fears of a nation in the throes of an identity crisis: was the Union a federation of self-interested states or a unified conglomerate? The real question to be determined, it seemed, was which party could best lead the nation as it grew and prospered? The partisan battles grew ever more fierce as the new nation struggled for its own identity.

However, the democracy of the antebellum period was clearly limited. People of color, women, immigrants, and organized labor still had to fight for equal rights as citizens. The eastern Native Americans lost their last battles to remain as separate nations, and the "Indian Removal" process wreaked devastating effects on their cultures and populations. The antebellum mercantile class rose in the urban areas alongside the new planter class of the south-western rural areas to create a demand for a more mechanized approach to labor. Just as the factory workers had to keep up with the new technologies in the more centralized mills, the enslaved field hands had to keep up with the demands for higher yields in cotton, rice, hemp, and tobacco. The rise of unions and organized slave conspiracies coincided with this increased control over worker productivity.

The new machines in industry and transportation had set about creating a new socio-economic milieu, and the new visions of democracy and opportunity framed a new American nation ready to take its place in the world order.

IDENTIFICATION: Briefly describe each term.

Andrew Jackson

Henry Clay

John C. Calhoun

Martin Van Buren

Nicholas Biddle

Osceola

Sequoyah

Richard M. Johnson

Whigs

Democrats

Common Man

Suffrage reform

Sunset laws

Political "treat"

Dorr's War

Tariff "of Abominations"

"Peggy" Eaton affair

"Kitchen" Cabinet

Secretary of the Treasury Roger Taney

"pet banks"

Specie Circular

Hayne-Webster debates

South Carolina's Ordinance of Nullification

Indian Removal Act

Cherokee Nation v. Georgia

Trail of Tears

Black Hawk War

Treaty of New Echota

<u>"wage slavery"</u>

<u>Commonwealth v. Hunt</u>

<u>Waltham System</u>

<u>Lowell Female Labor Reform Association</u>

<u>Spoils system</u>

<u>the Veto</u>

<u>the Bank War</u>

<u>Nicholas Biddle</u>

<u>Panic of 1837</u>

<u>"Turn outs"</u>

THINK ABOUT:

1. This era was a time of great change and the beginning of our national identity as a democracy for all people. How did Americans express their patriotism during this time period? Did different people have a different sense of what an "American citizen" was? Were there different types of citizens?

2. Imagine that you were a white male farmer running for political office at the local or state level. What would you need to have in your speeches that would help you become popular? How would you campaign? Which organizations would you target as you solicited support for your candidacy? What do you think would be the barriers to your success?

In 1830 President Jackson vetoed a bill that would have provided $150,000 for a federal government subscription of stock in a company that proposed to extend the Cumberland National Road with a sixty-mile road near Maysville, Kentucky. The project would have advanced Henry Clay's American System since the bill would have developed the National Road from an east-west orientation to include points in the South. Jackson's veto of this bill established a precedent, particularly in the case of roads, that made future federal support for internal improvements difficult to obtain. Jackson's message discussed the relationship between the federal government and the states and on the role of government in society in general. As you read, look for the points Jackson makes to defend his veto. Think about how he reflected the ideology of the Democratic Party at the time.

To the House of Representatives:

Gentlemen, I have maturely considered the bill proposing to authorize a "subscription of stock in the Maysville...Road Company," and now return the same to the House of Representatives, in which it originated, with my objections to its passage...

Such grants [of money by the federal government] have always been [passed] under the control of the general principle that the works which might be thus aided should be "of a general, not local, national, not State," character. A disregard of this distinction would of necessity lead to the subversion of the federal system.... I am not able to view [the Maysville Road Bill] in any other light than as a measure of purely local character.... It has no connection with any established system of improvements; [and] is exclusively within the limits of a State [Kentucky]....

...As great as this object [goal of internal improvements] undoubtedly is, it is not the only one which demands the fostering care of the government. The preservation and success of the republican principle rest with us. To elevate its character and its influence rank among our most important duties, and the best means to accomplish this desirable end are those which will rivet the attachment of our citizens to the Government of their choice by the comparative lightness of their public burthens [burdens] and by the attraction which the superior success of its operations will present to the admiration and respect of the world.

Through the favor of an overruling and indulgent Providence our country is blessed with a general prosperity and our citizens exempted from the pressure of taxation, which other less favored portions of the human family are obliged to bear; yet it is true that many of the taxes collected from our citizens through the medium of imposts have for a considerable period been onerous. In many particulars these taxes have borne severely upon the laboring and less prosperous classes of the community, being imposed on the necessaries of life, and this, too, in cases where the burden was not relieved by the consciousness that it would ultimately contribute to make us independent of foreign nation articles of prime necessity by the encouragement of growth and manufacture at home. They have been cheerfully borne because they were thought to be necessary to the support of government and the payments of debts unavoidably incurred in the acquisition and maintenance of our national rights and liberties. But have we a right to calculate on the same cheerful acquiescence when it is known that the necessity for their continuance would cease were it not for irregular, improvident, and unequal appropriations of public funds?...

...How gratifying the effect of presenting to the world the sublime spectacle of a Republic of more than 12,000,000 happy people, in the fifty-fourth year of her existence, after having passed through two protracted wars—one for the acquisition and the other for the maintenance of liberty—free from debt and all her immense resources unfettered! What a salutary influence would not such an exhibition exercise upon the cause of liberal principles and free government throughout the world! Would we not find ourselves in its effect an additional guarantee that our political institutions will be transmitted to the most remote posterity without decay? A course of policy destined to witness events like these cannot be benefited by a legislation which tolerates a scramble for appropriations that have no relation to any general system of improvement, and whose good effects must of necessity be very limited...

...If different impressions are entertained in any quarter; if it is expected that the people of this country, reckless of their constitutional obligations, will prefer their local interest to the principles of the Union...indeed has the world but little to hope from the example of free government. When an honest observance of constitutional compacts cannot be obtained from communities like ours, it need not be anticipated elsewhere... and the degrading truth that man is unfit for self-government [will be] admitted. And this will be the case if expediency be made a rule of construction in interpreting the Constitution. Power in no government could desire a better shield for the insidious advances which it is ever ready to make upon the checks that are designed to restrain its action...

Source: James D. Richardson, comp., *A Compilation of the Messages and Papers of the Presidents, Vol. 3.* In 20 volumes. (New York: Bureau of National Literature, 1897), pp. 1046-1055.

HOW WELL DID YOU UNDERSTAND THIS SELECTION?

1. What were Jackson's main reasons for vetoing the bill?

2. Point out in the text where Jackson is clearly using the Democratic Party platform to differentiate the Democrats from the Whigs on the basic assumptions about the role of government.

3. What do you think might have happened in the southern states if the National Road had been extended there? Would our nation's history have been different?

INDIAN REMOVAL: Two Sides of the Story

The Trail of Tears became a symbol of white injustice toward the Amerindians. Even though the Cherokee Nation had won a legal victory over the state of Georgia in the Supreme Court, the United States refused to acknowledge their rights. The so-called "removal" or forced marches to the so-called Indian Territory (later Oklahoma) was part of this era's attempt to define who was an American citizen... and who was not.

Andrew Jackson's 2nd Annual Message To Congress, December 7, 1830
.... It give me pleasure to announce to Congress that the benevolent policy of the Government .... in relation to the removal of the Indians beyond the white settlements is approaching to a happy consummation .... Toward the aborigines of the country no one can indulge a more friendly feeling than myself, or would go further in attempting to reclaim them from their wandering habits and make the a happy, prosperous people ....

Humanity has often wept over the fate of the aborigines of this country and Philanthropy has been long busily employed in devising means to avert it, but its progress has never for a moment been arrested, and one by one have many powerful tribes disappeared from the earth. To follow to the tomb the last of his race and to tread on the graves of extinct nations excites melancholy reflections. But true philanthropy reconciles the mind to these vicissitudes [change in luck] as it does to the extinction of one generation to make room for another .... Nor is there anything in this which, upon a comprehensive view of the general interests of the human race, is to be regretted. Philanthropy could not wish to see this continent restored to the condition in which it was found by our forefathers. What good man would prefer a country covered with forests and ranged by a few thousand savages to our extensive Republic, studded with cities, towns and prosperous farms .... ?

.... May we not hope, therefore, that all good citizens, and none more zealously than those who think the Indians oppressed by subjection to the laws of the states, will unite in attempting to open the eyes of those children of the forest to their true condition, and, by a speedy removal, to relieve them from the evils, real or imaginary, present or prospective, with which they maybe supposed to be threatened....

Source: "Message of the President of the U.S., to Both Houses of Congress, at the Commencement of the Second Session of the Twenty-First Congress, Dec. 7, 1830," *Register of Debates in Congress...* Vol. VII (Washington: Gales and Seaton, 1831), Appendix, pp. ix-x.

Memorial And Protest Of The Cherokee Nation, June 22, 1836

It would be useless to recapitulate the numerous provisions for the security and protection of the rights of the Cherokees, to be found in the various treaties between their nation and the United States. The Cherokees were happy and prosperous under a scrupulous observance of treaty stipulations by the government of the United States, and from the fostering hand extended over them, they made rapid advances in civilization, morals, and in the arts and sciences. Little did they anticipate, that when taught to think and feel as the American citizen, and to have with him a common interest, they were to be despoiled by their guardian, to become strangers and wanders in the land of their fathers, forced to return to the savage life, and to seek a new home in the wilds of the far west, and that without their consent.

An instrument purporting to be a treaty with the Cherokee people, has recently been made public by the President of the United States, that will have such an operation, if carried into effect. This instrument, ... [we] aver before the civilized world, and in the presence of Almighty God, is fraudulent, false upon its face, made by unauthorized individuals, without the sanction, and against the wishes, of the great body of the Cherokee people.

Source: "Memorial of Protest of the Cherokee Nation," June 22, 1836, U.S. Congress, House Document 286, 24th Cong., 1st sess.

HOW WELL DID YOU UNDERSTAND THIS SELECTION?

1. What was Jackson's benevolent policy? How, in Jackson's view, did the Indians live in 1830? What was the Indians' natural fate, and why was this not regrettable, according to Jackson?

2. Why were Cherokees happy and prosperous before 1830 (2 reasons)? How were they going to live after 1830?

3. Was the Indian Removal Act and Jackson's enforcement of it "for the common man"?

HENRY CLAY'S SPEECH ON THE COMPROMISE TARIFF, February 12, 1833

A tariff is a schedule of taxes on commodities crossing a political boundary. It can raise money to pay for the costs of government; it can protect domestic producers from foreign competitors; and it can serve as a way to get a foreign nation to change a particular policy. After the War of 1812, the U.S. began to use the tariff for protective purposes, especially against English competition. Henry Clay's "American System" relied on a heavy tariff, and he worked with John C. Calhoun to find a compromise during the Nullification Crisis that the anti-tariff Southerners might tolerate.

.... In presenting the modification of the tariff laws, which I am now about to submit, I have two great objects in view. My first object looks to the tariff. I am compelled to express the opinion ... that ... the sudden repeal of the tariff policy would bring ruin and destruction on the whole people of this country. There is no evil, in my opinion, equal to the consequences which would result from such a catastrophe.

What, sir, are the complaints which unhappily divide the people of this great country? On the one hand it is said, by those who are opposed to the tariff, that it unjustly taxes a portion of the people, and paralyzes their industry; .... that there is to be no end to the system; which, right or wrong is to be urged to their inevitable ruin. And what is the just complaint, on the other hand, of those who support the tariff? It is, that the policy of the government is vacillating and uncertain, and that there is no stability in our legislation .... On one side we are urged to repeal a system which is fraught with ruin; on the other side, the check now imposed on enterprise, and the state of alarm in which the public mind has been thrown, render all prudent men desirous, looking ahead a little way, to adopt a state of things, on the stability of which they may have reason to county. Such is the state of feeling on the one side and on the other. I am anxious to find out some principle of mutual accommodation, to satisfy, as far as practicable, both parties — to increase the stability of our legislation; and at some distant day — but not too distant, when we take into view the magnitude of the interests which are involved — to bring down the rate of duties to that revenue standard, for which our opponents have so long contended. The basis on which I wish to found this modification is one of time; and the several parts of the bill to which I am about to call the attention of the Senate, are founded on this basis. I propose to give protection to our manufactured articles, adequate protection for a length of time, ... securing the stability of legislation, and allowing time for a gradual reduction on one side, and on the other proposing to reduce the duties to that revenue standard, for which the opponents of the system have so long contended.

.... Let us have peace, and become once more united as a band of brothers.

.... When I came to take my seat on this floor, I had supposed that a member of this Union had taken an attitude of defiance and hostility against the authority of the general government. I had imagined that she had arrogantly required that we should abandon at once a system which had long been the settled policy of this country. Supposing that she had manifested this feeling, and taken up this position, I had in consequence, felt a disposition to hurl defiance back again, and to impress upon her the necessity of the performance of her duties as a member of this Union. But since my arrival here, I find that South Carolina does not contemplate force, for it is denied and denounced by that State. She disclaims it; and asserts that she is merely making an experiment .... Her appeal is not to arms, but to another power; not to the sword, but to the law .... She disclaims any intention of resorting to force unless we should find it indispensable to execute the laws of the Union by applying force to her. It seems to me the aspect of the attitude of South Carolina has changed; or rather, the new light which I have obtained, enables me to see her in a different attitude; and I have not truly understood her until she passed her laws, by which it was intended to carry her ordinance into effect. Now, I venture to predict that the State to which I have referred must ultimately fail in her attempt .... From one end to the other of this continent, by acclamation, as it were, nullification has been put down, and put down in a manner more effectually than by a thousand wars or a thousand armies — by the irresistible force, by the mighty influence of public opinion. Not a voice beyond the single State of South Carolina has been heard in favor of the principle of nullification, which she has asserted by her own ordinance; and I will say, that she must fail in her lawsuit ....

.... South Carolina must perceive the embarrassments of her situation. She must be desirous — it is unnatural to suppose that she is not — to remain in the Union. What! A State whose heroes in its gallant ancestry fought so many glorious battles along with those of the other States of this Union — a State with which this confederacy is linked by bonds of such a powerful character! I have sometimes fancied what would be her condition if she goes out of this Union; if her five hundred thousand people should at once be thrown upon their own resources. She is out of the Union. What is the consequence? She is an independent power. What then does she do? She must have armies and fleets, and an expensive government; have foreign missions; she must raise taxes; enact this very tariff which has driven her out of the Union, in order to enable her to raise money, and to sustain the attitude of an independent power. If she should have no force, no navy to protect her, she would be exposed to piratical incursions. Their neighbor, St. Domingo, might pour down a horde of pirates on her borders, and desolate her plantations. She must have her embassies; therefore must she have a revenue.

.... If there be any who want civil war, who want to see the blood of any portion of our countrymen spilt, I am not one of them. I wish to see war of no kind; but, above all, I do not desire to see civil war. When war begins, whether civil or foreign, no human sight is competent to foresee when, or how, or where it is to terminate. But when a civil war shall be lighted up in the bosom of our own happy land, and armies are marching, and commanders are winning their victories, and fleets are in motion on our coast, tell me, if you can, tell me, if any human being can tell its duration. God alone knows where such a war would end. In what a state will our institutions be left? In what a state our liberties? I want no war; above all, no war at home.

Sir, I repeat, that I think South Carolina has been rash, intemperate, and greatly in the wrong; but I do not want to disgrace her, nor any other member of this Union. No: I do not desire to see the luster of one single star dimmed of that glorious confederacy which constitutes our political sun; still less do I wish to see it blotted out, and its light obliterated forever. .... If we can forget for a moment — but that would be asking too much of human nature -- if we could suffer, for one moment, party feelings and party causes — and, as I stand here before my God, I declare I have looked beyond those considerations, and regarded only the vast interests of this united people — I should hope that under such feelings, and with such dispositions, we may advantageously proceed to the consideration of this bill, and heal, before they are yet bleeding, the wounds of our distracted country.

Source: Henry Clay, "On Introducing the Compromise Bill. In the Senate of the United States, February 12, 1833," pp. 139-156 in *The Life and Speeches of Henry Clay, Vol. 1*. Philadelphia: Leary, Getz & Co., 1860.

HOW WELL DID YOU UNDERSTAND THIS SELECTION?

1. How does Clay defend his belief in federal protection of the American economy?

2. When Clay described the government of South Carolina as a "she," do you think he consequently belittled or demeaned its actions — or was he simply showing inherent differences? How did the feminization of the nullification argument add to Clay's argument about what a true Union of the States should be?

3. Do you think Clay's vision of civil war was the clinching argument for consensus on the Compromise Tariff? What other factors, not mentioned by Clay, might have been involved?

HOW TO TREAT YOUR CONSTITUENTS AND BE A POPULAR PARTY HERO,
from *The Life of David Crockett,* 1834

David Crockett (1789-1836) was a frontiersman, congressman, and folk hero: half-horse, half-alligator, touched with the snapping turtle, who could leap the Ohio, wade the Mississippi, and whip his weight in wildcats. He was born in Tennessee and served in the militia there. After a successful career in local politics, he was elected to Congress in 1827 as a Democrat. When he started speaking out against Jackson, he was defeated in 1831, and in 1833 he was re-elected as a Whig. In 1835, he was again defeated; so, in disgust he left Tennessee, saying, "You can all go to Hell and I'm going to Texas." There he died as a defender of the Alamo.

.... I saw a number of young politicians around the table, [and] I told them, that I would lay down a few rules for their guidance, which, if properly attended to, could not fail to lead them on the highway to distinction and public honor. I told them, that I was an old hand at the business, and as I was about to retire for a time I would give them a little instruction gratis, for I was up to all the tricks of the trade, though I had practised (sic) but few.

"Attend all public meetings," says I "and get some friends to move that you take the chair; if you fail in this attempt, make a push to be appointed secretary; the proceedings of course will be published, and your name is introduced to the public. But should you fail in both undertakings, get two or three acquaintances, over a bottle of whisky, to pass some resolutions, no matter on what subject; publish them even if you pay the printer — it will answer the purpose of breaking the ice, which is the main point in these matters. Intrigue until you are elected an officer of the militia; this is the second step towards promotion, and can be accomplished with ease ....

"If your ambition or circumstances compel you to serve your country, and earn three dollars a day, by becoming a member of the legislature, you must first publicly avow that the constitution of the state is a shackle upon free and liberal legislation; and is, therefore, of as little use in the present enlightened age, as an old almanac of the year in which the instrument was framed. There is policy in this measure, for by making the constitution a mere dead letter, your headlong proceedings will be attributed to a bold and unshackled mind; whereas, it might otherwise be thought they arose from sheer mulish ignorance.

".... When the day of election approaches, visit your constituents far and wide. Treat liberally, and drink freely, in order to rise in their estimation, though you fall in your own. True, you may be called a drunken dog by some of the clean shirt and silk stocking gentry, but the real rough necks will style you a jovial fellow, their votes are certain, and frequently count double. Do all you can to appear to advantage in the eyes of the women. That's easily done you have but to kiss and slabber their children, wipe their noses, and pat them on the head; this cannot fail to please their mothers, and you may rely on your business being done in that quarter.

"Promise all that is asked," said I, "and more if you can think of anything. Offer to build a bridge or a church, to divide a county, create a batch of new offices, make a turnpike, or anything they like. Promises cost nothing, therefore deny nobody who has a vote or sufficient influence to obtain one.

"Get up on all occasions, and sometimes on no occasion at all, and make long-winded speeches, though composed of nothing else than wind — talk of your devotion to your country, your modesty and disinterestedness, or on any such fanciful subject. Rail against taxes of all kinds, office-holders, and bad harvest weather; and wind up with a flourish about the heroes who fought and bled for our liberties in the times that tried men's souls. To be sure you run the risk of being considered a bladder of wind, or an empty barrel, but never mind that, you will find enough of the same fraternity to keep you in countenance.

"If any charity be going forward, be at the top of it, provided it is to be advertised publicly; if not, it isn't worth your while. None but a fool would place his candle under a bushel on such an occasion.

"These few directions," said I, "if properly attended to, will do your business; and when once elected, why care a fig for the dirty children, the promises, the bridges, the churches, the taxes, the offices, and the subscriptions, for it is absolutely necessary to forget all these before you can become a thoroughgoing politician, and a patriot of the first water."

Source: David Crockett, *The Life of Colonel David Crockett* (Philadelphia: Porter and Coates, 1865), pp. 275-78.

HOW WELL DID YOU UNDERSTAND THIS SELECTION?

1. Davy Crockett had served in Congress since 1826 and although he portrayed himself as a backwoodsman hero, claiming to be "half-alligator, half-horse, with a touch of the snapping turtle," he was a wily politician. What does he recommend to do in order to succeed in democratic politics?

2. How do oratorical skills and whiskey figure in to the success of a young politician?

SETH LUTHER ON WAGE SLAVERY IN NEW ENGLAND, 1832

The earliest advocates for the labor reform movement were urban artisans even before the Revolution. Local craft unions worked hard to defend their trades against cheap, unskilled labor. Centralization came to organized labor in the antebellum era, and this early labor movement had everything to do with the American dream of social equality and virtuous independent citizens. Many of the early workingmen's parties of the 1830s were strong advocates of equal rights, and much of their literature mirrored the rhetoric of the many other antebellum reform movements.

A member of the United States Senate seems to be extremely pleased with cotton mills. He says in the Senate, "Who has not been delighted with the clockwork movements of a large cotton manufactory?" He had visited them often, and always with increased delight. He says the women work in large airy apartments, well warmed. They are neatly dressed, with ruddy complexions, and happy countenances. They mend the broken threads and replace the exhausted balls or broaches, and at stated period they go to and return from their meals with light and cheerful step. (While on a visit to that pink of perfection, Waltham [Lowell], I remarked that the females moved with a very light step, and well they might, for the bell rang for them to return to the mill from their homes in nineteen minutes after it had rung for them to go to breakfast. Some of these females boarded the largest part of a half a mile from the mill.)

And the grand climax is that at the end of the week, after working like slaves for thirteen or fourteen hours every day, "they enter the temples of God on the Sabbath, and thank him for all his benefits ..." We remark that .... we do not believe there can be a single person .... who ever thanked God for permission to work in a cotton mill ....

We would respectfully advise the honorable Senator to travel incognito when he visits cotton mills. If he wishes to come at the truth, he must not be known. Let him put on a short jacket and trousers, and join the "lower orders" for a short time .... In that case we could show him, in some of the prisons in New England called cotton mills, instead of rosy cheeks, the pale, sickly, haggard countenance of the ragged child — haggard from the worse than slavish confinement in the cotton mill. He might see that child driven up to the "clockwork" by the cowskin [whip], in some cases. He might see, in some instances, the child taken from his bed at four in the morning, and plunged into cold water to drive away his slumbers and prepare him for the labors of the mill. After all this he might see that

153

child robbed, yes, robbed of a part of his time allowed for meals by moving the hands of the clock backwards, or forwards, as would best accomplish that purpose .... He might see in some, and not infrequent, instances, the child, and the female child too, driven up to the "clockwork" with the cowhide, or well-seasoned strap of American manufacture.

We could show him many females who have had corporeal punishment inflected upon them; one girl eleven years of age who had her leg broken with billet of wood; another who had a board split over her head by a heartless monster in the shape of an overseer of a cotton mill "paradise."

We shall for want of time .... omit entering more largely into detail for the present respecting the cruelties practiced in some of the American mills. Our wish is to show that education is neglected, ... because if thirteen hours' actual labor is required each day, it is impossible to attend to education among children, or to improvement among adults.

Source: Seth Luther, *An Address to the Working Men of New England, on the State of Education, and on the Condition of the Producing Classes in Europe and America.* Second edition. (New York, The Office of the Working Man's Advocate by George H. Evans, 1833), pp. 17-21.

HOW WELL DID YOU UNDERSTAND THIS SELECTION?

1. How does Luther, a carpenter who was one of the earliest labor reformers, describe the conditions of the textile factories in New England? What does he say are the worst abuses?

2. Why are these conditions in his view harmful to the new democratic nation?

3. How might the factory owners or parents of the child laborers respond to Luther's pamphlet?

In the textile mills of Lowell, Massachusetts, a particular method of factory management was developed by the Boston Manufacturing Company. The production process was fully mechanized, and the only thing restricting profits was the limited availability of labor. The Lowell System was famous for its innovation in recruiting young farm girls and putting them in dormitories under close watch. Through the self-improvement programs and literary clubs, many of the Lowell women became a symbol of the new American industrial worker. However, the mills' wage cuts in the 1830s and the work speedups in the 1840s caused the women to form the Lowell Female Labor Reform Association. This union worked hard to negotiate better working conditions and even petitioned the state legislature for help.

Union is Power. — Our present object is to have union and exertion, and we remain in possession of our own unquestionable rights. We circulate this paper, wishing to obtain the names of all who imbibe the spirit of our patriotic ancestors, who preferred privation to bondage and parted with all that renders life desirable — and even life itself — to produce independence for their children. The oppressing hand of avarice would enslave us, and to gain their objective they very gravely tell us of the pressure of the times; this we are already sensible of and deplore it. If any are in want of assistance, the ladies will be compassionate and assist them, but we prefer to have the disposing of our charities in our own hands [In this strike, as in others, the strikers set up a fund to help those in need], and as we are free, we would remain in possession of what Kind Providence has bestowed upon us, and remain daughters of freemen still.

All who patronize this effort we wish to have discontinue their labor until terms of reconsiliation [sic] are made.

Resolved, that we will not go back into the mills to work unless our wages are continued to us as they have been.

Resolved, that none of us will go back unless they receive us all as one.

Resolved, that if any have not money enough to carry them home that they shall be supplied.

> Let Oppression shrug her shoulders
> And a haughty tyrant frown
> And little upstart Ignorance
> In mockery look down
>
> Yet I value not the feeble threats
> Of Tories in disguise,
> While the flag of Independence
> O'er our noble nation flies.

Source: "Daughters of Freemen Still," *The Man*, Boston, February 22, 1834 & *Boston Transcript*, February 18, 1834

HOW WELL DID YOU UNDERSTAND THIS SELECTION?

1. The "turn out" or strike that inspired this statement protested a 15% cut in wages. The leaders of the strike were fired, and the remaining workers forced to accept lower wages. How does the statement rely on the tradition of the American Revolution?

2. Compare and contrast this statement with Luther's statement in the previous section. How are working women portrayed?

AN ACCOUNT OF JACKSON'S INAUGURATION, March 1829

After losing the presidential election in 1824, Andrew Jackson expanded his political base in the lower and mid-South by playing on the general frustration against the old elite. He won in 1828 by emphasizing his image as a manly warrior who could lead a citizenry of economically independent men in a neverending struggle against the greedy and privileged who exploited the vast majority. This rhetoric served him well, and though his inauguration was a quiet and solemn ceremony (he was still in mourning for his wife), the reception afterwards turned into a huge mess from the crowds that crammed into the White House.

Margaret Bayard Smith to Mary Ann Kirkpatrick, [Washington D.C.], March 11, 1829

.... It was not a thing of detail of a succession of small incidents. No, it was one grand whole, an imposing and majestic spectacle and to a reflective mind one of moral sublimity. Thousands and thousands of people, without distinction of rank, collected in an immense mass round the Capitol, silent, orderly and tranquil, with their eyes fixed on the front of that edifice, waiting the appearance of the President in the portico. The door from the Rotunda opens, preceded by the marshals, surrounded by the Judges of the Supreme Court, the old man with his grey locks, that crown of glory, advances, bows to the people, who greet him with a shout that rends the air, the Cannons, from the heights around, from Alexandria and Fort Warburton proclaim the oath he has taken and all the hills reverberate the sound. It was grand, — it was sublime! An almost breathless silence, succeeded and the multitude was still, — listening to catch the sound of his voice, tho' it was so low, as to be heard only by those nearest to him. After reading his speech, the oath was administered to him by the Chief Justice. The Marshal presented the Bible. The President took it from his hands, pressed his lips to it, laid it reverently down, then bowed again to the people – Yes, to the people in all their majesty. And had the spectacle closed here, even Europeans must have acknowledged that a free people collected in their might, silent and tranquil, restrained solely by a moral power, without a shadow around of military force, was majesty, rising to sublimity, and far surpassing the majesty of Kings and Princes, surrounded with armies and glittering in gold ....

The men all walked. Julia, Anna Maria and I, (the other girls would not adventure) accompanied by Mr. Wood, ... rode round the whole square, taking a view of the animated scene. .... The day was warm and delightful, from the South Terrace we had a view of Pennsylvania and Louisiana Avenues, crowded with people hurrying towards the Capitol. It was a most exhilarating scene! Most of the ladies preferred being inside of the Capitol and the eastern portico, damp and cold as it was, had been fileed from 9 in the morning by ladies who wished to be near the General when he spoke. Every room was filled and the windows crowded. .... We stood on the South steps of the terrace; when the appointed hour came saw the General and his company advancing up the Avenue, slow, very slow, so impeded was his march by the crowds thronging around him. Even from a distance, he could be discerned from those who accompanied him, for he only was uncovered, (the Servant in presence of his Sovereign, the People). ....

At last he enters the gate at the foot of the hill and turns to the road that leads round to the front of the Capitol. In a moment every one who until then had stood like statues gazing on the scene below them, rushed onward, to right, to left, to be ready to receive him in the front. Our party, of course, were more deliberate, we waited until the multitude had rushed past us and then left the terrace and walked round to the furthest side of the square, where there were no carriages to impede us, and entered it by the gate fronting the Capitol. Here was a clear space, and stationing ourselves on the central gravel walk we stood so as to have a clear, full view of the whole scene. The Capitol in all its grandeur and beauty. The Portico and grand steps leading to it, were filled with ladies. Scarlet, purple, blue, yellow, white draperies and waving plumes of every kind and colour, among the white marble pillars, had a fine effect. In the center of the portico was a table covered with scarlet, behind it the closed door leading into the rotunda, below the Capitol and all around, a mass of living beings, not a ragged mob, but well dressed and well behaved respectable and worthy citizens. ....

At the moment the General entered the Portico and advanced to the table, the shout that rent the air, still resounds in my ears. When the speech was over, and the President made his parting bow, the barrier that had separated the people from him was broken down and they rushed up the steps all eager to shake hands with him. It was with difficulty he made his way through the Capitol and down the hill to the gateway that opens on the avenue. Here for a moment he was stopped. The living mass was impenetrable. After a while a passage was opened, and he mounted his horse which had been provided for his return (for he had walked to the Capitol) then such a cortege as followed him! Country men, farmers, gentlemen, mounted and dismounted, boys, women and children, black and white. Carriages, wagons and carts all pursuing him to the President's house .... Here was a perfect levee, at least a hundred ladies and gentlemen, all happy and rejoicing, — wine and cake was handed in profusion. We sat with this company and stopped on the summit of the hill until the avenue was comparatively clear, tho' at any other time we should have thought it terribly crowded. Streams of people on foot and of carriages of all kinds, still pouring towards the President's house. ....

The day was delightful, the scene animating, so we walked backward and forward at every turn meeting some new acquaintance and stopping to talk and shake hands. .... [The Smiths finally got into the President's house soon after 3:00 in the afternoon.] But what a scene did we witness! The *Majesty of the People* [italics hers] had disappeared, and a rabble, a mob, of boys, negros, women, children, scrambling fighting, romping. What a pity what a pity! No arrangements had been made no arrangements had been made no police officers placed on duty and the whole house had been inundated by the rabble mob. We came too late. The President, after having been *literally* nearly pressed to death and almost suffocated and torn to pieces by the people in their eagerness to shake hands with Old Hickory, had retreated through the back way or south front and had escaped to his lodgings at Gadsby's. Cut glass and china to the amount of several thousand dollars had been broken in the struggle to get the refreshments, punch and other articles had been carried out in tubs and buckets, but had it been in hogsheads it would have been insufficient, ice-creams, and cake and lemonade, for 20,000 people, for it is said that number were there, tho' I think the estimate exaggerated. Ladies fainted, men were seen with bloody noses and such a scene of confusion took place as is impossible to describe, — those who got in could not get out by the door again, but had to scramble out of windows. At one time, the President who had retreated and retreated until he was pressed against the wall, could only be secured by a number of gentlemen forming round him and making a kind of barrier of their own bodies, and the pressure was so great that Col[.] Bomford who was one said that at one time he was afraid they should have been pushed down, or on the President. It was then the windows were thrown open, and the torrent found an outlet, which otherwise might have proved fatal.

This concourse had not been anticipated and therefore not provided against. Ladies and gentlemen, only had been expected at this Levee, not the people en masse. But it was the People's day, and the People's President and the People would rule. God grant that one day or other, the People, do not put down all rule and rulers. I fear, enlightened Freemen as they are, they will be found, as they have been found in all ages and countries where they get the Power in their hands, that of all tyrants, they are the most ferocious, cruel and despotic. The noisy and disorderly rabble in the President's House brought to my mind descriptions I had read, of the mobs in the Tuileries and at Versailles ....

Source: Margaret Bayard Smith, *The First Forty Years of Washington Society; Portrayed by the Family Letters of Mrs. Samuel Harrison Smith (Margaret Bayard) from the Collection of her Grandson, J. Henley Smith,* edited by Gaillard Hunt (New York: Charles Scribner's Sons, 1906), pp. 290-96.

HOW WELL DID YOU UNDERSTAND THIS SELECTION?

1. What does Smith mean by "majesty" when describing Jackson's swearing-in ceremony?

2. Why, since women couldn't vote at this time, were the "ladies" so anxious to be near and hear the new president? Why was it so important for Smith to describe the waiting crowd as "well dressed and well behaved respectable and worthy citizens"?

3. How does Smith describe the "rabble" in the president's house in the late afternoon? Why does she relate this mob with the thirty thousand French peasants who storm the Tuileries Palace in France in 1792 to capture King Louis XVI?

4. Do you think that the way Smith portrays the presidential inauguration was affected by the fact that Smith was a friend with the Calhouns and the Clays?

U.S. TRANSPORTATION REVOLUTION AS PERCEIVED BY A EUROPEAN TRAVELER IN 1832

Fanny Kemble, an internationally popular English actress, toured the U.S. with her father, Charles Kemble. She wrote a journal that described her adventures, and the following excerpts are accounts of her various journeys in New York by steamboat, stagecoach, horse-drawn train, and canal.

Monday [October] 8th [1832] .... The steamboat was very large and commodious as all these conveyances are.... These steamboats have three stories; the upper one is, as it were, a roofing or terrace on the leads of the second, a very desirable station when the weather is neither too foul, nor too fair; a burning sun being, I should think, as little desirable there, as a shower of rain. The second floor or deck, has the advantage of the ceiling above, and yet, the sides being completely open, it is airy, and allows free sight of the shores on either hand. Chairs, stools and benches are the furniture of these two decks. The one below, or third floor, downwards, in fact, the ground floor, being the one near the water, is a spacious room completely roofed and walled in, where the passengers take their meals, and resort if the weather is unfavorable. At the end of this room, is a smaller cabin for the use of the ladies, with beds and sofa, and all the conveniences necessary, if they should like to be sick; whither I came and slept till breakfast time. Vigne's account of the pushing, thrusting, rushing, and devouring on board a western steamboat at meal times, had prepared me for rather an awful spectacle; but_-this, I find, is by no means the case in these civilized parts, and everything was conducted with perfect order, propriety and civility. The breakfast was good, and was served and eaten with decency enough.

At about half past ten, we reached the place where we leave the river, to proceed across a part of the State of New Jersey, to the Delaware.... Oh, these coaches! English eye hath not seen, English ear hath not heard, nor hath it entered into the heart of Englishmen to conceive the surpassing clumsiness and wretchedness of these leathern inconveniences. They are shaped something like boats, the sides being merely leathern pieces, removable at pleasure, but which in bad weather are buttoned down to protect the inmates from the wet. There are three seats in this machine, the middle one having a movable leathern strap, by way of a dossier, runs between the carriage doors, and lifts away, to permit the egress and ingress of the occupants of the other seats.... For the first few minutes, I thought I must have fainted from the intolerable sensation of smothering which I experienced. However, the leathers having been removed, and a little more air obtained, I took heart of grace, and resigned myself to my fate. Away wallopped the four horses, trotting with their front, and galloping with their hind legs: and away went we after them, bumping, thumping, jumping, jolting, shaking, tossing and tumbling, over the wickedest road, I do think, the cruellest, hard_heartedest road that ever wheel rumbled upon. Through bog and marsh and ruts, wider and deeper than any Christian ruts I ever saw, with the roots of trees protruding across our path, their boughs every now and then giving us an affectionate scratch through the windows; and, more than once, a half_demolished trunk or stump lying in the middle of the road lifting us up, and letting us down again, with most awful variations of our poor coach body from its natural position. Bones of me! What a road! Even my father's solid proportions could not keep their level, but were jerked up to the roof and down again every three minutes. Our companions seemed nothing dismayed by these wondrous performances of a coach and four, but laughed and talked incessantly, the young ladies, at the very top of their voices, and with the national nasal twang....

At the end of fourteen miles we turned into a swampy field, the whole fourteen coachfuls of us, and by the help of heaven, bag and baggage were packed into the coaches which stood on the railway ready to receive us. The carriages were not drawn by steam, like those on the Liverpool railway, but by horses, with the mere advantage in speed afforded by iron ledges, which, to be sure, compared with our previous progress through the ruts, was considerable. Our coachful got into the first carriage of the train, escaping, by way of especial grace, the dust which one's predecessors occasion. This vehicle had but two seats, in the usual fashion; each of which held four of us. The whole inside was lined with blazing scarlet leather, and the windows shaded with stuff curtains of the same refreshing color; which with full complement of passengers, on a fine, sunny, American summer's day, must make as pretty a little miniature held as may be, I should think.... This railroad is an infinite blessing; 'tis not yet finished, but shortly will be so, and then the whole of that horrible fourteen miles will be performed in comfort and decency, in less than half the time. In about an hour and a half, we reached the end of our railroad part of the journey, and found another steamboat waiting for us, when we all embarked on the Delaware.... At about four o'clock, we reached Philadelphia, having performed the journey between that and New York (a distance of a hundred miles,) in less than ten hours, in spite of bogs, ruts and all other impediments.

.... July 10 [1833] .... We proceeded by canal to Utica, which distance we performed in a day and a night, starting at two from Schenectady, and reaching Utica the next day at about noon. I like traveling by the canal boats very much. Ours was not crowded, and the country through which we passed being delightful, the placid moderate gliding through it, at about four miles and a half an hour, seemed to me infinitely preferable to the noise of wheels, the rumble of a coach, and the jerking of bad roads, for the gain of a mile an hour. The only nuisances are the bridges over the canal, which are so very low, that one is obliged to prostrate oneself on the deck of the boat, to avoid being scraped off it; and this humiliation occurs, upon an average, once every quarter of an hour....

The valley of the Mohawk, through which we crept the whole sunshining day, is beautiful from beginning to end; fertile, soft, rich, and occasionally approaching sublimity and grandeur, in its rocks and hanging woods. We had a lovely day, and a soft blessed sunset, which, just as we came to a point where the canal crosses the river, and where the curved and wooded shores on either side recede, leaving a broad smooth basin, threw one of the most exquisite effects of light and color, I ever remember to have seen, over the water, and through the sky.... We sat in the men's cabin until they began making preparations for bed, and then withdrew into a room about twelve feet square, where a whole tribe of women were getting to their beds. Some half undressed, some brushing, some curling, some washing, some already asleep in their narrow cribs, but all within a quarter of an inch of each other; it made one shudder....

. . . At Utica we dined; and after dinner I slept profoundly. The gentlemen, I believe, went out to view the town, which, twenty years ago, was not, and now is a flourishing place, with fine-looking shops, two or three hotels, good broad streets, and a body of lawyers, who had a supper at the house where we were staying, and kept the night awake with champagne, shouting, toasts, and clapping of hands: so much for the strides of civilization through the savage lands of this new world....

Source: Fanny Kemble, *Journal of a Residence in America by Frances Anne Butler (Miss Fanny Kemble)* (Paris : A. and W. Galignani, 1835), pp. 86-93, 303-05.

HOW WELL DID YOU UNDERSTAND THIS SELECTION?

1. How did Kemble describe the differences between traveling in the stagecoach and the horse-drawn train?

2. Why were bridges a "nuisance" to Kemble?

3. Which transportation resource would most Americans be able to afford to use in order to travel across the country?

Ralph Waldo Emerson (1803-1882) was an essayist and poet. He advocated self-reliance and urged his readers to give less deference to institutions or traditions. He was the leading figure in the literary and philosophical movement known as Transcendentalism, and he influenced such thinkers as Henry David Thoreau, Margaret Fuller, Nathaniel Hawthorne, and Walt Whitman. At the time, his ideas were considered dangerous and radical, but over time he won increasing respect.

.... I have now spoken of the education of the scholar by nature, by books, and by action. It remains to say somewhat of his duties.

They are such as become Man Thinking. They may all be comprised in self-trust. The office of the scholar is to cheer, to raise, and to guide men by showing them facts amidst appearances. He plies the slow, unhonored, and unpaid task of observation. .... He is one, who raises himself from private considerations and breathes and lives on public and illustrious thoughts. He is the world's eye. He is the world's heart. He is to resist the vulgar prosperity that retrogrades ever to barbarism, by preserving and communicating heroic sentiments, noble biographies, melodious verse, and the conclusions of history. Whatsoever oracles the human heart in all emergencies, in all solemn hours, has uttered as its commentary on the world of actions, — these he shall receive and impart. And whatsoever new verdict Reason from her inviolable seat pronounces on the passing men and events of today, — this he shall hear and promulgate.

These being his functions, it becomes him to feel all confidence in himself, and to defer never to the popular cry. He and he only knows the world. The world of any moment is the merest appearance. Some great decorum, some fetish of a government, some ephemeral trade, or war, or man, is cried up by half mankind and cried down by the other half, as if all depended on this particular up or down. The odds are that the whole question is not worth the poorest thought which the scholar has lost in listening to the controversy. Let him not quit his belief that a popgun is a popgun, though the ancient and honorable of the earth affirm it to be the crack of doom. In silence, in steadiness, in severe abstraction, let him hold by himself; add observation to observation, patient of neglect, patient of reproach, and bide his own time, — happy enough, if he can satisfy himself alone, that this day he has seen something truly. Success treads on every right step. For the instinct is sure, that prompts him to tell his brother what he thinks. He then learns, that in going down into the secrets of his own mind he has descended into the secrets of all minds.

.... Free should the scholar be, — free and brave. Free even to the definition of freedom, "without any hindrance that does not arise out of his own constitution." Brave; for fear is a thing which a scholar by his very function puts behind him. Fear always springs from ignorance. It is a shame to him if his tranquillity, amid dangerous times, arise from the presumption that, like children and women, his is a protect class; or if he seek a temporary peace by the diversion of his thoughts from politics or vexed questions, hiding his head like an ostrich in the flowering bushes, peeping into microscopes, and turning rhymes, as a boy whistles to keep his courage up. So is the danger a danger still; so is the fear worse. Manlike let him turn and face it. Let him look into its eye and search its nature, inspect its origin, — see the whelping of this lion, — which lies no great way back; he will then find in himself a perfect comprehension of its nature and extent; he will have made his hands meet on the other side, and can henceforth defy it, and pass on superior. The world is his, who can see through its pretension. What deafness, what stone-blind custom, what overgrown error you behold, is there only by sufferance, — by your sufferance. See it to be a lie, and you have already dealt it its mortal blow.

.... Men are become of no account. Men in history, men in the world of to-day are bugs, are spawn, and are called "the mass" and "the herd." In a century, in a millennium, one or two men; that is to say, — one or two approximations to the right state of man. All the rest behold in the hero or the poet their own green and crude being, — ripened; yes, and are content to be less, so *that* may attain to its full stature. What a testimony, — full of grandeur, full of pity, — is borne to the demands of his own nature, by the poor clansman, the poor partisan, who rejoices in the glory of his chief. The poor and the low find some amends to their immense moral capacity, for the acquiescence in a political and social inferiority. They are content to be brushed like flies from the path of a great person, so that justice shall be done by him to that common nature which it is the dearest desire of all to see enlarged and glorified. They sun themselves in the great man's light, and feel it to be their own element. They cast the dignity of man from their downtrod selves upon the shoulders of a hero, and will perish to add one drop of blood to make that great heart beat, those giant sinews combat and conquer. He lives for us, and we live in him.

Men such as they are, very naturally seek money or power; and power because it is as good as money, — the "spoils," so called, "of office." And why not? for they aspire to the highest, and this, in their sleep-walking, they dream is highest. Wake them and they shall quit the false good and leap to the true, and leave governments to clerks and desks. This revolution is to be wrought by the gradual domestication of the idea of Culture. The main enterprise of the world for splendor, for extent, is the upbuilding of a man. Here are the materials strown along the ground. The private life of one man shall be a more illustrious monarchy, — more formidable to its enemy, more sweet and serene in its influence to its friend, than any kingdom in history. For a man, rightly viewed, comprehendeth the particular natures of all men. Each philosopher, each bard, each actor, has only done for me, as by a delegate, what one day I can do for myself. The books which once we valued more than the apple of the eye, we have quite exhausted. What is that but saying, that we have come up with the point of view which the universal mind took through the eye of one scribe; we have been that man, and have passed on. First, one; then, another; we drain all cisterns, and, waxing greater by all these supplies, we crave a better and more abundant food. The man has never lived that can feed us ever. The human mind cannot be enshrined in a person, who shall set a barrier on any one side to this unbounded, unboundable empire. It is one central fire, which, flaming now out of the lips of Etna, lightens the capes of Sicily; and now out of the throat of Vesuvius, illuminates the towers and vineyards of Naples. It is one light which beams out of a thousand stars. It is one soul which animates all men.

Source: Ralph Waldo Emerson, "An Oration delivered before the Phi Beta Kappa Society, at Cambridge [Mass.], Aug. 31, 1837" in *American Prose,* edited by George Rice Carpenter (New York: Macmillan Co., 1903), pp. 194-98.

HOW WELL DID YOU UNDERSTAND THIS SELECTION?

1. What's the difference between the lessons taught the young politicians tutored by Davy Crockett in the section and the young students of Ralph Waldo Emerson?

2. How does Emerson's speech reflect or reinforce democratic ideals of his day?

MULTIPLE CHOICE: Circle the correct response. The correct answers are given at the end.

1. What did the Jacksonians want to do to the Second Bank of the U.S.?
    a. add more investors to its board
    b. destroy it
    c. force it to lower interest rates
    d. strengthen it

2. The spoils system
    a. led to the Indian Removal Act
    b. protected officeholders appointed by President Adams
    c. put President Jackson's supporters in the government bureaucracy
    d. required all politicians to be native born

3. What gave birth to the Whig Party?
    a. the "corrupt bargain"
    b. the election of William Henry Harrison
    c. the Indian Removal Act
    d. Jackson's extraordinary use of the presidential veto

4. Andrew Jackson founded the
    a. American Party
    b. Anti-Masonic movement
    c. Democratic Party
    d. Locofocos

5. The first true factory in the U.S. was founded by
    a. Andrew Carnegie
    b. Joseph Sutter
    c. Noah Webster
    d. Samuel Slater

6. Which court case aided organized labor?
    a. *Commonwealth v. Hunt*
    b. *Gibbons v. Ogden*
    c. *McCulloch v. Maryland*
    d. *Worcester v. Georgia*

7. The earliest most famous American invention was the
    a. cotton gin
    b. electric light bulb
    c. rotary engine
    d. thresher

8. Who issued the Specie Circular?
    a. Henry Clay
    b. Andrew Jackson
    c. Winfield Scott
    d. Roger Taney

9. Who was Margaret Timberlake Eaton?
   a. the best friend of Vice-President Calhoun's wife
   b. the biggest stockholder in the Bank of the U.S.
   c. the president of the Virginia Association of Ladies for the Erecting of a Statue to Henry Clay
   d. the wife of Jackson's secretary of war

10. What was Martin Van Buren's partisan state political machine called?
   a. Federalists
   b. Lowell Reform Association
   c. Old Hickory
   d. the Albany Regency

Answers:
   1-b; 2-c; 3-d; 4-c; 5-d; 6-a; 7-a; 8-b; 9-d; 10-d.

ESSAYS:

1. Are political parties necessary in the United States? Why did they emerge in the 1820s and 30s? How did the new American republic get along without them before the War of 1812? How does the party system affect democratic ideals?

2. Discuss the controversy surrounding the Indian Removal Act. How were the arguments for and against the process formulated? How persuasive was the argument regarding private property (vs. tribal lands) and that the Native Americans were not putting the land to good use?

3. Debate Jackson's own definition of Jacksonian Democracy found in his Farewell Address: "To you everyone placed in authority is ultimately responsible...[Be vigilant and jealous of rights, stay]...uncorrupted and incorruptible...[and the nation would be safe]. The cause of freedom will continue to triumph over all its enemies."

OPTIONAL ACTIVITIES: Use your knowledge **and** imagination

1. Imagine you are Andrew Jackson in 1832 during the Nullification Crisis. Would you have taken a stronger position in public against South Carolina? Would you have used force? Would a civil war have happened if you did? Write a series of private journal entries that trace your ideas and the events that transpired in that fateful year.

2. Debate the following statement by James Fenimore Cooper (1838): "The tendency of democracies is, in all things, to mediocrity."

WEB SITE LISTINGS:

The Hermitage, Tennessee home of Andrew Jackson
http://www.thehermitage.com/

Martin Van Buren National Historic Site, New York
http://www.nps.gov/mava/

Ashland, The Henry Clay Estate
http://www.henryclay.org

National Portait Gallery, Hall of Presidents, Smithsonian Institute
http://www.npg.si.edu/exh/hall2/

The Internet Public Library's Presidents of the United States (POTUS)
http://www.potus.com/

"The Panic of 1837", an excerpt from "Life of Martin Van Buren," by Edward M. Shepard (1888-1899), The Legacy Preservation Library
http://www.usgennet.org/usa/topic/preservation/epochs/vol6/pg178.htm

"President's Levee, or all Creation going to the White House," painting by Robert Cruikshank, Library of Congress's American Memory website
http://www.loc.gov/exhibits/treasures/trr074.html

Jackson's 1st & 2nd Inaugural Addresses
http://www.bartleby.com/124/pres23.html
http://www.bartleby.com/124/pres24.html

Tales of the Early Republic
http://www.earlyrepublic.net

The Cherokee "Trail of Tears" National Historic Trail
http://rosecity.net/tears

The People's Paths, North American and Indigenous People
http://www.thepeoplespaths.net/mainindex.html

From Revolution to Reconstruction, "A Brief Biography of Andrew Jackson," by Hal Morris
http://odur.let.rug.nl/~usa/P/aj7/about/bio/jackxx.htm

"Andrew Jackson and the Bankwar" by Tony D'Urso
http://odur.let.rug.nl/~usa/E/bankwar/bankwarxx.htm

"Andrew Jackson" audio seminar by Robert Remini, September 7, 2002
http://www.teachingamericanhistory.org/seminars/2002/remini.html

Chapter Eight

AGE OF REFORM

In the early nineteenth century, organized groups of reformers worked at local, state, and federal levels to create what they imagined to be a more moral social order in the new nation. They highlighted the growing disparities between the rich and the poor, between the pious and the irreligious, and between the free and the enslaved or otherwise oppressed populations. Most antebellum reformers believed that with persuasive appeals to individual conscience, that is, moral suasion, the U.S. could become a "more perfect" nation.

Activists, philanthropists, voluntary associations, and individual intellectuals supported crusades for temperance (banning alcoholic beverages), public education, humane asylums for the poor and disabled, and abolitionism (ending slavery). These reformers optimistically believed in the certainty of human progress, and they fought for radical change in the individual, the family, and the state in order to effect this change. Public attention to an individual's morals could manifest itself in home visits to the very poor, informational tours of state and local penitentiaries, Washingtonian or "Cold Water Army" parades and public confessions of alcoholism, and missionary activities.

The impetus for reform came mainly from the Second Great Awakening, a Protestant revivalist fervor that emphasized salvation for all who fought against sin. One of the leading evangelicals was the Presbyterian minister, Charles G. Finney. In 1824 Finney went as missionary to the settlers of upstate New York, where revivals followed under his preaching, and the area between Albany and Buffalo became known as the "Burnt-Over District." Western New York also was where Joseph Smith dug up the *Book of Mormon* on a hillside near Palmyra, beginning the Church of Jesus Christ of Latter Day Saints. The new religion of Spiritualism was also founded in this area when the three Fox sisters of Hydesville created an international stir in 1848, with their claims to have heard "rappings" from beyond the grave and their public exhibitions of their ability to communicate with the dead. Revivals swept through urban centers such as New York, Philadelphia, and Boston, and the revivalist spirit gained strength in the rural Midwest and South.

Among Charles Finney's most ardent followers were Arthur and Lewis Tappan, philanthropists who helped create a loose association of reformers known as the Benevolent Empire. The Tappan brothers spent much of their energy in the cause of abolitionism. Along with Theodore Weld, they formed the American Anti-Slavery Society in 1833 and backed the most widely circulated anti-slavery journal, *The Emancipator*. In the same year they founded Oberlin College, open to blacks and whites alike. With the passage of the Fugitive Slave Act of 1850, they actively supported the efforts of the Underground Railroad. But by then, the Tappan brothers had split with the more radical William Lloyd Garrison, who believed in immediate emancipation of all slaves and who wanted to branch off into other kinds of reform, including women's rights.

By the 1840s the moral reform movement was mainly run by women's campaigns. The American Female Moral Reform Society had thousands of members who worked to persuade both men and women to adhere to a higher standard of moral purity, and, in particular, they focused on ending prostitution. The rise of the women's rights movement came out of a variety of causes, including abolitionism and temperance. Sarah and Angelina Grimké, two sisters from South Carolina who had converted to Quakerism, were the first official female antislavery agents. However, like the Scottish crusader and utopianist, Frances Wright, before them, the Grimké sisters met up with outrage and dismay from the more conservative reformers who believed that women should not speak out in public forums that included men as well as women. By the 1840s the focus for women's rights rested mainly on legal reform for married women. Leaders in New York and Massachusetts, such as Ernestine Rose, Lucretia Mott, Elizabeth Cady Stanton, and Lucy Stone, lobbied state legislatures to gain better protection for wives and mothers by allowing property ownership or legal guardianship of their children. Stanton's "Declaration of Sentiments and Resolutions" formulated at Seneca Falls, New York, in 1848, has become the classic statement for this reform effort. However, black women were also speaking out at this time: Sojourner Truth and Harriet Tubman were popular speakers for both abolitionism and women's rights.

The temperance crusade, however, was probably the largest organized reform movement of all. By 1851, temperance societies had successfully lobbied the Maine legislature to pass a law that banned the manufacture and sale of alcoholic beverages. Thereafter, the temperance lobby, together with the Sabbatarian movement to halt any type of business transactions on Sundays, succeeded in creating local and state "Maine" laws that curtailed legal access to alcohol.

Other reform efforts to restrain human licentiousness included the establishment of public schools that would help create a moral and virtuous society. Horace Mann was the most influential in this effort to create free schools and to reform school curriculum so to encourage cooperation, righteousness, and deference in all American citizens, male and female. White women's educational opportunities also expanded: Emma Willard opened her successful Troy Female Seminary in New York in 1821, and in 1837 Mary Lyon founded the Mt. Holyoke Female Seminary, which later became the first women's college in the nation.

Unfortunately, most of these reform efforts were aimed at the white populace, and unless an effort was made to free blacks from slavery, many of the opportunities for better education and moral uplift were reserved mainly for whites. While pointing out the physical, mental, and spiritual horrors of being or owning a slave, most abolitionist reformers could not conceive of a society in the near future that treated blacks and whites equally. One of the earliest anti-slavery movements was founded by a group of wealthy Southerners: the American Colonization Society. This voluntary association proposed emancipation of slaves only upon the masters' own volition or upon compensation by charitable organizations or the state. The freed slaves, or free blacks who wanted to emigrate, were then transported to the newly established nation of Liberia, located on the west coast of Africa. The more militant abolitionists, such as the immediatists Frederick Douglass, David Walker, and William Lloyd Garrison, felt the brunt of most Americans' anger at the idea of black equality. Whether they were slaveowners or not, most whites believed that blacks were racially inferior and equal rights would lead to anarchy. Ironically, the anti-abolitionist censorship and violence reflected greater disregard for law and order than the dissenters they hated. The Revolutionary ideals of individual rights such as freedom of public speech and assembly to protest injustices were trampled by lynchings and riots, mail censorship, and even "gag rules" in legislatures to halt debate.

This era also birthed the literary and artistic revolution, which has come to be described as the "American Renaissance." This era boasted of literary giants, such as Washington Irving, James Fenimore Cooper, Henry Wadsworth Longfellow, and Nathaniel Hawthorne, to the philosophers of the transcendental movement founded by Ralph Waldo Emerson and carried on by Henry David Thoreau and Margaret Fuller. Some of these thinkers formed the core of the more radical dissenters who chose to live their everyday lives in a more "perfect" society. The transcendentalist experiment "Brook Farm," like the Owenite communities New Harmony and Nashoba, lasted for a very short time, but many other utopianists succeeded. John Humphrey Noyes' Oneida Community in New York flourished economically in a communal setting that allowed for plural or "complex" marriages and a system of self-assessment called "mutual criticism." The Society of True Believers, a religious-based communistic group more commonly known as the Shakers, reached their height in the 1840s with at least twenty communities across the U.S. Along with the Mormons, these dissenters believed in human perfectibility and rejected the secular world in order to create their own more authoritarian communities that would protect their followers from the immoralities and disorder of the rest of America.

IDENTIFICATION: Briefly describe each term.

American Anti-Slavery Society

American Colonization Society

American Female Moral Reform Society

American Renaissance

Benevolent Empire

Brook Farm

Charles Grandison Finney

David Walker

Dorothea Dix

Elizabeth Blackwell

Elizabeth Cady Stanton

Emma Willard

Frederick Douglass

Fugitive Slave Law of 1850

The Grimké sisters

Harriet Tubman

Horace Mann

Liberty Party

Lucretia Mott

Lucy Stone

Mary Lyon

Mormonism

Nashoba

New Harmony

Oberlin College

Oneida Community

Ralph Waldo Emerson

Sabbatarianism

Second Great Awakening

Shakers

Sojourner Truth

The Tappan brothers

Temperance

Transcendentalism

Washington Societies

William Lloyd Garrison

THINK ABOUT:

1. This era of reform was a time of great fervor and passionate public debate. How did Americans express their beliefs in a more moral order? Describe at least three major reform movements and their leaders. Include in your discussion your assessment of how successful these efforts were in both the short and long term.

2. Why did the social and legal conditions of women lead to political lobbying by women activists? What were some of the key reforms desired by leaders of the pre-Civil War women's rights movement?

3. Compare and contrast three major utopian communities of this time period: for example, Mormon, Shaker, Oneida, Brook Farm, New Harmony, Nashoba.

4. Why did the American Colonization Society fail?

ABOLITIONISM IN THE MIDWEST

The following excerpt is from a book published in 1905 during Theodore Roosevelt's run for the presidency. The author, a former abolitionist, wrote the book to counter Roosevelt's charge that antebellum reformers were criminals and extremists and that they had received "an immense amount of hysterical praise which they do not deserve." (See Roosevelt's biography of Thomas H. Benton, published in 1887.)

It is customary to speak of our Civil War as a four years' conflict. It was really a thirty years' war, beginning when the pioneer Abolitionists entered the field and declared for a life-and-death struggle... The general public has now [1905] but slight comprehension of the trials endured by the Abolitionists for principle's sake. In many ways they were persecuted. In society they were tabooed; in business shunned. By the rabble they were hooted and pelted. Clowns in the circus made them the subjects of their jokes. Newspaper scribblers lampooned and libelled them. Politicians denounced them. By the Church they were regarded as very black sheep, and sometimes excluded from the fold. And this state of things lasted for years, during which they kept up a steady agitation with the help of platform lecturers, and regularly threw away their votes — so it was charged — in a "third party" movement that seemed to be a hopeless venture.

Another inducement to the writer to take up the cause of the Abolitionists is the fact that he has always been proud to class himself as one of them. He came into the world before Abolitionism, by that name, had been heard of; before the first Abolition Society was organized; before William Lloyd Garrison founded his *Liberator* and before (not the least important circumstance) John Quincy Adams entered Congress. He cannot remember when the slavery question was not discussed. His sympathies at an early day went out to the slave. He informed himself on the subject as well as a farmer boy might be expected to do in a household that received the most of its knowledge of current events from the columns of one weekly newspaper. He cast his first vote for the ticket of the Abolitionists while they were yet a "third party [Liberty Party]."

The community in which he then lived, although in the free State of Ohio, was strongly pro-slavery, being not far from the Southern border. The population was principally from Virginia and Kentucky. There were a few Abolitionists, and they occasionally tried to hold public meetings, but the gatherings were always broken up by mobs.

The writer very well remembers the satisfaction with which he, as a schoolboy, was accustomed to hear that there was to be another Abolition "turnout." The occasion was certain to afford considerable excitement that was dear to the heart of a boy, and it had another recommendation. The only room in the village — "town" we called it — for such affairs, except the churches, which were barred against "fanatics," was the district schoolhouse, which, by common consent was open to all comers, and as the windows and doors, through which missiles were hurled during Anti-Slavery gatherings were always more or less damaged, "we boys" usually got a holiday or two while the building was undergoing necessary repairs.

As might be surmised, the lessons I learned at school were not all such as are usually acuired at such institutions. My companions were like other children, full of spirit and mischief, and not without their prejudices. They hated Abolitionists because they — the Abolitionists — wanted to compel all white people to marry "niggers." Although not naturally unkind, they did not always spare the feelings of "the son of an old Abolitionist." We had our arguments. Some of them were of the knock-down kind. In more than one shindy, growing out of the discussion of the great question of the day, I suffered the penalty of a bloody nose or a blackened eye for standing up for my side.

The feeling against the negroes' friends — the Abolitionists — was not confined to children in years. It was present in all classes. It entered State and Church alike, and dominated both of them. The Congressional Representative from the district in which I lived in those days was an able man and generally held in high esteem. He made a speech in our village when a candidate for re-election. In discussing the slavery question — everybody discussed it then — he spoke of the negroes as being "on the same footing with other cattle." I remember the expression very well because it shocked me, boy that I was. It did not disturb the great majority of those present, however. They cheered the sentiment and gave their votes for the speaker, who was re-elected by a large majority.

About the same time I happened to be present where a General Assembly of one of our largest religious denominations was in session, and listened to part of an address by a noted divine — the most distinguished man in the body — which was intended to prove that slavery was an institution existing by biblical authority. He spent two days in a talk that was mostly made up of scriptural texts and his commentaries upon them. This was in Ohio, and there was not a slave-owner in the assembly, and yet a resolution commendatory of the views that had just been declared by the learned doctor, was adopted by an almost unanimous vote.

In the neighborhood in which I lived was an old and much respected clergyman who was called upon to preach a sermon on a day of some national significance. He made it the occasion for a florid panegyric upon American institutions, which, he declared, assured freedom to all men. Here he paused, "When I spoke of all men enjoying freedom under our flag," he resumed, "I did not, of course, include the Ethiopians whom Providence has brought to our shores for their own good as well as ours. They are slaves by a divine decree. As descendants of Ham, they are under a curse that makes them the servants of their more fortunate white brethren." Having thus put himself right on the record, he proceeded with his sermon. No one seemed to take exception to what he said.

In the same neighborhood was a young preacher who had shortly before come into it from somewhere farther North. In the course of one of his regular services he offered up a prayer in which he expressed the hope that the good Lord would find a way to break the bands of all who were in bondage. That smacked of Abolitionism and at once there was a commotion. The minister was asked to explain. This he declined to do, say that he petition was a matter between him and his God, and he denied the right of others to question him That only increased the opposition, and in a short time the spunky young man was compelled to resign his charge.

About that time there appeared a lecturer on slavery — which meant against slavery — who carried credentials showing that he was a clergyman in good standing in one of the leading Protestant denominations. In our village was a church of that persuasion, whose pastor was not an Abolitionist. As in duty bound, the visiting brother called on his local fellow-laborer, and informed him that on the following day, which happened to be Sunday, he would be pleased to attend service at his church. On the morrow he was on hand and occupied a seat directly in front of the pulpit; but, notwithstanding his conspicuousness, the home minister, who should, out of courtesy, have invited him to a seat in the pulpit, if to no other part in the services, never saw him. He looked completely over his head,

171

keeping his eyes, all through the exercises, fixed upon the back pews, which happened, on that occasion, to be chiefly unoccupied.

Such incidents, of themselves, were of no great importance. Their significance was in the fact that they all occurred on the soil of a free State. They showed the state of feeling that then and there existed.

Source: John F. Hume, *The Abolitionists* (New York: G.P. Putnam's Sons, 1905), pp. 20-25.

HOW WELL DID YOU UNDERSTAND THIS SELECTION?

1. Determine when the author of the above excerpt "came into the world."

2. How did popular politicians get elected, according to Hume?

3. According to this excerpt, what was a common lesson told by white ministers about African Americans and their place in society? What happened if someone hinted of a difference of opinion on this issue?

PROTESTING CENSORSHIP OF THE U.S. MAIL AND THE "GAG" RULES IN THE U. S. HOUSE OF REPRESENTATIVES

In a number of procedural rules adopted from 1836 to 1844, the U.S. House of Representatives tried to exclude from consideration by the House, or by House committees, any petitions asking for the abolition of slavery. Congressman Henry Laurens Pinckney (1794-1863) of South Carolina introduced the first one in response to a petition about slavery in the District of Columbia. Both southern congressmen and many northern representatives supported the rules since they regarded the antislavery petitions as inflammatory. The former president of the U.S., John Quincy Adams, was then a member of the House from Massachusetts and led the fight to rescind the gag rules. At the beginning of each session, when the House regularly adopted its rules of procedure, Adams moved to strike out the offending gag rule. Finally, on Dec. 3, 1844, he was successful. The following excerpt is from a speech given before the U.S. House of Representatives by Judge William Jay. Jay was a founder of the American Bible Society, life director for the American Tract Society, president of the American Peace Society, and ally of the philanthropist reformers, the Tappan brothers.

172

"Address to the Friends of Constitutional Liberty, on the Violation by the United States House of Representatives of the Right of Petition, 1840."

To the Friends of Constitutional Liberty: —

There was a time, fellow citizens, when the above address would have included the People of the United States. But, alas! the freedom of the press, freedom of speech, and the right of petition, are now hated and dreaded by our Southern citizens, as hostile to the perpetuity of human bondage; while, by their political influence in the Federal Government, they have induced members at the North to unite with them in their sacrilegious crusade against these inestimable privileges.

On the 28th of January last, the House of Representatives, on motion of Mr. Johnson, from Maryland, made it a standing rule of the House that "no petition, memorial, resolution, or other paper, praying the abolition of slavery in the District of Columbia, or any State or Territory of the United States, in which it now exists, shall be received by the House, or entertained in any way whatever."

Thus has the right of petition been immolated in the very Temple of Liberty, and offered up, a propitiatory sacrifice to the demon of slavery. Never before has an outrage so unblushingly profligate been perpetrated upon the Federal Constitution. Yet, while we mourn the degeneracy which this transaction evinces, we behold, in its attending circumstances, joyful omens of the triumph which awaits our struggle with the hateful power that now perverts the General Government into an engine of cruelty and loathsome oppression.

Before we congratulate you on these omens, let us recall to your recollection the steps by which the enemies of human rights have advanced to their present rash and insolent defiance of moral and constitutional obligation.

In 1831, a newspaper was established in Boston, for the purpose of disseminating facts and arguments in favor of the duty and policy of immediate emancipation. The Legislature of Georgia, with all the recklessness of despotism, passed a law, offering a reward of $5000, for the abduction of the editor, and his delivery in Georgia. As there was no law by which a citizen of Massachusetts could be tried in Georgia, for expressing his opinions in the capital of his own State, this reward was intended as the price of BLOOD. Do you start at the suggestion? Remember the several sums of $25,000, of $50,000, and of $100,000, offered in Southern papers for kidnapping certain abolitionists. Remember the horrible inflictions by Southern Lynch clubs. Remember the declaration, in the United States Senate, by the brazen-fronted Preston, that, should an abolitionist be caught in Carolina, he would be HANGED. But, as the slave-holders could not destroy the lives of the abolitionists, they determined to murder their characters. Hence, the President of the United States was induced, in his Message of 1835, to Congress, to charge them with plotting the massacre of the Southern planters; and even to stultify himself, by affirming that, for this purpose, they were engaged in sending, by *mail*, inflammatory appeals to the *slaves* — sending papers to men who could not read them, and by a conveyance through which they could not receive them! He well knew that the papers alluded to were appeals on the immorality of converting men, women, and children, into beasts of burden, and were sent to the masts for *their* consideration. The masts in Charleston, dreading the moral influence of these appeals on the conscience of the slaveholding community, forced the Post Office, and made a bonfire of the papers. The Postmaster-General, with the sanction of the President, also hastened to their relief, and, in violation of oaths, and laws, and the Constitution, established ten thousand censors of the press, each one of whom was authorized to abstract from the mail every paper which *he* might think too favorable to the rights of man.

For more than twenty years, petitions have been presented to Congress, for the abolition of slavery in the District of Columbia. The right to present them, and the power of Congress to grant their prayer, were, until recently, unquestioned. But the rapid multiplication of these petitions alarmed the slaveholders, and, knowing that they tended to keep alive at the North, an interest in the slave, they deemed it good policy to discourage and, if possible, suppress all such applications. Hence Mr. Pinckney's famous resolution, in 1836, declaring, "that all petitions, or papers, relating *in any way, or to any extent* whatever to the *subject of slavery*, shall, without being printed or referred, be laid on the table; and no further action whatever shall be had thereon!"

The peculiar atrocity of this resolution was, that it not merely trampled upon the rights of the petitioners, but took from each member of the House his undoubted privilege, as a legislator of the District, to introduce any proposition he might think proper, for the protection of the slaves. In every slave state there are laws affording, at least, some nominal protection to these unhappy beings; but, according to this resolution, slaves might be flayed alive in the streets of Washington, and no representative of the people could offer even a resolution for inquiry. And this vile outrage upon constitutional liberty was avowedly perpetrated "to repress agitation, to allay excitement, and reestablish harmony and tranquillity among the various sections of the Union!!"

But this strange opiate did not produce the stupefying effects anticipated from it. In 1836, the petitioners were on 37,000 — the next session they numbered 110,000. Mr. Hawes, of Kentucky, now essayed to restore tranquillity by gagging the uneasy multitude; but, alas! at the next Congress, more than 300,000 petitioners carried new terror to the hearts of the slaveholders. The next anodyne was prescribed by Mr. Patten, of Virginia, but its effect was to rouse from their stupor some of the northern Legislatures [Massachusetts and Connecticut, in April and May 1838], and to induce them to denounce his remedy as "a usurpation of power, a violation of the Constitution, subversive of the fundamental principles of the government, and at war with the prerogatives of the people."

Source: William Jay, *Miscellaneous Writings on Slavery* (Boston: John P. Jewett & Co., 1853), pp. 397-400.

HOW WELL DID YOU UNDERSTAND THIS SELECTION?

1. Why did Pinckney call in 1836 for abolitionist petitions to be tabled? What, according to Jay, was the problem with this strategy in principle?

2. What arguments do you think abolitionists gave in particular about the institution of slavery in the District of Columbia?

THE CALL FOR THE FIRST NATIONAL CONVENTION FOR WOMEN'S RIGHTS,
Worcester, Mass., 1850

The women's rights movement formally began with a series of local public action conventions. The most famous of these local conventions was held in 1848 at Seneca Falls, New York, and today we mark this as the official beginning of the women's rights movement. At that convention, the Declaration of Sentiments and Resolutions, authored by Elizabeth Cady Stanton, was presented as a general call for the extension of the natural rights of men to women. In October 1850, the first National Women's Rights Convention was held at Worcester, Massachusetts. At this convention, the women's rights movement achieved additional definition from activist Paulina Wright Davis. Unlike the local conventions, the Worcester convention organized the establishment of permanent, standing committees that would work on implementing specified political strategies at the local, state, and national levels.

A CONVENTION Will be held at Worcester, Mass., on the twenty-third and twenty-fourth of October next, (agreeably to appointment by a preliminary meeting held at Boston, on the thirtieth of May last,) to consider the great question of Woman's Rights, Duties, and Relations; and the Men and Women of our country who feel sufficient interest in the subject, to give an earnest thought and effective effort to its rightful adjustment, are invited to meet each other in free conference, at the time and place appointed.

The upward tending spirit of the age, busy in a hundred forms of effort for the world's redemption from the sins and sufferings which oppress it, has brought this one, which yields to none in importance and urgency, into distinguished prominence. One half of the race are its immediate objects, and the other half are as deeply involved, by that absolute unity of interest and destiny which nature has established between them.

The neighbor is near enough to involve every human being in a general equality of rights and community of interests; but, Men and Women, in their reciprocities of love and duty are one flesh and one blood-mother, wife, sister, and daughter come so near the heart and mind of every man that they must be either his blessing or his bane. Where there is such mutuality of interests, such an interlinking of life, there can be no real antagonism of position and action. The sexes should not, for any reason or by any chance, take hostile attitudes towards each other, either in the apprehension or amendment of the wrongs which exist in their necessary relations; but they should harmonize in opinion and co-operate in effort, for the reason that they must unite in the ultimate achievement of the desired reformation.

Of the many points now under discussion and demanding a just settlement, the general question of Woman's Rights and Relations comprehends these:- Her Education, Literary, Scientific , and Artistic; -Her Avocations, Industrial, Commercial, and Professional; -Her Interests, Pecuniary, Civil, and Political; in a word -Her Rights as an Individual, and her Functions as a Citizen.

No one will pretend that all these interests, embracing, as they do, all that is not merely animal in a human life, are rightly understood or justly provided for in the existing social order. Nor is it any more true that the constitutional differences of the sexes, which should determine, define, and limit the resulting differences of office and duty, are adequately comprehended and practically observed.

Woman has been condemned for her greater delicacy of physical organization, to inferiority of intellectual and moral culture, and to the forfeiture of great social, civil, and religious privileges. In the relation of marriage she has been ideally annihilated, and actually enslaved in all that concerns her personal and pecuniary rights; and even in widowhood and single life, she is oppressed with such limitation and degradation of labor and avocation as clearly and cruelly mark the condition of a disabled caste. But, by the inspiration of the Almighty, the beneficent spirit of reform is roused to the redress of these wrongs. The tyranny which degrades and crushes wives and mothers, sits no longer lightly on the world's conscience; the heart's home-worship feels the stain of stooping at a dishonored altar; Manhood begins to feel the shame of muddying the springs from which it draws its highest life; and Womanhood is everywhere awakening to assert its divinely chartered rights, and to fulfil its noblest duties. It is the spirit of reviving truth and righteousness which has moved upon the great deep of the public heart and aroused its redressing justice; and, through it, the Providence of God is vindicating the order and appointments of his creation.

The signs are encouraging; the time is opportune. Come, then, to this Convention. It is your duty, if you are worthy of your age and country. Give the help of your best thought to separate the light from the darkness. Wisely give the protection of your name and the benefit of your efforts to the great work of settling the principles, devising the method, and achieving the success of this high and holy movement.

The President elect, Paulina W. Davis, took the Chair and offered the following ADDRESS.

Usage assigns to the Chair of such Conventions as this, the duty of stating the objects of the meeting. But the published call under which we are convened presents such a summary of our objects as may suffice for mere statement; and the subject matters to be submitted, the points to be discussed, and the action contemplated by this Convention, are equally familiar to us all.

This leaves me at liberty to occupy your attention for a few moments with some general reflections upon the attitude and relations of our movement to our times and circumstances, and upon the proper spirit and method of promoting it.

I do not even intend to treat these topics formally, and I do not hope to do it successfully; for nothing less than a complete philosophy of reform could answer such inquiries, and that philosophy, it is very certain, the world has not yet discovered.

Human rights, and the reasons on which they rest, are not difficult of comprehension. The world has never been ignorant of them, nor insensible to them; and human wrongs and their evils are just as familiar to experience and as well understood; but all this is not enough to secure to mankind the possession of the one, or to relieve them from the felt burden and suffering of the other. A creed of abstract truths, or a catechism of general principles, and a completely digested list of grievances, combined, are not enough to adjust a practical reform to its proper work, else Prophets and Apostles and earnest world-menders in general would have been more successful, and left us less to wish and to do.

It is one thing to issue a declaration of rights or a declaration of wrongs to the world, but quite another thing wisely and happily to commend the subject to the world's acceptance, and so to secure the desired reformation. Every element of success is, in its own place and degree, equally important; but the very starting point is the adjustment of the reformer to his work, and next after that is the adjustment of his work to those conditions of the times which he seeks to influence.

Those who prefer the end in view to all other things, are not contented with their own zeal and the discharge of their duty to their conscience. They desire the highest good for their follow-beings, and are not satisfied with merely clearing their own skirts; and they esteem martyrdom a failure at least, if not a fault, in the method of their action. It is not the salvation of their own souls they are thinking of, but the salvation of the world; and they will not willingly accept a discharge or a rejection in its stead. It is their business to preach righteousness and rebuke sin, but they have no quarrel with "the world that lieth in wickedness," and their mission is not merely to judge and condemn, but to save alike the oppressor and the oppressed. Right principles and conformable means are the first necessities of a great enterprise, but without right apprehensions and tempers and expedient methods, the most beneficent purposes must utterly fail. Who is sufficient for these things?

Divine Providence has been baffled through all the ages of disorder and suffering for want of fitting agents and adapted means. Reformations of religion have proved but little better than the substitution of a new error for an old one, and civil revolutions have resolved themselves into mere civil insurrections, until history has become but a monument of buried hopes.

The European movement of 1848 was wanting neither in theory nor example for its safe direction, but it has nevertheless almost fallen into contempt. We may not, therefore, rely upon a good cause and good intentions alone, without danger of deplorable disappointment. The reformation which we purpose, in its utmost scope, is radical and universal. It is not the mere perfecting of a progress already in motion, a detail of some established plan, but it is an epochal movement-the emancipation of a class, the redemption of half the world, and a conforming re-organization of all social, political, and industrial interests and institutions. Moreover, it is a movement without example among the enterprises of associated reformations, for it has no purpose of arming the oppressed against the oppressor, or of separating the parties, or of setting up independence, or of severing the relations of either.

Its intended changes are to be wrought in the intimate texture of all societary organizations, without violence, or any form of antagonism. It seeks to replace the worn out with the living and the beautiful, so as to reconstruct without overturning, and to regenerate without destroying; and nothing of the spirit, tone, temper, or method of insurrection, is proper or allowable to us and our work.

Human societies have been long working and fighting their way up from what we scornfully call barbarism, into what we boastfully call modern civilization; but, as yet, the advancement has been chiefly in ordering and methodizing the lower instincts of our nature, and organizing society under their impulses. The intellect of the masses has received immense development, and the gentler affections have been somewhat relieved from the dominion of force; but the institutions among men are not yet modelled after the highest laws of our nature. The masterdom of the strong hand and bold spirit is not yet over, for men have not yet established all those natural claims against each other, which seem to demand physical force and physical courage for their vindication. But the age of war is drawing towards a close, and that of peace (whose methods and end alike are harmony) is dawning, and the uprising of womanhood is its prophecy and foreshadow.

The first principles of human rights have now for a long time been abstractly held and believed, and both in Europe and America whole communities have put them into practical operation in some of their bearings. Equality before the law, and the right of the governed to choose their governors, are established maxims of reformed political science; but in the countries most advanced, these doctrines and their actual benefits are as yet enjoyed exclusively by the sex that in the battle-field and the public forum has wrenched them from the old time tyrannies. They are yet denied to Woman, because she has not yet so asserted or won them for herself; for political justice pivots itself upon the barbarous principle that "Who would be free, themselves must strike the blow." Its furthest progress toward magnanimity is to give arms to helplessness. It has not yet learned to give justice. For this rule of barbarism there is this much justification, that although every human being is naturally entitled to every right of the race, the enjoyment and administration of all rights require such culture and conditions in their subject as usually lead him to claim and struggle for them; and the contented slave is left in slavery, and the ignorant man in darkness, on the inference that he cannot use what he does not desire. This is indeed true of the animal instincts, but it is false of the nobler soul; and men must learn that the higher faculties must be first awakened, and then gratified, before they have done their duty to their race. The ministry of angels to dependent humanity is the method of Divine Providence, and among men the law of heaven is, that the "elder shall serve the younger." But let us not complain that the hardier sex overvalue the force which heretofore has figured most in the world's affairs. "They know not what they do," is the apology that crucified womanhood must concede in justice and pity to the wrong doers. In the order of things, the material world was to be first subdued. For this coarse conflict, the larger bones and stronger sinews of manhood are especially adapted, and it is a law of muscles and of all matter that might shall overcome right. This is the law of the vegetable world, and it is the law of the animal world, as well as the law of the animal instincts and of the physical organization of men; but it is not the law of spirit and affection. They are of such a nature as to charge themselves with the atonement for all evils, and to burden themselves with all the sufferings which they would remove.

This wisdom is pure, and peaceable, and gentle, and full of mercy and of good fruits. Besides the feebler frame, which under the dynasty of muscles is degraded, there remains, even after justice has got the upper hand of force in the world's judgments, a mysterious and undefined difference of sex that seriously embarrasses the question of equality; or, if that is granted in terms, of equal fitness for avocations and positions which heretofore have been the monopoly of men. Old ideas and habits of mind survive the facts which produced them, as the shadows of night stretch far into the morning, sheltered in nooks and valleys from the rising light; and it is the work of a whole creation-day to separate the light from the darkness.

The rule of difference between the sexes must be founded on the traits which each estimates most highly in the other; and it is not at all wonderful that some of woman's artificial incapacities and slaveries may seem to be necessary to some of her excellencies; just as the chivalry that makes man a butcher of his kind still glares like a glory in the eyes of admiring womanhood, and all the more because it seems so much above and unlike her own powers and achievements. Nature does not teach that men and women are unequal, but only that they are unlike; an unlikeness so naturally related and dependent that their respective differences by their balance establish, instead of destroying, their equality.

Men are not in fact, and to all intents, equal among themselves, but their theoretical equality for all the purposes of justice is more easily seen and allowed than what we are here to claim for women. Higher views, nicer distinctions, and a deeper philosophy are required to see and feel the truths of woman's rights; and besides, the maxims upon which men distribute justice to each other have been battle-cries for ages, while the doctrine of woman's true relations in life is a new science, the revelation of an advanced age, - perhaps, indeed, the very last grand movement of humanity towards its highest destiny, - too new to be yet fully understood, too grand to grow out of the broad and coarse generalities which the infancy and barbarism of society could comprehend.

The rule of force and fraud must be well nigh overturned, and learning and religion and the fine arts must have cultivated mankind into a state of wisdom and justice tempered by the most beneficent affections, before woman can be fully installed in her highest offices. We must be gentle with the ignorance and patient under the injustice which old evils induce. Long suffering is a quality of the highest wisdom, and charity beareth all things for it hopeth all things. It will be seen that I am assuming the point that the redemption of the inferior, if it comes at all, must come from the superior. The elevation of a favored caste can have no other providential purpose than that, when it is elevated near enough to goodness and truth, it shall draw up its dependents with it

But, however this may be in the affairs of men as they are involved with each other, it is clearly so in the matter of woman's elevation. The tyrant sex, if such we choose to term it, holds such natural and necessary relations to the victims of injustice, that neither rebellion nor revolution, neither defiance nor resistance, nor any mode of assault or defence incident to party antagonism, is either possible, expedient, or proper. Our claim must rest on its justice, and conquer by its power of truth. We take the ground, that whatever has been achieved for the race belongs to it, and must not be usurped by any class or caste. The rights and liberties of one human being cannot be made the property of another, though they were redeemed for him or her by the life of that other; for rights cannot be forfeited by way of salvage, and they are in their nature unpurchasable and inalienable.

We claim for woman a full and generous investiture of all the blessings which the other sex has solely or by her aid achieved for itself. We appeal from men's injustice and selfishness to their principles and affections.

For some centuries now, the best of them have been asserting, with their lives, the liberties and rights of the race; and it is not for the few endowed with the highest intellect, the largest frame, or even the soundest morals, that the claim has been maintained, but broadly and bravely and nobly it has been held that wherever a faculty is given, its highest activities are chartered by the Creator, and that all objects alike - whether they minister to the necessities of our animal life or to the superior powers of the human soul and so are more imperatively needed, because nobler than the bread that perishes in the use - are, of common right, equally open to ALL; and that all artificial restraints, for whatever reason imposed, are alike culpable for their presumption, their folly, and their cruelty.

It is pitiable ignorance and arrogance for either man or woman now to prescribe and limit the sphere of woman. It remains for the greatest women whom appropriate culture, and happiest influences shall yet develope, to declare and to prove what are woman's capacities and relations in the world.

I will not accept the concession of any equality which means identity or resemblance of faculty and function. I do not base her claims upon any such parallelism of constitution or attainment. I ask only freedom for the natural unfolding of her powers, the conditions most favorable for her possibilities of growth, and the full play of all those incentives which have made man her master, and then, with all her natural impulses and the whole heaven of hope to invite, I ask that she shall fill the place that she can attain to, without settling any unmeaning questions of sex and sphere, which people gossip about for want of principles of truth, or the faculty to reason upon them.

But it is not with the topics of our reform and the discussion of these that I am now concerned. It is of its position in the world's opinion, and the causes of this, that I am thinking; and I seek to derive hints and suggestions as to the method and manner of successful advocacy, from the inquiry. Especially am I solicitous that the good cause may suffer no detriment from the theoretical principles its friends may assume, or the spirit with which they shall maintain them. It is fair to presume that such causes as have obscured these questions in the general judgment of the governing sex, must also more or less darken the counsels of those most anxious for truth and right. If our demand were simply for chartered rights, civil and political, such as get acknowledgment in paper constitutions, there would be no ground of doubt. We could plead our common humanity, and claim an equal justice. We might say that the natural right of self-government is so clearly due to every human being alike, that it needs no argument to prove it; and if some or a majority of women would not exercise this right, this is no ground for taking it from those who would. And the right to the control and enjoyment of her own property and partnership in all that she helps her husband to earn and save, needs only to be stated to command instant assent. Her appropriate avocations might not be so easily settled that a programme could be completed on theoretical principles merely; but we need discuss no such difficulties while we ask only for liberty of choice, and opportunities of adaptation; and the question of her education is solved by the simple principle, that whatever she can receive is her absolute due.

Yet all these points being so easily disposed of, so far as they are mere matters of controversy, the advocates of the right need none the less the wisest and kindest consideration for all the resistance we must encounter, and the most forbearing patience under the injustice and insolence to which we must expose ourselves. And we can help ourselves to much of the prudence and some of the knowledge we shall need, by treating the prejudices of the public as considerately as if they were principles, and the customs of society as if they once had some temporary necessity, and so meet them with the greater force for the claim to respect which we concede to them. For a prejudice is just like any other error of judgment, and a custom has sometimes had some fitness to things more or less necessary, and is not an utter absurdity, even though the reason on which it was based is lost or removed. Who shall say that there is nothing serious, or respectable, or just, in the repugnance with which our propositions are received? The politician who knows his own corruption may be excused for an earnest wish to save his wife and daughter from the taint, and he must be excused, too, for not knowing that the corruption would be cured by the saving virtue which he dreads to expose to risk.

There may be real though very foolish tenderness in the motive which refuses to open to woman the trades and professions that she could cultivate and practice with equal profit and credit to herself. The chivalry that worships womanhood is not mean, though it at the same time enslaves the objects of its overfond care.

And it is even possible that men may deprive women of their property and liberties, personal and political, with the kindly purpose of accommodating their supposed incapacities for the offices and duties of human life. Harsh judgments and harsh words will neither weaken the opposition, nor strengthen our hands. Our address is to the highest sentiment of the times; and the tone and spirit due to it and becoming in ourselves, are courtesy and respectfulness. Strength and truth of complaint, and eloquence of denunciation, are easy of attainment; but the wisdom of affirmative principles and positive science, and the adjustment of reformatory measures to the exigencies of the times and circumstances, are so much the more useful as they are difficult of attainment. A profound expediency, as true to principle as it is careful of success, is, above all things, rare and necessary. We have to claim liberty without its usually associated independence. We must insist on separate property where the interests are identical, and a division of profits where the very being of the partners is blended. We must demand provisions for differences of policy, where there should be no shadow of controversy; and the free choice of industrial avocations and general education, without respect to the distinctions of sex and natural differences of faculty.

In principle these truths are not doubtful, and it is therefore not impossible to put them in practice, but they need great clearness in system and steadiness of direction to get them allowance and adoption in the actual life of the world. The opposition should be consulted where it can be done without injurious consequences. Truth must not be suppressed, nor principles crippled, yet strong meat should not be given to babes. Nor should the strong use their liberties so as to become a stumbling block to the weak. Above all things, we owe it to the earnest expectation of the age, that stands trembling in mingled hope and fear of the great experiment, to lay its foundations broadly and securely in philosophic truth, and to form and fashion it in practical righteousness. To accomplish this, we cannot be too careful or too brave, too gentle or too firm; and yet with right dispositions and honest efforts, we cannot fail of doing our share of the great work, and thereby advancing the highest interests of humanity.

Source: "The Proceedings of the Woman's Rights Convention, held at Worcester, October 23d & 24th, 1850" (Boston: Prentiss & Sawyer, 1851), pp. 3-5 and 6-13.

HOW WELL DID YOU UNDERSTAND THIS SELECTION?

1. Find a print copy (or go to the World Policy Institute's web site for their "Americas Project: Democracy and Human Rights in the USA" where they have an on-line copy available at <http://worldpolicy.org/americas/usa/declofsentiments.html>) to read the "Declaration of Rights and Sentiments" written by Elizabeth Cady Stanton and signed by members of the Seneca Falls convention in 1848. Compare and contrast this document with the speech by Paulina Davis at the national convention in Worcester in 1850.

2. What strategies does Davis recommend women's rights activists take?

The Shakers, formally the United Society of Believers in Christ's Second Appearing, originated in 1747, in Manchester, England. These separatists from the Church of England were called "Shaking Quakers" because of their ecstatic and violent body agitation during worship. In 1770 Ann Lee (1736-1784) was imprisoned for her religious views and there she experienced a series of visions. From that date on, Ann Lee was acknowledged as their leader and known as Mother Ann. By 1776 they had emigrated to New York and built their own community to live separately from "the world." Persecuted and harassed, the Shakers nevertheless grew in numbers (eventually twenty-eight communities) and gained economic strength as they successfully evangelized their millennial message: the Shakers believed they lived in the era mentioned in Revelation 20, a thousand years of great happiness and human perfection during which Christ reigns on earth. The following account describes a Shaker service in the 1840s, which shows the continued reliance on the ecstatic form of worship.

When a tune was started they began a march in a circle around the centre of the room, the brethren two abreast, leading the column, the sisters following after in sections of three abreast. In this march there was a waving movement of the hands by drawing inward, as if gathering in spiritual good and storing it up for the necessities of the week.

Occasionally there was a clapping of hands in perfect concert, this being repeated for several times in succession. In the marching and counter-marching, the worshippers frequently changed their positions, the brethren reducing their ranks to two abreast, while the sisters increased their ranks to three, and while in this position the singers stood in the centre, the others encircling them twice in their marching. Then again they formed in single file and marched around the central body ultimately forming into four circles, with the singers as a common centre. This was afterwards explained as symbolical of the four 'dispensations' as expounded in Shakerism. The first from Adam to Abraham; the second from Abraham to Jesus; the third from Jesus to Mother Ann; and the fourth, the 'Millennial' which the Shakers claim they are now enjoying as the triumphs of their religion.

The following hymn was usually sung to the marching: —

I shall march through Mount Zion
With my angelic band,
I shall pass through the city
With my fan in my hand,
And around thee, O Jerusalem,
My armies will encamp,
While I search my Holy Temple
With my bright burning lamp.

At the close of the singing, one of the sisters began to rock her body to and fro; at first gently, then in a more violent manner, until two of the sisters, one on each side, supported her else she would have fallen to the floor. She appeared to be wholly unconscious of her surroundings, and to be moved by an invisible power. The shaking of the subject continued to increase in violence, and it was with great difficulty that she could be restrained from throwing herself forcibly to the floor. Her limbs became rigid, her face took on an ashen hue, her lips moved, and she began to speak in a clear distinct voice, every word of which penetrated every part of the room which was as still as death. Every eye was on the recipient of the gift, every ear open to catch each word as it fell from her lips. She spoke of the shortness of life, of the absolute necessity of abandoning the world and its sinful pleasures before it was too late; that in Shakerism was embodied all the virtues, and none of the vices of mankind; that through her the spirit of Mother Ann was speaking to every Shaker present to remain steadfast to the faith and they would enjoy the richest of Heaven's blessings — an eternity of bliss.

For the space of fifteen minutes she spoke rapidly, yet impressively, her whole frame shaking from head to foot. Gradually the "spell" left her, and her limbs relaxed as she sank into a seat completely exhausted.

Source: Clara Endicott Sears, *Gleanings from Old Shaker Journals* (Boston and New York: Houghton Mifflin Co., 1916), pp. 206-208.

HOW WELL DID YOU UNDERSTAND THIS SELECTION?

1. How does Shakerism reflect the antebellum desire for perfectionism?

2. Compare and contrast the Shaker account of a spiritual visitation with the account by Joseph Smith below.

Origin of *THE BOOK OF MORMON*

*Mormons believe that Joseph Smith's 1830 translation of the **Book of Mormon** was based on writings he found on gold plates left by Hebrews who migrated to the Americas in 600 BCE and were later visited by a resurrected Jesus Christ. The name of the church he then founded began as the Church of Christ. By 1834 in Ohio it became known as the Church of Latter-Day Saints and finally by 1838 in Missouri as the Church of Jesus Christ of Latter-day Saints. In 1993 a group of researchers contended that Joseph Smith's 1830 translation was based less on writings he found on gold plates than on the King James version of the Bible. Nevertheless, like most Christians, modern mainstream Mormons emphasize faith and prayer over a scholarly scrutiny of spiritual texts (including the Bible) as literary history.*

Joseph Smith, through whom, by the gift and power of God, the ancient Scripture, known as THE BOOK OF MORMON, has been brought forth and translated into the English tongue, made personal and circumstantial record of the matter. He affirmed that during the night of September 21, 1823, he sought the Lord in fervent prayer, having previously received a Divine manifestation of transcendent import. His account follows:

"While I was thus in the act of calling upon God, I discovered a light appearing in my room, which continued to increase until the room was lighter than at noonday, when immediately a personage appeared at my bedside, standing in the air, for his feet did not touch the floor.

"He had on a loose robe of most exquisite whiteness. It was a whiteness beyond anything earthly I had ever seen; nor do I believe that any earthly thing could be made to appear so exceedingly white and brilliant. His hands were naked, and his arms also, a little above the wrists; so, also, were his feet naked, as were his legs, a little above the ankles. His head and neck were also bare. I could discover that he had no other clothing on but this robe, as it was open, so that I could see into his bosom.

"Not only was his robe exceedingly white, but his whole person was glorious beyond description, and his countenance truly like lightning. The room was exceedingly light, but not so very bright as immediately around his person. When I first looked upon him, I was afraid; but the fear soon left me.

"He called me by name, and said unto me that he was a messenger sent from the presence of God to me, and that his name was Moroni: that God had a work for me to do; and that my name should be had for good and evil among all nations, kindreds, and tongues, or that it should be both good and evil spoken of among all people.

"He said there was a book deposited, written upon gold plates, giving an account of the former inhabitants of this continent, and the source from whence they sprang. He also said that the fulness of the everlasting Gospel was contained in it, as delivered by the Savior to the ancient inhabitants;

"Also, that there were two stones in silver bows — and these stones, fastened to a breastplate, constituted what is called the Urim and Thummim — deposited with the plates; and the possession and use of these stones were what constituted *Seers* in ancient or former times; and that God had prepared them for the purpose of translating the book.

* * * * * * * *

"Again, he told me, that when I got those plates of which he had spoken — for the time that they should be obtained was not yet fulfilled — I should not show them to any person; neither the breastplate with the Urim and Thummim; only to those to whom I should be commanded to show them; if I did I should be destroyed. While he was conversing with me about the plates, the vision was opened to my mind that I could see the place where the plates were deposited, and that so clearly and distinctly that I knew the place again when I visited it.

"After this communication, I saw the light in the room begin to gather immediately around the person of him who had been speaking to me, and it continued to do so, until the room was again left dark, except just around him, when instantly I saw, as it were, a conduit open right up into heaven, and he ascended until he entirely disappeared, and the room was left as it had been before this heavenly light had made its appearance.

"I lay musing on the singularity of the scene, and marveling greatly at what had been told to me by this extraordinary messenger; when, in the midst of my meditation, I suddenly discovered that my room was again beginning to get lighted, and in an instant, as it were, the same heavenly messenger was again by my bedside.

"He commenced, and again related the very same things which he had done at his first visit, without the least variation; which having done, he informed me of great judgments which were coming upon the earth, with great desolations by famine, sword, and pestilence; and that these grievous judgments would come on the earth in this generation. Having related these things, he again ascended as he had done before.

"By this time, so deep were the impressions made on my mind, that sleep had fled from my eyes, and I lay overwhelmed in astonishment at what I had both seen and heard. But what was my surprise when again I beheld the same messenger at my bedside, and heard him rehearse or repeat over again to me the same things as before; and added a caution to me, telling me that Satan would try to tempt me (in consequence of the indigent circumstances of my father's family), to get the plates for the purpose of getting rich. This he forbade me, saying that I must have no other object in view in getting the plates but to glorify God, and must not be influenced by any other motive than that of building His kingdom; otherwise I could not get them.

"After this third visit, he again ascended into heave as before, and I was again left to ponder on the strangeness of what I had just experienced; when almost immediately after the heavenly messenger had ascended from me the third time, the cock crowed, and I found that day was approaching, so that our interviews must have occupied the whole of that night.

"I shortly after arose from my bed, and, as usual, went to the necessary labors of the day; but, in attempting to work as at other times, I found my strength so exhausted as to render me entirely unable. My father, who was laboring along with me, discovered something to be wrong with me, and told me to go home. I started with the intention of going to the house; but, in attempting to cross the fence out of the field where we were, my strength entirely failed me, and I fell helpless on the ground, and for a time was quite unconscious of anything.

"The first thing that I can recollect was a voice speaking unto me, calling me by name. I looked up, and beheld the same messenger standing over my head, surrounded by light as before. He then again related unto me all that he had related to me the previous night, and commanded me to go to my father and tell him of the vision and commandments which I had received.

"I obeyed; I returned to my father in the field, and rehearsed the whole matter to him. He replied to me that it was of God, and told me to go and do as commanded by the messenger. I left the field, and went to the place where the messenger had told me the plates were deposited; and owing to the distinctness of the vision which I had had concerning it, I knew the place the instant that I arrived there.

"Convenient to the village of Manchester, Ontario county, New York, stands a hill of considerable size, and the most elevated of any in the neighborhood. On the west side of this hill, not far from the top, under a stone of considerable size, lay the plates, deposited in a stone box. This stone was thick and rounding in the middle part of it was visible above the ground, but the edge all around was covered with earth.

"Having removed the earth, I obtained a lever, which I got fixed under the edge of the stone, and with a little exertion raised it up. I looked in, and there indeed did I behold the plates, the Urim and Thummim, and the breastplate, as stated by the messenger. The box in which they lay was formed by laying stones together in some kind of cement. In the bottom of the box were laid two stones crossways of the box, and on these stones lay the plates and the other things with them.

"I made an attempt to take them out, but was forbidden by the messenger, and was again informed that the time for bringing them forth had not yet arrived, neither would it, until four years from that time; but he told me that I should come to that place precisely in one year from that time, and that he would there met with me, and that I should continue to do so until the time should come for obtaining the plates.

"Accordingly, as I had been commanded, I went at the end of each year, and at each time I found the same messenger there, and received instruction and intelligence from him at each of our interviews, respecting what the Lord was going to do, and how and in what manner His kingdom was to be conducted in the last days.

****

"At length the time arrived for obtaining the plates, the Urim and Thummim, and the breastplate. On the twenty-second day of September, one thousand eight hundred and twenty-seven, having gone as usual at the end of another year to the place where they were deposited, the same heavenly messenger delivered them up to me with this charge: That I should be responsible for them; that if I should let them go carelessly, or through any neglect of mine, I should be cut off; but that if I would use all my endeavors to preserve them, until he, the messenger, should call for them, they should be protected.

"I soon found out the reason why I had received such strict charges to keep them safe, and why it was that the messenger had said that when I had done what was required at my hand, he would call for them. For no sooner was it known that I had them, than the most strenuous exertions were used to get them from me. Every stratagem that could be invented was resorted to for that purpose. The persecution became more bitter and severe than before, and multitudes were on the alert continually to get them from me if possible. But by the wisdom of God, they remained safe in my hands, until I had accomplished by them what was required at my hand. When according to arrangements, the messenger called for them, I delivered them up to him; and he has them in his charge until this day, being the second day of May, one thousand eight hundred and thirty-eight."

Source: *The Book of Mormon, An Account Written by the Hand of Mormon upon Plates Taken from the Plates of Nephi.* Translated by Joseph Smith, Jun. (Salt Lake City, Utah: Church of Jesus Christ of Latter-day Saints, 1920; first edition published in 1830).

HOW WELL DID YOU UNDERSTAND THIS SELECTION?

1. What did the messenger tell Joseph Smith in each of the first three visitations? What was important about the fourth time?

2. Smith wrote that though he had found the plates in 1823, the messenger did not allow him to remove them from their hiding place until 1827 — and then, what happened?

3. Where in this passage can be found the message of millennialism that was common among many of the religious revivalists of this era?

*The widow Mary Owen "Polly" Todd Russell was a wealthy slaveowner in Lexington, Kentucky. When she married Robert Wickliffe in 1826, she insisted on the emancipation of several slaves whom she believed would be able to carry out her missionary goals for Africa. Milly Crawford, a light-skinned young woman, and her white son, Alfred, lived as slaves in the Russell-Wickliffe mansion. In between their duties as house servants, they learned to read and write. Polly Wickliffe hoped that Milly would become a teacher and Alfred would become a minister … in Africa. In March of 1833, Milly and Alfred finally left for Liberia with their cousin, Lucy Russell, and her four children (Sinthia, Gilbert, George and Henry). Milly's husband, George Crawford, who was emancipated by another Lexingtonian slaveowner, later joined them. Milly wrote a long letter of thanks from their first stop in Frankfort (reproduced below), revealing their fears of being two women alone with children. They traveled overland to Frankfort, and then to Louisville to get on the riverboat, **Mediterranean**. They sailed down the Ohio & Mississippi Rivers to New Orleans where other emigrants joined them. They boarded the brig "Ajax" on April 20, 1833, with the white missionary A.H. Savage & H.D. King, agent for the Tenn. Colonization Society. The cost of the expedition ($5,000) was defrayed by the American Colonization Society with a donation of $2,300 from the Ky. Colonization Society. Cholera, whooping cough, or a bowel disorder forced the brig to put in for many days at a West Indian island and 30 (mostly children) died during the passage. On July 11, 1833, 146 new settlers (31 men, 42 women, 74 children age 12 & under, mostly farmers) arrived in Liberia after 3 months aboard the brig. See the online roll of emigrants to Liberia, "Brig Ajax's Company" at <http://www.ccharity.com/Liberia/ajax07111833.html>. They were put under quarantine upon arrival by Dr. Mechlin who then sent them to Caldwell & Millsburg on the St. Paul's River (formerly Bassa country) where 26 soon died, two others returned to the U.S., and one migrated to Sierra Leone. See the 17th Annual Report of the A.C.S., 11; African Repository, IX (Oct. 1833), 243.*

Milly Crawford and Lucy Russell on their way to Liberia from Lexington Kentucky
A letter to Mary Owen Todd Russell Wickliffe
*** [the letter is transcribed as written without any changes in punctuation or spelling] ***

March 10 1833 Saterday night

My Dear Misstress we have all arrived at frankfort in safety and health little George Lucy and all the children are well. My dear Misstress how shall we thank you for all your kindness too us. We sometimes despond being all females and children haveing no male protecter of our own. but we try to put our trust in the Almighty and go on in his srength. whatever betide us.

My Dear Mystress you have done your whole duty. and may the [Almighty] bless and reward you a thousand fold.

[this section is from] Lucy all love and thanks to you for your goodness care and kindness to us all. the children all desires me remember them to Mystress.

Mystress we all desire you thank Mayster for his goodness and kindness to us.

I hope the Lord will bless him give our love to miss Margaret miss Mary Mys Sally Wooly [Robert Wickliffe's three living white children] and all our friends. the Lord has raised up manny friend to us in fankford we are treated with so much kindness by all who see us. the gentleman at whose house we now lodge Mr Gray trets us with the utmost kindness - he had us all in his dining room prayed with and for us - the gentleman you wrote too received your letter recommending us to him he took us home with him gave us supper and we returned again mr grays you will hear again from us att Louisville May the [Lord] bless preserve and reward you for all kindness is the prare of your unworthy but affecunate servant

Milly C

Source: Wickliffe-Preston Family Papers, Box 39, University of Kentucky Special Collections and Archives, Lexington, Kentucky.

HOW WELL DID YOU UNDERSTAND THIS SELECTION?

1. Why was it significant that the "gentleman" Mr. Gray took the emigrants into his dining room? Can you imagine why they had to leave Mr. Gray's house to go to another man's house to eat and sleep?

2. Re-read the letter and identity several instances of Christian piety. This language is similar to that used by many teachers in the U.S. (of any color) at this time. What kind of lessons do you think Milly will teach her students in Liberia?

THE PROTEST OF LUCY STONE AND HENRY BLACKWELL UPON THEIR MARRIAGE
on May 2, 1855

The minister who married them, the Reverend Thomas Wentworth Higginson, an abolitionist reformer, published their statement in the **Worcester Spy**. *It was reprinted in newspapers and journals across the nation. Married women who kept their given names became known as Lucy Stoners.*

While we acknowledge our mutual affection by publicly assuming the relationship of husband and wife, yet, in justice to ourselves and a great principle, we deem it a duty to declare that this act on our part implies no sanction of, nor promise of voluntary obedience to, such of the present laws of marriage as refuse to recognize the wife as an independent, rational being, while they confer upon the husband an injurious and unnatural superiority, investing him with legal power which no honorable man would exercise, and which no man should possess. We protest especially against the laws which give to the husband:

1. The custody of the wife's person.
2. The exclusive control and guardianship of their children.
3. The sole ownership of her personal and use of her real estate, unless previously settled upon her, or placed in the hands of trustees, as in the case of minors, lunatics, and idiots.
4. The absolute right to the product of her industry.
5. Also against laws which give to the widower so much larger and more permanent an interest in the property of his deceased wife than they give to the widow in that of the deceased husband.
6. Finally, against the whole system by which 'the legal existence of the wife is suspended during marriage,' so that, in most States, she neither has a legal part in the choice of her residence, nor can she make a will, nor sue or be sued in her own name, nor inherit property.

We believe that personal independence and equal human rights can never be forfeited, except for crime; that marriage should be an equal and permanent partnership, and so recognized by law; that until it is so recognized, married partners should provide against the radical injustice of present laws, by every means in their power.

We believe that, where domestic difficulties arise, no appeal should be made to legal tribunals under existing laws, but that all difficulties should be submitted to the equitable adjustment of arbitrators mutually chosen. Thus, reverencing law, we enter our earnest protest against rules and customs which are unworthy of the name, since they violate justice, the essence of all law.

Source: Alice Stone Blackwell, *Lucy Stone: Pioneer of Woman's Rights* (Boston: Little, Brown, and Co., 1930), pp. 166-68.

HOW WELL DID YOU UNDERSTAND THIS SELECTION?

1. How do Stone and Blackwell protest against the laws of marriage in principle? How might a counter-argument be framed?

2. How is this statement different from Stanton's "Declaration of Rights and Sentiments" published in 1848?

3. What do they mean when they say they believe that if married couples are having trouble, they should not ask for help from "legal tribunals under existing laws" but from "arbitrators mutually chosen"?

SELF TEST:

MULTIPLE CHOICE: Circle the correct response. The correct answers are given at the end.

1. Which of the following reform movements was concerned most about alcoholism?
   a. asylums
   b. penitentiaries
   c. temperance
   d. women's rights

2. Which of the following authors believed in the overall benefits of "woman's sphere" of moral purity and superiority over women's equality with men?
   a. Catherine Beecher
   b. Frances Wright
   c. Elizabeth Cady Stanton
   d. William Lloyd Garrison

3. Which one of the following were NOT advocates for black civil rights?
   a. David Walker
   b. Frederick Douglass
   c. Henry Clay
   d. Sojourner Truth

4. Who was America's first great philosopher?
   a. Herman Melville
   b. Nathaniel Hawthorne
   c. Ralph Waldo Emerson
   d. Walt Whitman

5. Which of the following utopias practiced complete celibacy?
   a. Brook Farm
   b. New Harmony
   c. Oneida Community
   d. Shakers

6. *The Book of Mormon* was written by
   a. Frederick Douglass
   b. Horace Mann
   c. Joseph Smith
   d. Mother Ann Lee

7. William Lloyd Garrison wanted
   a. free public education for all white Americans
   b. immediate freedom and civil rights for black Americans
   c. slavery to be extended into the northern states
   d. the annexation of Texas so to increase the number of slaveholders in the U.S.

8. Revivalist preachers during the Second Great Awakening generally all
   a. believed in perfectionism
   b. insisted on total immersion for baptism
   c. interpreted the Bible in a symbolic way
   d. practiced celibacy

9. Dorothea Dix was a leader of
   a. Brook Farm
   b. mesmerism
   c. the movement for mental health reform
   d. the public school movement

10. The "gag" rule in the House of Representatives tried to stop the debates about
   a. abolitionism
   b. phrenology
   c. prostitution
   d. unionism

Answers:
        1-c; 2-a; 3-c; 4-c; 5-d; 6-c; 7-b; 8-a; 9-c; 10-a.

ESSAYS:

1. How did most free blacks react to the goals of the American Colonization Society?

2. How might one argue that radical activists like Garrison were simply irrational fanatics? What would be the counter-arguments?

3. Describe two major goals, two tactics, and two problems that antebellum reform movements shared.

4. Why did people turn to revivalism to help them understand their world, and how well did it work?

OPTIONAL ACTIVITIES: Use your knowledge **and** imagination

1. Imagine your own utopian community. What principles, rules and policies, and goals would you want to see? What problems should you anticipate?

2. Read a reformer's autobiography (e.g., Frederick Douglass and Elizabeth Cady Stanton wrote about their life experiences). Then imagine if you met that person! Write a series of diary entries that reflect upon the first meeting (be sure to describe when and where the meeting took place); and also tell how that person's reform message did or did not convince you to act. How would you have acted after this meeting? What are the supports and barriers to your actions?

WEB SITE LISTINGS:

"Votes for Women," Library of Congress selections from NAWSA Collection, 1848-1921
   http://memory.loc.gov/ammem/naw/nawshome.html
Worcester Women's History Project: Online celebration of the first national women's rights convention
   http://www.assumption.edu/HTML/Academic/history/WWHP/why1850.html
Women's Rights National Historic Park, Seneca Falls, NY
   http://www.nps.gov/wori/
National Women's Hall of Fame, online biographical portraits
   www.greatwomen.org/grtwmn.htm
The Walt Whitman Archive, edited by Ed Folsom and Kenneth M. Price
   http://www.iath.virginia.edu/whitman/
Nathaniel Hawthorne's "The Blithedale Romance," including weblogs
   http://www.online-literature.com/hawthorne/blithedale_romance/
"African-American Mosaic," A Library of Congress Resource Guide for the Study of Black History and Culture
   http://www.loc.gov/exhibits/african/intro.html
"The Role of Literature and Philosophy in Building up the National Identity of early 19th century America,"
by Keijo Vertanen for *From Revolution to Reconstruction*, a Hypertext on American History
   http://odur.let.rug.nl/~usa/E/identity/philosxx.htm
"African American Voices" from Digital History website
   http://www.digitalhistory.uh.edu/black_voices/black_voices.cfm
Amistad America's website, including information about the Freedom Schooner "Amistad" and an online
version of curriculum about its history
   http://www.amistadamerica.org/
Radicalism and Reform History hubsite, *Virtual Library*, University of Kansas
   www.ukans.edu/history/VL/USA/radicalism.html
The Prophet Joseph Smith
   http://www.mormons.org/learn/0,8672,957-1,00.html

Chapter Nine

AMERICAN LIFE:
1840-1860

In the two decades before the Civil War, the United States grew at an extraordinary rate. Along with land acquisitions in the West and the boom in population growth, the new market economy developed a sense of American pride and international power. At the same time, economic and social inequalities increased: most people of color were denied landownership and basic human rights, immigrants were forced into unspeakable living conditions, and the very richest segment of society reaped unprecedented percentages of the country's total wealth. Meanwhile, however, the literature of the day trumpeted the positive feelings of most who struggled to realize some part of the American dream of "equality of condition." By 1850 over 70 percent of the U.S. population was under 30, perhaps accounting for the national exuberance and westward spirit for individual socio-economic upward mobility.

The growth of cities crafted a new type of American norm. By 1860 the Census Bureau determined that 20 percent of the American population lived in "urban" areas, that is, towns and cities with populations of 2,500 or more. City populations doubled or tripled in the decade after 1840; this was, in proportion, the greatest growth of city populations in the nation's history. Eight cities had populations of more than 150,000 — and three of them were in the West. The growth of mass transit, e.g., the street railway, helped allow cities to expand, and the professional and upper classes moved to exclusive areas separate from the poor and from commercial centers. Other important transportation advances, such as the development of canals, clipper ships, steamboats, and railroads, also supported the rapid urbanization across the U.S. Basic services, such as sewers, lighting, and fire prevention, were quickly outstripped, and most urban areas were centers of disease and crime. Rioting focused on ethnic populations, such as Irish Catholics or Germans, becoming a major problem.

At the same time, an extraordinary agricultural expansion into the West and Old Southwest proved that the majority of Americans continued to depend on farming for their livelihoods. New heights in the production of surplus food crops helped fuel the urban growth, but, more importantly, the European market demand for American wheat and cotton led to a reliance on mono-crop agriculture. Using the new "right of preemption" established in 1841 to allow access to cheap public lands, new settlers in the western lands planted more and fertilized less. The technological revolution in agriculture supported the tendency of the profit-driven farmer to go deep into debt to produce more cash crops, especially wheat and cotton, even when the market price went down.

By 1850, however, the value of American industrial output surpassed all of that of agriculture, including cotton. Yearly numbers of patent applications increased exponentially, and American "know-how" developed all sorts of new inventions: from the electric telegraph, to vulcanization of rubber, to the six-shooter pistol. These technological advances, along with the high literacy rates of white Americans, promoted a new pride in the "modernization" of America. The popularity of "how to succeed" books reflected a growing value system that emphasized hard work, self-discipline, and thrift.

But white Americans were not the only ones to believe in this work ethic. People of color, especially free blacks in the cities, while segregated and restricted in multiple ways by the laws and social mores of the day, helped establish their own support systems to allow for success. In urban America, a black elite began to emerge, and they helped establish important community institutions such as mutual aid societies and independent black churches. Key black spokespersons, such as Harriet Tubman, Sojourner Truth, and Frederick Douglass, helped raise the spirits not only of those who attended antislavery and women's rights conventions but also those who heard of their public appearances and knew they spoke out for their civil rights.

White middle-class women were increasingly identified with "the home": an icon of refuge from the instability and competition of the new American industrial age. Popular literature, sermons, and advice books stressed the importance of a pure and chaste woman for the benefit not only of herself and her family but also for society as a whole. Middle-class women's average birthrate dropped, and, even as they had fewer children, they became engrossed with the idea of childhood as a separate stage of life needing particular types of nurturing. At the same time as the rise of the "cult of domesticity," there was a rise in female illnesses in the middle and upper classes.

American popular culture reflected the changes in the role of the common people in society. Entertainments, such as sporting events, theatre, opera, and even county fairs, all generated heavy audience participation. Sometimes the immense crowds of spectators turned into riots.

The regional differences between the North and the South grew more obvious in the different economies and lifestyles. Southerners tended to stress tradition and stability more than the type of progress and change that many Northerners pursued. Southerners also rejected many of the reform movements popular in the North. The relative shortage of white free labor and dependence on black slave labor, along with the growth of the Cotton Kingdom in the Southwest, helped create a different economic future as well. Though the slave economy was clearly profitable only to the few large planters and their northern financiers, even the poorer southern whites strove to support the system, hoping to become rich themselves someday. Most Southerners came to believe that slavery was indeed a "positive good," since it kept their society stable. The southern planters' paternalism dominated the political and social life of the South even though most southern whites were yeoman farmers who did not own any slaves. A full 25 percent of the southern white population did not own any land and either worked as day laborers or rented property. By 1860, only 25 percent of the white families in the South owned slaves but they controlled 95 percent of the South's agricultural wealth.

At least half of the slave population of the South lived on plantations where all-black communities could provide important cultural support to offset the dehumanizing effects of slavery. The slaves' religion, music, and folk tales helped provide a key sense of identity separate from that imposed on them by their masters and the white community around them. The slave family was vulnerable to the whims and economic needs of their master, but the African heritage of extended kin-systems helped bolster the bereaved when their family members were sold away or killed. Though armed slave rebellions, such as those by Denmark Vesey or Nat Turner, were less common than in the slave societies of Central and South Americas, southern blacks found many ways to resist the overwhelming odds against them. Slave resistance found many forms, including running away.

IDENTIFICATION: Briefly describe each term

Associated Press

Catherine Beecher

Charles Goodyear

Children's Aid Society

Cult of domesticity ("woman's sphere")

Denmark Vesey

Eli Whitney

Elias Howe

Elizabeth Blackwell

Erie Canal

Europe's Revolutions of 1848

F.B. Morse

Godey's Lady's Book

"Golden Mountain"

Ireland's Great Famine of 1845

John Deere

McCormick Reaper

McGuffey's Readers

Mesmerism

Minstrel shows

Nat Turner

New York's Five Points

The North Star

Oberlin College

P.T. Barnum

Patrollers

Phrenology

"the Protestant work ethic"

Robert Fulton

Samuel Colt

Slave codes

Turnpike

THINK ABOUT:

Key Technological Inventions

Norbert Rillieux	Multiple-effect vacuum evaporator (to process sugar cane)
Henry Blair	Corn harvester
Peter Cooper	Railroad steam locomotive
Cyrus McCormick	Grain reaper
Samuel Colt	Repeating pistol
John Deere	Steel plow
Charles Goodyear	Vulcanization of rubber
Gail Borden	Condensed milk and concentrated coffee
Crawford Long	Use of ether in surgery
Samuel F.B. Morse	Telegraph
Elias Howe	Sewing machine
Richard M. Hoe	Rotary printing press
Oliver Evans	First American steam engine
Eli Whitney	Cotton gin

1. Look at the table of technological inventions above to answer the following questions.
   a) Choose which invention you think was most important for American progress and explain why.
   b) How might a particular region of the U.S. benefit by each of the inventions listed? How might that invention make a region vulnerable economically?
   c) Which invention, if it had not existed, do you think would have most affected the course of American labor history?

2. How might southern political leaders argue that slavery was a "positive good"?

3. Describe the "cult of true womanhood," and explain how this mainly affected middle-class white women.

PLANTATION SONG: "My Old Kentucky Home, Good Night!" 1853

Stephen Collins Foster, a popular songwriter in Pennsylvania, wrote this plantation song. Foster was deeply affected by Harriet Beecher Stowe's **Uncle Tom's Cabin** *published in 1852. His original sketches for the song showed that he did not start the song with the present opening lines but with words that echoed the plot of Stowe's story about a saintly slave sold to the cotton plantations of the deep South where he is killed by overwork and exposure. "Oh good night, good night, good night / Poor Uncle Tom / Grieve not for your old Kentucky home / You're bound for a better land / Old Uncle Tom." The Kentucky legislature adopted it as a state song in 1928. The old Rowan mansion in Bardstown, Kentucky is maintained as an official state shrine to the song, though no one can prove that Foster himself ever visited his slaveowning cousins there. In recent years, the word "darkies" was substituted with "old folks," but the racist assumptions of the song's original story remain obvious to any careful observers.*

The sun shines bright in the old Kentucky home
'tis summer, the darkies are gay,
the corn top's ripe and the meadow's in the bloom
while the birds make music all the day.
The young folks roll on the little cabin floor
all merry, all happy, and bright.
By'n by hard times comes a-knocking at the door,
then my old Kentucky home, good night.

Chorus:
Weep no more, my lady,
oh weep no more today.
We will sing on song for the old Kentucky home,
for the old Kentucky home far away.

They hunt no more for the 'possum and the coon
on meadow, the hill and the shore.
They sing no more by the glimmer of the moon
on the bench by that old cabin door.
The day goes by like a shadow o'er the heart
with sorrow where all was delight.
The time has come when the darkies have to part
then my old Kentucky home, good night.

The head must bow and the back will have to bend
wherever the darky may go.
A few more days and the trouble all will end
in the field where sugar-canes may grow.
A few more days for to tote the weary load.
No matter, 'twill never be light.
A few more days till we totter on the road,
then my old Kentucky home, good night.

Source: *A Treasury of Stephen Foster* (New York: Random House, 1946), pp. 95-97.

HOW WELL DID YOU UNDERSTAND THIS SELECTION?

1. In Foster's original notes on this song, the narrator is identified as "Old Tom" — the saintly Kentuckian in Stowe's book, a slave sold South. What are "the hard times" that he bemoans in the first verse (*Hint: see the second verse, second to last line*)?

2. Who do you think is "my lady" and why is she weeping?

3. How is the slave experience in Kentucky portrayed, and how does the narrator see this as different from slavery in the Deep South?

4. The plantation song was a popular part of the blackface minstrel show, and often-white middle-class women purchased this sheet music to perform in their parlors. Its popularity was not restricted to any particular region of the U.S. How does this sentimental portrayal of Kentucky slavery reflect racist assumptions that were shared by most white Americans, North and South?

The historic interaction between African and African-American cultural traditions can be observed in specific forms of music. The cultural connection is not the retention of particular African songs but of a conceptual framework that distinguishes them from Western European cultural forms. The African-American songs whose words are written below were most likely sung with a great deal of improvisation. These religious folk songs used Biblical imagery but also emphasized the everyday life of the slaves who created them. So, white singers might think freedom meant religious salvation, African-American singers meant physical and psychic liberation from the bondage of chattel slavery.

Nobody Knows the Trouble I've Had
Chorus:
Nobody knows de trouble I've had [or, I've seen],
   Nobody knows but Jesus
Nobody knows de trouble I've had
   Glory hallelu.

One morning I was a-walking down,
   O yes, Lord!
I saw some berries a-hanging down,
   O yes, Lord!
Chorus

I pick de berry and I suck de juice,
   O yes, Lord!
Just as sweet as the honey in de comb,
   O yes, Lord!
Chorus

Sometimes I'm up, sometimes I'm down,
Sometimes I'm almost on de groun'.
Chorus

What make ole Satan hate me so?
Cause he got me once and he let me go.
Chorus

Deep River
Deep river, my home is over Jordan, Deep river,
Lord, I want to cross over into campground,
Lord, I want to cross over into campground,
Lord, I want to cross over into campground.
Oh, chillun, Oh, don't you want to go to that gospel feast,
That promised land, that land, where all is peace?
Walk into heaven, and take my seat,
And cast my crown at Jesus feet,
Lord, I want to cross over into campground,
Lord, I want to cross over into campground.

195

Deep river, my home is over Jordan, Deep river,
Lord, I want to cross over into campground,
Lord, I want to cross over into campground,
Lord, I want to cross over into campground, Lord!

Go Down, Moses
When Israel was in Egypt's land,
    Let my people go;
Oppressed so hard they could not stand,
    Let my people go.

Chorus:
Go down, Moses, way down in Egypt's land;
Tell old Pharaoh, to let my people go.

Thus saith the Lord, bold Moses said,
    Let my people go;
If not I'll smite your first born dead,
    Let my people go. *Chorus*
No more shall they in bodage toil,
    Let my people go;
Let them come out with Egypt's spoil,
    Let my people go. *Chorus*
O 'twas a dark and dismal night,
    Let my people go;
When Moses led the Israelites,
    Let my people go. *Chorus*
The Lord told Moses what to do,
    Let my people go;
To lead the children of Israel through,
    Let my people go. *Chorus*
O come along, Moses, you won't get lost,
    Let my people go;
Stretch out your rod and come across,
    Let my people go. *Chorus*
As Israel stood by the water side,
    Let my people go;
At the command of God it did divide,
    Let my people go. *Chorus*
And when they reached the other side,
    Let my people go;
They sang a song of triumph o'er,
    Let my people go. *Chorus*
You won't get lost in the wilderness,
    Let my people go;
With a lighted candle in your breast,
    Let my people go. *Chorus*
O let us all from bondage flee,
    Let my people go;
And let us all in Christ be free,
    Let my people go. *Chorus*

We need not always weep and moan,
    Let my people go;
And wear these slavery chains forlorn,
    Let my people go. *Chorus*
What a beautiful morning that will be,
    Let my people go;
When time breaks up in eternity,
    Let my people go. *Chorus*

Source: *Slave Songs of the United States.* William Francis Allen, et al., comp. New York, A. Simpson, 1867.

HOW WELL DID YOU UNDERSTAND THIS SELECTION?

1.   Spirituals sung by slaves often depicted a Christian redemption and deliverance from the earthly life into paradise. How would slaves have used these messages? Why were Biblical heroes like Moses popular?

2.   How much can historians learn about slave communities by studying music? What other information (besides the words of a song) would you need to have in order to attempt an analysis of African-American music and culture?

John C. Calhoun (1782-1850) was not only an American statesman but also a political philosopher. Calhoun's first national leadership role came as a "war hawk" when serving in the U.S. House of Representatives during the War of 1812. It cost him the vice presidency to express his views on nullification and to become the leading defender of a minority Southern cause against a commercial, industrial North. This speech made while he was a Senator is widely considered the most clear expression of the pro-slavery stance taken by antebellum southern conservative leaders.

I do not belong, said Mr. C., to the school which holds that aggression is to be met by concession... If we concede an inch, concession would follow concession - compromise would follow compromise, until our ranks would be so broken that effectual resistance would be impossible. We must meet the enemy on the frontier, with a fixed determination of maintaining our position at every hazard. Consent to receive these insulting petitions [from anti-slavery associations], and the next demand will be that they be referred to a committee in order that they may be deliberated and acted upon. At the last session we were modestly asked to receive them, simply to lay them on the table, without any view to ulterior action. . . . I then said, that the next step would be to refer the petition to a committee, and I already see indications that such is now the intention. If we yield, that will be followed by another, and we will thus proceed, step by step, to the final consummation of the object of these petitions. We are now told that the most effectual mode of arresting the progress of abolition is, to reason it down; and with this view it is urged that the petitions ought to be referred to a committee. That is the very ground which was taken at the last session in the other House, but instead of arresting its progress it has since advanced more rapidly than ever. The most unquestionable right may be rendered doubtful, if once admitted to be a subject of controversy, and that would be the case in the present instance. The subject is beyond the jurisdiction of Congress - they have no right to touch it in any shape or form, or to make it the subject of deliberation or discussion. . . .

As widely as this incendiary spirit has spread, it has not yet infected this body, or the great mass of the intelligent and business portion of the North; but unless it be speedily stopped, it will spread and work upwards till it brings the two great sections of the Union into deadly conflict. ... They who imagine that the spirit now abroad in the North, will die away of itself without a shock or convulsion, have formed a very inadequate conception of its real character; it will continue to rise and spread, unless prompt and efficient measures to stay its progress be adopted. Already it has taken possession of the pulpit, of the schools, and, to a considerable extent, of the press; those great instruments by which the mind of the rising generation will be formed.

However sound the great body of the non-slaveholding States are at present, in the course of a few years they will be succeeded by those who will have been taught to hate the people and institutions of nearly one-half of this Union, with a hatred more deadly than one hostile nation ever entertained towards another. It is easy to see the end. By the necessary course of events, if left to themselves, we must become, finally, two people. It is impossible under the deadly hatred which must spring up between the two great nations, if the present causes are permitted to operate unchecked, that we should continue under the same political system. The conflicting elements would burst the Union asunder, powerful as are the links which hold it together. Abolition and the Union cannot coexist. As the friend of the Union I openly proclaim it, - and the sooner it is known the better. The former may now be controlled, but in a short time it will be beyond the power of man to arrest the course of events. We of the South will not, cannot, surrender our institutions. To maintain the existing relations between the two races, inhabiting that section of the Union, is indispensable to the peace and happiness of both. It cannot be subverted without drenching the country or the other of the races. . . . But let me not be understood as admitting, even by implication, that the existing relations between the two races in the slaveholding States is an evil: - far otherwise; I hold it to be a good, as it has thus far proved itself to be to both, and will continue to prove so if not disturbed by the fell spirit of abolition. I appeal to facts. Never before has the black race of Central Africa, from the dawn of history to the present day, attained a condition so civilized and so improved, not only physically, but morally and intellectually. In the meantime, the white or European race, has not degenerated. It has kept pace with its brethren in other sections of the

Union where slavery does not exist. It is odious to make comparison; but I appeal to all sides whether the South is not equal in virtue, intelligence, patriotism, courage, disinterestedness, and all the high qualities which adorn our nature.

But I take higher ground. I hold that in the present state of civilization, where two races of different origin, and distinguished by color, and other physical differences, as well as intellectual, are brought together, the relation now existing in the slaveholding States between the two, is, instead of an evil, a good - a positive good. I feel myself called upon to speak freely upon the subject where the honor and interests of those I represent are involved. I hold then, that there never has yet existed a wealthy and civilized society in which one portion of the community did not, in point of fact, live on the labor of the other. Broad and general as is this assertion, it is fully borne out by history. This is not the proper occasion, but, if it were, it would not be difficult to trace the various devices by which the wealth of all civilized communities has been so unequally divided, and to show by what means so small a share has been allotted to those by whose labor it was produced, and so large a share given to the non-producing classes. The devices are almost innumerable, from the brute force and gross superstition of ancient times, to the subtle and artful fiscal contrivances of modern. I might well challenge a comparison between them and the more direct, simple, and patriarchal mode by which the labor of the African race is, among us, commanded by the European. I may say with truth, that in few countries so much is left to the share of the laborer, and so little exacted from him, or where there is more kind attention paid to him in sickness or infirmities of age. Compare his condition with the tenants of the poor houses in the more civilized portions of Europe - look at the sick, and the old and infirm slave, on one hand, in the midst of his family and friends, under the kind superintending care of his master and mistress, and compare it with the forlorn and wretched condition of the pauper in the poorhouse.

But I will not dwell on this aspect of the question; I turn to the political; and here I fearlessly assert that the existing relation between the two races in the South, against which these blind fanatics are waging war, forms the most solid and durable foundation on which to rear free and stable political institutions. It is useless to disguise the fact. There is and always has been in an advanced stage of wealth and civilization, a conflict between labor and capital. The condition of society in the South exempts us from the disorders and dangers resulting from this conflict; and which explains why it is that the political condition of the slaveholding States has been so much more stable and quiet than that of the North. . . . Surrounded as the slaveholding States are with such imminent perils, I rejoice to think that our means of defense are ample, if we shall prove to have the intelligence and spirit to see and apply them before it is too late. All we want is concert, to lay aside all party differences and unite with zeal and energy in repelling approaching dangers. Let there be concert of action, and we shall find ample means of security without resorting to secession or disunion. I speak with full knowledge and a thorough examination of the subject, and for one see my way clearly. . . . I dare not hope that anything I can say will arouse the South to a due sense of danger; I fear it is beyond the power of mortal voice to awaken it in time from the fatal security into which it has fallen.

Source: *Register of Debates in Congress...1824-1837*. Vol. 14. 24th Cong. 2nd Sess. (Washington: Gales & Seaton, 1837), cols. 2184-2188.

HOW WELL DID YOU UNDERSTAND THIS SELECTION?

1. Who is "the enemy" of Mr. Calhoun? Why doesn't he want to allow their "insulting petitions" to be referred to a congressional committee?

2. Mr. Calhoun predicts that, if left unchecked, the present course of events would lead to civil war. Who in his scenario would have started this war and for what reason?

3. What are Calhoun's arguments for keeping the institution of slavery intact in the South?

4. How does Calhoun contrast the conditions of southern slaves with European peasants? the political stability of the southern states to that of the northern states?

SPIRITUALISM AND CORA L. V. SCOTT of New York, 1851

Spiritualists and social reformers had many connections from the beginning of the movement. In many ways, the Spiritualist movement became an integral part of the romantic faith of white American Christians. The following excerpt is from a biography of Cora L.V. (Scott) Richmond, a spiritualist from Cadytown (North Cuba), New York. During the summer of 1850 her father, David Scott, a lumbermill owner, visited Hopedale, Mass., a Christian socialist utopian community established by Universalist Rev. Adin Ballou. Scott brought his family to live there for the next six months, and while there he attended a Spiritual séance. The next summer he traveled to Wisconsin to try and find an alternative site for the Hopedale Community, and he moved his family back to New York. That fall, his eleven-year-old daughter began experiencing trances as a medium. One of her "spirit controls" was Adin Agustus Ballou, the deceased son of the Hopedale founder. The more famous Fox sisters, Margerhetta (8) and Katherine (10), had begun their work also in western New York (Rochester) only three years before Scott.

In the fall of 1851 the first visitation came to this household. The young girl was seated in an arbor fashioned of young oak trees that were growing in the garden, they having been purposely left to form this arbor. She was preparing in her crude way, as a girl of eleven years will, her composition upon her slate for school, intending to copy it afterwards. As she supposed, she fell asleep, and on her return to consciousness found the slate was covered with writing not her own. Supposing some one had been there and done the writing in sport or as a joke, she hastened to the house to show the slate to her mother and to tell her that some one had been there writing while she was asleep. The mother was slightly shocked when she told her this, for the little children playing around had come in a short time before and told her that "Cora was in the arbor writing in her sleep." Thinking this mere play she had said nothing about it, but when the slate was presented covered with writing, which commenced, "My dear sister," and was signed with the name of a deceased sister of the mother whom Cora had never seen nor scarcely heard of, as she had passed away in early childhood, the mother became frightened, put the slate away and said nothing to Cora of what the children had told her.

A few days later Cora was seated at the feet of her mother sewing when again sleep overcame her, and the mother thinking she had fainted or was ill, applied the usual restoratives; but meanwhile discovered a trembling motion of the right hand, and instantly remembered the slate. As soon as she placed slate and pencil in her hands, Cora began to write, this time before the very eyes of her mother. She rapidly wrote one message after another signed by different members of the family who had departed to spirit life, all of whom united in saying: "We are not dead." They also assured the anxious mother that they would not harm the child, for they had found through her a means of communicating with those on earth, and wished her to aid them in carrying out this work. The influence at intervals continued, sometimes once in two or three days, until at last the house was thronged with curious friends and neighbors who came in to see "Cora write in her sleep." There was no knowledge of Spiritualism in the neighborhood, no realization of what these manifestations might mean on the part of the people, yet persons of all creeds alike came and not infrequently received messages from their own friends. They were often called upon to ask questions, mentally or otherwise, which would be promptly answered in writing and the answers handed to them. Of course the sensitive organism [body] of the child, the unusual surroundings and the excitement incident to these occurrences must have brought about serious results to the medium had there not been a strong band of influences around her who had complete control of her organism and were able to dictate what her line of work should be. These guides would not permit the child-medium to overtax her physical strength, and made such conditions possible through the unconscious trance state as would least affect the medium's health and general power of endurance. By taking complete possession of the medium the maximum effort had to be made from the spirit side, which left but little for the medium to do herself.

Source: *Life Work of Mrs. Cora L. V. Richmond.* Compiled and edited by Harrison D. Barrett. Published under the Auspices of the National Spiritualists Association of the U.S.A. (Chicago: Hack & Anderson, Printers, 1895), pp. 9-11.

HOW WELL DID YOU UNDERSTAND THIS SELECTION?

1. The narrative of the origin of Cora Richmond's spiritualism begins with a romantically pastoral scene complete with arbor and innocently playing children. How is the portrayal of the young girl and her mother in keeping with images of respectable, domestic images of the day?

2. Why was the young Cora's work as a medium so believable to so many?

3. What do you think made Spiritualism acceptable to some religious denominations and unacceptable to others?

FROM A BROKEN SAWMILL BLADE TO A STEEL PLOW: The Story of John Deere's Invention, 1837

A skilled mechanic and blacksmith in Grand Detour, Michigan, John Deere (1804-1886) used "Yankee know-how" to turn a sawmill blade into a plow that would conquer the tough prairie sod of the antebellum frontier. While blacksmithing for his regular customers, he built one plow at a time. By selling them out on condition of customer satisfaction, he continually tested them in different soils and under different conditions. The key was to make a plow that was "self-scouring" — that is, it would turn the sod cleanly and not leave gobs of earth on the plow, getting it stuck in the furrow. Often his earliest sales came from early adopters who convinced their neighbors of the better quality plow by Deere. By 1848 he and his family had moved to Moline, Illinois, to establish a factory and there, on the Mississippi River and near the rapidly growing frontier, the Deere manufacturing business flourished. Deere was barely literate and did not write his own story, however, many of the men around him told the story later in life. The following excerpt used oral history accounts of what Deere did after he brought home a circular saw blade made of Sheffield steel broken and discarded at a sawmill.

"I cut the teeth off the mill-saw with a hand-chisel," John Deere said. "I cut a pattern out of paper for the mold-board and share." (One account says that he bent his first plow to a form which he carved out of wood.) "I laid the pattern on the saw and cut out around it with a hand chisel, with the help of a striker and a sledge. I then laid the piece on the fire of the forge and heated it, a little at a time, shaping it as best I could with the hand hammer." (According to one story, he used a wooden mallet to avoid denting the surface of the steel.)

"After making the upright standards out of bar iron," the account continues, "I was ready for the wood parts. I went out to the timber, dug up a sapling, and used the crooks of the roots for handles. I shaped the beam out of a stick of timber" (a fence rail, in one version) "with an axe and a drawing-knife. In this fashion, I succeeded in constructing a very rough plow." … On that bright morning in 1837, when John Deere wiped the sweat from his brow with the back of his hand and said proudly, "She's finished" — it was an implement that caught and held the eye; new, sturdy, but light enough for a strong man to carry on his shoulder, the sun flashing from the polished steel as light from a mirror.

Farmers roundabout had heard what the blacksmith was up to. For the most part, they were skeptical, but willing to be shown. So, some of them, together with a number of villagers, assembled to watch John Deere's promised test of the new plow. … They climbed into the boat with John Deere and his precious plow, or followed in other boats, and rowed across to the far bank, calling jokes to one another, warning the curly-headed blacksmith not to be too down in the mouth when his plow proved itself no whit better than the plows brought from "back East." John was not given to light talk, but he sent as good chaff as he received; and, single-handed, he carried the plow across his shoulder to the field where Lewis Crandall was waiting with the necessary horse, and where it was said that no plow would ever scour. … Hitching up was no long process. In five minutes, all was ready.

"Want me to take her?" Crandall asked.

"I will," said John, "you drive."

Crandall slapped the reins on the horse's back. They were off. John Deere held the handles which he had fashioned from sapling roots and polished smooth. The plowshare bit deep into black soil. The horse put his withers into the pull. Soil began to cut and curl from the moldboard in a neat, smooth furrow. The spectators trudged behind, mostly silent, watching and wondering. After an eighth of a mile, they all stopped to appraise the performance.

"By cracky!" exclaimed one bystander, after a good look at the plow, "She's *clean*!"

There were several echoes of this approval — and some shouts of doubt.

"So *fur* she's clean," said one of the doubters, "but you wait!"

Crandall turned the horse, and they trudged back across the field, cutting another furrow. It was an ideal field, ideal weather for the test. The earth was still a little too moist; if ever it would stick to a plow, it should stick now. At the end of the second furrow, they stopped for a further examination. Moldboard was surprisingly clean. The gummy soil seemed unable to cling to it. A farmer turned to his neighbor:

"No need of your [cleaning] paddle with *that* plow!" he remarked triumphantly. "She moves right along, and polishes herself as she moves."

The one spoken to had broken many a prairie acre. "Aye," he said drily, "so it seems, but I *still* don't believe it!"

Round and round the field they went. Half a dozen times. A dozen. John Deere relinquished his place at the handles and let others take a turn at holding the plow. The worst pessimists finally had to admit that his plow scoured better than any plow they had ever seen. The optimists, on the other hand, were enthusiastic. John Deere himself was pleased; but not *too* pleased.

"I'm making you a present of this plow, Lewis," he said to Crandall, "for loaning the use of your land and the horse. But I'd like well to take it back with me to the shop for a few days. I doubt not I'll build another, and I will wish to study this. Maybe ways of improving it will occur to me."

So ended the test of John Deere's first steel plow.

Source: Neil M. Clark, *John Deere: He Gave to the World the Steel Plow* ([Moline, Ill.]: Priv. Print. [Desaulniers], [1937]), pp. 35-38.

HOW WELL DID YOU UNDERSTAND THIS SELECTION?

1. What are the pros and cons of the development of a steel plow?

2. American inventors prided themselves on their ability to create and adapt their machines from what they saw around them. What moral lesson of the history of "Yankee know-how" is in this story of Deere's first plow?

3. Compare and contrast this hero's story of American inventiveness with American tall tales' heroes such as Davy Crockett, John Henry, or Paul Bunyon.

A MUSLIM ENSLAVED IN NORTH CAROLINA TOLD HIS OWN STORY, 1831

*The usual depiction of antebellum African Americans emphasizes the strong Christian beliefs that helped keep family and community ties strong. However, upon studying West African history, Americans are often surprised to learn that Christianity came to that part of the African continent late, and missionary activity was of little effect until the imperialist European governments fully enforced a Christian Victorian morality on their African subjects. At this time, West Africans were more likely to believe either in Islam or an indigenous African religion (or both) than Christianity. Omar ibn Said described in his autobiography his life as an African textile merchant and how during a war he was captured and enslaved. Said was a Fula from a region now in Senegal. He wrote the original manuscript in Arabic, and it included quotations he remembered from the Qur'an. The Rev. Isaax Bird, a former missionary in Syria and with a working knowledge of Arabic, translated this version in 1848 for the anti-slavery writer, Theodore Dwight. Dwight published excerpts of Omar's autobiography in the **Methodist Review** in 1864.*

Then there came to our place a large army, who killed many men, and took me, and brought me to the great sea, and sold me into the hands of the Christians, who bound me and sent me on board a great ship and we sailed upon the great sea a month and a half, when we came to a place called Charleston in the Christian language. There they sold me to a small, weak, and wicked man, called Johnson, a complete infidel, who had no fear of God at all. Now I am a small man, and unable to do hard work so I fled from the hand of Johnson and after a month came to a place called Fayd-il [Fayetteville]. There I saw some great houses. On the new moon I went into a church to pray. A lad saw me and rode off to the place of his father and informed him that he had seen a black man in the church. A man named Handah (hunter?) and another man with him on horseback, came attended by a troop of dogs. They took me and made me go with them twelve miles to a place called Fayd-il, where they put me into a great house from which I could not go out. I continued in the great house (which, in the Christian language, they called *jail*) sixteen days and nights. One Friday the jailor came and opened the door of the house and I saw a great many men, all Christians, some of whom called out to me, "What is your name? Is it Omar or Seid?" I did not understand their Christian language. A man called Bob Mumford took me and led me out of the jail, and I was very well pleased to go with them to their place. I stayed at Mumford's four days and nights, and then a man named Jim Owen, son-in-law of Mumford, having married his daughter Betsey, asked me if I was willing to go to a place called Bladen. I said, Yes, I was willing. I went with them and have remained in the place of Jim Owen until now.

Before I came into the hand of Gen. Owen a man by the name of Mitchell came to buy me. He asked me if I were willing to go to Charleston City. I said, "*No, no, no, no, no, no, no,* I not willing to go to Charleston. I stay in the hand of Jim Owen."

O ye people of North Carolina, O ye people of S. Carolina, O ye people of America all of you; have you among you any two such men as Jim Owen and John Owen? These men are good men. What food they eat they give to me to eat. As they clothe themselves they clothe me. They permit me to read the gospel of God, our Lord, and Saviour, and King; who regulates all our circumstances, our health and wealth, and who bestows his mercies willingly, not by constraint. According to power I open my heart, as to a great light, to receive the true way, the way of the Lord Jesus the Messiah.

Before I came to the Christian country, my religion was the religion of "Mohammed, the Apostle of God — may God have mercy upon him and give him peace." I walked to the mosque before day-break, washed my face and head and hands and feet. I prayed at noon, prayed in the afternoon, prayed at sunset, prayed in the evening. I gave alms every year, gold, silver, seeds, cattle, sheep, goats, rice, wheat, and barley. I gave tithes of all the above-named things. I went every year to the holy war against the infidels. I went on pilgrimage to Mecca, as all did who were able. — My father had six sons and five daughters, and my mother had three sons and one daughter. When I left my country I was thirty-seven years old; I have been in the country of the Christians twenty-four years.

Source: "Autobiography of Omar ibn Said," *American Historical Review,* 30 (July 1925): pp. 793-94. For more information on Omar, see the above source, pp. 787-795; and see also "Meroh, a Native African," New York, *Observer,* (January 8, 1863). This article was written by Rev. William S. Plumer who met Omar in Wilmington, North Carolina.

HOW WELL DID YOU UNDERSTAND THIS SELECTION?

1.   In the last paragraph of the above excerpt, Said describes his life in Africa before he was captured and enslaved. What clues did he give us about his economic and social status at this time in his life? What did he mean when he said his father had eleven children and his mother had four children? Who are "the infidels" in this section of the narrative?

2.   Clearly, this educated and cosmopolitan man could distinguish between the different white captors who demanded his labor. Compare and contrast his descriptions of Johnson, Handah, the mob at the jail, and Mitchell. How were Jim and John Owen different from the others? What Christian denomination do you think the Owens were?

TRUE WOMANHOOD IN ANTEBELLUM AMERICA:
Two Perspectives

Social Expectations of White Women (Charleston *Mercury*, October 10, 1837)

Using documents such as advice books, sermons, or the poem below, historians have described a "cult of domesticity" centered in antebellum white middle-class culture. It is a construction of Euro-American femininity, which emphasizes almost exclusively women's maternal qualities. A "true" woman then is seen as more morally responsible and more chaste than men, even while they are dependent and cloistered within an ideal "home." This is opposed to a particular type of masculinity that makes white men as the actors in the public sphere where they are providers for, and protectors of, women.

> Man is great in action - Woman in suffering.
> Man shines abroad - Woman at home.
> Man talks to convince - Woman to persuade and please.
> Man has a rugged heart - Woman a soft and tender one.
> Man prevents misery - Woman relieves it.
> Man has science - Woman taste.
> Man has judgment - Woman sensibility.
> Man is a being of justice - Woman an angel of mercy.

Source: reprinted from the *North American Review* in the Charleston *Mercury* (October 10, 1837).

A Reply from Soujourner Truth (1795-1883)

This speech by the great African-American woman orator was recorded by Frances D. Gage, Chair Presiding of the Woman's Convention at Akron, Ohio, 1851.

Well, children, where there is so much racket there must be something out of kilter. I think that 'twixt the negroes of the south and the women at the North, all talking about rights, the white men will be in a fix pretty soon. But what's all this here talking about?

That man over there says that women need to be helped into carriages, and lifted over ditches, and to have the best place everywhere. Nobody ever helps me into carriages, or over mud-puddles, or gives me any best place! And ain't I a woman? Look at me! Look at my arm! I have ploughed and planted and gathered into barns, and no man could head me! And ain't I a woman? I could work as much and eat as much as a man - when I could get it - and bear the lash as well! And ain't I a woman? I have borne thirteen children, and seen them most all sold off to slavery, and when I cried out with my mother's grief, none but Jesus heard me! And ain't I a woman?

Then they talk about this thing in the head; what's this they call it? [Intellect, someone whispers.] That's it, honey. What's that got to do with women's rights or negro's rights? If my cup won't hold but a pint, and yours holds a quart, wouldn't you be mean not to let me have my little half-measure full?

Then that little man in black there, he says women can't have as much rights as men, 'cause Christ wasn't a woman! Where did your Christ come from? Where did your Christ come from? From God and a woman! Man had nothing to do with Him.

If the first woman God ever made was strong enough to turn the world upside down all alone, these women together ought to be able to turn it back, and get it right side up again! And now they is asking to do it, the men better let them.

Obliged to you for hearing me, and now old Sojourner ain't got nothing more to say.

Source: *The Proceedings of the Woman's Rights Convention, held at Akron, Ohio, May 28 and 29, 1851.* Cincinnati: B. Franklin Book and Job Office, 1851.

HOW WELL DID YOU UNDERSTAND THIS SELECTION?

1.   Compare and contrast selections (a) and (b). What besides the obvious differences in racialized experiences can be examined here?

2.   How much are the two gendered lists of antebellum ideals in selection (a) continue to be prescriptive for men's and women's roles today?

3.   Delineate Truth's logic to argue women's rights using Christian theology. Was it a cogent argument?

SELF TEST:

MULTIPLE CHOICE: Circle the correct response. The correct answers are given at the end.

1.   McGuffey Readers taught
     a.   how to succeed in college
     b.   national pride and individual morality
     c.   the science of evolution
     d.   the value of equal rights for black Americans

2.   What percentage of the white population of the U.S. owned slaves?
     a.   5%
     b.   25%
     c.   55%
     d.   80%

3.   A yeoman was a southern farmer who
     a.   owned twenty or more slaves
     b.   was indentured to another farmer
     c.   worked a family farm without the aid of slaves
     d.   worked to raise enough crops to be self-sufficient

4. Nat Turner
   a. exposed the Vesey-led conspiracy in Charleston
   b. led an army of rebellious slaves in Virginia
   c. was denied entrance to Oberlin College
   d. wrote a book about his experiences as a slave in Maryland

5. Extensive cotton plantations were most often located in which region?
   a. coastal South
   b. Mississippi Delta
   c. Old Southwest
   d. upper South

6. How much could a healthy, enslaved, field worker be auctioned off for in New Orleans in 1860?
   a. $100
   b. $1000
   c. $5000
   d. $10,000

7. The development of steamboats
   a. forced the eastern port cities out of the competition for international trade
   b. led to a decline in the development of railroads
   c. made it economically feasible to bring products from the interior to market
   d. was a threat to "King Cotton."

8. The waves of immigrants who came to the U.S. in the period between 1840-1860 were looking for jobs and they
   a. cooperated with the new unions
   b. immediately went West
   c. threatened the high prices for southern slaves
   d. were easily exploited by manufacturers looking for higher profits

9. Which one of the following ethnic groups was used primarily as skilled workers when they arrived in the U.S. as immigrants in the 1840s-50s?
   a. Chinese
   b. English
   c. Irish
   d. Slavs

10. What percentage of Americans still lived in rural areas before the Civil War?
    a. 20%
    b. 50%
    c. 80%
    d. 95%

Answers:1-b; 2-a; 3-d; 4-b; 5-c; 6-b; 7-c; 8-d; 9-b; 10-c.

ESSAYS:

1. The mass immigration in the mid-nineteenth century vastly changed the regional distribution of American population and laid stress on the dwindling services available in the new cities. Describe some of these immigrant groups and explain why many of them were forced to live in areas of crime and disease.

2. How did pro-slavery advocates prove their arguments? What principle was at the basis of their assumptions? Why would non-slaveholders support their arguments?

OPTIONAL ACTIVITIES: Use your knowledge **and** imagination

1. The new transportation technologies invented and bolstered during the antebellum period opened up new geographical areas, but did this bring Americans together or split them into new regions of interdependence? Imagine you are in Pittsburgh and want to go to New Orleans to do some trading. What merchandise might you trade, how would you get there, and what would you do while you were there?

2. If you were a black preacher in the slave state of Kentucky (where blacks were not forbidden by law to read and write), how might you take a leadership role in trying to gain basic human rights for blacks? Would you participate in organizing a rebellion? Would you help fugitives? Would you speak out or write about violence against blacks? Would you work with whites to get political and economic support for your ideas?

3. Find some folktales from different ethnic origins (e.g., African-American, Irish, French, German, Scandinavian, Chinese) and read them aloud to a group of children. What kinds of cultural lessons do each of these tales teach to young children? How different or similar are these lessons to ideals and values of mainstream, Protestant, Anglo-America?

4. Are there any historical sites in your area that portray how it might have been to live in the period between 1840-60? Research the site and then take a tour. Be sure to bring a camera and a tape recorder, and ask the proprietors if you can take pictures or tape the docent's lecture. Create a website that re-creates the tour virtually, lists your additional resources you found in your research, and analyze the historical lessons taught at that site. Are the displays, tour guide information, and site literature balanced and accurate?

WEB SITE LISTINGS:

The Alexis de Tocqueville Tour Exploring Democracy in America: C-SPAN's re-creation of Tocqueville's Tour of the U.S. and primary sources including an online version of the book
    http://www.tocqueville.org/
Stratford Hall Plantation, the birthplace of Robert E. Lee
    http://www.stratfordhall.org/
Old Sturbridge Village (a small New England community of the 1830s)
    http://www.osv.org/
Tales of the Early Republic
    http://www.earlyrepublic.net
"Democratic Origins and Revolutionary Writers, 1776-1820: James Fenimore Cooper (1789-1851)" by Kathryn VanSpanckeren
    http://odur.let.rug.nl/~usa/LIT/cooper.htm
"Immigrant and Ethnic America," portrayed in Harper's Weekly (1857-1916)
    http://immigrants.harpweek.com/
Urban history hubsite, Virtual Library, University of Kansas
    http://www.ukans.edu/history/VL/USA/urban.html
Chesapeake and Ohio Canal (1820)
    http://www.fred.net/kathy/canal.html
"A House Divided: America in the Age of Lincoln" a digital history and exhibition by the Chicago Historical Society and the Gilder Lehrman Institute
    http://www.digitalhistory.uh.edu/ahd/index.html
Women in America (U.Va.'s Crossroads hypertext of literary texts on antebellum women's experiences)
    http://xroads.virginia.edu/~HYPER/DETOC/fem/

Chapter Ten

THE ROAD TO WAR

The two-party system of Whigs and Democrats that had developed in the 1830s promoted national unity by ignoring the dangerous issue of slavery's expansion, thought to have been settled by the 1820 Missouri Compromise. Both parties had northern and southern wings. Both advocated American expansionism, the Whigs through economic growth and the Democrats through territorial expansion. As the American people continued to push westward, most believed it was America's "Manifest Destiny" to occupy the entire continent, ignoring the claims of Mexico, England, and Native Americans. Americans interpreted the victory of Texans against a larger Mexican army as a vindication of that destiny. Southerners felt that the annexation of Texas was an essential step in the protection of slavery. In the 1844 election, the Democratic platform called for the reannexation of Texas and, to win northern support, the reoccupation of Oregon.

Democrats interpreted the victory of James K. Polk in that election as a mandate to pursue Manifest Destiny. After rapidly annexing Texas, Polk wisely agreed to compromise with the British over Oregon. He was far more aggressive in his dealing with Mexico, seeking to obtain the territory west of Texas to the Pacific. When negotiations failed, Polk sent General Zachary Taylor and his troops into disputed territory near the Rio Grande River. Despite the opposition of anti-slavery Whigs, the inevitable military clash led to the short-lived Mexican War, easily won by the United States. The Treaty of Guadalupe Hidalgo ceded vast new territories from the Rocky Mountains to the Pacific Coast to the United States. Settlers poured into the Mexican Cession, particularly after the discovery of gold in California.

The public had been divided over the war, and those disagreements deepened over issues involving slavery in the new territories. Northerners, as demonstrated by the Wilmot Proviso proposing to ban slavery in territories acquired from Mexico, were determined to build a barrier against the spread of slavery. They were animated by an increasing distaste for the institution of slavery and a determination to prevent competition with slave labor in the free lands of the West. Southerners, like their northern counterparts, fervently believed that slavery must continue to expand to survive. Their spokesman, John C. Calhoun, even argued that slavery had to be protected in all the territories. Those who hoped to avoid the divisive issue argued that the settlers in each territory should decide whether it should be slave or free ("popular sovereignty").

The Compromise of 1850 attempted to settle the conflict, but it offered only a temporary reprieve, rather than a permanent settlement of the underlying issues. The northern opposition to enforcement of the Fugitive Slave laws, as shown in the passage of personal liberty laws and the publication of the best-seller *Uncle Tom's Cabin*, demonstrated the shaky foundations of the compromise. The two-party system, based on avoidance of the slavery issue, collapsed in the 1850s. The Whig Party, with irreconcilable northern and southern wings, disintegrated. The Know-Nothing Movement, appealing to fears about foreign-born Catholics, further weakened the existing party system that had restrained sectional conflict.

The Kansas-Nebraska Act, introduced by Senator Stephen Douglas, provided the final blow in the destruction of that system. The act, organizing the two territories of Kansas and Nebraska on the basis of popular sovereignty, violated the Missouri Compromise. Angry Northerners became increasingly convinced of the growing dangers of the "Slave Power." A new northern political party, the Republicans, appealed to those sentiments. The violence between proslavery and anti-slavery forces that followed the push of settlers into Kansas convinced each side of the untrustworthiness of the other. The violence spilled over from the struggle in Kansas onto the floors of Congress, where a southern congressman beat antislavery Senator Charles Sumner with a cane.

The Kansas issue also fractured the last truly national institution, the Democratic Party, now increasingly dominated by proslavery forces. Divisions worsened with the issuance of the *Dred Scott* decision, declaring that slavery could not be excluded from the territories, even by popular sovereignty. The implications of this decision became a central issue in the 1858 Illinois senatorial contest between Stephen Douglas and his Republican opponent, Abraham Lincoln. Douglas was forced to argue that the decision did not destroy popular sovereignty because the right to take slaves into a territory meant little without the support of local laws and police enforcement. Lincoln maintained that Douglas' amorality on the issue of slavery made him unfit for national leadership. Lincoln, while agreeing that the national government could not interfere with slavery in southern states, expressed a deeply held belief that slavery was morally wrong. He argued that prohibiting slavery's expansion would lead to its inevitable extinction. The debates propelled Lincoln onto the national stage and destroyed any southern support for Douglas.

The reaction to John Brown's raid on Harper's Ferry revealed the extent of sectional divisions. While Southerners viewed his actions as proof of an evil northern conspiracy against the South, some Northerners praised his courage and lamented his "martyrdom." The charged atmosphere caused the destruction of the national Democratic Party. The election of 1860 dissolved into two sectional contests: Lincoln vs. Douglas in the North and southern Democrat Breckinridge vs. moderate Bell in the South. Lincoln's victory rested entirely on northern votes. In reaction to the triumph of a party devoted to free labor and the belief that slavery was a moral evil, South Carolina seceded from the union. It was quickly followed by the other states of the Lower South who established the Confederate States of America. President Buchanan, while declaring that secession was illegal, also maintained that the federal government could do nothing to stop it. When Lincoln took office in March, he ordered that the federal military base at Fort Sumter be resupplied. When the Confederates fired at the fort, Lincoln called for troops to put down the "insurrection." The Confederates quickly called for their own volunteers. The bloodiest war in American history had begun.

IDENTIFICATION: Briefly describe each term

Charles Sumner

Henry Clay

William Henry Harrison

John Tyler

Daniel Webster

Manifest Destiny

James K. Polk

Liberty Party

Slave Power conspiracy

Mexican War

Zachary Taylor

Winfield Scott

Treaty of Guadalupe Hidalgo

the Wilmot Proviso

"popular sovereignty"

Free Soil Party

the Compromise of 1850

John C. Calhoun

William Seward

Millard Fillmore

Stephen Douglas

the Fugitive Slave Act

"personal liberty laws"

Harriet Beecher Stowe's *Uncle Tom's Cabin*

Franklin Pierce

Know-Nothings

Kansas-Nebraska Act

Republican Party

John C. Fremont

James Buchanan

"Bleeding Kansas"

the Lecompton Constitution

the Dred Scott decision

the "house divided" speech

Lincoln-Douglas debates

John Brown's raid on Harper's Ferry

the Election of 1860

secession

Confederate States of America

Fort Sumter

THINK ABOUT:

1.   How did the northern concept of a Slave Power develop? Why did Northerners fear it, and what events caused that fear to increase?

2.   Once abolitionists implanted the issue of slavery into national politics, how could the nation deal with the issue? Was there any way the differences between anti-slavery and pro-slavery forces could have been compromised?

3.   Was John Brown crazy or were his actions logically designed to ultimately destroy slavery?

4.   Could the Civil War have been averted or was the conflict inevitable? Were there any actions Lincoln could have taken to avoid war?

5.   What strategies did southern extremists employ to destroy the Union? Why were their strategies successful in spite of opposition to secession in the South?

FALL OF THE ALAMO

There were about 25,000 Americans living in Mexican territory in Texas by the mid-1830s. They had been attracted by cheap land. Many came with their slaves and were angered when Mexico abolished slavery. Others found their independent spirit in conflict with Santa Anna, Mexico's new dictator. War erupted in 1835 as Texans declared their independence. Some 3,000 Mexican troops besieged 187 defenders barricaded in the Alamo mission. All the defenders died in the battle that followed, except for six who were executed after they had surrendered. The gallant defense of the Alamo became a potent symbol in the Texas struggle for independence. Filisola was one of the Mexican soldiers.

March 6, 1836
Bexar, Texas

VICENTE FILISOLA

On this same evening, a little before nightfall, it is said that Barret Travis, commander of the enemy, had offered to the general-in-chief, by a woman messenger, to surrender his arms and the fort with all the materials upon the sole condition that his own life and the lives of his men be spared. But the answer was that they must surrender at discretion, without any guarantee, even of life, which traitors did not deserve. It is evident, that after such an answer, they all prepared to sell their lives as dearly as possible. Consequently, they exercised the greatest vigilance day and night to avoid surprise.

On the morning of March 6, the Mexican troops were stationed at 4 o'clock, A.M., in accord with Santa Anna's instructions. The artillery, as appears from these same instructions, was to remain inactive, as it received no order; and furthermore, darkness and the disposition made of the troops which were to attack the four fronts at the same time, prevented its firing without mowing down our own ranks. Thus the enemy was not to suffer from our artillery during the attack. Their own artillery was in readiness. At the sound of the bugle they could no longer doubt that the time had come for them to conquer or to die. Had they still doubted, the imprudent shouts for Santa Anna given by our columns of attack must have opened their eyes. As soon as our troops were in sight, a shower of grape and musket balls was poured upon them from the fort, the garrison of which at the sound of the bugle, had rushed to arms and to their posts. The three columns that attacked the west, the north, and the east fronts, fell back, or rather, wavered at the first discharge from the enemy, but the example and the efforts of the officers soon caused them to return to the attack. The columns of the western and eastern attacks, meeting with some difficulties in reaching the tops of the small houses which formed the walls of the fort, did, by a simultaneous movement to the right and to left, swing northward till the three columns formed one dense mass, which under the guidance of their officers, endeavored to climb the parapet on that side..

Our loss was very heavy. Colonel Francisco Duque was mortally wounded at the very beginning, as he lay dying on the ground where he was being trampled by his own men, he still ordered them on to the slaughter. This attack was extremely injudicious and in opposition to military rules, for our own men were exposed not only to the fire of the enemy but also to that of our own columns attacking the other fronts; and our soldiers being formed in close columns, all shots that were aimed too low, struck the backs of our foremost men. The greatest number of our casualties took place in that manner; it may even be affirmed that not one fourth of our wounded were struck by the enemy's fire, because their cannon, owing to their elevated position, could not be sufficiently lowered to injure our troops after they had reached the foot of the walls. Nor could the defenders use their muskets with accuracy, because the wall having no inner banquette, they had, in order to deliver their fire, to stand on top where they could not live one second.

The official list of casualties, made by General Juan de Andrade, shows: officers 8 killed, 18 wounded; enlisted men 5 2 killed, 233 wounded. Total 311 killed and wounded. A great many of the wounded died for want of medical attention, beds, shelter, and surgical instruments.

The whole garrison were killed except an old woman and a negro slave for whom the soldiers felt compassion, knowing that they had remained from compulsion alone. There were 150 volunteers, 32 citizens of Gonzales who had introduced themselves into the fort the night previous to the storming, and about 20 citizens or merchants of Bexar.

Finally, the place remained in the power of the Mexicans, and all the defenders were killed. It is a source of deep regret, that after the excitement of the combat, many acts of atrocity were allowed which are unworthy of the gallantry and resolution with which this operation had been executed, and stamp it with an indelible stain in the annals of history. These acts were reproved at the time by those who had the sorrow to witness them, and subsequently by the whole army, who certainly were not habitually animated by such feelings, and who heard with disgust and horror, as becomes brave and generous Mexicans who feel none but noble and lofty sentiments, of certain facts which I forebear to mention, and wish for the honor of the Mexican Republic had never taken place.

In our opinion the blood of our soldiers as well as that of the enemy was shed in vain, for the mere gratification of the inconsiderate, puerile, and guilty vanity of reconquering Bexar by force of arms, and through a bloody contest. As we have said, the defenders of the Alamo, were disposed to surrender, upon the sole condition that their lives should be spared. Let us even grant that they were not so disposed what could the wretches do, being surrounded by 5,000 men, without proper means of resistance, no possibility of retreating, nor any hope of receiving proper and sufficient reinforcements to compel the Mexicans to raise the siege? Had they been supplied with all the resources needed, that weak enclosure could not have withstood for one hour the fire of our twenty pieces of artillery which if properly directed would have crushed it to atoms and leveled down the inner buildings . . . .

The massacres of the Alamo, of Goliad, of Refugio, convinced the rebels that no peaceable settlement could be expected, and that they must conquer, or die, or abandon the fruits of ten years of sweat and labor, together with their fondest hopes for the future.

Source: Amelia Williams, "A Critical Study of the Siege of the Alamo and of the Personnel of its Defenders," *Southwestern Historical Quarterly*, July 1933.

HOW WELL DID YOU UNDERSTAND THIS SELECTION?

1. How would this view of events at the Alamo from the Mexican point of view have differed from that of Americans?

2. What error of judgment does Filisola feel the general-in-chief made?

3. What is his opinion about the famous massacre at the Alamo and its results?

4. What do you think was the main consequence of the events at the Alamo?

James K. Polk, who was elected president in 1844, was a firm believer in Manifest Destiny. He was committed to obtaining American territory in the Southwest to the Pacific Ocean. After the failure of his efforts to purchase this land from Mexico, he was willing to use other methods to achieve his goals. He ordered American troops into a disputed region between the Rio Grande River, which the U.S. claimed constituted the southwestern boundary of the new state of Texas, and the Nueces River, Mexico's stated boundary. Shots were fired in the disputed area, and Polk used the clash as a pretext to declare war.

While most Americans enthusiastically supported the war, many Whigs and northern antislavery advocates were vocal in their opposition. The poet James Russell Lowell was one of the latter. Lowell wrote many poems in a rural Yankee dialect spoken by a fictional spokesman, Hosea Biglow.

Polk's War Message

JAMES K. POLK

The strong desire to establish peace with Mexico on liberal and honourable terms, and the readiness of this Government to regulate and adjust our boundary and other causes of difference with that power on such fair and equitable principles as would lead to permanent relations of the most friendly nature, induced me in September last [1845] to seek the reopening of diplomatic relations between the two countries. Every measure adopted on our part had for its object the furtherance of these desired results. In communicating to Congress a succinct statement of the injuries we had suffered from Mexico, and which have been accumulating during a period of more than twenty years, every expression that could tend to inflame the people of Mexico or defeat or delay a pacific result was carefully avoided. An envoy of the United States [John Slidell] repaired to Mexico with full powers to adjust every existing difference. But though present on Mexican soil by agreement between the two Governments, invested with full powers, and bearing evidence of the most friendly dispositions, his mission has been unavailing. The Mexican Government not only refused to see him or listen to his propositions, but after a long-continued series of menaces have at last invaded our territory and shed the blood of our fellow-citizens on our own soil ....

Thus the Government of Mexico, though solemnly pledged by official acts in October last to receive and accredit an American envoy, violated their plighted faith and refused the offer of a peaceful adjustment of our difficulties. Not only was the offer rejected, but the indignity of its rejection was enhanced by the manifest breach of faith in refusing to admit the envoy who came because they had bound themselves to receive him . . .In my message at the commencement of the present session [of Congress] I informed you that upon the earnest appeal of the Congress and the convention of Texas I had ordered an efficient military force to take a position between "the Nueces and the [Rio Grande] Del Norte." This had become necessary to meet a threatened invasion of Texas by the Mexican forces, for which extensive military preparations had been made. The invasion was threatened solely because Texas had determined, in accordance with a solemn resolution of the Congress of the United States, to annex herself to our Union, and under these circumstances it was plainly our duty to extend our protection over her citizens and soil ....

The movement of the troops to the Del Norte was made by the commanding general under positive instructions to abstain from all aggressive acts toward Mexico or Mexican citizens and to regard the relations between that Republic and the United States as peaceful unless she should declare war or commit acts of hostility indicative of a state of war. He was specially directed to protect private property and respect personal rights.

The Army moved from Corpus Christi on the 11th of March, and on the 28th of that month arrived on the left bank of the Del Norte opposite to Matamoras, where it encamped on a commanding position, which has since been strengthened by the erection of fieldworks. A depot has also been established at Point Isabel, near the Brazos Santiago, 30 miles in rear of the encampment. The selection of his position was necessarily confided to the judgment of the general in command.

The Mexican forces at Matamoras assumed a belligerent attitude, and on the 12th of April General Ampudia, then in command, notified General [Zachary] Taylor to break up his camp within twenty-four hours and to retire beyond the Nueces River, and in the event of his failure to comply with these demands announced that arms, and arms alone, must decide the question. But no open act of hostility was committed until the 24th of April. On that day General Arista, who had succeeded to the command of the Mexican forces, communicated to General Taylor that "he considered hostilities commenced and should prosecute them." A party of dragoons of 63 men and officers were on the same day dispatched from the American camp up the Rio del Norte, on its left bank, to ascertain whether the Mexican troops had crossed or were preparing to cross the river, "became engaged with a large body of these troops, and after a short affair, in which some 16 were killed and wounded, appear to have been surrounded and compelled to surrender."

The grievous wrongs perpetrated by Mexico upon our citizens throughout a long period of years remain unredressed, and solemn treaties pledging her public faith for this redress have been disregarded. A government either unable or unwilling to enforce the execution of such treaties fails to perform one of its plainest duties.
Our commerce with Mexico has been almost annihilated. It was formerly highly beneficial to both nations, but our merchants have been deterred from prosecuting it by the system of outrage and extortion which the Mexican authorities have pursued against them, whilst their appeals through their own Government for indemnity have been made in vain. Our forbearance has gone to such an extreme as to be mistaken in its character. Had we acted with vigor in repelling the insults and redressing the injuries inflicted by Mexico at the commencement, we should doubtless have escaped all the difficulties in which we are now involved.

Instead of this, however, we have been exerting our best efforts to propitiate her good will. Upon the pretext that Texas, a nation as independent as herself, thought proper to unite its destinies with our own, she has affected to believe that we have severed her rightful territory, and in official proclamations and manifestoes has repeatedly threatened to make war upon us for the purpose of reconquering Texas. In the meantime we have tried every effort at reconciliation. The cup of forbearance had been exhausted even before the recent information from the frontier of the. Del Norte. But now, after reiterated menaces, Mexico has passed the boundary of the United States, has invaded our territory and shed American blood upon the American soil. She has proclaimed that hostilities have commenced, and that the two nations are now at war.

As war exists, and, notwithstanding all our efforts to avoid it, exists by the act of Mexico herself, we are called upon by every consideration of duty and patriotism to vindicate with decision the honor, the rights, and the interests of our country.

James D. Richardson ed., *A Compilation of the Messages and Papers of the Presidents* (New York: Bureau of National Literature 1896), vol. 5, pp. 2287-93.

HOW WELL DID YOU UNDERSTAND THIS SELECTION?

1.   Do you think Polk was sincere in his list of grievances against Mexico? Which argument was most convincing?

2.   Do you believe Polk really wanted "to establish peace with Mexico on liberal and honorable terms" ? Or was he merely using this as an excuse to fulfill his territorial goals?

3.   How would this message have been received in the United States? In Mexico?

THE MEXICAN WAR IS ON BEHALF OF SLAVERY
By James Russell Lowell

'T would n't suit them Southun fellers,
  They're a dreffle' graspin'set,
We must ollers' blow the bellers'
  Wen they want their irons het';
May be it's all right ez preachin ;
  But my narves it kind o'grates,
Wen I see the overreachin'
  O' them nigger-driven' States . . .

Ez fer war, I call it murder,
  There you hev it plain an' flat;
I don't want to go no furder
  Than my Testyment fer that;
God hez sed so plump an' fairly,
  It's ez long ez it is broad,
An' you've gut to git up airly
  Ef you want to take in God ....

Wut's the use o'meetin-goin'
    Every Sabbath, wet or dry,
Ef it's right to go amowin'
    Feller-men like oats an' rye?
I dunno but wet it's pooty
    Trainin' round in botail coats,
But it's curus Christian dooty
    This 'ere cuttin' folks's throats.
They may talk o'Freedom's airy'
    Tell they're pupple in the face,
It's a grand gret eemetary
    For the barthrights of our race;
They jest want this Californy
    So's to lug new slave-states in
To abuse ye, an' to scorn ye,
    An' to plunder ye like sin.

Aint it cute' to see a Yankee
    Take sech everlastin' pains,
All to get the Devil's thankee
    Helpin' on 'em weld their chains!
Wy, it's jest ez clear ez figgers,
    Clear ez one an' one make two,
Chaps thet make black slaves o' niggers
    Want to make wite slaves o' you.

James Russell Lowell, *The Biglow Papers* (Boston: Houghton Mifflin Company, 1891), pp. 64-70.

HOW WELL DID YOU UNDERSTAND THIS SELECTION?

1. What theory about the real cause of the Mexican War does "Biglow" advance? Who would have agreed with that theory?

2. What do the last two lines tell you about the reasons for northern opposition to new slave territory?

3. What does the use of the word "nigger" by a fervent antislavery supporter tell you about racism in America at the time?

The voting public in the 1850s grew increasingly disgusted with the refusal of political parties to take stands on significant issues. Selling of votes and continuing evidence of corruption angered people. In the decade before 1855 more than three million immigrants entered the United States, the largest proportional increase in American history. More than half of these were Catholics. Many native-born Protestants believed that these Catholics were responsible for the ills infecting American society. The angry nativists turned to the secret anti-Catholic American Party, called the "Know-Nothings." By 1855 the Know-Nothings had won control of most of New England and provided the main opposition to the Democrats in much of the rest of the nation. By 1856, they were largely absorbed by the more politically savvy new Republican Party.

The American Party (the Know Nothings) Defend Their Movement, 1855

The American Party can date its existence as far back as the day and hour when the "one idea" of deliverance from foreign influence, rule, and dictation, first found birth in the head and heart of a true patriot. When first the idea of a distinctive nationality was broached by a native of this country, then the American party had its beginning; and from such beginnings have many nations sprung-many whose national individualities are as strongly defined as are the English, the French, or the Scotch. Let those who scoff at, and laugh to scorn the idea of an American nationality, remember how few of the modern nations can claim a consanguineous connection with the aborigines of the territories they inhabit. If it is desirable that a beginning should be made, that a foundation for a nationality should be laid, we cannot commence the work too soon,-but if this country is to be a thing without a name, or, having a name-America-signifying nothing; if this territory is to be considered by the nations of the world as a common property, to be claimed by anything bearing the human form, however beastly, degraded and vile,-then let us understand it, and govern ourselves accordingly. But let us see if it has not from our beginning, as a nation, been a prominent principle with our best men that native hearts and native heads should govern the hand. American or native legislation was adopted while the country was yet in its infancy-as the records will show; and the older we have grown, the more determination have the people, and the purer public men, manifested in their efforts to secure an American nationality. WASHINGTON proclaimed those principles embodied in the ideas of the present American party, and were the father of his country now living, he, too, would come in for a share of the abuse arid vilification poured out from the husky throats of the besotted party hacks, upon those who have resolved on having a country which they can call their own.

Revolutions never go backward. For many years the American Party has continued to struggle for the preservation of American institutions. It has been again and again defeated-yet never has defeat caused its advocates, for a moment, to despair, or to surrender one iota of principle. So far from this, each successive defeat, whilst it has demonstrated the necessity, has also inspired the firmness to demand such further remedial measures as in the altered circumstances of the case appeared to be required.

Revolutions in public sentiment are necessarily of slow development, yet they are ever onward. The American party in its first movement claimed only a guarantee for the purity of the ballot-box. That guarantee was resisted by all the political demagogues of the old parties, and the Native American party, as if in scorn of the baseness that could tamely surrender the palladium of our Republican Government to the scum of Europe, advanced another principle, more distasteful still to the trading politicians, who at present control the policy of our government-a requirement of twenty-one years residence before a foreigner should be permitted to thrust their unhallowed hands into the ark of our political covenant. Then the party demanded a capitation tax, that should restrain the most worthless and vicious of foreign emigrants from debarking on our shores. That, too, encountered the bitter hostility of the money-making politicians of one school, and the officeseeking and spoils-devouring cormorants of the other. Still the American Party, undismayed by the hostility it encountered, and undaunted by the reverses which befel it, moved forward, and demanded a capitation tax to an amount that should virtually check the unprecedented current of emigration, which, if not soon arrested and turned back to its source, must inevitably lead to that abasement of the people, which such an infusion must certainly produce. It was a glorious step, which, in after times,-when the whirlwind of passion has subsided,-will be remembered with gratitude by every American, in whose bosom the love of country is stronger than the love of money, and the lust of office. It is a position which no sophistry can undermine, and that will not be abandoned, cost what it may to maintain it. It is the first blow of the axe at the root of the deadly upas, whose pestilential influence cramps the genius of our government, and filches their birthright from the native sons of the soil. Revolutions are still onward. The sublime idea of deliverance from foreign influence, which first prompted an exclusion of the hordes of Europe from the elective franchise until they had resided twenty-one years in the country, now counsels still another and a bolder measure-a partition of the public domain among the native born, male and female, in quantities of 160 acres to each, to the end that it may not be seized by the swarms of aliens, who are hastening to secure possession of our heritage. The American mechanics and working men, with their wives and children, require something to fall back upon when they are ousted from their employments by the terrible competition of pauper laborers from the Old World. Then let the public lands be appropriated to the use of those Americans who are compelled to give way to pauper prices, and retire from their various callings in the cities before the onward march of foreign labor. Give the Americans some kind of protection against European competition in the home marts of industry, or else apportion out to them the public domain, on which they may build permanent homes at once, and abandon the cities for ever to the foreign hordes now pouring in upon us in a continuous stream.

Revolutions never go backward. The Americans now demand inalienable homesteads for all time-never to be driven therefrom. They require at the hands of the American Government, homes on their own soil-their portion of their birthright to the land of their forefathers.

Source: *Know Nothing Almanac and True Americans' Manual for 1855* (New York: DeWitt & Davenport, 1855).

HOW WELL DID YOU UNDERSTAND THIS SELECTION?

1. How does the party define "American nationality"? Who would this definition appeal to?

2. The American Party advocated what limitations on foreign immigrants?

3. Are there any groups demanding protection against "foreign hordes" in America today?

SOUTHERN REACTIONS TO THE CANING OF SENATOR SUMNER

After the passage of the Kansas-Nebraska Act, suspicion and anger directed by Northerners and Southerners at each other continued to build, even infected the halls of Congress. After Senator Charles Sumner delivered a bitter and provocative speech, "The Crime Against Kansas," an angry young congressman from South Carolina, Preston Brooks, viciously attacked Sumner on the floor of the Senate with a gold-headed walking stick. Sumner was seriously injured. Southerners celebrated this "defense of southern honor."

A glorious deed! A most glorious deed!! Mr. Brooks, of South Carolina, administered to Senator Sumner, a notorious abolitionist from Massachusetts, an effectual and classic caning. We are rejoiced. The only regret we feel is that Mr. Brooks did not employ a slave whip instead of a stick. We trust the ball may be kept in motion. Seward [another antislavery senator] should catch it next.

The RICHMOND WHIG, 1856

We entirely concur with the Richmond Whig, that if thrashing is the only remedy by which the abolitionists can be controlled, that it will be well to give Senator William H. Seward a double dose at least every other day until it operates freely on his political bowels.

The PETERSBURG INTELLIGENCER, May 1856

Good! - good!! -very good!!! 'The abolitionists have been suffered to run too long without collars. They must be lashed into submission. Sumner, in particular, ought to have nine-and-thirty (lashes] every morning .... Senator Wilson . .. [is] also dying for a beating. Will not somebody take him in hand .... If need be, let us have a caning or cowhiding every day.

The RICHMOND EXAMINER, May 1856

HOW WELL DID YOU UNDERSTAND THIS SELECTION?

1. Why did these southern newspapers rejoice in the beating of Sumner?

2. How do you think Northerners would have reacted both to the event and to southern response to the beating?

3. What light does this event shed on relations between the North and South by 1856? Did war seem inevitable?

It had seemed, for a while, that the Compromise of 1850 had settled the issue of whether slavery would be allowed to expand into the western territories. When Senator Stephen Douglas of Illinois introduced the Kansas-Nebraska Act in 1854 to organize the territories of Kansas and Nebraska, he reopened the issue by providing that the settlers themselves, through "popular sovereignty," would decide the status of slavery. The unintended result was that Northerners and Southerners rushed into Kansas and sought to implement the decision by means of rifles. The continuing conflict led people to describe the territory as "Bleeding Kansas." Eventually, after a bitter struggle, the antislavery forces won, and Kansas finally entered the Union in 1861. The authors of these letters from Kansas eventually fought on opposite sides in the Civil War. While John Lawrie survived, Axalla John Hoole died at Chickamauga in 1863.

LETTER FROM JOHN LAWRIE: A NORTHERNER'S VIEW

Wolf Mound Farm, White Co., Indiana
Apl. 16th, 1857
Dear Art,

After an absence of ten months I now find myself again at home, and surrounded by old associations, among which prominently stands my long-neglected correspondence with you. It was my hope on my way home that when I reached it I would find you with Bob and Lizzy of the Georgian block house, yet some twenty-five miles distant, and met with no incidents worthy of note until we reached the vicinity of the block house, where we were all rather anxious to see how the boys would behave under fire, many of them never having as yet heard singing lead. The night was rather dark, and the enemy showed no light and made no noise. Our captain (who by the way was an old man of wars man) reconnoitered the ground and concluded to lead us right on to the place and take it by assault as we had no artillery to storm the place with. The battalion was divided into two platoons, and the block house approached from toward its front and left so that in case we found it necessary to fire we could give them a destructive cross-fire. We went up as well as old veterans ever dared to go; and if there was any disorder at all whatever, it was occasioned by some of the boys rushing ahead too fast. The sound of our steady tramp! tramp! was too much for the garrison and they incontinently fled. We found about ten hundred pounds of bacon, some meal, several sacks of flour, a barrel of sugar, [and?] various articles recognized by many of our men as having been taken from Lawrence on the 21st of May, besides a number of letters written by Free-State men to their friends in the states which had been mailed in U. S. post offices, and probably had been abstracted in Missouri and forwarded to the Robbers of the Blue Lodge in order to give them whatever information they might possess of the prospects and conditions of their writers. After taking out all the provisions and military stores, we fired the block house and started home again by the light of it. On our return we had a most fatiguing time, but reached Lawrence without any incident occurring worthy of note ....

I found all our people well. I shall remain here until the middle of June when I intend returning to Kansas.

Your affectionate brother
John Lawrie

LETTERS FROM AXALLA JOHN HOOLE: A SOUTHERNER'S VIEW

Kansas City, Missouri,
Apl. 3d., 1856
My Dear Brother

It has cost me over $102 to get here, besides about $25 which I have spent for necessaries, &c. We have been quite well since we left-with the exception of one day that I had a headache and fever, caused I guess from losing so much sleep, and the fatigue of travelling. We did not get to Nashville until Sunday evening; we left that place Monday about 12 o'clock and went down the Cumberland river on the steamer City of Huntsville to Cairo, at the junction of the Mississippi and the Ohio rivers, where we changed boats and went up to St. Louis, Mo., where we arrived Friday morning about 8 o'clock. We remained there about two hours, in which time I purchased a six-shooter for $20, and some other things. We then changed boats and sailed up the Missouri river to this place.
The boats travel very slow up this river at this time, as it is very low and swift.
I have seen none of the country except along the banks of the river, which is, with very little exceptions, nothing but lofty, rugged rocks, sometimes two or three hundred feet high. It was quite a sight to me at first, but I got very tired of looking at them. I saw thousands of wild geese in the Missouri river; I shot at them once about 200 yards, and of course missed. I saw duck also in abundance....

The banks of the river were low and I could see for miles, but there were houses scattered all over the prairie. I fell in company with a young man who had just married, from Georgia, who said he was going to Kansas, but there were other families along from Georgia, who were going to Missouri, and when they left the boat about 60 miles from here, he left with them and I was not sorry for it, as I did not fancy him much; neither did I fancy his wife. I would have but little to do with them - one objection I had to him was, he drank liquor

The Missourians (all of whom I have conversed with, with the exception of one who, by the way, I found out to be an Abolitionist) are very sanguine about Kansas being a slave state & I have heard some of them say it shall be. I have met with warm reception from two or three, but generally speaking, I have not met with the reception which I expected. Everyone seems bent on the Almighty Dollar, and as a general thing that seems to be their only thought-There was a large box on one of the boats about a week ago coming up the river, which some of the Missourians thought contained Sharp's Rifles, so they sent a deputation to its destination, which was at this place, to have it opened. When they arrived here the person to whom it was consigned refused to let them open it, where-upon they opened it by force-when lo! it contained nothing but a piano. There was a box containing a cannon which a confounded Yankee opened, but closed it up again before any of them could examine it, saying that it was nothing but some cartwheels. His daughter-in-law told me this this morning, hesitatingly, as if her father-in-law had done a smart trick. If she had been a man, I don't know what I should have said, but she was a pretty young woman.

Well, dear brother, the supper bell has rung, so I must close. Give my love to [the immediate family] and all the Negroes .... Excuse bad writing for I am very nervous. I am anxious to hear from home . . . direct to Lawrence City, Kansas Territory, as I shall leave word there for my letters to be forwarded to whatever place I go.
Your ever affectionate brother,

Axalla.

Douglas, K. T., July the 5th., 1857

Dear Sister

I fear, Sister, that coming here will do no good at last, as I begin to think that this will be made a Free State at last. 'Tis true we have elected Proslavery men to draft a state constitution, but I feel pretty certain, if it is put to the vote of the people, it will be rejected, as I feel pretty confident they have a majority here at this time. The South has ceased all efforts, while the North is redoubling her exertions. We nominated a candidate for Congress last Friday-Ex-Gov. Ransom of Michigan. I must confess I have not much faith in him, tho he professes to hate the Abolitionists bitterly, and I have heard him say that Negroes were a great deal better off with Masters. Still, I fear him, but it was the best we could do. If we had nominated a Southern man, he would have been sure to have been beaten, and I doubt whether we can even elect a Northerner who favors our side.

One of our most staunch Proslavery men was killed in Leavensworth a few days ago. It is hard to ascertain the facts in relation to the murder correctly, but as far as I can learn, there was an election for something. The man who was killed (Jas. Lyle) went up to the polls and asked for a ticket. An Abolitionist handed him one which he, Lyle, tore in two. The other asked him why he did that; he replied he did all such tickets that way. The Abolitionist told him he had better not do so again, when Lyle told him if he would give him another he would. It was given him, and he tore it also, at which the Abolitionist drew a bowie knife and stabbed Lyle to the heart, then ran a few paces, drew a revolver, and commenced firing at the dying man. The fellow was taken prisoner and eighty men were sent from Lawrence that night, by Jim Lane, to keep Lyle's friends from hanging him. Gov. Walker put out for Leavensworth on Friday to have the prisoner carried to the fort, in order to keep the Abolitionists from rescuing him, or prevent Lyle's friends from hanging him by mob law.

There was a big ball in Lecompton on the night of the 3d., but they had no celebration there yesterday. The Abolitionists had a barbecue at Bloomington, about 8 miles south of this, but it was a party thing, I hear. There was a big celebration at Tecumseh and all were invited to attend, tho it was given by Proslavery men. Judge Cato was the orator of the day. I celebrated the day by hard work . . . so you may guess I felt like sleeping last night . . . .

You must give my love to all .... Tell all the Negroes a hundred Howdies for us ....

Your Affectionate Brother, Axalla.

P. S. 6th. Mr. Smith, the man engaged with me in work, was bit by a rattlesnake last night about midnight. He got up to give his child a drink of water, & stepped on the snake on the floor. He drank a pint of whiskey and got drunk. He has the Doctor with him this morning, and I hope he will be up in a day or two.

Source: V. E. Gibbons (editor), "Letters on the War in Kansas in 1856," In *Kansas Historical Quarterly*, 1941, 10: 370-373. William Stanley Hoole (editor), "A Southerner's Viewpoint of the Kansas Situation, 1856-1857," In *Kansas Historical Quarterly*, 1934, 3: 43-45; 64-65; 164-166.

HOW WELL DID YOU UNDERSTAND THIS SELECTION?

1. How do the views of the two men differ about conditions in Kansas?

2. Why do think Axalla Hoole's view of which way Kansas would go changed so much between April and July?

3. How did events in Kansas reflect the conditions in the rest of the country?

After President Buchanan sought to bring Kansas into the Union as a slave state, against the clear mandate of its settlers, the Supreme Court issued the Dred Scott decision, which declared that Congress had no right to bar slavery from the territories. These two events put Senator Douglas's cherished idea of "popular sovereignty" in serious jeopardy. Against this background, Senator Douglas ran for re-election in 1858. His opponent, a shrewd Republican lawyer, Abraham Lincoln, argued that Douglas's policy could lead only to chaos. The two men had a series of intense and well-attended debates. Gustave Koerner, a witness to these debates, was an Illinois political leader.

July 1858 GUSTAVE KOERNER

The first speech Judge Douglas made was at Chicago. His friends had made the most ample preparations for an ovation. Notice had been given for weeks, half-price excursion trains carried large numbers from the country into town. Bands of music and torch-light processions brought large masses to the front of the Tremont House, from the balcony of which he addressed the crowd. Bengal fires illuminated the scene, and when he appeared he was greeted with tumultuous cheers. He was fighting for his political life. His massive form supported his ample head, covered with a thick growth of black hair. His deep-set, dark blue eyes shed their lustre under his heavy brows. The features of his firm, round face were wonderfully expressive of the working of his feelings. Calm in stating facts, passionate when he attacked, disdainful when he was forced to defend, his gestures were sometimes violent and often exceptionally so. His voice was strong, but not modulated. Bold in his assertions, maledictory in his attacks, impressive in language, not caring to persuade, but intent to force the assent of his hearers, he was the Danton, not the Mirabeau, of oratory . . . .

Lincoln, who happened to be in the city, sat quietly on the same balcony. After Douglas got through, he was loudly called for. He rose and stated that this ovation was gotten up for his friend Judge Douglas, but that if the good people of Chicago would listen to him, he would speak to them to-morrow evening at the same time and place. Without time for parade or showy demonstration the throng that listened to Lincoln next evening, as might have been expected from the political complexion of the city, was larger and really more enthusiastic than the one of the night before.

No greater contrast could be imagined than the one between Lincoln and Douglas. The latter was really a very little giant physically, measuring five feet and nothing, while Lincoln, when standing erect, towered to six feet three inches. (Actually, Douglas was five feet four and Lincoln six feet four – editor.) Lincoln, awkward in his posture and leaning a little forward, stood calm and collected, addressing his hearers in a somewhat familiar, yet very earnest, way, with a clear, distinct, and far-reaching voice, generally well modulated, but sometimes rather shrill. When unmoved, his features seemed overshadowed by an expression of sadness, though at times he could assume a most humorous, and even comical, look; but, when aroused, he appeared like a prophet of old. Neither he nor Douglas indulged in rhetoric; both were mainly argumentative. But while Douglas, powerful as was his speech, never showed anything like genius, there came from Lincoln occasionally flashes of genius and burning words, revelations as it were from the unknown, that will live as long as the English language lives. Lincoln was deeply read in the Bible and Shakespeare. He did not quote from them, but his style showed plainly his close intimacy with the Scriptures and the great bard. Douglas was eminently talented, Lincoln was original. But what made Lincoln vastly more effective in this contest was that even the most obtuse hearer could see at once that Douglas spoke for himself, and Lincoln for his cause.

Source: Memoirs of Gustave Koerner, II.

SOME OF THE DEBATE

Lincoln, at Springfield

"A house divided against itself cannot stand." I believe this government cannot endure permanently half slave and half free .... I do not expect the house to fall; but I do expect it will cease to be divided. It will become all one thing, or all the other.

Douglas, of Chicago

Mr. Lincoln advocates boldly and clearly a war of sections, a war of the North against the South, of the Free States against the Slave States . . . . He objects to the Dred Scott decision because it does not put the negro in the possession of citizenship on an equality with the white man. I am opposed to negro equality .... I am in favor of preserving, not only the purity of the blood, but the purity of the government from any mixture or amalgamation with inferior races.

Lincoln, at Chicago

I protest, now and forever, against that counterfeit logic which presumes that because I do not want a negro woman for a slave, I do necessarily want her for a wife. My understanding is that I need not have her for either, but, as God made us separate, we can leave one another alone, and do one another much good thereby .... The Judge regales us with the terrible enormities that take place by the mixture of races . . . . Why, Judge, if we do not let them get together in the Territories, they won't mix there.

From *Political Debates between Abraham Lincoln and Stephen A. Douglas in the Celebrated Campaign of 1858 in Illinois* (Cleveland, Ohio: The Arthur H. Clark Company, 1902), pp. 1, 14, 18, 33.

HOW WELL DID YOU UNDERSTAND THIS SELECTION?

1. How does Koerner describe the scene of the debates and the candidates?

2. Who does he think was the more effective debater? Why?

3. Douglas won re-election. Do you feel he won the debate? Why or why not?

4. How did the two men differ on issues like slavery, race, and the possibilities of war?

5. Some modern commentators have argued that Lincoln was a racist. If that is so, how would you describe Douglas?

John Brown, a fanatic antislavery activist who had been involved in bloody exploits in Kansas, seized the federal arsenal at Harper's Ferry, Virginia. His ostensible plan was to distribute arms to slaves who would join him in rebellion. His long-term goal was to cause a violent showdown that would ultimately free the slaves. His small "army" was easily defeated, and all the raiders were killed or captured. To Southerners, Brown symbolized everything evil and dangerous in abolitionism. But many Northerners, particularly abolitionists and African Americans, thought of Brown and his raiders as heroes. The first letter was sent to Brown from a northern black woman. The second letter came from John Copeland, a fugitive slave, who was one of Brown's men. He was captured and sentenced to death.

Dear Friend:

Although the hands of Slavery throw a barrier between you and me, and it may not be my privilege to see you in the prison house, Virginia has no bolts or bars through which I dread to send you my sympathy. In the name of the young girl sold from the warm clasp of a mother's arms to the clutches of a libertine or profligate ,—in the name of the slave mother, her heart rocked to and fro by the agony of her mournful separations—I thank you that you have been brave enough to reach out your hands to the crushed and blighted of my race. You have rocked the bloody Bastille; and I hope from your sad fate great good may arise to the cause of freedom. Already from your prison has come a shout of triumph against the giant sin of our country ....

We may earnestly hope that your fate will not be a vain lesson, that it will intensify our hatred of Slavery and love of Freedom, and that your martyr grave will be a sacred altar upon which men will record their vows of undying hatred to that system which tramples on man and bids defiance to God. I have written to your dear wife, and sent her a few dollars, and I pledge myself to you that I will continue to assist her ....

Letter to John Brown, in prison, from a free black woman,
FRANCES ELLEN WATKINS,
Kendallville, Indiana, November 25, 1859

Dear Brother:

. .. It was a sense of the wrongs that we have suffered that prompted the noble but unfortunate John Brown and his associates to attempt to give freedom to a small number, at least, of those who are now held by cruel and unjust laws, and by no less cruel and unjust men. To this freedom they were entitled by every known principle of justice and humanity, and for the enjoyment of it God created them. And now, dear brother, could I die in a more noble cause? Could I, brother, die in a manner and for a cause which could induce true and honest men more to honor me, and the angels more readily to receive me to their happy home of everlasting joy above... ? And were it not that I know that the hearts of those to whom I am attached by the nearest and most enduring ties of blood relationship-yea by the closest and strongest ties that god has instituted-will be filled with sorrow, I would almost as soon die now as at any time, for I feel that I am now prepared to meet my maker ....

JOHN A. COPELAND,
sentenced to death for participating in the Harpers Ferry Raid, in a letter to his brother,
December 10, 1859

HOW WELL DID YOU UNDERSTAND THIS SELECTION?

1. Why did John Brown seem to strike such an emotional chord among African Americans?

2. What reaction do you think Southerners would have to his exploits?

3. Why did this man excite such emotion among his opponents and defenders?

Although the states of the lower South seceded immediately after Lincoln's election, he still hoped to avoid confrontation, preserve the loyalty of the states of the upper South, and allow eventual voluntary reunion. Fort Sumter, in Charleston harbor, had become a symbol of Union presence and resolve. Major Robert Anderson, in command of the fort, sent word that the garrison would have to evacuate unless its supplies were restocked. Lincoln notified the governor of South Carolina that he was sending "provisions only" to the fort. In response, the Confederates demanded its surrender and opened fire when Anderson failed to give a satisfactory response. On April 14, the garrison surrendered after 33 hours of bombardment. The war had begun. Mary Chestnut was a southern diarist known for her pointed and perceptive comments.

April 8-15, 1861
Charleston, South Carolina
MARY BOYKIN CHESTNUT

APRIL 8, 1861

Went to see Miss Pinckney one of the last o the old-world Pinckneys. Governor Manning walked in, bowed gravely, and seated himself by me. Again he bowed low in mock-heroic style and with a grand wave of his hand said, "Madam, your country is invaded." When I had breath to speak I asked, "What does he mean?" He meant this: There are six men-of war outside the bar. Talbot and Chew have come to say that hostilities are to begin. Governor Pickens and Beauregard are holding a council of war.

Mr. Chesnut then came in and confirmed the story. Wigfall next entered in boisterous spirits and said, "There was a sound of revelry by night." The men went off almost immediately. And I crept silently to my room, where I sat down to a good cry.

Mrs. Wigfall came in, and we had it out on the subject of civil war. We solaced ourselves with dwelling on all its known horrors, and then we added what we had a right to expect with Yankees in front and Negroes in the rear. "The slaveowners must expect a servile insurrection, of course," said Mrs. Wigfall, to make sure that we were unhappy enough. Suddenly loud shouting was heard. We ran out. Cannon after cannon roared. We met Mrs. Allen Green in the passageway, with blanched cheeks and streaming eyes. Governor Means rushed out of his room in his dressing gown and begged us to be calm. "Governor Pickens," said he, "has ordered, in the plenitude of his wisdom, seven cannon to be fired as a signal to the Seventh Regiment. Anderson [Major Robert Anderson, commander of the fort) will hear as well as the Seventh Regiment. Now you go back and be quiet; fighting in the streets has not begun yet."

So we retired. No sleep for anybody last night. The streets were alive with soldiers, men shouting, marching,-singing. Wigfall, the stormy petrel, is in his glory, the only thoroughly happy person I see. Today things seem to have settled down a little. One can but hope still. Lincoln or Seward has made such silly advances and then far sillier drawings back. There may be a chance for peace after all. Things are happening so fast. My husband has been made an aide-de-camp to General Beauregard . . . . Governor Means has rummaged a sword and red sash from somewhere and brought it for Colonel Chesnut, who had gone to demand the surrender of Fort Sumter. And now, patience we must wait.

Why did that green goose Anderson go into Fort Sumter? Then everything began to go wrong. Now they have intercepted a letter from him, urging them to let him surrender. He paints the horrors likely to ensue if they will not. He ought to have thought of all that before he put his head in the hole.

Anderson will not capitulate. Yesterday's was the merriest, maddest dinner we have had yet. Men were audaciously wise and witty. We had an unspoken foreboding that it was to be our last pleasant meeting. Mr. Miles dined with us today. Mrs. Henry King rushed in saying: "The news, I come for the latest news! All the men of the King family are on the island," of which fact she seemed proud.

I do not pretend to go to sleep. How can I? If Anderson does not accept terms at four, the orders are he shall be fired upon. I count four, St. Michael's bells chime out, and I begin to hope. At half past four the heavy booming of a cannon. I sprang out of bed, and on my knees prostrate I prayed as I never prayed before.

There was a sound of stir all over the house, pattering of feet in the corridors. All seemed hurrying one way. I put on my double gown and a shawl and went too. It was to the housetop. The shells were bursting. In the dark I heard a man say, "Waste of ammunition." I knew my husband was rowing a boat somewhere in that dark bay. If Anderson was obstinate, Colonel Chesnut was to order the fort on one side to open fire. Certainly fire had begun. The regular roar of the cannon, there it was. And who could tell what each volley accomplished of death and destruction?

The women were wild there on the housetop. Prayers came from the women and imprecations from the men. And then a shell would light up the scene. Tonight they say the forces are to attempt to land. We watched up there, and everybody wondered that Fort Sumter did not fire a shot . . . .

We hear nothing, can listen to nothing; boom, boom, goes the cannon all the time. The nervous strain is awful, alone in this darkened room.

APRIL 13

Nobody has been hurt after all. How gay we were last night! Reaction after the dread of all the slaughter we thought those dreadful cannon were making. Not even a battery the worse for wear. Fort Sumter has been on fire. Anderson has not yet silenced any of our guns. So the aides, still with swords and red sashes by way of uniform, tell us. But the sound of those guns makes regular meals impossible. None of us goes to table. Tea trays pervade the corridors, going everywhere. Some of the anxious hearts lie on their beds and moan in solitary misery. Mrs. Wigfall and I solace ourselves with tea in my room. These women have all a satisfying faith. "God is on our side," they say. When we are shut in Mrs. Wigfall and I ask, "Why?" "Of course, He hates the Yankees," we are told, "You'll think that well of Him."

Not by one word or look can we detect any change in the demeanor of these Negro servants. Lawrence sits at our door, sleepy and respectful, and profoundly indifferent. So are they all, but they carry it too far. You could not tell that they even heard the awful roar going on in the bay, though it has been dinning in their ears night and day. People talk before them as if they were chairs and tables. They make no sign. Are they stolidly stupid? or wiser than we are; silent and strong, biding their time?

APRIL 15

I did not know that one could live such days of excitement. Some one called: "Come out! There is a crowd coming." A mob it was, indeed, but it was headed by Colonels Chesnut and Manning. The crowd was shouting and showing these two as messengers of good news. They were escorted to Beauregard's headquarters. Fort Sumter had surrendered! Those upon the housetops shouted to us, "The fort is on fire." That had been the story once or twice before. But it is all confusion. Our flag is flying there. Fire engines have been sent for to put out the fire.

Everybody tells you half of something and then rushes off to tell something else or to hear the last news.

Source: Mary Boykin Chesnut, *A Diary from Dixie* (New York, 1905).

HOW WELL DID YOU UNDERSTAND THIS SELECTION?

1. How did the people of Charleston react to the events at Fort Sumter? Why did they seem so happy and excited?

2. How did the Negro servants react? What did their response indicate?

SLAVERY IS THE CORNERSTONE OF THE CONFEDERACY
By Alexander H. Stephens

In many ways, slavery was the key to southern secession. Both sides acknowledged its importance. In his 1861 speech, Alexander Stephens, vice president of the Confederate States of America, describes the Confederate Constitution and compares it to the Constitution of the United States. He reaffirms the total commitment to slavery in the Confederate Constitution.

But not to be tedious in enumerating the numerous changes for the better, allow me to allude to one other-though last, not least. The new constitution has put at rest, *forever*, all the agitating questions relating to our peculiar institution-African slavery as it exists amongst us-the proper status of the negro in our form of civilization. This was the immediate cause of the late rupture and present revolution. Jefferson in his forecast, had anticipated this, as the "rock upon which the old Union would split." He was right. What was conjecture with him, is now a realized fact. But whether he fully comprehended the great truth upon which that rock *stood* and *stands*, may be doubted. The prevailing ideas entertained by him and most of the leading statesmen at the time of the formation of the old constitution, were that the enslavement of the African was in violation of the laws of nature; that it was wrong in principle, socially, morally, and politically. It was an evil they knew not well how to deal with, but the general opinion of the men of that day was that, somehow or other in the order of Providence, the institution would be evanescent and pass away. This idea, though not incorporated in the constitution, was the prevailing idea at that time. The constitution, it is true, secured every essential guarantee to the institution while it should last, and hence no argument can be justly urged against the constitutional guarantees thus secured, because of the common sentiment of the day. Those ideas, however, were fundamentally wrong. They rested upon the assumption of the equality of races. This was an error. It was a sandy foundation, and the government built upon it fell, when the "storm came and the wind blew."

Our new government is founded upon exactly the opposite idea; its foundations are laid, its corner-stone rests upon the great truth, that the negro is not equal to the white man; that slavery-subordination to the superior race-is his natural and normal condition.

This, our new government, is the first, in the history of the world, based upon this great physical, philosophical, and moral truth. This truth has been slow in the process of its development, like all other truths in the various departments of science. It has been so even amongst us. Many who hear me, perhaps, can recollect well, that this truth was not generally admitted, even within their day. The errors of the past generation still clung to many as late as twenty years ago. Those at the North, who still cling to these errors, with a zeal above knowledge, we justly denominate fanatics. All fanaticism springs from an aberration of the mind-from a defect in reasoning. It is a species of insanity. One of the most striking characteristics of insanity, in many instances, is forming correct conclusions from fancied or erroneous premises; so with the anti-slavery fanatics; their conclusions are right if their premises were. They assume that the negro is equal, and hence conclude that he is entitled to equal privileges and rights with the white man. If their premises were correct, their conclusions would be logical and just-but their premise being wrong, their whole argument fails. I recollect once of having heard a gentleman from one of the northern States, of great power and ability, announce in the House of Representatives, with imposing effect, that we of the South would be compelled, ultimately, to yield upon this subject of slavery, that it was as impossible to war successfully against a principle in politics, as it was in physics or mechanics. That the principle would ultimately prevail. That we, in maintaining slavery as it exists with us, were warring against a principle, a principle founded in nature, the principle of the equality of men. The reply I made to him was, that upon his own grounds, we should, ultimately, succeed, and that he and his associates, in this crusade against our institutions, would ultimately fail. The truth announced, that it was as impossible to war successfully against a principle in politics as it was in physics and mechanics, I admitted; but told him that it was he, and those acting with him, who were warring against a principle. They were attempting to make things equal which the Creator had made unequal.

In the conflict thus far, success has been on our side, complete throughout the length and breadth of the Confederate States. It is upon this, as I have stated, our social fabric is firmly planted; and I cannot permit myself to doubt the ultimate success of a full recognition of this principle throughout the civilized and enlightened world.

As I have stated, the truth of this principle may be slow in development, as all truths are and ever have been, in the various branches of science. It was so with the principles announced by Galileo-it was so with Adam Smith and his principles of political economy. It was so with [William] Harvey, and his theory of the circulation of the blood. It is stated that not a single one of the medical profession, living at the time of the announcement of the truths made by him, admitted them. Now, they are universally acknowledged. May we not, therefore, look with confidence to the ultimate universal acknowledgment of the truths upon which our system rests? It is the first government ever instituted upon the principles in strict conformity to nature, and the ordination of Providence, in furnishing the materials of human society. Many governments have been founded upon the principle of the subordination and serfdom of certain classes of the same race; such were and are in violation of the laws of nature. Our system commits no such violation of nature's laws. With us, all of the white race, however high or low, rich or poor, are equal in the eye of the law. Not so with the negro. Subordination is his place. He, by nature, or by the curse against Canaan, is fitted for that condition which he occupies in our system. The architect, in the construction of buildings, lays the foundation with the proper material-the granite; then comes the brick or the marble. The substratum of our society is made of the material fitted by nature for it, and by experience we know that it is best, not only for the superior, but for the inferior race, that it should be so. It is, indeed, in conformity with the ordinance of the Creator. It is not for us to inquire into the wisdom of his ordinances, or to question them. For his own purposes, he has made one race to differ from another, as he has made "one star to differ from another star in glory."

The great objects of humanity are best attained when there is conformity to his laws and decrees, in the formation of governments as well as in all things else. Our confederacy is founded upon principles in strict conformity with these laws. This stone which was rejected by the first builders "is become the chief of the corner"-the real "corner-stone"-in our new edifice.

I have been asked, what of the future? It has been apprehended by some that we would have arrayed against us the civilized world. I care not who or how many they may be against us, when we stand upon the eternal principles of truth, if we are true to ourselves and the principles for which we contend, we are obliged to, and must triumph.

Thousands of people who begin to understand these truths are not yet completely out of the shell; they do not see them in their length and breadth. We hear much of the civilization and christianization of the barbarous tribes of Africa. In my judgment, those ends will never be attained, but by first teaching them the lesson taught to Adam, that "in the sweat of his brow he should eat his bread," and teaching them to work, and feed, and clothe themselves.

Henry Cleveland, *Alexander H. Stephens in Public and Private* (Philadelphia: National Publishing Company, 1866), pp. 721-23.

HOW WELL DID YOU UNDERSTAND THIS SELECTION?

1. What great truth does Stephens say is the "corner-stone" of the new government?

2. What arguments does Stephens give to support the institution of slavery?

3. Do you think that slavery was the basic cause of the Civil War? Why or why not?

SELF TEST:

MULTIPLE CHOICE: Circle the correct response. The correct answers are given at the end.

1. The election of James K. Polk as president in 1844 was widely regarded as a popular mandate for
   a. going to war with Mexico
   b. reintroducing the slave trade
   c. expanding American territory westward
   d. spreading slavery into the territories

2. The most significant question that arose from the results of the Mexican War was
   a. how to prevent another deadly war
   b. what to do about slavery in the new territories gained from the war
   c. how to restrain the president's ability to start wars
   d. how to deal with the citizenship of Mexicans in the territories

3. The idea of "popular sovereignty" was that the issue of slavery in the territories would be decided by
   a. votes by residents in each territory
   b. an amendment to the Constitution
   c. a national referendum
   d. a congressional resolution

4. The Wilmot Proviso, if passed, would have
   a. annexed most of northern Mexico to the United States
   b. prevented another war with Mexico
   c. banned slavery in all territories transferred from Mexico to the United States
   d. allowed the citizens of the territories to decide the issue of slavery

5. The section of the Compromise of 1850 that led to the greatest sectional controversy was
   a. California's admission to the Union as a free state
   b. the abolition of the slave trade in the District of Columbia
   c. the settlement of the Texas-New Mexico boundary controversy
   d. the enforcement of the Fugitive Slave Act

6. Opponents of the Kansas-Nebraska Act were angry because they believed it
   a. repealed the Missouri Compromise
   b. would destroy the Compromise of 1850
   c. was contrary to the *Dred Scott* decision
   d. mandated slavery in Kansas and Nebraska

7. Members of the new Republican Party in the 1850s agreed that
   a. slavery should be abolished immediately
   b. blacks should be given full civil and voting rights
   c. slavery in the territories should be determined by popular sovereignty
   d. slavery should be banned in all territories in the West

8. In his raid on Harper's Ferry, John Brown seemed to expect
   a. the Southerners to agree to compromise on the issue of slavery
   b. the northern public to rise up in his support
   c. the slaves to revolt against their masters
   d. Congress to admit Kansas to the union as a free state

9. The clearest differences between Lincoln and Douglas in their famous debates concerned
   a. the immediate abolition of slavery
   b. the morality of slavery
   c. the belief that voters in territories should not bar slavery
   d. support for settlers in Kansas

10. Southern "fire eaters" and northern Republicans seemed in agreement that
    a. the *Dred Scott* decision mandated the federal government to protect slavery in the territories
    b. Stephen Douglas's plan for popular sovereignty in the territories was unworkable
    c. the survival of slavery depended on its continuous expansion
    d. all of the above

Answers: 1-c; 2-b; 3-a; 4-c; 5-d; 6-a; 7-d; 8-c; 9-b; 10-d.

ESSAYS:

1. What was the relationship between America's territorial expansion in the 1840s and slavery? Why was it so much more difficult to settle the conflict over the expansion of slavery in the 1850s than it had been in the 1820s when the Missouri Compromise had been accepted?

2. Explain how each of the following caused increasing tension and distrust between the North and South
    A. California's bid for admission to the Union
    B. the Fugitive Slave Act
    C. the publication of *Uncle Tom's Cabin*
    D. "Bleeding Kansas"
    E. the *Dred Scott* decision
    F. John Brown's raid on Harper's Ferry

3. Can it be argued that there was no single factor that caused the Civil War? What do you feel was the basic cause(s) of the Civil War? Give at least five specific events to support your point of view.

OPTIONAL ACTIVITIES: (Use your imagination **and** knowledge.)

1. Imagine that you are a writer for an abolitionist newspaper in Massachusetts. Write an editorial about the Fugitive Slave Law and the experience of one specific fugitive slave (such as Anthony Burns).

2. Assume you are a Southerner who is writing a letter to a national magazine in response to *Uncle Tom's Cabin*. Include your main arguments against the book's point of view.

4. Pretend that you are a member of John Brown's band at Harper's Ferry. Write a diary of your experiences.

WEB SITE LISTINGS:

Mexican War: This is the most complete site with links to numerous sites, images, maps, and documents.
    http://www.dmwv.org/mexwar
Documenting the American South
    http://metalab.unc.edu/docsouth/
Library of Congress includes excellent material on African Americans before the Civil War
    http://lcweb.loc.gov/exhibits/african/intro.html
Causes of the Civil War:
    http://www.civilwarhome.com (includes many links to other sites)
    http://www.lincoln.lib.niu.edu
Sites covering specific events such as Abolitionism, Kansas, Dred Scott
    /speeches/garrison.htm" http://www.historyplace.com/lincoln/kansas.htm
                                 /speeches/garrison.htm
                                 /dred.htm
     http://grid.let.rug.nl/~usa/E/dred_scott/scottxx.htm
                            /D/1826-1850/slavery/contesxx.htm
                                /fugitxx.htm

Chapter Eleven

THE CIVIL WAR

The most devastating war in American history had begun. The initial calls for troops, issued by both Abraham Lincoln and his Confederate counterpart, Jefferson Davis, were met with overwhelming enthusiasm in both the North and South. Sharing a common culture, both governments and peoples reacted to the economic, military, and political problems arising from the war in remarkably similar ways. Both were confronted with major organizational problems in forming effective governments: the Confederacy because it lacked any formal national structure and the Union because Lincoln was the nation's first Republican president and was faced with the novel problem of secession.

After the Lower South had seceded and fighting broke out when Fort Sumter was fired upon, the loyalties of the Upper South became a key issue. The secession of Virginia, as well as Arkansas, Tennessee, and North Carolina, strengthened the Confederacy in population and resources. Lincoln succeeded in keeping Maryland and Kentucky, along with Delaware and Missouri, in the Union. The continued loyalty of these states was so important that Lincoln was careful to avoid any antislavery action that might have threatened their allegiance.

At first glance, it would have seemed as if the advantages of the North should have easily overwhelmed the South. The North maintained an immense superiority in population, industrial system, transportation system, and capital resources. The advantages of fighting a defensive war on its own extensive territory with superior officers, however, ensured that the South would be able to hold out for a lengthy period of time. As the war dragged on, the northern material superiority became increasingly decisive.

As the early enthusiasm began to fade, both governments were faced with the problem of raising troops. In early 1862, the Confederacy enacted a conscription act with many exemptions, designed to encourage reenlistments. Later that year, the Union followed with its own draft law that, with its exemptions for those able to buy their way out, was met with public outrage. This anger erupted in the brutal New York City Draft Riots of 1863. Both governments encountered as much difficulty in financing their war efforts, as they did in raising armies. Neither had a national bank or a viable national currency. Both were faced with the reality that burdensome taxes would have dampened ardor for the war and substantial borrowing was impossible. (Eventually, the Union did find an important source of revenue in the issuance of bonds.) By 1862 both began to depend on the issuing of paper money, backed only by the promise to redeem the notes someday in the future. The resulting inflation, far more damaging in the South, was particularly harmful to poorer people.

Both sides also had to deal with issues in foreign relations. The South hoped for European intervention based on the supposed dependency of industrial economies on "King Cotton." Northern efforts were directed at ensuring European neutrality. In the end, the stance of various European nations arose from each government's view of its own national self-interest.

After the surprising rout of Union troops at the first Battle of Bull Run, the war settled into a stalemate in 1861 and 1862. One reason was that most of the generals on both sides had been trained at West Point and thought alike in stressing seizing the enemy's capital and conquering territory. Lincoln had particular problems in finding a general who was daring, original, and intelligent enough to use the North's natural superiority in resources to advantage. The North settled on a three-part strategy. The first was to divide the South in half by controlling the Mississippi River. The second was to blockade the Confederate coastline to prevent the export of southern cotton and tobacco and the import of essential manufactured goods. As the war progressed, the blockade became increasingly effective. The third element was to capture the Confederate capital, Richmond, temptingly close to the nation's capital of Washington D.C. The North hoped to combine exhaustion and destruction to achieve victory.

After a series of bitter and costly battles, the war's momentum began to gradually shift. Union forces stopped Lee's advance into Maryland at the bloody Battle of Antietam in September 1862. Although the Union fumbled its chance to win a major triumph, Lincoln used this "victory" as the opportunity to announce his Emancipation Proclamation to take effect January 1, 1863. Justified as an act of "military necessity," it declared that slaves would be freed in states still in rebellion. It also authorized the enlistment of blacks into the Union army. The excellent battle record of black regiments in the latter parts of the war helped moderate views about black inferiority. The Proclamation also brought about a new war aim, transforming the Union army into an army of liberation. This, in turn, made it impossible for the European public, overwhelmingly antislavery, to support the South.

Decisive Union victories in July 1863 seemed to foreshadow the beginning of the end. General Ulysses S. Grant, after a lengthy siege at Vicksburg, won a daring victory and control of the Mississippi River. At the same time, Robert E. Lee's audacious gamble led to a conclusive Confederate defeat at Gettysburg. Lee hobbled back to defend Richmond. Grant became the Union commander-in-chief and adopted Lincoln's strategy of simultaneous advances.

As the northern economy boomed to meet wartime needs, the South's resources eroded and economic devastation loomed, leading to civilian discontent and military desertions. By the end of 1864, Davis was actually considering a suggestion to arm slaves, a desperate move that would have undermined the very existence of slavery. Davis, further undermined by southern attachment to states rights, faced division and criticism. Lincoln also was attacked by southern sympathizers ("copperheads"), critics of his violations of civil liberties, and radicals who disliked his cautiousness. The growing weariness with Grant's war of attrition and its resulting appalling casualty lists even seemed to threaten Lincoln's reelection in 1864. His political fortunes and the continued pursuit of the war were rescued by news of Sherman's occupation of Atlanta. Sherman's punishing "March to the Sea" and Grant's devastating push to Richmond finally sealed the fate of the Confederacy, leading to the surrender at Appomattox.

Thus ended the terrible and bloody conflict that caused the deaths of more Americans than in all other wars combined up to Vietnam. The slave-based economy of the South lay in ruins. The power of the federal government increased, and the northern ideology of inevitable progress and modernization was triumphant. Four million black slaves were now free, and the nation faced the issue of what their place would be in America in the future. The necessity of finding a balance between punishment and restoration of the Union also would remain the task of Reconstruction.

IDENTIFICATION: Briefly describe each term

Ulysses S. Grant

Robert E. Lee

First Battle of Bull Run

George McClellan

Suspension of the writ of *habeas corpus*

"King Cotton"

Jefferson Davis

William Seward

Salmon Chase

Edwin Stanton

"Greenbacks"

The blockade

The Trent Affair

William Tecumseh Sherman

Battle of Shiloh

The *Merrimack* and the *Monitor*

Stonewall Jackson

Second Battle of Bull Run

Battle of Antietam

Battle of Fredericksburg

"Copperheads"

The Homestead Act

The Morrill Act

The Emancipation Proclamation

The U.S. Sanitary Commission

The New York Draft Riot

Black troops

Andersonville prison

Dorothea Dix

Clara Barton

Battle of Chancellorsville

Gettysburg

Vicksburg

The Gettysburg Address

Battle of the Wilderness

Petersburg

Sherman's March to the Sea

The Election of 1864

THINK ABOUT:

1. It has been said that the Civil War was the first modern war in weapons, techniques, and tactics. To what extent was that true? In what other ways was the Civil War similar to the world wars of the twentieth century? How did it differ from those wars?

2. Why did President Lincoln narrow his war aims to the single one of saving the Union in 1861? Why did he then widen those objectives in 1863 to include freeing the slaves?

3. Had you been a resident of a border state in 1861 would you have favored or opposed secession? Why? Would you have fought for one side or the other in the war? Why?

4. Why was the war stalemated for so long? What changes in military strategies or tactics might have hastened the end of the war?

5. If the Union had not won major victories in late 1864 and Lincoln had lost his bid for reelection, what would the consequences have been for the rest of the war? How would the history of America have been changed?

FIRST BATTLE OF BULL RUN

When the war began, both North and South were overcome with enthusiasm. Each assumed the war would be over in a few weeks. The first battle and its unheard-of casualties, a decisive Union debacle, which the Confederate army was unable to capitalize on, quickly sobered the public. William Russell, a well-known correspondent of the London Times, *wrote this account of the battle, which angered many Northerners, including President Lincoln.*

July 21, 1861
Manassas, Virginia

WILLIAM HOWARD RUSSELL

Centreville appeared in sight-a few houses on our front, beyond which rose a bald hill, the slopes covered with bivouac huts, commissariat carts, and horses, and the top crested with spectators of the fight.

The scene was so peaceful a man might well doubt the evidence of one's sense that a great contest was being played out below in bloodshed . . . . But the cannon spoke out loudly from the green bushes, and the plains below were mottled, so to speak, by puffs of smoke and by white rings from bursting shells and capricious howitzers . . . . With the glass I could detect now and then the flash of arms through the dust clouds in the open, but no one could tell to which side the troops who were moving belonged, and I could only judge from the smoke whether the guns were fired towards or away from the hill. In the midst of our little reconnaissance Mr. Vizetelly, who has been living and, indeed, marching with one of the regiments as artist of the Illustrated London News, came up and told us the action had been commenced in splendid style by the Federalists, who had advanced steadily, driving the Confederates before them-a part of the plan, as I firmly believe, to bring them under the range of their guns. He believed the advantages on the Federalist side were decided, though won with hard fighting.

As I turned down into the narrow road, or lane, there was a forward movement among the large four-wheeled tilt waggons, when suddenly there arose a tumult in front of me at a small bridge across the road, and then I perceived the drivers of a set of waggons with the horses turned towards me, who were endeavouring to force their way against the stream of vehicles setting in the other direction. By the side of the new set of waggons there were a number of commissariat men and soldiers, whom at first sight I took to be the baggage guard. They looked excited and alarmed and were running by the side of the horses-in front the dust quite obscured the view. At the bridge the currents met in wild disorder. "Turn back! Retreat!" shouted the men from the front, "We're whipped, we're whipped!" They cursed and tugged at the horses' heads, and struggled with frenzy to get past.

I got my horse up into the field out of the road, and went on rapidly towards the front. Soon I met soldiers who were coming through the corn, mostly without arms; and presently I saw firelocks, cooking tins, knapsacks, and great-coats on the ground, and observed that the confusion and speed of the baggage-carts became greater, and that many of them were crowded with men, or were followed by others, who clung to them. The ambulances were crowded with soldiers, but it did not look as if there were many wounded. Negro servants on led horses dashed frantically past; men in uniform, whom it were a disgrace to the profession of arms to call "soldiers," swarmed by on mules, chargers, and even draught horses, which had been cut out of carts or waggons, and went on with harness clinging to their heels, as frightened as their riders. Men literally screamed with rage and fright when their way was blocked up. On I rode, asking all "What is all this about?" and now and then, but rarely, receiving the answer, "We're whipped;" or, "We're repulsed." Faces black and dusty, tongues out in the heat, eyes staring-it was a most wonderful sight.

All the road from Centreville for miles presented such a sight as can only be witnessed in the track of the runaways of an utterly demoralized army. Drivers flogged, lashed, spurred, and beat their horses, or leaped down and abandoned their teams, and ran by the side of the road; mounted men, servants, and men in uniform, vehicles of all sorts, commissariat waggons thronged the narrow ways. At every shot a convulsion as it were seized upon the morbid mass of bones, sinew, wood, and iron, and thrilled through it, giving new energy and action to its desperate efforts to get free from itself . . . . The Federalists, utterly routed, had fallen back upon Arlington to defend the capital, leaving nearly five batteries of artillery, 8,000 muskets, immense quantity of stores and baggage, and their wounded and prisoners in the hands of the enemy!

Source: The London *Times*, August 6, 1861.

HOW WELL DID YOU UNDERSTAND THIS SELECTION?

1. How does Russell characterize the actions of the "Federalist" (Union) army?

2. What impact do you think his report would have had in England?

3. How would the outcome of this first battle of the war have affected the attitudes and actions of both sides?

Although Lincoln declared that the war was a "struggle to save the Union and is not either to save or destroy slavery," the issue of slavery, the basic cause of the war, continued to linger above the conflict. Early in the war, Southerners continued to argue that slavery was a source of strength to them. Northern officers increasingly noticed that the slaves were taking matters into their own hands by fleeing to Union lines.

A UNION GENERAL ON THE SIGNIFICANCE OF SLAVES

In September and October last, and perhaps as late as November (1861) in two or three instances, orders came from the headquarters of the army of the Potomac, directing that such and such persons naming them-claiming to have slaves in one of my camps. .. should be permitted to search the camp, and reclaim their slaves. I addressed a communication. . . stating that such steps would likely lead to disorder and mischief in the camps; because in several instances the sympathies of the men [Union soldiers] had been excited by seeing slaves, reclaimed under such circumstances, very harshly treated ....

The most valuable and reliable information of the enemy's movements in our vicinity that we have been able to get derived [originated] from Negroes who came into our lines ....

...They will submit to any privation, perform any duty, incur any danger. I know an instance in which four of them recently carried a boat from the Rappahannock River [Virginia], passing through the enemy's pickets successfully, to the Potomac and crossed over to my camp and reported themselves there. They gave us information of the enemy's force which was communicated to headquarters; a service upon which it would be difficult to fix a price. These services rendered by these men are known to the soldiers, and contribute, I presume, largely to the sympathy they feel for them ....

...There was one case in the 5th regiment where a man named Cox claimed some slaves. He was very badly treated by the soldiers. He came there with an order from the division headquarters for two or three slaves. He pointed out who they were and undertook to take them away; but the soldiers pounced upon him and beat him severely ....He went away without his slaves.

With our people there was a feeling of indignation against it, from the lowest to the highest; it was a universal feeling.

Testimony of GENERAL DANIEL E. SICKLES before the *Joint Committee on the Conduct of the War, 37th [US] Congress, Third Session 1862*

A SOUTHERN NEWSPAPER ON THE "ADVANTAGES" OF SLAVERY

The total white population of the eleven States now comprising the Confederacy is 6,000,000, and therefore to fill up the ranks of the proposed army (600,000) about ten per cent of the entire white population will be required. In any other country but our own such a draft could not be met, but the Southern States can furnish that number of men, and still not leave the material interests of the country in a suffering condition. Those who are incapacitated for bearing arms can oversee the plantation, and the Negroes can go on undisturbed in their usual labors. In the North, the case is different; the men who join the army of subjugation are the laborers, the producers and the factory operatives. Nearly every man from that section, especially those from the rural districts, leaves some branch of industry to suffer during his absence. The institution of slavery in the South alone enables her to place in the field a force much larger in proportion to her white population in the North ....The institution is a tower of strength to the South, particularly at the present crisis, and our enemies will be likely to find that the "moral cancer" about which their orators are so fond of prating, is really one of the most effective weapons employed against the union by the South.

Editorial in the MONTGOMERY ADVERTISER,
Alabama, November 6, 1861

A NORTHERN GENERAL ON SLAVERY AS A MILITARY QUESTION

Sir:

Since I wrote my last dispatch the question in regard to slave property is becoming one of very serious magnitude. The inhabitants of Virginia are using their Negroes in the batteries, and are preparing to send the women and children South. The escapes [of slaves] from them are very numerous and a squad [of escaped slaves] has come in this morning to my pickets bringing their women and children ....Twelve of these Negroes I am informed have escaped from the erection of batteries on Sewall's Point which this morning fired upon my expedition as it passed by out of range. As a means of offense therefore in the enemy's hands these Negroes when able bodied are of... importance. Without them the batteries could not have been erected at least for many weeks. As a military question it would seem to be a measure of necessity to deprive their masters of their services. How can this be done? As a political question and as a question of humanity can I receive the services of a father and mother and not take the children? Of the humanitarian aspect I have no doubt. Of the political one I have no right to judge. I therefore submit all of this to your better judgement ....

Letter from GENERAL BENJAMIN BUTLER to General-in-Chief Winfield Scott, May 27, 1861

HOW WELL DID YOU UNDERSTAND THIS SELECTION?

1. What attitude towards slavery does General Sickles attribute to his men?

2. How would such an attitude affect the actions of Union troops and the treatment of slaves?

3. Why does the southern newspaper consider slavery to be an advantage for the South?

4. What flaws, if any, do you find in its argument?

5. What actions by slaves does General Butler report?

6. In the long run, how do you think slavery and the reaction of slaves would affect the outcome of the war?

As the war dragged on with its appalling casualties, many people realized that there was a large source of manpower still unused: African Americans. However, allowing blacks to be soldiers would seem to suggest that white Northerners were willing to recognize them as equals. Blacks, like the great abolitionist leader, Frederick Douglass, argued passionately for the use of African-American soldiers. Many white Northerners were equally vehement in their opposition.

Newspaper Editorial by Frederick Douglass

Our Presidents, Governors, Generals and Secretaries are calling, with almost frantic vehemence, for men- "Men! men! send us men!" they scream, or the cause of the Union is gone; ... and yet these very officers, representing the people and Government, steadily and persistently refuse to receive the very class of men which have a deeper interest in the defeat and humiliation of the rebels, than all others .... What a spectacle of blind, unreasoning prejudice and pusillanimity is this! The national edifice is on fire. Every man who can carry a bucket of water, or remove a brick, is wanted; but those who have the care of the building, having a profound respect for the feeling of the national burglars who set the building on fire are determined that the flames shall only be extinguished by Indo-Caucasian hands, and to have the building burnt rather than save it by means of any other. Such is the pride, the stupid prejudice and folly that rules the hour.

　　　Why does the Government reject the negro? Is he not a man? Can he not wield a sword, fire a gun, march and countermarch, and obey orders like any other? . . . If persons so humble as we can be allowed to speak to the President of the United States, we should ask him if this dark and terrible hour of the nation's extremity is a time for consulting a mere vulgar and unnatural prejudice? . . . We would tell him that this is no time to fight with one hand, when both are needed; that this is no time to fight only with your white hand, and allow your black hand to remain tied .... While the Government continues to refuse the aid of colored men, thus alienating them from the national cause, and giving the rebels the advantage of them, it will not deserve better fortunes than it has thus far experienced.-Men in earnest don't fight with one hand, when they might fight with two, and a man drowning would not refuse to be saved even by a colored hand.

Source: *Douglass' Monthly*, September 1861.

PUBLIC OPPOSITION TO USE OF BLACK TROOPS

Letter to the Editor,

I am quite sure there is not one man in ten but would feel himself degraded as a volunteer if negro equality is to be the order in the field of battle .... I take the liberty of warning the abettors of fraternizing with the blacks, that one negro regiment, in the present temper of things, put on equality with those who have the past year fought and suffered, will withdraw an amount of life and energy in our army equal to disbanding ten of the best regiments we can now raise.

Source: *New York Tribune*, August 16, 1862.

HOW WELL DID YOU UNDERSTAND THIS SELECTION?

1.　What argument does Frederick Douglass put forward for using black troops in the war?

2. Why does the letter writer oppose the use of such troops?

3. Which argument do you think would win out in the long run? Why?

As the war continued, northern public opinion gradually moved to an acceptance of emancipation. European public opinion strongly supported freedom for the slaves, and it seemed as though measures taken to free them would positively impact Union foreign policy efforts. The slaves own actions in fleeing their plantations to follow northern armies made the end of slavery seem more inevitable. Lincoln, in his cautious way, had come to the conclusion that it was time to take action. He was convinced to wait until after a Union victory, so a proclamation of emancipation would not seem like an act of desperation. After the Union "victory" at Antietam in September 1862, Lincoln issued his proclamation, which applied only to areas still in rebellion. It was not until the passage of the Thirteenth Amendment in 1865 that slavery was ended throughout the United States.

ABRAHAM LINCOLN

Whereas on the 22d day of September, A.D. 1862, a proclamation was issued by the President of the United States, containing among other things, the following, to wit:

"That on the 1st day of January, A.D. 1863, all persons held as slaves within any State or designated part of a State the people whereof shall then be in rebellion against the United States shall be then, thenceforward, and forever free; and the executive government of the United States, including the military and naval authority thereof, will recognize and maintain the freedom of such persons and will do no act or acts to repress such persons, or any of them, in any efforts they may make for their actual freedom.

"That the executive will on the 1st day of January aforesaid, by proclamation, designate the States and parts of States, if any, in which the people thereof, respectively, shall then be in rebellion against the United States; and the fact that any State or the people thereof shall on that day be in good faith represented in the Congress of the United States by members chosen thereto at elections wherein a majority of the qualified voters of such States shall have participated shall, in the absence of strong countervailing testimony, be deemed conclusive evidence that such State and the people thereof are not then in rebellion against the United States."

Now, therefore, I, Abraham Lincoln, President of the United States, by virtue of the power in me vested as Commander-in-Chief of the Army and Navy of the United States in time of actual armed rebellion against the authority and government of the United States, and as a fit and necessary war measure for suppressing said rebellion, do, on this 1st day of January, A.D. 1863, and in accordance with my purpose so to do, publicly proclaimed for the full period of one hundred days from the first day above mentioned, order and designate as the States and parts of States wherein the people thereof, respectively, are this day in rebellion against the United States .... (Here he lists the states – ed.)

And by virtue of the power and for the purpose aforesaid, I do order and declare that all persons held as slaves within said designated States and parts of States are, and henceforward shall be, free; and that the Executive Government of the United States, including the military and naval authorities thereof, will recognize and maintain the freedom of said persons.

And I hereby enjoin upon the people so declared to be free to abstain from all violence, unless in necessary self-defense; and I recommend to them that, in all cases when allowed, they labor faithfully for reasonable wages.

And I further declare and make known that such persons of suitable condition will be received into the armed service of the United States to garrison forts, positions, stations, and other places, and to man vessels of all sorts in said service.

And upon this act, sincerely believed to be an act of justice, warranted by the Constitution upon military necessity, I invoke the considerate judgment of mankind and the gracious favor of Almighty God.

Source: John Nicolay and John Hay, eds., *Complete Works of Abraham Lincoln* (Lincoln Memorial University, 1894), VIII: 161-164.

HOW WELL DID YOU UNDERSTAND THIS SELECTION?

1. The Emancipation Proclamation has been characterized as about as exciting as a cargo bill. Do you think that is true? Why do you think Lincoln, a master of wonderful language, made the language of the proclamation so ordinary?

2. Upon what presidential power does the president base his action?

3. Why would some observers criticize the principle of the proclamation as declaring that one human being cannot own another "unless he is loyal to the United States"?

4. In that case, why did so many abolitionists and blacks celebrate the issuance of the Proclamation?

5. Which view do you think has more validity?

In July 1863 the Confederate army, which had moved into Pennsylvania, was decisively defeated in a bitter and bloody battle at Gettysburg. This was the last Confederate invasion of the North. The disheartening sight of thousands of rotting corpses became a national scandal. Four months later, a national cemetery was finally dedicated. After a lengthy oration by famed public speaker, Edward Everett, Lincoln delivered a 272-word address that articulated the feelings of the northern public.

ABRAHAM LINCOLN

Fourscore and seven years ago our fathers brought forth on this continent a new nation, conceived in liberty, and dedicated to the proposition that all men are created equal.

Now we are engaged in a great civil war, testing whether that nation, or any nation so conceived and so dedicated, can long endure. We are met on a great battle-field of that war. We have come to dedicate a portion of that field as a final resting-place for those who here gave their lives that that nation might live. It is altogether fitting and proper that we should do this.

But, in a larger sense, we cannot dedicate—we cannot consecrate—we cannot hallow—this ground. The brave men, living and dead, who struggled here, have consecrated it far above our poor power to add or detract. The world will little note nor long remember what we say here, but it can never forget what they did here. It is for us, the living, rather, to be dedicated here to the unfinished work which they who fought here have thus far so nobly advanced. It is rather for us to be here dedicated to the great task remaining before us—that from these honored dead we take increased devotion to that cause for which they gave the last full measure of devotion; that we here highly resolve that these dead shall not have died in vain; that this nation, under God, shall have a new birth of freedom; and that government of the people, by the people, for the people, shall not perish from the earth.

Source: John Nicolay and John Hay, eds., *Complete Works of Abraham Lincoln* (Lincoln Memorial University, 1894), IX: 209-210.

HOW WELL DID YOU UNDERSTAND THIS SELECTION?

1. Why do you think that Edward Everett, a famed orator who spoke for two hours at the dedication of the cemetery, told Lincoln that while his speech would be rapidly forgotten, Lincoln's would never be and he would "gladly exchange my hundred pages for your twenty lines"?

2. What does Lincoln suggest was the real underlying meaning of the Civil War?

3. Why do you believe that this brief speech has resonated through the years?

The Emancipation Proclamation provided for the use of black troops by the Union army. Many Union soldiers remained resentful. Most, however, came to understand that blacks could help fill the Union's manpower needs. By the war's end, there were 180,000 blacks in the Union army. Many northern districts filled their troop quota with blacks. Despite this, they were treated unequally, receiving far lower pay. After protests, Congress eventually voted to equalize military salaries. Those blacks used as combat soldiers quickly proved their toughness and effectiveness in a series of engagements.

Reminiscence of a Former Black Soldier in the Union Army

At first the faintest intimation that Negroes should be employed as soldiers in the Union Army was met with derision. By many it was regarded as a joke. The idea of arming the ex-slaves seemed ridiculous to most civil and military officers ....

Most observing and thoughtful people concluded that centuries of servitude had rendered the Negro slave incapable of any civil or military service .... Some officers talked of resigning if Negroes were to be called upon to fight the battles of a free republic. The privates in regiments from large cities and border States were bitter and demonstrative in their opposition. The Negro volunteers themselves were subjected to indignities from rebel civilians within the Union lines, and obtained no protection from the white troops.

Source: George Washington Williams, *A History of the Negro Troops in the War of the Rebellion, 1861-65* (New York, 1888), pp. 66-67, 90-91.

Letter written by an UNNAMED SOLDIER IN THE MASSACHUSETTS FIFTY-FIFTH INFANTRY

Why are we not worth as much as white soldiers? We do the same work they do, and do what they cannot... just let them think of the charge at Fort Wagner, where the colored soldiers were cruelly murdered by the notorious rebels. Why is it that they do not want to give us our (just] pay when they have already witnessed our deeds of courage and bravery .... If we had staid at home with our fathers and mothers, wives and sisters, and dear ones at home, we could have received from $1 00 to $1-50 per day.   [African-American troops received $7 a month – ed.]

Source: The *Christian Recorder*, March 5,1864.

BLACK SOLDIERS TRIUMPH AT BATTLE OF PETERSBURG, JULY 1864

...The rebel cannon opened. The sons of Africa did not flinch, but took their positions with deliberation. They had been slaves; they stood face to face with their former master ....The [Confederate] flag in front of them waving in the morning breeze was the emblem of oppression; the banner above them was the flag of the free ....

The Rebels were on a knoll in the field, and had a clear sweep of all the approaches. The advancing troop must come out of the woods, rush up the slope, and carry it at the point of bayonet, receiving the tempest of musketry and canister.

[General] Hinks deployed his line. At the word of the command the colored men stepped out from the woods, and stood before the enemy. They gave a volley, and received one in return. Shells crashed through them, but unheeding the storm with a yell they started up the slope upon the run. They received one charge of canister, one scathing volley of musketry. Seventy of their number went down, but the living hundreds rushed on. The Rebels did not wait their coming, but fled towards Petersburg, leaving one of the pieces of artillery in the hands of assailants, who leaped over the works, turned it in a twinkling, but were not able to fire upon the retreating foe, fleeing in consternation [confusion] towards the main line of entrenchments two miles east of the city.

The colored troops were wild with joy. They embraced the captured cannon with affectionate enthusiasm, patting it as if it were animate, and could appreciate the endearment.

"Every soldier of the colored division was two inches taller for that achievement," said an officer describing it.

Source: Charles Carleton Coffin, *Four Years of Fighting*, 1866

HOW WELL DID YOU UNDERSTAND THIS SELECTION?

1. According to the first memoir, what was the initial reaction of Union soldiers to the enlistment of black troops?

2. What injustice(s) did black troops protest against?

3. How did the black troops perform in combat, according to the last writer?

4. What long-term results do you think would flow from the performance of black troops in the war?

THE HOME FRONTS

*The seemingly endless slaughter and inconclusive engagements hurt civilian morale on both sides. In the North, the conscription law with its obvious class bias in its exemption and substitution clauses led to popular indignation. The worst explosion occurred in New York City on July 13, 1863 – one of the bloodiest riots of American history. The **New York Times**, like most opinion leaders, was vehement in its condemnation of the riots.*

Suffering was far worse in the South where the morale of soldiers was undermined by the misery of their loved ones at home. Those in the paths of invading armies struggled to exist from day to day. Eliza Andrews, the 24-year-old daughter of a Unionist slaveholder, described the destruction in the wake of Sherman's "March to the Sea."

THE NEW YORK CITY DRAFT RIOTS

The mob in our city is still rampant ....The monster grows more dangerous as he grows desperate ....

It is too true that there are public journals who try to dignify the mob by some respectable appellation. The Herald characterizes it as the people and the World as the laboring men of the City.... The people of New-York and the laboring men of New-York are not incendiaries, nor robbers, nor assassins. They do not hunt down men whose only offense is the color God gave them: they do not chase and insult and beat women; they do not pillage [loot] an asylum for orphan children, and burn the very roof over those orphans' heads. They are civilized beings, valuing law and respecting decency: and they regard with unqualified abhorrence the doings of the tribe of savages...in their midst.

...You may as well reason with the wolves in the forest as with these men in their present mood ....-*Give them grape and plenty of it.*

OBJECT OF THE MOB . If this mob was originated in a passionate spirit of resistance to the Conscription law, it very soon changed its purpose, and assumed the character of merely a mob for robbery, plunder and arson. This is shown in the rifling of houses, hotels and stores, and the assaults and felonies upon the persons of unoffending citizens. Some of the ringleaders are noted thieves, who have served out several terms in Sing Sing and other penitentiaries and prisons. Hundreds of the workmen who joined with the crowd on Monday, were, of course, as honest as the average of us, but they were at once joined by all the knaves of the City who saw...an opportunity for plunder ....

LAW AND LIBERTY ....A mob is un-American, antiAmerican. Every grievance can here be remedied, every wrong can here be righted by laze, which has its power in the will of the people and "its fountain in the bosom of God." It will be a dark day for the liberties of America, for its honor, its greatness, its power, its glory, when this excrescence of European despotism fastens itself upon our free institutions and society. Every man who prides himself in the name of an American must use his determined efforts to drive back this black and deadly tide of human depravity.

Source: Editorial in the *New York Times*, Wednesday, July 15, 1863

RESPONSE OF A RIOTER

You will no doubt be hard on us rioters tomorrow morning,, but that 300-dollar law has made us nobodies, vagabonds and cast-outs of society, for whom nobody cares when we must go to war and be shot down. We are the poor rabble, and the rich rabble is our enemy by this law. Therefore we will give our enemy battle right here, and ask no quarter. Although we got hard fists, and are dirty without, we have soft hearts and have clean consciences within, and that's the reason we love our wives and children more than the rich, because we got not much besides them, and we will not go and leave them at home for to starve .... Why don't they let the nigger kill the slave-driving race and take possession of the South, as it belongs to them.

Source: Letter to the editor of the *New York Times*, by "A POOR MAN, BUT A MAN FOR ALL THAT," July 15, 1863

PROBLEMS IN THE SOUTH

After an absence of ten months in the army, I obtained a furlough and what joy did I anticipate in once more pressing my wife and little ones to my bosom. But imagine my feelings when told by my wife that she could not get bread enough for my children. She said that she had been to five gentlemen and could get no corn, while some in her immediate neighborhood had been known to ship corn to Augusta that they might get extortionate prices. Most of the time of my absence I have been on the march through Mississippi, Alabama and upper Georgia, many times with nothing but wet clay for my bed. I have seen my comrades fall on my right and my left, I have heard the whistling of bullets and seen them strike within a few inches of me; but all those hardships and dangers only nerved my arm to strike one more blow for my country and her honor. But, sir, when I am told that my little ones are suffering for want through the avarice of those for whom I stand as a wall between the enemy and their property, I feel this the greatest hardship of all. Why, Mr. Editor, the Beast Butler [a Union general] with all his refinements of cruelty could not serve them worse.

Source: Letter to the *Savannah Republican*, February 23,1864

Diary of a Georgia Girl (1864)

ELIZA ANDREWS

December 24, 1864.-About three miles from Sparta we struck the "burnt country;" as it is well named by the natives, and then I could better understand the wrath and desperation of these poor people. I almost felt as if I should like to hang a Yankee myself. There was hardly a fence left standing all the way from Sparta to Gordon. The fields were trampled down and the road was lined with carcasses of horses, hogs, and cattle that the invaders, unable either to consume or to carry away with them, had wantonly shot down, to starve out the people and prevent them from making their crops. The stench in some places was unbearable; every few hundred yards we had to hold our noses or stop them with the cologne Mrs. Elzey had given us, and it proved a great boon. The dwellings that were standing all showed signs of pillage, and on every plantation we saw the charred remains of the ginhouse and packing screw, while here and there lone chimney stacks, "Sherman's sentinels," told of homes laid in ashes. The infamous wretches! I couldn't wonder now that these poor people should want to put a rope round the neck of every red-handed "devil of them" they could lay their hands on. Hayricks and fodder stacks were demolished, corncribs were empty, and every bale of cotton that could be found was burnt by the savages. I saw no grain of any sort except little patches they had spilled when feeding their horses and which there was not even a chicken left in the country to eat. A bag of oats might have lain anywhere along the road without danger from the beasts of the field, though I cannot say it would have been safe from the assaults of hungry man.

Crowds of soldiers were tramping over the road in both directions; it was like traveling through the streets of a populous town all day. They were mostly on foot, and I saw numbers seated on the roadside greedily eating raw turnips, meat skins, parched corn-anything they could find, even picking up the loose grains that Sherman's horses had left. I felt tempted to stop and empty the contents of our provision baskets into their laps, but the dreadful accounts that were given of the state of the country before us made prudence get the better of our generosity.

Before crossing the Oconee at Milledgeville we ascended an immense hill, from which there was a fine view of the town, with Governor Brown's fortifications in the foreground and the river rolling at our feet. The Yankees had burnt the bridge; so we had to cross on a ferry. There was a long train of vehicles ahead of us, and it was nearly an hour before our turn came; so we had ample time to look about us. On our left was a field where thirty thousand Yankees had camped hardly three weeks before. It was strewn with the debris they had left behind, and the poor people of the neighborhood were wandering over it, seeking for anything they could find to eat, even picking up grains of corn that were scattered around where the Yankees had fed their horses. We were told that a great many valuables were found there at first, plunder that the invaders had left behind, but the place had been picked over so often by this time that little now remained except tufts of loose cotton, piles of half-rotted grain, and the carcasses of slaughtered animals, which raised a horrible stench. Some men were plowing in one part of the field, making ready for next year's crop.

Source: Eliza Andrews, *The War-Time Diary of a Georgia Girl* (Appleton, New York, 1908).

HOW WELL DID YOU UNDERSTAND THIS SELECTION?

1. How does the *New York Times* characterize the actions of the New York draft rioters?

2. What are the explanations of the rioter/letter-writer for the actions of the rioters?

3. What problem did the southern soldier find when he came home on a furlough?

4. What conditions does the Georgian, Eliza Andrews, find in the wake of Sherman's march?

5.   Unlike the North, there were no government sponsored wartime organizations that employed women in the South. How did they cope with conditions?

6. In which section do you feel the home front problems were more severe? Why?

As manpower shortages worsened in the South, some leaders argued that the Confederate army should also recruit blacks, guaranteeing freedom "to every slave in the South who shall remain true to the Confederacy in this war." Naturally, this proposal was met with powerful resistance. At the very end of the war, however, the desperation was so great that the Confederate Congress authorized the recruiting of black companies. Although such companies were actually raised, the war ended before they could be used.

OPPOSITION TO THE IDEA

The proposition is so strange—so unconstitutional—so directly in conflict with all of our former practices and teachings—so entirely subversive of our social and political institutions—and so completely destructive of our liberties, that we stand completely appalled [and] dumfounded at its promulgation.

They propose that Congress shall conscribe two hundred and fifty thousand slaves, arm, equip and fight them in the field. As an inducement of them to be faithful, it is proposed that, at the end of the war, they shall have their freedom and live amongst us. "The conscription of negroes," says the Enquirer, "should be accompanied with freedom and the privilege of remaining in the States." This is the monstrous proposition. The South went to war to defeat the designs of the abolitionists, and behold! in the midst of the war, we turn abolitionists ourselves! We went to war because the Federal Congress kept eternally meddling with our domestic institutions, with which we contended they had nothing to do, and now we propose to end the war by asking the Confederate Congress to do precisely what Lincoln proposes to do-free our negroes and make them the equals of the white man! We have always been taught to believe that slaves are property, and under the exclusive control of the States and the courts. This new doctrine teaches us that Congress has a right to free our negroes and make them the equals of their masters ....

Source: *Lynchburg (Va.) Republican*, November 2, 1864.

A WOMAN FAVORS THE IDEA

Mr. Editor:

A lady's opinion may not be worth much in such an hour as this, but I cannot resist the temptation of expressing my approbation of "The crisis the Remedy," copied from the Mobile Register. Would to God our Government would act upon its suggestions at once. The women of the South are not so in love with their negro property, as to wish to see husbands, fathers, sons, brothers, slain to protect it; nor would they submit to Yankee rule, could it secure to them a thousand waiting maids, whence now they possess one ....

Source: *Macon (Ga.) Telegraph and Confederate*, January 11, 1865.

CONFEDERATE CONGRESS APPROVES USE OF BLACK TROOPS

The Congress of the Confederate States of America do enact, That in order to provide additional forces to repel invasion, maintain the rightful Possession of the Confederate States, secure their independence, and preserve their institutions, the President be, and he is hereby, authorized to ask for and accept from the owners of slaves, the services of such number of able-bodied negro men as he may deem expedient, for and during the war, to perform military service in whatever capacity he may direct.

Source: Confederate Congress, "An Act to Increase the Military Force of the Confederate States," March 13, 1865.

HOW WELL DID YOU UNDERSTAND THIS SELECTION?

1. What argument against the use of slaves as troops does the *Lynchburg Republican* advance?

2. Why does the woman letter-writer favor the idea of using such troops?

3. Why do you think the Confederate Congress ultimately approved of such an action?

4. Had the war lasted long enough for such troops to actually be used, what impact would this have had upon the South and upon the rest of the war?

RECOLLECTIONS OF THE WAR'S HORRORS :1875

The great American poet, Walt Whitman, served as a nurse in Union Army hospitals. Ten years later, when he wrote these recollections, the horrors of the war still remained vivid to him.

Walt Whitman

The dead in this war-there they lie, strewing the fields and woods and valleys and battle-field's of the South-Virginia, the Peninsula-Malvern Hill and Fair Oaks-the banks of the Chickahominy-the terraces of Fredericksburg-Antietam bridge-the grisly ravines of Manassas-the bloody promenade of the Wilderness-the varieties of the strayed dead, (the estimate of the War Department is 25,000 national soldiers kill'd in battle and never buried at all, 5,000 15,000 inhumed by strangers, or on the march in haste, in hitherto unfound localities-2,000 graves cover'd by sand and mud by Mississippi freshets, 3,000 carried away by caving-in of banks, &c.,)-Gettysburg, the West, Southwest-Vicksburg--Chattanooga-the trenches of Petersburg-the numberless battles, camps, hospitals everywhere-the crop reap'd by the mighty reapers, typhoid, dysentery, inflammations-and blackest and loathsomest of all, the dead and living burial-pits, the prison-pens of Andersonville, Salisbury, Belle Isle, &c., (not Dante's pictured hell and all its woes, its degradations, filthy torments, excell'd those prisons)-the dead, the dead, the dead-our dead-or South or North, ours all, (all, all, all, finally dear to me)-or East or West-Atlantic coast or Mississippi valley-somewhere they crawl'd to die, alone, in bushes, low gullies, or on the sides of hills-(there, in secluded spots,

253

their skeletons, bleach'd bones, tufts of hair, buttons, fragments of clothing, are occasionally found yet)-our young men once so handsome and so joyous, taken from us-the son from the mother, the husband from the wife, the dear friend from the dear friend-the clusters of camp graves, in Georgia, the Carolinas, and in Tennessee-the single graves left in the woods or by the roadside, (hundreds, thousands, obliterated)-the corpses floated down the rivers, and caught and lodged, (dozens, scores, floated down the upper Potomac, after the cavalry engagements, the pursuit of Lee, following Gettysburg)-some lie at the bottom of the sea-the general million, and the special cemeteries in almost all the States-the infinite dead-(the land entire saturated, perfumed with their impalpable ashes' exhalation in Nature's chemistry distill'd, and shall be so forever, in every future grain of wheat and ear of corn, and every flower that grows, and every breath we draw) not only Northern dead leavening Southern soil-thousands, aye tens of thousands, of Southerners, crumble to-day in Northern earth.

And everywhere among these countless graves-everywhere in the many soldier Cemeteries of the Nation, (there are now, I believe, over seventy of them)-as at the time in the vast trenches, the depositories of slain, Northern and Southern, after the great battles-not only where the scathing trail passed those years, but radiating since in all the peaceful quarters of the land-we see, and ages yet may see, on monuments and gravestones, singly or in masses, to thousands or tens of thousands, the significant word Unknown ....

Source: *The Complete Works of Walt Whitman* (New York, 1902): 137-139.

HOW WELL DID YOU UNDERSTAND THIS SELECTION?

1. What are the main images Walt Whitman retained of the war?

2. What impact do you think these images and similar ones by other observers would have had on public opinion in the years after the war?

3. Why do you think Walt Whitman served as a nurse during the war?

SECOND INAUGURAL ADDRESS (1865)
Abraham Lincoln

Although the depressing events on the military front convinced Lincoln that he would not be reelected in 1864, victories in Atlanta and Mobile Bay swung public opinion back to Lincoln. He won a substantial victory in the election. In his Second Inaugural Address on March 4, 1865, Lincoln looked forward to peace and the elimination of slavery. At an April 14 cabinet meeting, he implored these leaders to reject animosity and reprisals. He was assassinated that evening.

FELLOW-COUNTRYMEN:-At this second appearing to take the oath of the presidential office there is less occasion for an extended address than there was at the first. Then a statement somewhat in detail of a course to be pursued seemed fitting and proper. Now, at the expiration of four years, during which public declarations have been constantly called forth on every point and phase of the great contest which still absorbs the attention and engrosses the energies of the nation, little that is new could be presented. The progress of our arms, upon which all else chiefly depends, is as well known to the public as to myself, and it is, I trust, reasonably satisfactory and encouraging to all. With high hope for the future, no prediction in regard to it is ventured.

On the occasion corresponding to this four years ago all thoughts were anxiously directed to an impending civil war. All dreaded it, all sought to avert it. While the inaugural address was being delivered from this place, devoted altogether to saving the Union without war, insurgent agents were in the city seeking to destroy it without war-seeking to dissolve the Union and divide effects by negotiation. Both parties deprecated war, but one of them would make war rather than let the nation survive, and the other would accept war rather than let it perish, and the war came.

One eighth of the whole population was colored slaves, not distributed generally over the Union, but localized in the southern part of it. These slaves constituted a peculiar and powerful interest. All knew that this interest was somehow the cause of the war. To strengthen, perpetuate, and extend this interest was the object for which the insurgents would rend the Union even by war, while the Government claimed no right to do more than to restrict the territorial enlargement of it. Neither party expected for the war the magnitude nor the duration which it has already attained. Neither anticipated that the cause of the conflict might cease with or even before the conflict itself should cease. Each looked for an easier triumph, and a result less fundamental and astounding. Both read the same Bible and pray to the same God, and each invokes His aid against the other. It may seem strange that any men should dare to ask a just God's assistance in wringing their bread from the sweat of other men's faces, but let us judge not, that we be not judged. The prayers of both could not be answered. That of neither has been answered fully. The Almighty has His own purposes. "Woe unto the world because of offenses; for it must needs be that offenses come, but woe to that man by whom the offense cometh." If we shall suppose that American slavery is one of those offenses which, in the providence of God, must needs come, but which, having continued through His appointed time, He now wills to remove, and that He gives to both North and South this terrible war as the woe due to those by whom the offense came, shall we discern therein any departure from those divine attributes which the believers in a living God always ascribe to Him? Fondly do we hope, fervently do we pray, that this mighty scourge of war may speedily pass away. Yet, if God wills that it continue until all the wealth piled by the bondsman's two hundred and fifty years of unrequited toil shall be sunk, and until every drop of blood drawn with the lash shall be paid by another drawn with the sword, as was said three thousand years ago, so still it must be said, "The judgments of the Lord are true and righteous altogether."

With malice toward none, with charity for all, with firmness in the right as God gives us to see the right, let us strive on to finish the work we are in, to bind up the nation's wounds, to care for him who shall have borne the battle and for his widow and his orphan, to do all which may achieve and cherish a just and lasting peace among ourselves and with all nations.

Source: James D. Richardson, ed., *A Compilation of the Messages and Papers of the Presidents* (Government Printing Office, Washington, D.C., 1897-1907), VIII: 3477-3478.

HOW WELL DID YOU UNDERSTAND THIS SELECTION?

1. What does Lincoln seem to suggest was the basic cause of the Civil War?

2. How does this differ from what he had originally suggested caused the war?

3. Why, do you think, this Second Inaugural Address, is considered one of the greatest American speeches?

4. What future does Lincoln want to create after the war ends?

5. How might his assassination have changed the history of America after the war?

SELF TEST:

MULTIPLE CHOICE: Circle the correct response. The correct answers are given at the end.

1. After Fort Sumter was fired upon, the calls for volunteers by both presidents were greeted with
   a. lack of interest in both North and South.
   b. great enthusiasm in both North and South.
   c. enthusiasm in the South, but disinterest in the North.
   d. enthusiasm in the North and anger in the South.

2. When the war began, the South appeared to have its greatest superiority in its
   a. industrial might.
   b. available capital.
   c. military leadership.
   d. accessible railroads.

3. When they first assumed office, both Jefferson Davis and Abraham Lincoln
   a. faced serious organizational problems.
   b. reserved major political offices for their friends.
   c. had very well-organized governments in place.
   d. demonstrated their extensive military training.

4. During the Civil War, abolitionists
   a. supported northern Democrats who urged negotiation to end the war immediately.
   b. felt both sides of the war were equally guilty of violating human rights.
   c. led the campaign to prevent Lincoln's re-election in 1864.
   d. campaigned to convert the war into a struggled against slavery.

5. In order to finance the war, both the North and South ultimately turned to
   a. collecting tariffs from foreign trade.
   b. borrowing from banks in Europe.
   c. issuing paper money.
   d. taxing states and individuals directly.

6. The caution President Lincoln demonstrated in embracing the goal of abolishing slavery
   a. caused the war to drag out longer than might have been expected.
   b. arose from his fear of losing the allegiance of the slave-holding border states.
   c. came from his own mixed feelings about the morality of slavery.
   d. angered most Northerners and disappointed Union soldiers.

7. When Lincoln did issue the Emancipation Proclamation, he justified it on the grounds of
   a. biblical commandments.
   b. slavery's fundamental immorality.
   c. the natural rights of man.
   d. military necessity.

8. All of the following were considered Union victories in the Civil War **EXCEPT**
   a. First Bull Run.
   b. Gettysburg.
   c. Antietam
   d. Atlanta.

9. Lincoln's reelection in 1864 was assured by the
   a. immediate success of Grant's northern Virginia campaign.
   b. public enthusiasm for the Emancipation Proclamation.
   c. Confederate defeat at Gettysburg.
   d. news that Sherman had captured Atlanta.

10. The result of Sherman's "March to the Sea" was to
    a. get his troops entangled in deadly trench warfare.
    b. create an orgy of troops engaged in plunder, rape and murder.
    c. destroy the ability of the South to continue to fight the war.
    d. distract the attention of Lee's army away from the actions in Virginia.

Answers: 1-b; 2-c; 3-a; 4-d; 5-c; 6-b; 7-d; 8-a; 9-d; 10-c.

ESSAYS:

1. Compare the resources and advantages of the North and South at the beginning of the war? Why, with its obvious disadvantages, was the South able to continue its struggle for four years? What were the main reasons for the Union's eventual victory?

2. Explain the changes the war brought in views about slavery and black soldiers in both the North and South? What were the reasons for changes in policy? What were the results?

3. Which do you consider to be the four most significant battles of the Civil War? Explain why you picked each and why each was important in the eventual outcome of the war.

4. Compare and contrast the economic and social impact of the Civil War on the North and the South. Examine the impact of these changes on the lives of ordinary people.

OPTIONAL ACTIVITIES: Use your knowledge **and** imagination.

1. Mary Chestnut wrote a diary describing the impact of the war on her life. Imagine you are a northern or southern woman and write diary entries showing how the war affects you.

2. Write a letter home describing experiences at a Civil War battle. (You can be either a northern or southern soldier.)

3. As a black leader write a letter to the president or a speech to other African Americans explaining why you favor allowing black troops to fight for the Union in the Civil War.

WEB SITE LISTINGS:

A premier Civil War site - it links to dozens of other sites
>   http://www.civilwarhome.com
>>>>   /sanitarycommission.htm
>>>>   /medicinehistory.htm
>>>>   /confederateoverview.htm

The Valley of the Shadow: A Northern and a Southern Community during the War
>   http://www.valley.vcdh.virginia.edu

Sampler of Civil War Literature from Harper's Weekly
>   http://www.civilwarliterature.com

American Memory National Digital Library (earlier sections cover slavery, free blacks and abolition):
>   http://memory.loc.gov/ammem/aaohtml/exhibit/aopart4.html

This Week in the Civil War
>   http://www.civileek.com/index.htm

The Civil War Preservation Trust
>   http://www.civilwar.org/historyctandclassrm.htm

A Tour of the Lincoln White House
>   www.mrlincolnswhitehouse.org

Civil War Times on the History Net
>   http://www.thehistorynet.com/cwt.acwu

Furman University Secession Era Editorials Project:
>   http://history.furman.edu/~benson/docs

Washington State University documents:
>   http://www.wsu.edu:8080/%7Eamerstu/19th/docs.html#civilwar

University of Michigan Making of America has thousands of sources:
>   http://www.umdl.umich.edu/moa

Louisiana State University Civil War Center:
>   http://www.cwc.lsu.edu

Dakota State:
>   http://homepages.dsu.edu/jankej/civilwar/civilwar.htm

Chapter Twelve

RECONSTRUCTION: The Turning Point That Never Turned

The Civil War was over. It ended both secession and slavery, but it did not settle the fate of the former slaves or that of the former Confederate states. What labor system would arise in the South to replace slavery? What rights and privileges would be given to the newly freed people? How could governments be reestablished in the South and who would control them?

Unfortunately Lincoln, the man best equipped to deal with these thorny issues, was assassinated. His mantle fell to Andrew Johnson, a southern Democratic Union supporter, a man ill-fitted to handle the give and take of political compromise. The new president and Congress rapidly moved further and further apart on how to recon-struct the South. Johnson supported the establishment of new state governments headed by former Confederate leaders who had been pardoned by the president. The intransigence of these governments was demonstrated by the passage of Black Codes that sought to severely limit the freed slaves. Congress reacted to this challenge by passing the Freedman's Bureau and Civil Rights Bills, both of which were vetoed by Johnson.

The congressional Joint Committee on Reconstruction developed its own reconstruction plan that was based upon acceptance of the Fourteenth Amendment guaranteeing citizenship rights to black Americans. At Johnson's urging, ten of the eleven ex-confederate states rejected the amendment. In the congressional elections of 1866 the president strenuously campaigned against the Republicans. His efforts were a disaster that led to the dominance of radical Republicans in Congress. In 1867, they passed a more demanding Reconstruction Act, dividing the ten recalcitrant states into five military districts. New state governments would be created guaranteeing black men the right to vote and ratifying the Fourteenth Amendment.

President Johnson continued to fight the radicals at every turn and attempted to sabotage their reconstruction efforts. Finally, he challenged Congress by removing Secretary of War Edwin Stanton, violating the Tenure of Office Act. He was impeached by the House, but the Senate narrowly failed to convict him. However, his power was destroyed, and he was followed in office by Republican Ulysses S. Grant, the former commander of the Union Army.

The radical governments in the South, set up by the Reconstruction Act, depended on a fragile alliance of northern "carpetbaggers," southern "scalawags," and the votes of the freedmen. These governments accomplished substantial social and political progress including universal manhood suffrage, the establishment of public school systems, institutions for the poor and handicapped, and the rebuilding of roads and railroads. Their image was tarnished, however, by widespread corruption, which also existed in the North and in the federal government. A more serious limitation was the widely held conviction of the limited role of government and the sanctity of private property. This meant that land would not be distributed to former slaves, limiting their possibilities for economic advancement. The South would have to rely on its own limited resources in dealing with postwar economic adapta-tions. The economic pattern that developed in the South was based upon sharecropping and one-crop agriculture. This not only obstructed black economic opportunity, it also assured the South's continuing poverty.

Despite the passage of the Fifteenth Amendment that seemed to guarantee the right of blacks to vote, the alliance supporting reconstruction began to disintegrate. Feminists, who had once been ardent supporters of rights for freed people, balked when women's suffrage was not included. The old Radicals, who were committed to racial equality, died out. Most Northerners, themselves firm believers in black inferiority, lost interest in the issue, particularly as economic depression took center stage. Southern Democratic "redeemers" regained control of one state after another utilizing racism, intimidation, and terror. They were aided by terrorist organizations like the Ku Klux Klan that frightened prospective Republican voters.

The disputed presidential election of 1876 undermined the few remaining radical governments in Louisiana, South Carolina, and Florida. Under the "Compromise of 1877," Southerners agreed to withdraw opposition to the election of the Republican, Rutherford B. Hayes, in return for the removal of federal troops from those last few states.

The nation entered an astonishing period of economic progress and vigor. Despite the proclamation of a "New South," the economic and social system of the South remained backward and mired in poverty. "Jim Crow" laws created a rigid system of segregation. The Supreme Court in the *Plessy v. Ferguson* case validated this system of segregation.

Reconstruction was unable to deliver in its promise of permanent change in race relations in America. Although the amendments and civil rights acts passed during this era became the basis for later struggles for equality, blacks remained second-class citizens for many years to come.

IDENTIFICATION: Briefly describe each term.

Andrew Johnson

Thirteenth Amendment

Radical Republicans

Thaddeus Stevens

Black Codes

Freedmen's Bureau

Joint Committee on Reconstruction

Fourteenth Amendment

Reconstruction Act of 1867

Secretary of War Edwin Stanton

Tenure of Office Act

Impeachment of President Johnson

"Waving the bloody shirt"

Ku Klux Klan

Fifteenth Amendment

Carpetbaggers

Scalawags

Sharecropping

Black churches

Credit Mobilier scandal

Whiskey Ring

Elizabeth Cady Stanton

Susan B. Anthony

Civil Rights Act of 1875

Charles Sumner

"redeemers"

Disputed Election of 1876

Compromise of 1877

"New South"

Booker T. Washington

Jim Crow

Plessy v. Ferguson

THINK ABOUT:

1. If Lincoln had not been assassinated, would the story of Reconstruction had been different? In what ways? How would the relations between Congress and the president have been affected? Would there have been a different process in reintegrating the South into the union and the former slaves into the South?

2. If you could have been in charge of Reconstruction, what actions would you have taken? How would these have differed from what was actually done? What do you think the long-term results would have been for the future of America?

A LETTER "TO MY OLD MASTER," c. 1865

The newly freed slaves had struggled for their freedom. They aided the Union cause during the Civil War. At the war's end, they were overjoyed by their hard-won liberty. In this letter, Jourdon Anderson lets his former master know exactly how he really felt about being a slave and what he thinks about his new life.

TO MY OLD MASTER, COLONEL P.H. ANDERSON, BIG SPRING, TENNESSEE

Sir: I got your letter, and was glad to find that you had not forgotten Jourdon, and that you wanted me to come back and live with you again, promising to do better for me than anybody else can. I have often felt uneasy about you. I thought the Yankees would have hung you long before this, for harboring Rebs they found at your house. I suppose they never heard about your going to Colonel Martin's to kill the Union soldier that was left by his company in their stable. Although you shot at me twice before I left you, I did not want to hear of your being hurt, and am glad you are still living. It would do me good to go back to the dear old home again, and see Miss Mary and Miss Martha and Allen, Esther, Green, and Lee. Give my love to them all, and tell them I hope we will meet in the better world, if not in this. I would have gone back to see you all when I was working in the Nashville Hospital, but one of the neighbors told me that Henry intended to shoot me if he ever got a chance.

I want to know particularly what the good chance is you propose to give me. I am doing tolerably well here. I get twenty-five dollars a month, with victuals and clothing; have a comfortable home for Mandy—the folks call her Mrs. Anderson—and the children—Milly, Jane, and Grundy—go to school and are learning well. The teacher says Grundy has a head for a preacher. They go to Sunday school, and Mandy and me attend church regularly. We are kindly treated. Sometimes we overhear others saying, "Them colored people were slaves" down in Tennessee. The children feel hurt when they hear such remarks; but I tell them it was no disgrace in Tennessee to belong to Colonel Anderson. Many darkeys would have been proud, as I used to be, to call you master. Now if you will write and say what wages you will give me, I will be better able to decide whether it would be to my advantage to move back again.

As to my freedom, which you say I can have, there is nothing to be gained on that score, as I got my free papers in 1864 from the Provost-Marshal General of the Department of Nashville. Mandy says she would be afraid to go back without some proof that you were disposed to treat us justly and kindly; and we have concluded to test your sincerity by asking you to send us our wages for the time we served you. This will make us forget and forgive old scores, and rely on your justice and friendship in the future. I served you faithfully for thirty-two years, and Mandy twenty years. At twenty-five dollars a month for me, and two dollars a week for Mandy, our earnings would amount to eleven thousand six hundred and eighty dollars. Add to this the interest for the time our wages have been kept back, and deduct what you paid for our clothing, and three doctor's visits to me, and pulling a tooth for Mandy, and the balance will show what we are in justice entitled to. Please send the money by Adam's Express, in care of V. Winters, Esq., Dayton, Ohio. If you fail to pay us for faithful labors in the past, we can have little faith in your promises in the future. We trust the good Maker has opened your eyes to the wrongs which you and your fathers have done to me and my fathers, in making us toil for you for generations without recompense. Here I draw my wages every Saturday night; but in Tennessee there was never any pay-day for the Negroes any more than for the horses and cows. Surely there will be a day of reckoning for those who defraud the laborer of his hire.

In answering this letter, please state if there would be any safety for my Milly and Jane, who are now grown up, and both good-looking girls. You know how it was with poor Matilda and Catherine. I would rather stay here and starve—and die, if it come to that—than have my girls brought to shame by the violence and wickedness of their young masters. You will also please state if there has been any schools opened for the colored children in your neighborhood. The great desire of my life now is to give my children an education, and have them form virtuous habits.

Say howdy to George Carter, and thank him for taking the pistol from you when you were shooting at me.

FROM YOUR OLD SERVANT,
JOURDON ANDERSON

HOW WELL DID YOU UNDERSTAND THIS SELECTION?

1. What point do you think Jourdon Anderson was trying to make to his old master?

2. Do you think he ever intended to go back? Why or why not?

3. What does this letter tell you about freed people and their aspirations?

At the end of the war, in 1865 and 1866, southern state legislatures passed a series of "Black Codes," supposedly to codify legal rights for newly freed blacks. In reality, most of the codes denied blacks many basic rights. Many Northerners believed that the provisions of the codes foreshadowed an attempt to reinstitute plantation slavery.

The Black Code of
St. Landry's Parish, 1865

Whereas it was formerly made the duty of the police jury to make suitable regulations for the police of slaves within the limits of the parish; and whereas slaves have become emancipated by the action of the ruling powers; and whereas it is necessary for public order, as well as for the comfort and correct deportment of said freedmen, that suitable regulations should be established by their government in their changed condition, the following ordinances are adopted, with the approval of the United States military authorities commanding in said parish, viz:

SECTION *1. Be it ordained by the police jury of the parish of St. Landry,* That no negro shall be allowed to pass within the limits of said parish without a special permit in writing from his employer. Whoever shall violate this provision shall pay a fine of two dollars and fifty cents, or in default thereof shall be forced to work four days on the public road, or suffer corporeal punishment as provided hereinafter.

SECTION *2. Be it further ordained,* That every negro who shall be found absent from the residence of his employer after 10 o'clock at night, without a written permit from his employer, shall pay a fine of five dollars, or in default thereof, shall be compelled to work five days on the public road, or suffer corporeal punishment as hereinafter provided.

SECTION *3. Be it further ordained,* That no negro shall be permitted to rent or keep a house within said parish. Any negro violating this provision shall be immediately ejected and compelled to find an employer; and any person who shall rent, or give the use of any house to any negro, in violation of this section, shall pay a fine of five dollars for each offence.

SECTION *4. Be it further ordained,* That every negro is required to be in the regular service of some white person, or former owner, who shall be held responsible for the conduct of said negro. But said employer or former owner may permit said negro to hire his own time by special permission in writing, which permission shall not extend over seven days at any one time. Any negro violating the provisions of this section shall be fined five dollars for each offence, or in default of the payment thereof shall be forced to work five days on the public road, or suffer corporeal punishment as hereinafter provided.

SECTION *5. Be it further ordained,* That no public meetings or congregations of negroes shall be allowed within said parish after sunset; but such public meetings and congregations may be held between the hours of sunrise and sunset, by the special permission of writing of the captain of patrol, within whose beat such meetings shall take place. This prohibition, however, is not intended to prevent negroes from attending the usual church services, conducted by white ministers and priests. Every negro violating the provisions of this section shall pay a fine of five dollars, or in default thereof shall be compelled to work five days on the public road, or suffer corporeal punishment as hereinafter provided.

SECTION *6. Be it further ordained,* That no negro shall be permitted to preach, exhort, or otherwise declaim to congregations of colored people, without a special permission in writing from the president of the police jury. Any negro violating the provisions of this section shall pay a fine of ten dollars, or in default thereof shall be forced to work ten days on the public road, or suffer corporeal punishment as hereinafter provided.

SECTION *7. Be it further ordained,* That no negro who is not in the military service shall be allowed to carry fire-arms, or any kind of weapons, within the parish, without the special written permission of his employers, approved and indorsed by the nearest or most convenient chief of patrol. Any one violating the provisions of this section shall forfeit his weapons and pay a fine of five dollars, or in default of the payment of said fine, shall be forced to work five days on the public road, or suffer corporeal punishment as hereinafter provided.

SECTION 8. *Be it further ordained,* That no negro shall sell, barter, or exchange any articles of merchandise or traffic within said parish without the special written permission of his employer, specifying the articles of sale, barter or traffic. Any one thus offending shall pay a fine of one dollar for each offence, and suffer the forfeiture of said articles' or in default of the payment of said fine shall work one day on the public road, or suffer corporeal punishment as hereinafter provided.

SECTION 9. *Be it further ordained,* That any negro found drunk within the said parish shall pay a fine of five dollars, or in default thereof shall work five days on the public road, or suffer corporeal punishment as hereinafter provided.

SECTION 10. *Be it further ordained,* That all the foregoing provisions shall apply to negroes of both sexes.

SECTION 11. *Be it further ordained,* That it shall be the duty of every citizen to act as a police officer for the detection of offences and the apprehension of offenders, who shall be immediately handed over to the proper captain or chief of patrol.

SECTION 12. *Be it further ordained,* That the aforesaid penalties shall be summarily enforced, and that it shall be the duty of the captains and chiefs of patrol to see that the aforesaid ordinances are promptly executed.

SECTION 13. *Be it further ordained,* That all sums collected from the aforesaid fines shall be immediately handed over to the parish treasurer.

SECTION 14. *Be it further ordained,* That the corporeal punishment provided for in the foregoing sections shall consist in confining the body of the offender within a barrel placed over his or her shoulders, in the manner practiced in the army, such confinement not to continue longer than twelve hours, and for such time within the aforesaid limit as shall be fixed by the captain or chief of patrol who inflicts the penalty.

HOW WELL DID YOU UNDERSTAND THIS SELECTION?

1. What do you think was the real purpose of this Black Code?

2. Which provisions would be most troubling to freedmen? To northern public opinion?

It was clear to some Radical Republicans that the only way freed people could expect to achieve real independence was if they could have their own land to farm. This land would have to be taken from plantation owners and Confederate leaders. Most Americans believed that such a policy was contrary to deeply-held ideas about economic rights. Radical Republican congressman, Thaddeus Stevens argued in favor of confiscation and redistribution of southern land. The New York Times opposed such redistribution, while the former slaves expressed their deep desire to own their own land.

From a speech by THADDEUS STEVENS, 1865
Published in the Congressional Record

We especially insist that the property of the chief rebels should be seized and appropriated to the payment of the national debt, caused by the unjust and wicked war they instigated [started] .... There are about 6,000,000 of freedmen in the South. The number of acres of land is 465,000,000. Of this those who own above 200 acres each number about 70,000 persons, holding in the aggregate—together with the states—about 394,000,000 acres. By forfeiting the estates of the leading rebels the government would have 394,000,000 of acres besides their town property, and yet nine-tenths of the people would remain untouched. Divide the land into convenient farms. Give, if you please, forty acres to each adult male freedman. Suppose there are 1,000,000 of them. That would require 40,000,000 acres, which deducted from 394,000,000 leaves 354,000,000 acres for sale. Divide it into suitable farms, and sell it to the highest bidders. I think it, including town property, would average at least $10 per acre. That would produce $3,540,000.

The whole fabric of southern society must be changed and never can it be done if this opportunity is lost. Without this, this government can never be, as it has never been, a true republic.... How can republican institutions, free schools, free churches, free social intercourse exist in a mingled community of nabobs [men of wealth and high position] and serfs [tillers of the land]? If the South is ever made a safe republic let her lands be cultivated by the toil of .. free labor....

Nothing is so likely to make a man a good citizen as to make him a freeholder. Nothing will so multiply the production of the South as to divide it into small farms. Nothing will make men so industrious and moral as to let them feel that they are above want and are the owners of the soil which they till.... No people will ever be republican in spirit and practice where a few own immense manors and the masses are landless. Small and independent land-holders are the support and guardians of republican liberty.

NEW YORK TIMES, July 9, 1867:

[Land confiscation] is a question not of humanity, not of loyalty, but of fundamental relation of industry to capital; and sooner or later, if begun at the South, it will find its way into the cities of the North.... An attempt to justify the confiscation of Southern land under the pretense of doing justice to the freedmen, strikes at the root of property rights in both sections. It concerns Massachusetts as much as Mississippi.

A Conversation between a Freedman and a General at Fort Smith Arkansas
Reported by the JOINT CONGRESSIONAL COMMITTEE ON RECONSTRUCTION, 1867:

FREEDMAN: Sir, I want you to help me in a personal matter.
GENERAL: Where is your family?
FREEDMAN: On the Red River.

GENERAL: Have you not everything you want?

FREEDMAN: No sir.

GENERAL: You are free!

FREEDMAN: Yes sir, you set me free, but you left me there.

GENERAL: What do you want?

FREEDMAN: I want some land; I am helpless; you do nothing for me but give me freedom.

GENERAL: Is not that enough?

FREEDMAN: It is enough for the present; but I cannot help myself unless I get some land; then I can take care of myself and my family; otherwise I cannot do it.

HOW WELL DID YOU UNDERSTAND THIS SELECTION?

1. What was Thaddeus Steven's plan? To whom do you think the plan would appeal?

2. What are the grounds for his argument that his plan would strengthen democracy and agricultural production? Do you agree?

3. What is the basis for the *New York Times'* opposition to confiscation and redistribution of southern lands? Who would find its argument convincing? Why?

4. How does the freedman look at this issue?

Most Americans believed in a close connection between education and democracy. Under slavery laws, masters had been prohibited from teaching reading and writing to slaves. Now that they were free, blacks thirsted for the knowledge that had once been denied to them.

Dedicated Teachers,
Determined Students, 1869

RALEIGH, N.C., FEB 22, 1869

It is surprising to me to see the amount of suffering which many of the people endure for the sake of sending their children to school. Men get very low wages here—from $2.50 to $8 per month usually, while a first-rate hand may get $10, and a peck or two of meal per week for rations—and a great many men cannot get work at all. The women take in sewing and washing, go out by day to scour, etc. There is one woman who supports three children and keeps them at school; she says, "I don't care how hard I has to work, if I can only send Sallie and the boys to school looking respectable." Many of the girls have but one decent dress; it gets washed and ironed on Saturday, and then is worn until the next Saturday, provided they do not tear it or fall in the mud; when such an accident happens there is an absent mark on the register.... One may go into their cabins on cold, windy days, and see daylight between every two boards, or feel the rain dropping through the roof; but a word of complaint is rarely heard. They are anxious to have the children "get on" in their books, and do not seem to feel impatient if they lack comforts themselves. A pile of books is seen in almost every cabin, though there be no furniture except a poor bed, a table and two or three broken chairs.

> MISS M. A. PARKER
> In *American Freedman, April 1869*

SYDNEY ANDREWS quoted in the Joint Report
on Reconstruction, 39th (U.S.) Congress, 1st Session, 1866:

Many of the negroes ... common plantation negroes, and day laborers in the towns and villages, were supporting little schools themselves. Everywhere I found among them a disposition to get their children into schools, if possible. I had occasion very frequently to notice that porters in stores and laboring men in warehouses, and cart drivers on the streets, had spelling books with them, and were studying them during the time they were not occupied with their work. Go into the outskirts of any large town and walk among the negro inhabitants, and you will see children and in many instances grown negroes, sitting in the sun alongside their cabins studying.

CAPTAIN C. M. HAMILTON in a letter to the Office
of the Adjutant General in Washington, D.C., 1866:

The night school has been frequently disturbed. One evening a mob called out of the school house, the teacher, who upon presenting himself was confronted with four revolvers, and menacing expressions of shooting him, if he did not promise to quit the place, and close the school. The freedmen promptly came to his aid and the mob dispersed.

About the 18th or 19th of the month, I was absent ... when a formidable disturbance took place at the school. The same mob threatened to destroy the school that night, and the freedmen, learning this, assembled... at their place of instruction in a condition of self-defense.

I understand that not less than forty colored men armed to protect themselves, but the preparation becoming known to the *respectable, rowdies,* they only maneuvered about in small squads, and were wise enough to avoid a collision.

HOW WELL DID YOU UNDERSTAND THIS SELECTION?

1. What evidence do the documents in this section show about the significance of education for freed people?

2. What barriers did these blacks have to overcome to get some education?

3. What is meant by "respectable rowdies"? Why would they assault a school?

THE SPLIT BETWEEN ADVOCATES OF WOMEN'S RIGHTS AND BLACK RIGHTS

The close alliance between women reformers and abolitionists was seriously tested by the dispute over universal suffrage. The women expected to see the right to vote extended to women, as well as blacks. Many advocates of rights for the freed people, however, argued that it was "the Negro's hour, not the woman's."

A petition drafted after the Civil War by ELIZABETH CADY STANTON and SUSAN B. ANTHONY, leaders of the women's movement and also abolitionists:

To the Senate and House of Representatives in Congress Assembled:
The undersigned citizens of the State of _____ earnestly but respectfully request that in any change or amendment of the Constitution you may propose to extend or regulate Suffrage, there shall be no distinction made between men and women.

Letter to Susan B. Anthony from abolitionist and advocate of suffrage for ex-slaves GERRITT SMITH, December 30, 1868

My Dear Susan B. Anthony: I this evening received your earnest letter. It pains me to be obliged to disappoint you. But I cannot sign the petition you sent me. Cheerfully, gladly can I sign a petition for the enfranchisement [granting the right to vote] of women. But I cannot sign a paper against the enfranchisement of the Negro man, unless at the same time woman shall be enfranchised. The removal of the political disabilities of race is my first desire, of sex my second. If put on the same level and urged in the same connection, neither will be soon accomplished. The former will very soon be, if untrammeled by the other, and its success will prepare the way for the other.

A Response by Elizabeth Cady Stanton

[Gerritt Smith] does not clearly read the sign of the times, or he would see that there is to be no reconstruction of this nation, except on the basis of Universal Suffrage, as the natural, inalienable right of every citizen to its exercise....

As the aristocracy of this country is the "male sex" and as Mr. Smith belongs to the privileged order, he naturally considers it important, for the best interests of the nation, that every type and shade of degraded, ignorant manhood should be enfranchised, before even the higher classes of womanhood should be admitted to the polls.

This does not surprise us. Men always judge more wisely of objective wrongs and oppressions, than of those in which they themselves are involved. Tyranny on a southern plantation is far more easily seen by white men... [in] the north than the wrongs of the women of their own households....

Again, Mr. Smith refuses to sign the petition because he thinks that to press the broader question of "Universal Suffrage" would defeat the partial one of "Manhood Suffrage"; in other words to demand protection for women against her oppressors would jeopardize the black man's chances for securing protection against his oppressors. If it is a question of precedence merely, on what principle of justice or courtesy should woman yield her right of enfranchisement to the Negro? If men cannot be trusted to legislate for their own sex, how can they legislate for the opposite sex, of whose wants and needs they know nothing! It has always been considered good philosophy in pressing any measure to claim the uttermost in order to get something .... Henry Ward Beecher advised abolitionists, right after the war, to demand "Universal Suffrage" if they wished to secure the ballot for the new made freedmen. "Bait your hooks," said he, "with a woman and perhaps you will catch a Negro." But their intense interest in the Negro blinded them, and they forsook principle for policy. In giving woman the cold shoulder they raised a more deadly opposition to the Negro than any we had encountered, creating an antagonism between him and the very element most needed, especially in the South, to be propitiated in his behalf...

... There is no other ground on which to debate the question. Every argument for the Negro is an argument for woman and no logician can escape it....

Although those who demand "Women's Suffrage" on principle are few, those who would oppose "Negro suffrage" from prejudice are many, hence the only way to secure the latter is to end all this talk of class legislation, bury the Negro in the citizen, and claim suffrage for all men and women as a natural, inalienable right.
- ELIZABETH CADY STANTON, January 14, 1869

"Being Persons, Then, Women are Citizens"

Though the words persons, people, inhabitants, electors, citizens, are all used indiscriminately in the national and State constitutions, there was always a conflict of opinion, prior to the war, as to whether they were synonymous terms, but whatever room there was for doubts, under the old regime, the adoption of the Fourteenth Amendment settled that question forever in its first sentence:
    All persons born or naturalized in the United States, and subject to the jurisdiction thereof, are citizens of
    the United States wherein they reside.
The second settles the equal status of all citizens:
    No state shall make or enforce any law which shall abridge the privileges or immunities of citizens of the
    United States; nor shall any State deprive any person of life, liberty, or property without due process of law;
    nor deny to any person within its jurisdiction the equal protection of the laws.
The only question left to be settled now is: Are women persons? I scarcely believe that any of our opponents will have the hardihood to say that they are not. Being persons, then, women are citizens and no State has a right to make any new law, or to enforce any old law, which shall abridge their privileges and immunities. Hence, every discrimination against women in the constitutions and laws of the several States is today null and void, precisely as is every one against Negroes.
    - SUSAN B. ANTHONY, November 1872

HOW WELL DID YOU UNDERSTAND THIS SELECTION?

1. Why wouldn't Gerritt Smith sign the petition? Why did he want to separate the issues of women and blacks getting the vote?

2. How does Elizabeth Cady Stanton respond to his argument? What aspect of her response do you find most troubling?

3. What is the basis of Susan B. Anthony's claim that the Fourteenth Amendment also guaranteed women's rights?

4. Why did the women's movement split with their former abolitionist allies?

DIFFERING VIEWS ABOUT BLACKS IN RECONSTRUCTION IN THE SOUTH

---

*Most white Southerners saw the Reconstruction era as a time period in which blacks, drunk with new-found power, lorded it over the oppressed white population. The reality, of course, was far different. Blacks never had real power in any state and were very moderate in their demands and votes. Albion Tourgee was a Northerner who served as a judge in the South, propelled by idealism. He was eventually disillusioned by the level of resistance to rights for freed people he found among southern whites. Thomas Dixon's bestselling novel, **The Clansman**, reflected the attitudes of southern whites. (It later became the basis for the popular movie, **Birth of a Nation**, which was instrumental in disseminating negative images of black-actions in Reconstruction.) The final document in this segment relates the experiences of a black man who gained some measure of authority during Reconstruction.*

From the Novel, *A Fool's Errand*
By the "carpetbagger," Albion Tourgee (1879)

When the second Christmas come, Metta wrote again to her sister:

"The feeling is terribly bitter against Comfort on account of his course towards the colored people. There is quite a village of them on the lower end of the plantation. They have a church, a sabbath school, and are to have next year a school. You can not imagine how kind they have been to us, and how much they are attached to Comfort.... I got Comfort to go with me to one of their prayer meetings a few nights ago. I had heard a great deal about them, but had never attended one before. It was strangely weird. There were, perhaps, fifty present, mostly middle-aged men and women. They were singing in a soft, low monotone, interspersed with prolonged exclamatory notes, a sort of rude hymn, which I was surprised to know was one of their old songs in slave times. How the chorus came to be endured in those days I can not imagine. It was—

'Free! free! free, my Lord, free!
An' we walks de hebben-ly way!'

"A few looked around as we came in and seated ourselves; and Uncle Jerry, the saint of the settlement, came forward on his staves, and said, in his soft voice, "'Ev'nin', Kunnel! Sarvant, Missus! Will you walk up, an' hev seats in front?'

'We told him we had just looked in, and might go in a short time; so we would stay in the back part of the audience.

"Uncle Jerry can not read nor write; but he is a man of strange intelligence and power. Unable to do work of any account, he is the faithful friend, monitor, and director of others. He has a house and piece of land, all paid for, a good horse and cow, and, with the aid of his wife and two boys, made a fine crop this season. He is one of the most promising colored men in the settlement: so Comfort says, at least. Everybody seems to have great respect for his character. I don't know how many people I have heard speak of his religion. Mr. Savage used to say he had rather hear him pray than any other man on earth. He was much prized by his master, even after he was disabled, on account of his faithfulness and character."

From the Novel, *The Clansman*
By Thomas Dixon Jr. (1905)

At noon Ben and Phil strolled to the polling-place to watch the progress of the first election under Negro rule. The Square was jammed with shouting, jostling, perspiring negroes, men, women, and children. The day was worm, and the African odour was supreme even in the open air....

The negroes, under the drill of the League and the Freedman's Bureau, protected by the bayonet, were voting to enfranchise themselves, disfranchise their former masters, ratify a new constitution, and elect a legislature to do their will. Old Aleck was a candidate for the House, chief poll-holder, and seemed to be in charge of the movements of the voters outside the booth as well as inside. He appeared to be omnipresent, and his self-importance was a sight Phil had never dreamed. He could not keep his eyes off him....

[Aleck] was a born African orator, undoubtedly descended from a long line of savage spell-binders, whose eloquence in the palaver houses of the jungle had made them native leaders. His thin spindle-shanks supported an oblong, protruding stomach, resembling an elderly monkey's, which seemed so heavy it swayed his back to carry it.

The animal vivacity of his small eyes and the flexibility of his eye-brows, which he worked up and down rapidly with every change of countenance, expressed his eager desires.

He had laid aside his new shoes, which hurt him, and went barefooted to facilitate his movements on the great occasion. His heels projected and his foot was so flat that what should have been the hollow of it made a hole in the dirt where he left his track.

He was already mellow with liquor, and was dressed in an old army uniform and cap, with two horse-pistols buckled around his waist. On a strap hanging from his shoulder were strung a half-dozen tin canteens filled with whiskey.

From—*The Autobiography of JOHN ROY LYNCH,*
an ex-slave appointed justice-of-the peace in Natchez, Mississippi at age 22
(he later was elected a three-term congressman)

[A] case of some significance that came before me was that of a white man that I knew unfavorably and well. He had cursed, abused, and threatened the life of an inoffensive old colored man on account of a misunderstanding over a small business transaction. Upon the complaint of the colored man, a warrant was issued for the arrest of the party against whom the complaint was made. When he was brought before the court and the charges had been read to him and he was asked whether or not he was guilty as charged, he seemed to be somewhat surprised. "Why," he re-marked, "do you mean to tell me that it is a crime for a white man to curse a nigger?" "Yes," the court replied. "It is a crime for a white man to curse a Negro as it is for a Negro to curse a white man." "Well," he exclaimed, "that's news to me. You certainly must be mistaken. If there is such a law, I never heard of it." The court then handed him the code and told him where he could find the section bearing upon the point at issue and requested him to read it for himself, which he did.

When he had finished, he exclaimed in a somewhat subdued tone: "Well, I'll be damned." The court then admonished him that if that remark should be repeated, he would be committed to the county jail for contempt of court. He quickly apologized and assured the court that no disrespect was intended. He said that he could not deny having used the language set forth in the affidavit, but he hoped the court would not be severe because he did not know and did not believe that in using that language he was violating any law. Since it was his first offense, he was let off with a fine of five dollars and costs which he promptly paid. It was the first and only time he was brought before me.

HOW WELL DID YOU UNDERSTAND THIS SELECTION?

1. What are the differences in the ways Tourgee and Dixon (in selections A and B) see freed people and their conduct? Why do you think there are such great differences in their points of view?

2. Whose description do feel is most accurate? Why?

3. Why do you think John Lynch considers his case to be "of some significance"? Do you agree or disagree?

4. What does his experience tell you about changes in the South during the era of Reconstruction?

Eventually, Americans grew weary with the struggle to maintain the rights of black people. The Civil Rights Act of 1875 was the last attempt to guarantee such rights. Northern white commitment faded as other issues, such as economic depression and political scandals, drew their attention. Southern white violence, directed at white and black Republicans and any blacks asserting their rights, was carried out by groups such as the Ku Klux Klan. Democratic opponents of Reconstruction returned to political control of the South.

An excerpt from the speech of black Congressman Richard Harvey Cain of South Carolina on the floor of the House in support of the Civil Rights Act of 1875.

All we ask is that you, the legislators of this nation, shall pass a law so strong and so powerful that no one shall be able to elude it and destroy our rights under the Constitution and laws of our country. That is all we ask....

We do not want any discriminations to be made. If discriminations arc made in regard to schools, then there will be accomplished just what we are fighting against. If you say that the schools in the State of Georgia, for instance, shall be allowed to discriminate against colored people, then you will have discriminations made against us. We do not want any discriminations. I do not ask any legislation for the colored people of this country that is not applied to the white people. All that we ask is equal laws, equal legislation, and equal rights throughout the length and the breadth of this land.

[Another congressman] says that the colored men should not come here begging at the doors of Congress for their rights. I agree with him. I want to say that we do not come here begging for our rights. We come here clothed in the garb of American citizenship. We come demanding our rights in the name of justice. We come, with no arrogance on our part, asking that this great nation, which laid the foundations of civilization and progress more deeply and more securely than any other nation on the face of the earth, guarantee us protection from outrage. We come here, five millions of people—more than composed this entire nation when it had its great tea-party in Boston Harbor, and demanded its rights at the point of a bayonet—asking that unjust discriminations against us be forbidden. We come here in the name of justice, equity, and law, in the name of our children, in the name of our country, petitioning for our rights.

Source: Congressional Record, 43rd Cong., 1st session, Vol. II, pg. 1

Political Terrorism by the Ku Klux Klan
Testimony by Harriet Hernandez

The following account by Harriet Hernandez, a former slave of Spartanburg, South Carolina, describes how the Klan used threats and violence to intimidate black Republican voters in the region. It is excerpted from her testimony in December 1871 before a congressional committee appointed to investigate Klan activities.

Question: Did the Ku-Klux: ever come to your house at any time?
Answer: Yes, Sir; twice.
Q.: Go on to the second time....
A.: They came in; I was lying in bed. Says he, "Come out here, Sir; Come out here, Sir!" They took me out of bed; they would not let me get out, but they took me up in their arms and toted me out—me and my daughter Lucy. He struck me on the forehead with a pistol, and here is the scar above my eye now. Says he, "Damn you, fall!" I fell. Says

he, "Damn you, get up!" I got up. Says he, "Damn you, get over this fence!" And he kicked me over when I went to get over; and then he went to a brush pile, and they laid us right down there, both together. They laid us down twenty yards apart, I reckon. They had dragged and beat us along. They struck me right on the top of my head, and I thought they had killed me; and I said, "Lord o' mercy, don't, don't kill my child!" He gave me a lick on the head, and it liked to have killed me; I saw stars. He threw my arm over my head so I could not do anything with it for three weeks, and there are great knots on my wrist now.

Q: What did they say this was for?

A: They said, "You can tell your husband that when we see him we are going to kill him."

Q: Did they say why they wanted to kill him?

A: They said, "He voted the radical ticket, didn't he?" I said, "Yes, that very way."

Q: When did your husband get back after this whipping? He was not at home, was he?

A: He was lying out; he couldn't stay at home, bless your soul

Q: Has he been afraid for any length of time?

A: He has been afraid ever since last October. He has been lying out. He has not laid in the house ten nights since October.

Q: Is that the situation of the colored people down there to any extent?

A: That is the way they all have to do—men and women both.

Q: What are they afraid of?

A: Of being killed or whipped to death.

Q: What has made them afraid?

A: Because men that voted radical tickets they took the spite out on the women when they could get at them.

Q: How many colored people have been whipped in that neighborhood?

A: It is all of them, mighty near.

Source: Report of the Joint Select Committee to Inquire into the Condition of Affairs in the Late Insurrectionary States (1872)

Excerpts from the original draft of the South Carolina 1876 Democratic party campaign plan formulated by ex-Confederate general MARTIN W. GARY

[It is decreed] That the Democratic Military Clubs are to be armed with rifles and pistols and such other arms as they may command. They are to be divided into two companies, one of the old men, the other of the young; an experienced captain or commander to be placed over each of them. That each company is to have a first and second lieutenant. That the number of ten privates is to be the unit of organization. That each captain is to see that his men are well armed and provided with at least thirty rounds of ammunition. That the Captain of the young men is to provide a Baggage wagon in which three days rations for the horses and three days rations for the men are to be stored on the day before the election in order that they may be prepared at a moment's notice to move to any point in the County when ordered by the Chairman of the Executive Committee....

Every Democrat must feel honor bound to control the vote of at least one Negro, by intimidation, purchase, keeping him away or as each individual may determine, how he may best accomplish it....

Never threaten a man individually. If he deserves to be threatened, the necessities of the times require that he should die. A dead Radical is very harmless—a threatened Radical or one driven off by threats from the scene of his operations is often very troublesome, sometimes dangerous, always vindictive [vengeful]....In the month of September, we ought to begin to organize Negro [Democratic] clubs, or pretend that we have organized them.... Those who join are to be taken on probation and are not to be taken into full fellowship until they have proven their sincerity by voting our ticket.

HOW WELL DID YOU UNDERSTAND THIS SELECTION?

1. What is the basis for Congressman Cain's pleas for the passage of the Civil Rights Act of 1875?

2. What was the purpose of Klan threats and violence as shown by Harriet Hernandez's testimony? What do you think would be the result of such tactics?

3. What were the key elements of South Carolina Democratic Party's 1876 election plan? In what way did it intend to "control the vote" of freedmen? Why do you think the plan included an organization of "Negro Democratic" clubs?

AFTER RECONSTRUCTION

Frederick Douglass had great hopes that his fellow blacks would gain full rights as American citizens after the Civil War. He had helped the Republican Party to win black votes and was rewarded by various government appointments. It soon became clear, however, that the hard-won gains of the Reconstruction era were rapidly being lost. In this keynote address to a convention of blacks, Douglass describes the discrimination faced by his people and hopes for its eventual elimination.

Address to the Louisville Convention (1883)
FREDERICK DOUGLASS

Born on American soil in common with yourselves, deriving our bodies and our minds from its dust, centuries having passed away since our ancestors were torn from the shores of Africa, we, like yourselves, hold ourselves to be in every sense Americans, and that we may, therefore, venture to speak to you in a tone not lower than that which becomes earnest men and American citizens. Having watered your soil with our tears, enriched it with our blood, performed its roughest labor in time of peace, defended it against war, and at all times been loyal and true to its best interests, we deem it no arrogance or presumption to manifest now a common concern with you for its welfare, prosperity, honor and glory ...

It is our lot to live among a people whose laws, traditions, and prejudices have been against us for centuries, and from these they are not yet free. To assume that they are free from these evils simply because they have changed their laws is to assume what is utterly unreasonable and contrary to facts. Large bodies move slowly. Individuals may be converted on the instant and change their whole course of life. Nations never. Time and events are required for the conversion of nations. Not even the character of a great political organization can be changed by a new platform. It will be the same old snake though in a new skin. Though we have had war, reconstruction and abolition as a nation, we still linger in the shadow and blight of an extinct institution. Though the colored man is no longer subject to be bought and sold, he is still surrounded by an adverse sentiment which fetters all his movements. In his downward course he meets with no resistance, but his course upward is resented and resisted at every step of his progress. If he comes in ignorance, rags, and wretchedness, he conforms to the popular belief of his character, and in that character he is welcome. But if he shall come as a gentleman, a scholar, and a statesman, he is hailed as a contradiction to the national faith concerning his race, and his coming is resented as impudence. In the one case he may provoke contempt and derision, but in the other he is an affront to pride, and provokes malice. Let him do what he will, there is at present, therefore, no escape for him. The color line meets him everywhere, and in a measure shuts him out from all respectable and profitable trades and callings. In spite of all your religion and laws he is a rejected man.

He is rejected by trade unions, of every trade, and refused work while he lives, and burial when he dies, and yet he is asked to forget his color, and forget that which everybody else remembers. If he offers himself to a builder as a mechanic, to a client as a lawyer, to a patient as a physician, to a college as a professor, to a firm as a clerk, to a Government Department as an agent, or an officer, he is sternly met on the color line, and his claim to consideration in some way is disputed on the ground of color.

Not even our churches, whose members profess to follow the despised Nazarene, whose home, when on earth, was among the lowly and despised, have yet conquered this feeling of color madness, and what is true of our churches is also true of our courts of law. Neither is free from this all pervading atmosphere of color hate. The one describes the Deity as impartial, no respecter of persons, and the other the Goddess of Justice as blindfolded, with sword by her side and scales in her hand held evenly between high and low, rich and low, white and black, but both are the images of American imagination, rather than American practices.

Taking advantage of the general disposition in this country to impute crime to color, white men color their faces to commit crime and wash off the hated color to escape punishment. In many places where the commission of crime is alleged against one of our color, the ordinary processes of law are set aside as too slow for the impetuous justice of the infuriated populace. They take the law into their own bloody hands and proceed to whip, stab, shoot, hang, or burn the alleged culprit, without the intervention of courts, counsel, judges, juries, or witnesses. In such cases it is not the business of the accusers to prove guilt, but it is for the accused to prove his innocence, a thing hard for him to do in these infernal Lynch courts. A man accused, surprised, frightened, and captured by a motley crowd, dragged with a rope about his neck in midnight-darkness to the nearest tree, and told in the coarsest terms of profanity to prepare for death, would be more than human if he did not, in his terror-stricken appearance, more confirm suspicion of guilt than the contrary. Worse still, in the presence of such hell-black outrages, the pulpit is usually dumb, and the press in the neighborhood is silent or openly takes side with the mob. There are occasional cases in which white men are lynched, but one sparrow does not make a summer. Every one knows that what is called Lynch law is peculiarly the law for colored people and for nobody else. If there were no other grievance than this horrible and barbarous Lynch law custom, we should be justified in assembling, as we have now done, to expose and denounce it. But this is not all. Even now, after twenty years of so-called emancipation, we are subject to lawless raids of midnight riders, who, with blackened faces, invade our homes and perpetrate the foulest of crimes upon us and our families. This condition of things is too flagrant and notorious to require specifications or proof. Thus in all the relations of life and death we are met by the color line.

While we recognize the color line as a hurtful force, a mountain barrier to our progress, wounding our bleeding feet with its flinty rocks at every step, we do not despair. We are a hopeful people. This convention is a proof of our faith in you, in reason, in truth and justice our belief that prejudice, with all its malign accomplishments, may yet be removed by peaceful means; that, assisted by time and events and the growing enlightenment of both races, the color line will ultimately become harmless. When this shall come it will then only be used, as it should be, to distinguish one variety of the human family from another. It will cease to have any civil, political, or moral significance, and colored conventions will then be dispensed with as anachronisms, wholly out of place, but not till then. Do not marvel that we are discouraged. The faith within us has a rational basis, and is confirmed by facts. When we consider how deep-seated this feeling against us is; the long centuries it has been forming; the forces of avarice which have been marshaled to sustain it; how the language and literature of the country have been pervaded with it; how the church, the press, the play-house, and other influences of the country have been arrayed in its support, the progress toward its extinction must be considered vast and wonderful....

We do not believe, as we are often told, that the Negro is the ugly child of the national family, and the more he is kept out of sight the better it will be for him. You know that liberty given is never so precious as liberty sought for and fought for. The man outraged is the man to make the outcry. Depend upon it, men will not care much for a people who do not care for themselves. Our meeting here was opposed by some of our members, because it would disturb the peace of the Republican party. The suggestion came from coward lips and misapprehended the character of that party. If the Republican party cannot stand a demand for justice and fair play, it ought to go down. We were men before that party was born, and our manhood is more sacred than any party can be. Parties were made for men, not men for parties.

The colored people of the South are the laboring people of the South. The labor of a country is the source of its wealth; without the colored laborer today the South would be a howling wilderness, given up to bats, owls, wolves, and bears. He was the source of its wealth before the war, and has been the source of its prosperity since the war. He almost alone is visible in her fields, with implements of toil in his hands, and laboriously using them to-day.

Let us look candidly at the matter. While we see and hear that the South is more prosperous than it ever was before and rapidly recovering from the waste of war, while we read that it raises more cotton, sugar, rice, tobacco, corn, and other valuable products than it ever produced before, how happens it, we sternly ask, that the houses of its laborers are miserable huts, that their clothes are rags, and their food the coarsest and scantiest? How happens it that the land-owner is becoming richer and the laborer poorer?

The implication is irresistible that where the landlord is prosperous the laborer ought to share his prosperity, and whenever and wherever we find this is not the case there is manifestly wrong somewhere....

Flagrant as have been the outrages committed upon colored citizens in respect to their civil rights, more flagrant, shocking, and scandalous still have been the outrages committed upon our political rights by means of bull-dozing and Kukluxing, Mississippi plans, fraudulent courts, tissue ballots, and the like devices. Three States in which the colored people outnumber the white population are without colored representation and their political voice suppressed. The colored citizens in those States are virtually disfranchised, the Constitution held in utter contempt and its provisions nullified. This has been done in the face of the Republican party and successive Republican administrations....

This is no question of party It is a question of law and government. It is a question whether men shall be protected by law, or be left to the mercy of cyclones of anarchy and bloodshed. It is whether the Government or the mob shall rule this land; whether the promises solemnly made to us in the constitution be manfully kept or meanly and flagrantly broken. Upon this vital point we ask the whole people of the United States to take notice that whatever of political power we have shall be exerted for no man of any party who will not, in advance of election, promise to use every power given him by the Government, State or National, to make the black man's path to the ballot-box as straight, smooth and safe as that Of any other American citizen....

We hold it to be self-evident that no class or color should be the exclusive rulers of this country. If there is such a ruling class, there must of course be a subject class, and when this condition is once established this Government of the people, by the people, and for the people, will have perished from the earth.

Source: *The Life and Writings of Frederick Douglass*, Philip Foner, ed., vol. IV (1955).

HOW WELL DID YOU UNDERSTAND THIS SELECTION?

1. To whom do you think Douglass is directing his speech?

2. What are five specific injustices he sees in the period following Reconstruction?

3. What does he believe the solution should be?

4. What does his description tell you about Reconstruction and its results?

SELF TEST

MULTIPLE CHOICE: Circle the correct response. The correct answers are given at the end.

1. Slavery was finally prohibited in all the states and territories of the United States by the
   a. Thirteenth Amendment.
   b. Fourteenth Amendment.
   c. Emancipation Proclamation.
   d. treaty ending the Civil War.

2. The Black Codes established in the South after the Civil War demonstrated that Southerners
   a. understood the need the newly freed people had for education.
   b. were happy to leave the future of blacks in the hands of blacks themselves.
   c. hoped to limit black rights and to restrict blacks to a servile position.
   d. were happy to grant blacks their full equality under the law.

3. The most important disagreement between President Johnson and Congress concerned
   a. how many representatives each state would be given.
   b. what to do with land seized from the Confederate leaders.
   c. how to demobilize the opposing armies.
   d. what the position of the former slaves would be in the reconstructed states.

4. After the Civil War, freed slaves
   a. upset Northerners due to their disinterest in any kind of education.
   b. put most of their efforts into creating racially integrated school systems.
   c. demonstrated a great desire for education as a means of upward mobility.
   d. felt that primary schools were more than adequate to meet their needs.

5. The three constitutional amendments that were ratified after the Civil War were designed to
   a. limit the powers of the federal government that had expanded during the war.
   b. grant the basic rights of citizenship to black Americans.
   c. punish the Confederates for their treason to their country.
   d. restore the country to exactly where it had been before the war.

6. Since most congressmen in the Reconstruction era were firm believers in laissez-faire, they resisted suggestions that
   a. plantation land be appropriated and redistributed to former slaves.
   b. former Confederate states be readmitted to the union.
   c. Northerners invest capital in southern railroads and industry.
   d. former slaves be given rights as citizens of the United States.

7. By the 1870s, northern public opinion
   a. continued to strongly back protection of the rights of blacks in the South.
   b. grew increasingly disinterested in black rights and southern Reconstruction.
   c. continued to strongly favor congressional reconstruction plans.
   d. grew increasingly angry at the political leaders who had led the nation into the Civil War.

8. By the end of Reconstruction most blacks worked as
   a. sharecroppers
   b. small farmers on their own land.
   c. domestic servants on their former plantations.
   d. industrial wage workers.

9. The most significant, long-lasting failure of southern Reconstruction governments was their
   a. unwillingness to rebuild and promote industrial development.
   b. failure to provide any support for a system of public education.
   c. inability to raise any taxes to support the needs of state budgets.
   d. failure to try to change the social and economic structure of southern society.

10. The Supreme Court, in the *Plessy v. Ferguson* case, authorized
    a. the prohibition of racial intermarriages.
    b. denying blacks the right to vote.
    c. state-mandated racial segregation.
    d. state efforts to create equal rights for all.

Answers:: 1-a; 2-c; 3-d; 4-c; 5-b; 6-a; 7-b; 8-a; 9-d; 10-c.

ESSAYS:

1. Describe the conflict between the president and Congress over Reconstruction and discuss the long and short-term consequences of this conflict.

2. Explain the following statement: "Reconstruction changed southern society in important but limited ways." What were the most important accomplishments of Reconstruction? Its failures? How would you evaluate its overall impact?

3. After the Civil War, the nation appeared to commit itself to equality for freed slaves through laws and constitutional amendments. Describe these laws and amendments. What caused the nation to retreat from this commitment?

OPTIONAL ACTIVITIES: (Use your knowledge **and** imagination.)

1. You are the prosecutor of Andrew Johnson in his impeachment trial **OR** his defense attorney. Write a two-page brief of the prosecution/defense strategy you would follow. What do you feel is the strongest point of your argument?

2. You live in a small southern town during Reconstruction. In a 2-3 page paper describe how a freedman/woman and a klansman would view the same events.

WEB SITE LISTINGS:

Harper's Weekly – America's Leading Magazine During Reconstruction
   http://www.harpweek.com

Library of Congress
   http://lcweb.loc.gov/exhibits/africa/intro.html
   http://memory.loc.gov/ammem/aaohtml/exhibit/aopart5.html
   http://scriptorium.lib.duke.edu/collections/african-american-women.html
                                          /franklin/af-am-mss.collections53.html

Many Specific Events
   http://www.channelone.com/fasttrack/ushistory/1800-1877/

Primary Sources including a Black Code and Sharecropper's Contract
   http://longman.awl.com/history/activities_16_20.htm

Report of the Joint committee on Reconstruction
   http://odur.let.rug.nl/~usa/usa.htm

Making of America – hundreds of articles and books in search
   www.hti.umcih.edu/m/moagrp
   http://moa.cit.cornell.edu/moa

Chapter Thirteen

INDUSTRIALIZATION

America's Industrial Revolution kicked into high gear about 1880. For the next forty years everything about the United States changed, including government, society, politics, work, and, most of all, the economy. The machine age embodied optimism and opportunity. Technological adaptation of existing devices, such as the steam engine and the sewing machine, as well as new discoveries and inventions in electricity, chemistry, physics, engineering, manufacturing, and agriculture, enabled the United States to move to the forefront of industrial nations. No people were more inventive and innovative than were Americans during this time. Between 1790 and 1860 the U. S. Patent Office granted a total of 36,000 patents. In 1897 alone it granted 22,000; by 1920, it had granted about 1.4 million patents.

Despite the optimism, industrialization did not proceed without problems. Cities experienced tremendous growth. Areas that before the Civil War had been, at best, small towns became bustling metropolitan areas almost overnight. New buildings had to be built, police forces enlarged, fire brigades created, streets enlarged, and new neighborhoods to house the growing population had to be constructed. Mayors and city councils sometimes struggled to find financing to pay for these projects.

Workers also experienced problems. Before the Industrial Revolution most products sold in the United States were produced by craftspeople working in shops near their houses. They set their own hours and worked when they had orders to fill. Mechanization changed methods of production, destroying time-honored crafts, such as glassmaking and iron molding, and subjecting workers to rigid schedules and repetitive routines they had never before experienced. Although mechanization created new jobs, it also produced low wages because most machines were labor saving devices that enabled fewer workers to produce more products. This created a situation workers had never experienced—unemployment and low wages. Workers responded by organizing unions such as the Knights of Labor and the American Federation of Labor. Their goals were generally to improve the lives of workers and eliminate evils like child labor.

Imperialism also came with industrialization. In 1898 the United States acquired its first overseas colonies and fought a war of seven years duration to prevent the Philippine Islands from gaining independence. Many Americans believed imperialism sullied America's reputation around the world and protested against it. Despite the protests, industrialists demanded that the United States acquire colonies so they could market products to additional populations.

Racism and Jim Crow segregation continued to play a prominent role in the South. Efforts by African Americans to overcome the racism, prejudice, and discrimination that were part of their everyday life generally centered on education. African-American leaders hoped that an educated population would be able to surmount racial barriers that white society had erected. Unfortunately, this was not reality.

IDENTIFICATION: Briefly describe each term.

Joseph Pulitzer

William Randolph Hearst

Andrew Carnegie

John D. Rockefeller

J. Pierpont Morgan

Cornelius Vanderbilt

Henry Huntington

Leland Stanford

Robber Barons

Standard Oil of Ohio

James Duke

Thomas Edison

Alexander Graham Bell

Vertical Integration

Horizontal Integration

Sherman Silver Purchase Act

Sherman Anti-Trust Act

Interstate Commerce Act

Queen Liliuokalani

Spanish-American War

Rough Riders

Emilio Aguinaldo

Gospel of Wealth

Ida B. Wells

Theodore Dreiser

Jacob Riis

Knights of Labor

Chinese Exclusion Act

Haymarket Square Bombing

American Federation of Labor

Mary Harris "Mother" Jones

Pullman Strike

Booker T. Washington

W.E.B. Du Bois

Women's Suffrage Movement

Lucy Stone

Susan B. Anthony

Elizabeth Cady Stanton

Francs Willard

Jane Addams

THINK ABOUT:

1. How did the Industrial Revolution change America? Could historians argue that modern America began with the Industrial Revolution? Why or why not? If not, when did modern America begin? What characteristics are part of modern America?

2. How did imperialism and the Spanish-American War change American foreign policy? What impact throughout the twentieth century did the Spanish-American War and imperialism have on American history?

3. What role did problems created by industrialism play in governmental regulation of the economy?

4. How did wealthy Americans deal with contradictions in American society produced by the concentration of wealth in the hands of a few while the masses remained poor? Does the same economic gap between rich and poor exist in the United States today? Why or why not?

THE SHERMAN ANTI-TRUST ACT OF 1890

Industrialization during the last half of the nineteenth century created the problem of trusts and monopolies. Big business faced cutthroat competition. They produced vast quantities of products and sold them quickly for small profits. To overcome the cutthroat competition, industrialists developed the pool, trust, and holding company. The purpose of these forms of business organizations was to eliminate or limit competition and thus raise profit margins. This was best done by getting rival businesses to cooperate or by driving competitors out of business. The first trust formed was Standard Oil in 1882. John D. Rockefeller's attorney, Samuel Dodd, thought of the idea. He created a board of trustees to control all companies Standard Oil had acquired, which allowed them to function as one company. Later, Rockefeller and Standard Oil created the Holding Company to serve the same purpose. Other corporations emulated Rockefeller, forming trusts of their own to restrain competition and raise prices.

By the mid 1880s the American public was fed up with monopolistic companies who drove up prices for products and services they produced. In 1888 both Democratic and Republican candidates for president promised to restrain the mo-

nopolies. This restraint occurred in 1890 when Congress passed the Sherman Anti-Trust Act by a vote of 51 to 1 in the Senate and 242 to 0 in the House of Representatives. President Harrison signed the bill into law, and trusts and monopolies became illegal forms of business.

SECTION ONE:

Every contract, combination in the form of trust or otherwise, or conspiracy, in restraint of trade or commerce among the several States, or with foreign nations, is declared to be illegal. Every person who shall make any contract or engage in any combination or conspiracy hereby declared to be illegal shall be deemed guilty of a felony, and, on conviction thereof, shall be punished by fine not exceeding ten million dollars if a corporation, or, if any other person, three hundred and fifty thousand dollars, or by imprisonment not exceeding three years, or by both said punishments, in the discretion of the court.

SECTION TWO:

Every person who shall monopolize, or attempt to monopolize, or combine or conspire with any other person or persons, to monopolize any part of the trade or commerce among the several States, or with foreign nations, shall be deemed guilty of a felony, and, on conviction thereof, shall be punished by fine not exceeding ten million dollars if a corporation, or, if any other person, three hundred and fifty thousand dollars or by imprisonment not exceeding three years, or by both said punishments, in the discretion of the court.

HOW WELL DID YOU UNDERSTAND THIS SELECTION?

1. What was the penalty corporations faced for violating the Sherman Anti-Trust Act?

2. What penalties did individuals face for violating the Sherman Anti-Trust Act?

3. Does the Sherman Anti-Trust Act define what a monopoly is? If so, what is a monopoly?

4. What weaknesses can you find in the Sherman Anti-Trust Act?

5. Look at the Constitution in the appendix to your textbook? What part of the Constitution gives Congress the power to pass the Sherman Anti-Trust Act?

Andrew Carnegie, a poor immigrant from Scotland, became one of the world's wealthiest men. He made his vast fortune in the steel industry, which he dominated through vertical integration until he sold the Carnegie Steel Company to J. P. Morgan, a New York financier, for nearly half a billion dollars. Carnegie felt guilty about acquiring such a vast fortune, especially when he had been poor in his native land and because workers who produced his vast wealth lived little better than animals. To ease his conscious, Carnegie devised an idea called the gospel of wealth. Late in life, he gave away much of his fortune, especially to libraries and churches.

The problem of our age is the administration of wealth, so that the ties of brotherhood may still bind together the rich and poor in harmonious relationship. The conditions of human life have not only been changed, but revolutionized, within the past few hundred years. In former days there was little difference between the dwelling, dress, food, and environment of the chief and those of his retainers.... The contrast between the...millionaire and the...laborer...today measures the change which has come with civilization.... This change, however, is not to be deplored, but welcomed as highly beneficial....

There are but three modes in which surplus wealth can be disposed of. It can be left to the families of the descendents; or it can be bequeathed for public purposes; or finally it can be administered during life by its possessors.... Let us consider each of these modes. The first is the most injudicious. In monarchial countries, the estates and the greatest portion of the wealth are left to the first son, that the vanity of the parent may be gratified by the thought that his name and title are to descend to succeeding generations unimpaired. The condition of this class in Europe today teaches the futility of such hopes or ambitions. The successors have become impoverished through their follies or from the fall in the value of land.... Why should men leave great fortunes to their children? If this is done from affection, is it not misguided affection? Observation teaches that, generally speaking, it is not well for the children that they be so burdened. Neither is it well for the state....

As to the second mode, that of leaving at death for public uses, it may be said that this is only a means for the disposal of wealth, provided a man is content to wait until he is dead before it becomes of much good....

The growing disposition to tax more and more heavily large estates left at death is a cheering indication of the growth of a salutary change in public opinion.... Of all forms of taxation, this seems the wisest. Men who continue hoarding great sums all their lives, the proper use of which for public ends would work good to the community, should be made to feel that the community, in the form of the state, cannot thus be deprived of its proper share. By taxing estates heavily at death, the state marks its condemnation of the selfish millionaire's unworthy life.

Source: Andrew Carnegie, "Wealth," *North American Review*, 1889

HOW WELL DID YOU UNDERSTAND THIS SELECTION?

1. How does Carnegie feel about the economic gap between rich and poor?

2. What does he think the problem of his (the industrial) age was?

3. What does Carnegie think caused the great disparity of wealth?

4. How does Carnegie define wealth? How does he define competence?

5. How does Carnegie believe wealth should be disposed of?

6. Why does Carnegie want to heavily tax large estates left at death?

A SELECTION FROM THE CONSTITUTION OF THE KNIGHTS OF LABOR

American workers faced numerous problems created by the Industrial Revolution. These included: low wages, long hours, unsafe working conditions, no job security, no health insurance, and few fringe benefits like paid vacations and sick leave. Laborers attempted to solve these and other problems by forming unions. An early and important union was the Knights of Labor. Initially the Knights of Labor practiced secret rituals much like fraternal lodges did, but Terence V. Powderly, who assumed the organization's presidency in 1879, moved the Knights away from fraternalism to unionism. Under Powderly's leadership the Knights of Labor advocated an eight-hour work day, a graduated income tax, and abolition of child labor. Membership approached one million in the mid-1880s. The Knights of Labor Constitution defines many of the objectives of the organization. Unlike most unions active in the nineteenth century, the Knights of Labor organized on an industry-wide basis rather than by crafts and accepted both skilled and unskilled workers as well as women. Philosophically the Knights opposed strikes in favor of organized boycotts, mediation and arbitration, and political involvement. Ultimately Powderly wanted to create a political party that would represent labor. He hoped workers could improve their economic situation by electing candidates to governmental office who would support labor issues. Ironically, the downfall of the Knights of Labor came as a result of their involvement in a strike against the McCormick Reaper Company and the Haymarket Square incident it produced.

PREAMBLE

The recent alarming development and aggression of aggregated wealth, which, unless checked, will invariably lead to the pauperization and hopeless degradation of the toiling masses, render it imperative, if we desire to enjoy the blessings of life, that a check should be placed upon its power and upon unjust accumulation, and a system adopted which will secure to the laborer the fruits of his toil, and as this much-desired object can only be accomplished by the thorough unification of labor, and the united efforts of those who obey the divine injunction that "in the sweat of thy brow shalt thou eat bread," we have formed the Knights of Labor with a view of securing the organization and direction, by cooperative effort, of the power of the industrial classes; and we submit to the world the objects sought to be accomplished by our organization, calling upon all who believe in securing "the greatest good to the greatest number" to aid and assist us:

I. To bring within the folds of organization every department of productive industry, making knowledge a stand-point for action, and industrial and moral worth, not wealth, the true standard of individual and national greatness.

II. To secure to the toilers a proper share of the wealth that they create: more of the leisure that rightfully belongs to them, more societary advantages; more of the benefits, privileges, and emoluments of the world: in a word, all those rights and privileges necessary to make them capable of enjoying, appreciating, defending and perpetuating the blessings of good government.

III. To arrive at the true condition of the producing masses in their educational, moral, and financial condition, by demanding from the various governments the establishment of bureaus of Labor Statistics.

IV. The establishment of co-operative institutions, productive and distributive.

V. The reserving of the public lands—the heritage of the people—or the actual settler—not another acre for railroads or speculators.

VI. The abrogation of all laws that do not bear equally upon capital and labor, the removal of unjust technicalities, delays, and discriminations in the administration of justice, and the adopting of measures providing for the health and safety of those engaged in mining, manufacturing, or building pursuits.

VII. The enactment of laws to compel chartered corporations to pay their employes weekly, in full, for labor performed during the preceding week, in the lawful money of the country.

VIII. The enactment of laws giving mechanics and laborers a first lien on their work for their full wages.

IX. The abolishment of the contract system on national, State, and municipal work.

X. The substitution of arbitration for strikes, whenever and wherever employers and employees are willing to meet on equitable grounds.

XI. The prohibition of the employment of children in workshops, mines and factories before attaining their fourteenth year.

XII. To abolish the system of letting out by contract the labor of convicts in our prisons and reformatory institutions.

XIII. To secure for both sexes equal pay for equal work.

XIV. The reduction of the hours of labor to eight per day, so that the laborers may have more time for social enjoyment and intellectual improvement, and be enabled to reap the advantages conferred by the labor-saving machinery which their brains have created.

XV. To prevail upon governments to establish a purely national circulating medium, based upon the faith and resources of the nation, and issued directly to the people, without the intervention of any system of banking corporations, which money shall be a legal tender in payment of all debts...

Source: Terence V. Powderly, *Thirty Years of Labor*, 1899

HOW WELL DID YOU UNDERSTAND THIS SELECTION?

1. What is the primary objective of the Knights of Labor?

2. Why do the Knights of Labor want state governments to create Bureaus of Labor Statistics?

3. How do the Knights of Labor propose to solve problems between labor and management?

4. What are the Knights of Labor's views regarding female workers? Does this surprise you?

5. What were the Knights of Labor's ideas regarding money and banks?

6. What problems did workers have that the Knights of Labor tried to address?

═══

EXCERPTS FROM JOHN MORRISON'S TESTIMONY BEFORE THE UNITED STATES SENATE

═══

John Morrison was one of hundreds of workers who testified before the Senate Committee upon the Relations between Labor and Capital in 1884 and 1885. This committee, which was convened to investigate the cause of strikes, concluded that strikes resulted because industrialization caused the workers' status to decline. Morrison, at the time of his testimony, was a young machinist in New York City. His testimony supports the conclusions about strikes drawn by the committee.

Q: Is there any difference between the conditions under which machinery is made now and those that existed ten years ago?

A: A great deal of difference.

Q: State the differences as well as you can.

A: Well, the trade has been subdivided and those subdivisions have been again subdivided, so that a man never learns the machinist's trade now. Ten years ago he learned, not the whole of the trade, but a fair portion of it. Also, there is more machinery used in the business, which again makes machinery. In the case of making the sewing-machine, for instance, you find that the trade is so subdivided that a man is not considered a machinist at all. Hence it is merely laborers' work and it is laborers that work at that branch of our trade. The different branches of the trade are divided and subdivided so that one man may make just a particular part of a machine and may not know anything whatever about another part of the same machine. In that way machinery is produced a great deal cheaper than it used to be formerly, and in fact through this system of work, 100 men are able to do now what it took 300 or 400 men to do fifteen years ago. By the use of machinery and the subdivision of the trade they so simplify the work that it is made a great deal easier and put together a great deal faster. There is no system of apprenticeship, I may say, in the business. You simply go in and learn whatever branch you are put at, and you stay at that unless you are changed to another.

Q: Does a man learn his branch very rapidly?

A: Yes, sir, he can learn his portion of the business very rapidly. Of course he becomes very expert at it, doing that all the time and nothing else, and therefore he is able to do a great deal more work in that particular branch than if he were a general hand and expected to do everything in the business as it came along.

Q: Do you know from reading the papers or from your general knowledge of the business whether there are other places in other cities or other parts of the country that those men could have gone and got work?

A: I know from general reports of the condition of our trade that the same condition existed throughout the country generally.

Q: Then those men could not have bettered themselves by going to any other place, you think?

A: Not in a body.

Q: I am requested to ask you this question: dividing the public, as is commonly done, into the upper, middle, and lower classes, to which class would you assign the average workingman of your trade at the time when you entered it, and to which class you would assign him now?

A: I now assign them to the lower class. At the time I entered the trade I should assign them as merely hanging on to the middle class, ready to drop out at any time.

Q: What is the character of the social intercourse of those workingmen? Answer first with reference to their intercourse with other people outside of their own trade—merchants, employers, and others.

A: Are you asking what sort of social intercourse exists between the machinists and the merchants? If you are, there is none whatever, or very little if any.

Q: What sort of social intercourse exists among the machinists themselves and their families, as to visiting, entertaining one another, and having little parties and other forms of sociability, those little things that go to make up the social pleasures of life?

A: In fact with the married folks that has died out—such things as birthday parties, picnics, and so on. The machinists today are on such small pay, and the cost of living is so high, that they have very little, if anything, to spend for recreation, and the machinist has to content himself with enjoying himself at home, either fighting with his wife or licking his children

Q: I hope that is not a common amusement in the trade. Was it so ten years ago?

A: It was not, from the fact that they then sought enjoyment in other places, and had a little more money to spend. But since they have had no organization worth speaking of, of course their pay has gone down. At that time they had a form of organization in some way or other which seemed to keep up the wages, and there was more life left in the machinist then, he had more ambition, he felt more like seeking enjoyment outside, and in reading and such things, but now it is changed to the opposite, the machinist has no such desires.

Q: What is the social air about the ordinary machinist's house? Are there evidences of happiness, and joy, and hilarity, or is the general atmosphere solemn, and somber, and gloomy?

A: To explain that fully, I would first of all state, that machinists have got to work ten hours a day in New York, and that they are compelled to work very hard. In fact the machinists of America are compelled to do about one-third more work than the machinists do in England in a day. Therefore, when they come home they are naturally played out from shoving the file, or using the hammer or the chisel, or whatever it may be, such long hours. They are pretty well played out when they come home, and the first thing they think of is having something to eat and sitting down, and resting, and then of striking a bed. Of course when a man is dragged out in that way he is naturally cranky, and he makes all around him cranky; so, instead of a pleasant house it is every day expecting to lose his job by competition from his fellow workman, there being so many out of employment, and no places for them, and his wages being pulled down through their competition, looking at all times to be thrown out of work in that way, and staring starvation in the face makes him feel sad, and the head of the house being sad, of course the whole family are the same, so the house looks like a dull prison instead of a home.

Q: Where do you work?

A: I would rather not have it in print. Perhaps I would have to go Monday morning if I did. We are so situated in the machinist's trade that we daren't let them know much about us. If they know that we open our mouths on the labor question, and try to form organizations, we are quietly told that "business is slack," and we have got to go.

Q: Do you know of anybody being discharged for making speeches on the labor question?

A: Yes, I do know of several. A little less than a year ago several members of the organization that I belong to were discharged because it was discovered that they were members of the organization.

Q: Do you say those men were members of the same organization that you belong to?

A: Yes sir; but not working in the same place where I work. And in fact many of my trade have been on the "black list," and have had to leave town to find work.

Q: Are the machinists here generally contented, or are they in a state of discontent and unrest?

A: There is mostly a general feeling of discontent, and you will find among the machinists the most radical workingmen, with the most revolutionary ideas. You will find that they don't so much give their thoughts simply to trades unions and other efforts of that kind, but they go far beyond that; they only look for relief through the ballot or through a revolution, a forcible revolution....

Q: You say they look for relief through a forcible revolution. In the alternative of a forcible revolution have they considered what form of government they would establish?

A: Yes; some of them have and some of them have not.

Q: What kind of government would they establish?

A: …They want to form a government such as this was intended to be, a government "of the people, for the people, and by the people"—different entirely from the present form of government.

Source: Report of the Committee of the Senate upon the Relations between Labor and Capital, 48th Congress, 1885

HOW WELL DID YOU UNDERSTAND THIS SELECTION?

1. What does Morrison think has happened to the machinist's trade?

2. What does Morrison say has happened to machinists as a result of the Industrial Revolution? What is their economic status?

3. How does Morrison describe the life of workers?

4. What would likely happen if workers joined a union?

5. What is a black list?

6. How does Morrison say workers will seek relief?

The Spanish-American War generated much controversy within the United States. Many Americans opposed going to war with Spain to acquire colonies because they believed it violated one of America's founding principles, that of self-determination. Americans had maintained for years that they believed all people should have the right to determine their own government. After all, this is why Americans had fought England for independence during the American Revolution. An organization called the Anti-Imperialist League was organized. Grover Cleveland, who served two nonconsecutive terms as president from 1885 to 1889 and from 1893 to 1897, was a member of this group, as well as other notable Americans, such as the author Mark Twain, the Supreme Court Justice Morfield Story, and Speaker of the House of Representatives Thomas Reed, who resigned after serving forty years in Congress because he believed the acquisition of colonies soiled America. Former President Cleveland served as vice president of the Anti-Imperialist League and spoke out forcefully against imperialism as the following speech indicates.

When our Government entered upon a war for the professed purpose of aiding self-government and releasing from foreign rule a struggling people whose cries for liberty were heard at our very doors, it rallied to its enthusiastic support a nation of freemen, in whose hearts and minds there was deeply fixed by heredity and tradition the living belief that all just powers of government are derived from the consent of the governed.

It was the mockery of fate that led us to an unexpected and unforeseen incident in this conflict, and placed in the path of our Government, while professing national righteousness, representing an honest and liberty-loving people, and intent on a benevolent, self-sacrificing errand, the temptation of sordid aggrandizement and the false glitter of world-power.

No sincerely thoughtful American can recall what followed without amazement, nor without sadly realizing how the apathy of our people's trustfulness and their unreflecting acceptance of alluring representations can be played upon.

No greater national fall from grace was ever known than that of the Government of the United States, when in the midst of high design, while still speaking words of sympathy with the weak who struggled against the strong, and while still professing to exemplify before the world a great Republic's love for self-government and its impulse to stay the bloody hand of oppression and conquest, it embraced an opportunity offered by the exigencies of its beneficent undertaking, to possess itself of territory thousands of miles from our coast, and to conquer and govern, without pretense of their consent, millions of resisting people—a heterogeneous population largely mixed with elements hardly within the light of civilization, and all far from the prospect of assimilation with anything American.

.... Refusing to accept the shallow and discreditable pretense that our conquest in the Philippines has gone so far beyond recall or correction, we insist that a nation as well as an individual is never so magnanimous or great as when false steps are retraced and the path of honesty and virtue is regained.

The message of the Democracy to the American people should courageously enjoin that, in sincere and consistent compliance with the spirit and profession of our interference in behalf of Cuba's self-government, our beneficent designs toward her should also extend to the lands which, as an incident of such interference, have come under our control; that the people of the Philippine Islands should be aided in the establishment of a government of their own; and that when this is accomplished our interference in their domestic rule should cease.

Source: "Ex-President Grover Cleveland on the Philippine Problem," Boston: Anti-Imperialist League, 1904

HOW WELL DID YOU UNDERSTAND THIS SELECTION?

1. What does President Cleveland consider wrong about America's acquisition of colonies such as the Philippines?

2. What does he think the United States government should do regarding the Philippines?

3. Where does Cleveland think government is derived from?

4. Would Cleveland think America's acquisition of colonies was hypocritical? Why or why not?

THE WIZARD OF OZ: Industrial Themes in a Child's Story
By Doug Cantrell

Practically everyone has either read the child's story, **The Wizard of Oz**, *by L. Frank Baum or viewed the movie starring Judy Garland. On the surface, this tale of witches and wizards appears to be a simple child's story complete with magic, intrigue, and good triumphing over evil. Beneath the simple tale, however, lies political metaphor. While it might appear that* **The Wizard of Oz** *is a child's story, it is really a potent story about the industrial revolution and its impact on workers and farmers. Contained within the child's story are powerful images and symbols drawn from the presidential election of 1900 pitting Republican William McKinley against Democrat William Jennings Bryan, the former Populist. These symbols and images reflect many of the issues facing Americans that arose during the Industrial Revolution. The following pages will examine* **The Wizard of Oz** *from the perspective of the Industrial Revolution, beginning with its author L. Frank Baum.*

Baum by profession was a journalist who experienced the Industrial Revolution first hand as a printer in the West and then a newspaper reporter in Chicago. As a printer in South Dakota, a state in which Populists were very active, Baum came to understand the problem farmers in the Great Plains states faced during the Industrial Revolution. He became aware of the importance farmers and Populists placed on inflation through their advocacy of the free coinage of silver. He also realized that the Industrial Revolution created a situation in which farmers saw their real incomes and social status decline because developments in agricultural technology enabled farmers to produce such a surplus that the market became glutted, driving down prices. It seemed as if the harder farmers worked the less compensation they received. As a printer, Baum experienced first hand the impact the Industrial Revolution had on skilled workers. Baum lost his printing business in South Dakota and had to move to Chicago and work for a big city newspaper (the equivalent of a blacksmith or tailor moving to the city to work in a factory). Like most skilled workers who were driven out of business by the factory, Baum's move to the city resulted in less income and a lowered social status. In the 1896 and 1900 presidential elections Baum actively supported the Populist/Democratic candidate, William Jennings Bryan. He wrote **The Wizard of Oz** *in the context of the 1900 presidential election, incorporating themes from the Industrial Revolution and issues in the 1896 and 1900 elections. An analysis of the story will reflect those themes.*

The story begins in Kansas, a farming state whose residents had experienced a decline in income and social status as a result of the Industrial Revolution. Baum describes everything in Kansas as gray. The sky is gray, people are gray, animals are gray, the landscape is gray. This image of gray is a metaphor for the negative impact the Industrial Revolution had on farmers in Kansas and elsewhere. Farmers have little to smile about. They are heavily in debt and are facing declining prices for farm produce as a result of the glut created by the use of industrial technology (machinery, fertilizer, hybrid seed, etc.) on the farm. Then, along comes a cyclone. The cyclone is symbolic of the presidential election of 1900. Baum believes that voters in the 1900 election will cleanse the political landscape much as a tornado cleanses the physical landscape. Everything will be swept clean in its path and Bryan's election to the presidency will represent a new beginning for Americans.

Dorothy, the central character in the story, and her little dog, Toto, hide in a farmhouse that is lifted high into the sky by the cyclone and deposited in a wonderful, magical land called Oz. There is much symbolism in this scene. Baum takes the name for his magical land, Oz, from the silver/gold issue so important to farmers and workers during the 1890s. Oz is the abbreviation for ounce and is taken from the formula Populists and workers urged the federal government to adopt to inflate the currency supply. They wanted sixteen ounces of silver to be equal to one ounce of gold. The fact that Oz is a magical land is also symbolic. Many farmers and workers believed that if the sixteen to one ratio was adopted and the nation got inflation many of their problems would magically disappear. Farmers would receive higher prices for their produce and could more easily pay debts with inflated currency while factory workers would see higher wages.

Dorothy's house had accidentally landed on a character called the Wicked Witch of the East, killing her. Dorothy emerges from the house and is greeted by small people called Munchkins who are dancing around the house expressing joy that Dorothy has killed the Wicked Witch of the East and hailing Dorothy as their liberator. Dorothy is taken aback. She quickly assures everyone that she did not mean to kill anyone, that it was an accident. The Wicked Witch of the East is symbolic for eastern capitalists, the so-called Robber Barons, the Rockefellers, the Carnegies, the Henry Fords, the corporations that oppressed workers and farmers. The witch's death represents what Baum believes will happen to the oppressors of workers and farmers when Bryan becomes president. He will crush them much as Dorothy's house crushed the Wicked Witch of the East. Munchkins, of course, are the common people who are oppressed by capitalism and conditions created by the Industrial Revolution.

Dorothy, after expressing remorse at the witch's death, becomes concerned about her family in Kansas. She asks the Munchkins if they can tell her how to return to Kansas. The Munchkins feel badly. They can't help their liberator. Suddenly, one of them has an idea. He tells Dorothy to see the Wizard. Dorothy is puzzled. She has never heard of the Wizard. The Munchkins explain that they have heard that a Wizard descended out of the clouds in Emerald City and that he is a good wizard who uses his magical powers to help common people. Dorothy agrees to see the Wizard but doesn't know how to get to Emerald City. The Munchkins tell her to take the yellow brick road. Dorothy, being a Midwestern farm girl, is bare footed (most rural residents did not wear shoes during warm months because leather was too expensive). The Munchkins tell her to take the shoes from the feet of the Wicked Witch of the East; after all, she is dead and will not need them. Dorothy takes the shoes from the witch's feet, which are made of silver (in the movie the slippers are ruby red because that color shows up better on the screen than does silver). She then proceeds to walk down the yellow brick road toward Emerald City wearing the silver slippers. There is a powerful metaphor here. Yellow is the color of gold. Dorothy wearing silver slippers walking down a golden road signifies the relationship between silver and gold so important to workers and farmers and the major issue in the 1896 and 1900 presidential elections.

After walking for a long time Dorothy and Toto stop to rest near a cornfield. As they are resting they hear a voice speaking to them. At first they can't figure out where the voice is coming from but finally determine it is that of the Scarecrow. The Scarecrow is in bad shape. He has had the straw that composed his body torn out by crows. Dorothy puts the straw back into the Scarecrow's body and he tells his tale. He says that the crows became so bold that they attacked him, the corn's guardian. After tearing out his stuffing, the crows stole the corn. The Scarecrow represents the American farmer and the fact that the stuffing is torn out of his body is symbolic of the negative impact the Industrial Revolution had on farmers. They were not in good shape. The crows are the factories that buy the farmer's produce—the canneries, the meat processors, and the tobacco companies. Farmers often believed that these companies stole from farmers by paying prices below what it cost to produce crops and livestock. The Scarecrow decides to go to Emerald City with Dorothy and Toto because he wants the Wizard to give him a brain. The journey to Emerald City represents the trek many farmers made to the city when their farms failed, as did the Scarecrows' when the crows stole his corn. Many farmers, like the Scarecrow, leave their farms, move to the city and

295

become factory workers. The brain the Scarecrow wants is symbolic of prejudices rural people faced as a result of the Industrial Revolution. Farmers were often viewed as "hicks," "hayseeds," and "country bumpkins" who were not as smart or sophisticated as city residents. Before the Industrial Revolution almost everybody was a farmer and farmers were the backbone of American society; afterward, their social status had fallen.

Dorothy, Toto, and the Scarecrow proceed down the yellow brick road toward Emerald City. On the way they encounter the Tin Woodsman. Like the farmer, the Tin Woodsman is in a bad way. He is rusted over. Dorothy and the Scarecrow apply oil to the Tin Woodsman's joints, loosening the rust. He then tells them his story. He says that once he was human until the Wicked Witch of the East cast a spell on him that caused him to cut off an appendage every time he swung his ax. Fortunately, however, tinsmiths in Oz can replace human parts with metal. Like other scenes in the *Wizard of Oz*, there are powerful metaphors in this one. The Tin Woodsman is the American worker. Metal (the steel industry) represents the American Industrial Revolution. The rust is symbolic of the impact the Industrial Revolution had on workers, low wages, long hours, and horrible working conditions and depressions the United States experienced in 1873 and 1893. His metal body reflects the impact the Industrial Revolution had on workers. Once he had been human but factory work had dehumanized him. He was no longer a man but a machine. Severing limbs by swinging the ax reflects the high rate of accidents industrial workers experienced. The application of oil represents what Baum thinks will happen once Bryan becomes president; he will institute policies that will benefit the worker and break the hold industrial capitalism has on them. The Tin Woodsman decides to join Dorothy, Toto, and the Scarecrow on their journey to Emerald City. He wants a heart, again symbolic of the dehumanizing affect the Industrial Revolution had on workers. Getting a heart will make the worker human again.

The group set off down the yellow brick road toward Emerald City. Taken together, they represent the political coalition Baum thinks will be important to Bryan's election. Of course, the Scarecrow represents farmers and the Tin Woodsman represents workers. Dorothy and Toto are part of the coalition too. Dorothy represents a feminist and Toto is short for a teetotaler (someone who does not believe in consuming alcoholic beverages). Both the feminist movement and the prohibition movement were active in the United States around the turn of the twentieth century. Women reformers were campaigning for suffrage, more liberal divorce laws and birth control while prohibitionists wanted to make the country dry. Bryan himself advocated national prohibition and was a teetotaler. All these groups, farmers, workers, feminists, and prohibitionists must unite behind Bryan before he can win the presidency, or so Baum thinks.

While traveling down the yellow brick road toward Emerald City the group next encounters the Cowardly Lion. He roars but frightens nobody; he scratched the Tin Woodsman but dulled his claws on the tin man's body. The Cowardly Lion is William Jennings Bryan. The roar is symbolic of his oratorical abilities. Bryan was often called the "boy orator from the Platt." He had crisscrossed the country making speech after speech during the 1896 campaign while his opponent, McKinley, had stayed home. Bryan's speeches appeared to have little effect. They had not persuaded workers to vote for him. He had dulled his claws on their armor. The Cowardly Lion wants courage. This reflects Baum's belief that Bryan needs to be more courageous in persuading workers to vote for him. He needs to promise workers more in the 1900 campaign than he promised in 1896.

The political coalition continues down the yellow brick road until finally it reaches Emerald City. A gatekeeper meets Dorothy and her friends and makes them put on green goggles (glasses), which they are required to wear while in Emerald City. They are told that they must not take the goggles off. The goggles make everything appear to be a bright shiny green. Curious, Dorothy lifts one corner of the goggles and peeks at the city through the naked eye. What she sees is not a city that is bright and shiny but one that is a dull, dirty white. Emerald City, the capitol of Oz, represents Washington, D.C., America's political capitol, during the Gilded Age. Just as America on the surface during the Gilded Age appeared to be bright and shiny, if one takes off the glasses and looks beneath the surface, corruption will be found in the government. Industrialists often bribed government officials. Things, as Mark Twain pointed out when he coined the term Gilded Age, were not what they appeared to be.

When the group gets an audience with the Wizard he appears to be all powerful and promises Dorothy and her friends what each one wants if they will do something for him—kill the Wicked Witch of the West. The Wizard represents President McKinley. A political deal has been struck. To gain the support of feminist, workers, farmers and others in the upcoming election, McKinley has made numerous promises that he will have trouble keeping, typical behavior for a politician.

Dorothy and her entourage head west where they are told they will find the Wicked Witch of the West. The Wicked Witch of the West, like her sister in the east, is the capitalist who oppresses common people. Dorothy, Toto, the Scarecrow, the Tin Woodsman, and the Cowardly Lion encounter the Wicked Witch of the West through characters identified as Flying Monkeys. The Flying Monkeys and their king appear to be vicious creatures. They take Dorothy to the Wicked Witch of the West where she is imprisoned. One day, while taking a bath, Dorothy splashes water on the witch, which causes her to melt. The water is symbolic that the drought, which had hurt farmers in the west during the 1880s, finally came to an end in the 1890s. Dorothy has destroyed the Wicked Witch of the West, freeing the Flying Monkeys from her spell. Again, when Bryan wins the 1900 election, Baum thinks the power of the capitalist will be broken over workers and farmers. The Flying Monkeys represent the American Indian confined to western reservations. The Flying Monkeys turn out to be good people who have been oppressed just as Native Americans were oppressed in the West. Dorothy asks the Flying Monkeys to return with her to Emerald City but they reply that they can't because they are bound to the land. The Indian was confined to the reservation.

Dorothy and her friends return to Emerald City, seeking an audience with the Wizard. He cannot believe that the group has destroyed the Wicked Witch of the West. He thought that task was impossible to achieve. Baum is saying here that Bryan has overcome impossible obstacles to win the 1900 election, defeating McKinley, the Wizard. At first, the Wizard tries to avoid Dorothy, the Scarecrow, the Tin Woodsman, and the Cowardly Lion. When they force an audience with him, he then tries to avoid keeping the promise he made to each of them, typical behavior for politicians who promise voters many things they can't deliver. Toto doesn't like the Wizard and knocks down a screen in the throne room. Instead of concealing a powerful wizard, the screen hides a short bald headed man that Baum describes as a humbug. McKinley has no real power. He is a fake, a fraud, and a ventriloquist who makes people believe he is a powerful man. This reflects the view many Americans had that President McKinley had no real power but was controlled by his handlers, such as the industrialists Mark Hanna. The Wizard attempts to keep his promise to Dorothy and each of her friends. Even here, he is a fake. Instead of giving the Scarecrow a real brain he fills his head with needles which will prick the skin and make him believe he has a brain. The lion's courage is merely a dose of cod liver oil and the Tin Woodsman gets a paper heart rather than a real one. Since the Wizard had been a carnival barker in the United States who drew a crowd by ascending aloft in a hot air balloon he decides he wants to return home with Dorothy. He makes a balloon that he and Dorothy plan to use to transport them home. Unfortunately, the balloon gets loose from its moorings while Dorothy is hunting for Toto and the Wizard leaves without her. Before departing the Wizard made some changes. He makes the Scarecrow the ruler of Oz; thus the farmer is restored to his lofty position at the top of society before the Industrial Revolution knocked him from that perch. The Wizard's departure is symbolic of McKinley leaving power after having lost the 1900 election.

Since the Wizard has left without her, Dorothy appears to be stuck in Oz. She encounters Glinda, the Good Witch of the North. Glinda tells Dorothy that the silver slippers she is wearing have magical powers that can be used to transport her anywhere in the world. This reflects the magical power of silver to solve the problems of farmers and workers. They believed their problems would magically disappear if America's currency were inflated by use of silver. Dorothy clicks her heels together, says magical words and is transported back to Kansas. When she arrives, the sun is shining and things are looking up for farmers and workers. Bryan is president and the power of the robber barons and corporations they control is broken. A new day has dawned for workers and farmers.

HOW WELL DID YOU UNDERSTAND THIS SELECTION?

1. What figures do the characters in *The Wizard of Oz* represent?

2. What themes from the Industrial Revolution are present in this child's story?

3. Can you find symbolism, other than the themes discussed by Cantrell in the above essay, reflected in issues or events from the Industrial Revolution?

4. Do politicians behave much like the Wizard?

5. What is a political coalition? Has Baum correctly identified the coalition needed to sweep Bryan into the White House?

6. Do you think Baum was disappointed when Bryan did not defeat McKinley in the 1900 election? Why or why not?

FORCED LABOR IN WEST VIRGINIA
By Gino C. Speranza

Gino C. Speranza was head of the Society for the Protection of Italian Immigrants in the United States. This organization existed to improve the lives of Italian immigrants in the United States. He wrote the following article for **The Outlook** *after conducting an investigation of working conditions and debt peonage in West Virginia coal mining and lumber camps.*

It is a far cry from Harmon's Camp in the lonely mountains of Raleigh County, West Virginia to New York City, yet it speaks well for the unceasing vigilance of our militant philanthropy that a cry from that camp in the wilderness was heard and heeded. The adventures of the twenty-three Italian laborers who were sent to Raleigh County from New York reads like a page from the history of the Middle Ages, except that the splendid animal courage of those days is replaced here by the all-absorbing sordid interest of money-making.

In the early part of March, 1903, twenty-three Italians were shipped (I use the word advisedly) from New York by one of those numberless "bankers" who infest the Italian colony, to Beckley, West Virginia, to work on a railroad in process of building in the Piney Creek District. They were told, as is often done and as must be done to induce men to go to that region, that Beckley was a few hours from New York and the approximate cost of transportation would be eighty cents. When they arrived at Beckley, after a journey of nearly two days, hungry, bewildered, and conscious already that they had been betrayed, they were driven to Harmon's Camp, some four miles from town. Those who have not been to the West Virginian labor camps can hardly understand how lonely and isolated some of them are. Even though geographically near each other, they are completely shut in by high mountains, and the surrounding country is practically uninhabited. Conscious of having been sold by the agents in New York, the lonesomeness of the camp naturally increased the apprehension of the laborers. But they started in on the work of drilling and grading, even thought the work was not as it had been represented. Perhaps they worked because the presence of some armed guards and the sight of the contractor with a revolver ostentatiously stuck in his breast pocket was not reassuring. Moreover, to make matters worse, though they were at liberty to "buy anywhere," they had to buy from the camp commissary, no matter how extortionate the prices were, as the nearest store was miles away. The day came when such conditions grew unbearable and the men left; they were not paid, but it seemed better to lose money than to remain. The contractor, however, having advanced transportation, was not going to stand a loss if he could help it. It is true that the Governor of West Virginia, stirred by constant complaints of abuse, had urged the use of legal process in such cases rather than a recourse to force. However hampered legally the contractor might be, the storekeeper had a ready remedy under the "Boarding-House Law" of West Virginia, which gives the right of arrest for non-payment of board. It did not matter that it applied with doubtful propriety to shanty board in a camp, once an accommodating squire could be found to grant a warrant. And so the twenty-three "insurgents" were arrested and locked over night in the Grand Jury room at the County Court House at Beckley, on the charge of non-payment of board. The next morning enters the contractor; he is a private citizen, he in not an officer, he is not even a party of record to the proceedings. What right has he in that Grand Jury room used as a jail? And when the prisoners, in the actual custody of the law, refuse to go back to his camp, he and his henchman, in that room set apart for what has been called "the bulwark of Anglo-Saxon liberty," proceed to bind six of the prisoner with ropes. I cite from the sworn statement of one of the men, "He had tied my wrists and had thrown the rope around my neck, when I shouted to the storekeeper, who was present and spoke Italian, "Not this, not this!" "It is Holy Week and I know Christ's hands were tied, but there was no rope around his neck." Thereupon the contractor, convinced that the binding of the arms was sufficient bunched together six of the bound men and marched them out into the public street. There, before "the whole town," not excluding certain sworn officers of the law, seeing that the prisoners still refused to march back to camp, the contractor hitched the rope by which they were tied to a mule, urging it on. The squire who had issued the warrant of arrest fortunately appeared then and cut the men free. Praise be to him for this act! But why did he urge these men to go back, as he did, with that brute of a contractor, and why did he, instead of trying the prisoners then and there according to law, go back to camp with them and help to induce them to "work out" their "board" and transportation? Why did he not take action against the contractor caught *in flagrante*? Why was there no entry made in his official docket of the disposition of this case till months after? Why did not the Prosecuting Officer at Beckley, who knew of this barbarity, take any action until two months after the event, when a society six hundred miles away submitted to him evidence which he could have gathered fifty yards from his office; and even then why did he merely promise to submit "this small matter" to the next Grand Jury?

Of the twenty-two men who worked out their "debts," one escaped and cannot be traced; eleven walked practically all the way from Charleston, West Virginia, to Washington, District of Columbia; two I found in a Washington hospital; the others had money enough to return to New York.

I have given this case at length, not because it is an example of exceptional cruelty and lawlessness, but because it is an uncommonly well substantiated and corroborated case of the system of intimidation in force in some labor camps of West Virginia, ranging from the silent intimidation of armed guards to an active terrorism of blows and abuse, of which the general public knows nothing.

It was in the latter part of April, 1903, that I was sent by the Society for the Protection of Italian Immigrants of New York to investigate a large number of complaints of alleged maltreatment suffered by Italians in certain counties of West Virginia. That State is developing her splendid resources of coal and lumber, and this necessitates the building of railroads for the transportation of such products. The demand for labor is tremendous and the supply totally inadequate. If it is true that too many immigrants come to our shores, it hardly holds good for West Virginia.

There capital is in danger of becoming paralyzed from lack of the labor supply. To supply the feverish demands, laborers of all conditions and classes have been literally dumped into that State by the brokers in human flesh in the cities—not only men unfit for the hard work required, but a lawless and criminal element as well. The problem for the contractor does not end with getting the men to West Virginia; an even harder task is to keep them there, for the isolation of the camps, the absence of human intercourse, and the hardships of life create a feeling of discontent among the laborers almost from the first day. It is not strange, under these circumstances, therefore, that contractors should resort to methods both to get and to keep laborers which are in defiance of law and repugnant to the moral sense. The temptation to illegitimate practices is further strengthened by the method employed of advancing transportation for the men. Thus, two hundred laborers at $10 each means an investment of $2,000; if the men become dissatisfied and leave, it means a clear loss to the contractor. Yet, however strong the temptation, it cannot justify acts of restraint which in practice amount to white slavery. The use of armed guards around the camps is notorious. Worse yet, the evidence seems to show that the men are charged for the expense of such unlawful surveillance.

Cases of brutality are frequent and inexcusable. One may find some palliation for the unlawful restraint exercised over men who wish to escape before they have "worked out" their transportation. But what can be said in extenuation of such acts of brutality as those of men felled with blows from iron bars or gun butts, or marched at the point of rifles and cursed and beaten if unable to keep up with the pace of the mounted overseers? I have before me the sworn declaration of one Girardi—a bright young Piedmontese, who had been employed by Boxley & Co. near Kayford. He was ordered to lift a heavy stone, and asked a negro co-laborer to help him. His was not, evidently, a permissible request, as his foreman, on hearing it, called him a vile name and thrust a revolver in his face. Thereupon Girardi lifted the stone, at the cost of a very bad rupture. That man to this day has had no redress.

"Tired of abuse," reads the sworn statement of another laborer, "we decided to escape from the camp; we had proceeded but a short distance when we were overtaken by several men armed with rifles and revolvers, who drove us back. One of the pursuing band took from me an iron rod which I held over my shoulder, over which I had slung my valise, and with it repeatedly struck several of my companions." Another, a splendid type of hardy Calabrian, described under oath the following picture: "My attention was drawn to the other side of the creek, where an Italian was shouting for help—appealing to us as fellow-countrymen to aid him. He had been felled by a blow of a heavy stick dealt him by one of the guards. Cervi, my friend, and I tried to cross over to help him, but were prevented by our boss, who drove us back at the point of a pistol; all I dared do was to shout to him not to resist or he would be killed, and to go back; the man who had struck him lifted him bodily by his coat and pushed him on, striking him every time he stumbled or fell from exhaustion."

These are a few of a number of well-substantiated cases. It will be hard for many of us to believe these facts; it will seem impossible that such barbarities should be allowed in a civilized community. Perhaps they would not be allowed if they were known. Publicity is the great hope for reform; a wide publicity that will, on the one hand, arouse public sentiment and react on the local authorities, and, on the other hand, that will further cut off the supply of laborers, thereby forcing the contractors to reform.

Little, if anything, can be hoped from the local officials. The Chief Executive of West Virginia admitted to me that it was practically impossible to obtain convictions through the local courts, and, however good his intentions, his powers seem very limited. In a recent letter the Governor of that State writes: "I am willing to do anything I can to bring about a better condition of affairs and to co-operate as I have the power in bringing to justice those guilty of the acts complained of, but you see my limitations. . . The executive in West Virginia has practically no power in controlling the administration of justice in our courts. . . .The legislature refused last winter to give me the necessary powers asked for in as grave a matter as lynching."

It is a reasonable presumption that contractors do not engage men with the express purpose of maltreating them, for it is a plain business principle that dissatisfied men make poor workers. I believe, therefore, that, with some few exceptions, these abuses are to a great extent due to that lack of mutual confidence and more especially of mutual understanding which is the basis of much of the unrest and spirit of reprisal in the labor situation. This lack of mutual understanding is especially evident in the relations between American employers and Italian laborers. It is not merely ignorance of the language, it is rather a lack of clear-sightedness and perception as regards what counts with these foreign laborers. Employers of Italian labor too often forget that their employees are proverbially sensitive, but are also susceptible to kind treatment. Courtesy and kindness will hold these men even in distant and isolated camps much better than curses and forcible threats. As a purely business proposition, the employment of a capable and honest interpreter or confidential secretary who knows both Italian and American ways, to whom laborers could go, would be a better and cheaper investment for contractors than the maintenance of armed guards or brutal foremen. As it is, not only in West Virginia but wherever Italian labor is employed the Italian is at the mercy of the middleman, without any right of appeal. Whether it be the fraud of his own countryman, the banker-agent who sells his labor under false pretenses, or the extortion of his countryman, the camp storekeeper to whom the contractor lets the commissary privileges, whether it be the "rake-off" of the foreman or the peculations of the paymaster, whether it be the brutality of the boss or the unlawful order of the gang-foremen—no matter what the injustice may be, the laborer has no opportunity to appeal to his employer, either because the employer recognizes the decision of his middleman as final or because he will not "bother with details." While this system, popularly called the "pardone system," is tolerated by contractors, abuses will continue. Much, however, can be done to lessen its evils by institutions like the Society for the Protection of Italian Immigrants, a society administered by Americans, which aims to destroy the padrone system by competing with padrone, using legitimate methods in supplying laborers and safeguarding their rights.

The responsibility, in the last instance, however, rests on the employers. Their duty to the men should not cease with the payment of agreed wages; without the careful, businesslike, and humane supervision, workmen are very likely to be abused by the middlemen. Especially is this true of the foreign workman whose helplessness in the face of unlawful and brutal treatment such as that in West Virginia would almost justify an extra-judicial reprisal. Certainly it is of vital importance that these numberless foreign laborers who come to us should learn, as a first step towards assimilation, that Americanism means honesty, regard for law, fair play, and plain dealing.

Source: *The Outlook*, June 13, 1908

HOW WELL DID YOU UNDERSTAND THIS SELECTION?

1. Who is Gino Speranza?

2. What is labor peonage?

3. What does Speranza find in West Virginia?

4. How are immigrant workers treated in West Virginia if they don't pay transportation charges?

5. What is "on transportation"?

6. What is the padrone system?

7. What does Speranza think will solve the problem of labor peonage?

THE AWAKENING OF THE NEGRO By Booker T. Washington

Booker T. Washington was an African-American leader who founded Tuskegee Institute in Alabama. A pioneer in education, he thought African Americans would best be served by obtaining a practical education in mechanical skills and agriculture. Washington was often accused of being an "Uncle Tom" because he was willing to accept racism and discrimination for slow economic gains for African Americans.

When a mere boy, I saw a young colored man, who had spent several years in school, sitting in a common cabin in the South, studying a French grammar. I noted the poverty, the untidiness, the want of system and thrift that existed about the cabin, notwithstanding his knowledge of French and other academic subjects. Another time, when riding on the outer edges of a town in the South, I heard the sound of a piano coming from a cabin of the same kind. Contriving some excuse, I entered, and began a conversation with the young colored woman who was playing, and who had recently returned from a boarding-school, where she had been studying instrumental music among other things. Despite the fact that her parents were living in a rented cabin, eating poorly cooked food, surrounded with poverty, and having almost none of the conveniences of life, she had persuaded them to rent a piano for four or five dollars per month. Many such instances as these, in connection with my own struggles, impressed upon me the importance of making a study of our needs as a race, and applying the remedy accordingly. Some one may be tempted to ask, Has not the negro boy or girl as good a right to study a French grammar and instrumental music as the white youth? I answer, Yes, but in the present condition of the negro race in this country there is need of something more. Perhaps I may be forgiven for the seeming egotism if I mention the expansion of my own life partly as an example of what I mean. My earliest recollection is of a small one-room log hut on a large slave plantation in Virginia. After the close of the war, while working in the coal-mines of West Virginia for the support of my mother, I heard in some accidental way of the Hampton Institute. When I learned that it was an institution where a black boy could study, could have a chance to work for his board, and at the same time be taught how to work and to realize the dignity of labor, I resolved to go there. Bidding my mother good-by, I started out one morning to find my way to Hampton, though I was almost penniless and had no definite idea where Hampton was. By walking, begging rides, and paying for a portion of the journey on the steam-cars, I finally succeeded in reaching the city of Richmond, Virginia. I was without money or friends. I slept under a sidewalk, and by working on a vessel next day I earned money to continue my way to the institute, where I arrived with a surplus of fifty cents. At Hampton I found the opportunity — in the way of buildings, teachers, and industries provided by the generous — to get training in the class-room and by practical touch with industrial life, to learn thrift, economy, and push. I was surrounded by an atmosphere of business, Christian influence, and a spirit of self-help that seemed to have awakened every faculty in me, and caused me for the first time to realize what it meant to be a man instead of a piece of property.

While there I resolved that when I had finished the course of training I would go into the far South, into the Black Belt of the South, and give my life to providing the same kind of opportunity for self-reliance and self-awakening that I had found provided for me at Hampton. My work began at Tuskegee, Alabama, in 1881, in a small shanty and church, with one teacher and thirty students, without a dollar's worth of property. The spirit of work and of industrial thrift, with aid from the State and generosity from the North, has enabled us to develop an institution of eight hundred students gathered from nineteen States, with seventy-nine instructors, fourteen hundred acres of land, and thirty buildings, including large and small; in all, property valued at $280,000. Twenty-five industries have been organized, and the whole work is carried on at an annual cost of about $80,000 in cash; two fifths of the annual expense so far has gone into permanent plant.

What is the object of all this outlay? First, it must be borne in mind that we have in the South a peculiar and unprecedented state of things. It is of the utmost importance that our energy be given to meeting conditions that exist right about us rather than conditions that existed centuries ago or that exist in countries a thousand miles away. What are the cardinal needs among the seven millions of colored people in the South, most of whom are to be found on the plantations? Roughly, these needs may be stated as food, clothing, shelter, education, proper habits, and a settlement of race relations. The seven millions of colored people of the South cannot be reached directly by any missionary agency, but they can be reached by sending out among them strong selected young men and women, with the proper training of head, hand, and heart, who will live among these masses and show them how to lift themselves up.

The problem that the Tuskegee Institute keeps before itself constantly is how to prepare these leaders. From the outset, in connection with religious and academic training, it has emphasized industrial or hand training as a means of finding the way out of present conditions. First, we have found the industrial teaching useful in giving the student a chance to work out a portion of his expenses while in school. Second, the school furnishes labor that has an economic value, and at the same time gives the student a chance to acquire knowledge and skill while performing the labor. Most of all, we find the industrial system valuable in teaching economy, thrift, and the dignity of labor, and in giving moral backbone to students. The fact that a student goes out into the world conscious of his power to build a house or a wagon, or to make a harness, gives him a certain confidence and moral independence that he would not possess without such training.

A more detailed example of our methods at Tuskegee may be of interest. For example, we cultivate by student labor six hundred and fifty acres of land. The object is not only to cultivate the land in a way to make it pay our boarding department, but at the same time to teach the students, in addition to the practical work, something of the chemistry of the soil, the best methods of drainage, dairying, the cultivation of fruit, the care of livestock and tools, and scores of other lessons needed by a people whose main dependence is on agriculture. Notwithstanding that eighty-five per cent of the colored people in the South live by agriculture in some form, aside from what has been done by Hampton, Tuskegee, and one or two other institutions practically nothing has been attempted in the direction of teaching them about the very industry from which the masses of our people must get their subsistence. Friends have recently provided means for the erection of a large new chapel at Tuskegee. Our students have made the bricks for this chapel. A large part of the timber is sawed by students at our own sawmill, the plans are drawn by our teacher of architecture and mechanical drawing, and students do the brick-masonry, plastering, painting, carpentry work, tinning, slating, and make most of the furniture. Practically, the whole chapel will be built and furnished by student labor; in the end the school will have the building for permanent use, and the students will have a knowledge of the trades employed in its construction. In this way all but three of the thirty buildings on the grounds have been erected. While the young men do the kinds of work I have mentioned, the young women to a large extent make, mend, and launder the clothing of the young men, and thus are taught important industries.

One of the objections sometimes urged against industrial education for the negro is that it aims merely to teach him to work on the same plan that he was made to follow when in slavery. This is far from being the object at Tuskegee. At the head of each of the twenty-five industrial departments we have an intelligent and competent instructor, just as we have in our history classes, so that the student is taught not only practical brick-masonry, for example, but also the underlying principles of that industry, the mathematics and the mechanical and architectural drawing. Or he is taught how to become master of the forces of nature so that, instead of cultivating corn in the old way, he can use a corn cultivator, that lays off the furrows, drops the corn into them, and covers it, and in this way he can do more work than three men by the old process of corn-planting; at the same time much of the toil is eliminated and labor is dignified. In a word, the constant aim is to show the student how to put brains into every process of labor; how to bring his knowledge of mathematics and the sciences into farming, carpentry, forging, foundry work; how to dispense as soon as possible with the old form of ante-bellum labor. In the erection of the chapel just referred to, instead of letting the money which was given us go into outside hands, we make it accomplish three objects: first, it provides the chapel; second, it gives the students a chance to get a practical knowledge of the trades connected with building; and third, it enables them to earn something toward the payment of board while receiving academic and industrial training.

Having been fortified at Tuskegee by education of mind, skill of hand, Christian character, ideas of thrift, economy, and push, and a spirit of independence, the student is sent out to become a centre of influence and light in showing the masses of our people in the Black Belt of the South how to lift themselves up. How can this be done? I give but one or two examples. Ten years ago a young colored man came to the institute from one of the large plantation districts; he studied in the class-room a portion of the time, and received practical and theoretical training on the farm the remainder of the time. Having finished his course at Tuskegee, he returned to his plantation home, which was in a county where the colored people outnumber the whites six to one, as is true of many of the counties in the Black Belt of the South. He found the negroes in debt. Ever since the war they had been mortgaging their crops for the food on which to live while the crops were growing. The majority of them were living from hand to mouth on rented land, in small, one-room log cabins, and attempting to pay a rate of interest on their advances that ranged from fifteen to forty per cent per annum. The school had been taught in a wreck of a log cabin, with no apparatus, and had never been in session longer than three months out of twelve. With as many as eight or ten persons of all ages and conditions and of both sexes huddled together in one cabin year after year, and with a minister whose only aim was to work upon the emotions of the people, one can imagine something of the moral and religious state of the community.

He took the three months' public school as a nucleus for his work. Then he organized the older people into a club, or conference, that held meetings every week. In these meetings he taught the people in a plain, simple manner how to save their money, how to farm in a better way, how to sacrifice, — to live on bread and potatoes, if need be, till they could get out of debt, and begin the buying of lands.

Soon a large proportion of the people were in condition to make contracts for the buying of homes (land is very cheap in the South), and to live without mortgaging their crops. Not only this: under the guidance and leadership of this teacher, the first year that he was among them they learned how, by contributions in money and labor, to build a neat, comfortable schoolhouse that replaced the wreck of a log cabin formerly used. The following year the weekly meetings were continued, and two months were added to the original three months of school. The next year two more months were added. The improvement has gone on, until now these people have every year an eight months' school.

I wish my readers could have the chance that I have had of going into this community. I wish they could look into the faces of the people and see them beaming with hope and delight. I wish they could see the two or three room cottages that have taken the place of the usual one-room cabin, the well-cultivated farms, and the religious life of the people that now means something more than the name. The teacher has a good cottage and a well-kept farm that serve as models. In a word, a complete revolution has been wrought in the industrial, educational, and religious life of this whole community by reason of the fact that they have had this leader, this guide and object-lesson, to show them how to take the money and effort that had hitherto been scattered to the wind in mortgages and high rents, in whiskey and gewgaws, and concentrate them in the direction of their own uplifting. One community on its feet presents an object-lesson for the adjoining communities, and soon improvements show themselves in other places.

Another student who received academic and industrial training at Tuskegee established himself, three years ago, as a blacksmith and wheelwright in a community, and, in addition to the influence of his successful business enterprise, he is fast making the same kind of changes in the life of the people about him that I have just recounted. It would be easy for me to fill many pages describing the influence of the Tuskegee graduates in every part of the South. We keep it constantly in the minds of our students and graduates that the industrial or material condition of the masses of our people must be improved, as well as the intellectual, before there can be any permanent change in their moral and religious life. We find it a pretty hard thing to make a good Christian of a hungry man. No matter how much our people "get happy" and "shout" in church, if they go home at night from church hungry, they are tempted to find something before morning. This is a principle of human nature, and is not confined to the negro.

The negro has within him immense power for self-uplifting, but for years it will be necessary to guide and stimulate him. The recognition of this power led us to organize, five years ago, what is now known as the Tuskegee Negro Conference, — a gathering that meets every February, and is composed of about eight hundred representative colored men and women from all sections of the Black Belt. They come in ox-carts, mule-carts, buggies, on muleback and horseback, on foot, by railroad: some traveling all night in order to be present. The matters considered at the conferences are those that the colored people have it within their own power to control: such as the evils of the mortgage system, the one-room cabin, buying on credit, the importance of owning a home and of putting money in the bank, how to build schoolhouses and prolong the school term, and how to improve their moral and religious condition.

As a single example of the results, one delegate reported that since the conferences were started five years ago eleven people in his neighborhood had bought homes, fourteen had got out of debt, and a number had stopped mortgaging their crops. Moreover, a schoolhouse had been built by the people themselves, and the school term had been extended from three to six months; and with a look of triumph he exclaimed, "We is done stopped libin' in de ashes!"

Besides this Negro Conference for the masses of the people, we now have a gathering at the same time known as the Workers' Conference, composed of the officers and instructors in the leading colored schools of the South. After listening to the story of the conditions and needs from the people themselves, the Workers' Conference finds much food for thought and discussion.

Nothing else so soon brings about right relations between the two races in the South as the industrial progress of the negro. Friction between the races will pass away in proportion as the black man, by reason of his skill, intelligence, and character, can produce something that the white man wants or respects in the commercial world. This is another reason why at Tuskegee we push the industrial training. We find that as every year we put into a Southern community colored men who can start a brick-yard, a sawmill, a tin-shop, or a printing-office, — men who produce something that makes the white man partly dependent upon the negro, instead of all the dependence being on the other side, — a change takes place in the relations of the races.

Let us go on for a few more years knitting our business and industrial relations into those of the white man, till a black man gets a mortgage on a white man's house that he can foreclose at will. The white man on whose house the mortgage rests will not try to prevent that negro from voting when he goes to the polls. It is through the dairy farm, the truck garden, the trades, and commercial life, largely, that the negro is to find his way to the enjoyment of all his rights. Whether he will or not, a white man respects a negro who owns a two-story brick house.

What is the permanent value of the Tuskegee system of training to the South in a broader sense? In connection with this, it is well to bear in mind that slavery taught the white man that labor with the hands was something fit for the negro only, and something for the white man to come into contact with just as little as possible. It is true that there was a large class of poor white people who labored with the hands, but they did it because they were not able to secure negroes to work for them; and these poor whites were constantly trying to imitate the slave-holding class in escaping labor, and they too regarded it as anything but elevating. The negro in turn looked down upon the poor whites with a certain contempt because they had to work. The negro, it is to be borne in mind, worked under constant protest, because he felt that his labor was being unjustly required, and he spent almost as much effort in planning how to escape work as in learning how to work. Labor with him was a badge of degradation. The white man was held up before him as the highest type of civilization, but the negro noted that this highest type of civilization himself did no labor; hence he argued that the less work he did, the more nearly he would be like a white man. Then, in addition to these influences, the slave system discouraged labor-saving machinery. To use labor-saving machinery intelligence was required, and intelligence and slavery were not on friendly terms; hence the negro always associated labor with toil, drudgery, something to be escaped. When the negro first became free, his idea of education was that it was something that would soon put him in the same position as regards work that his recent master had occupied. Out of these conditions grew the Southern habit of putting off till to-morrow and the day after the duty that should be done promptly to-day. The leaky house was not repaired while the sun shone, for then the rain did not come through. While the rain was falling, no one cared to expose himself to stop the leak. The plough, on the same principle, was left where the last furrow was run, to rot and rust in the field during the winter. There was no need to repair the wooden chimney that was exposed to the fire, because water could be thrown on it when it was on fire. There was no need to trouble about the payment of a debt to-day, for it could just as well be paid next week or next year. Besides these conditions, the whole South, at the close of the war, was without proper food, clothing, and shelter,— was in need of habits of thrift and economy and of something laid up for a rainy day.

This industrial training, emphasizing as it does the idea of economic production, is gradually bringing the South to the point where it is feeding itself. Before the war, and long after it, the South made what little profit was received from the cotton crop, and sent its earnings out of the South to purchase food supplies, — meat, bread, canned vegetables, and the like; but the improved methods of agriculture are fast changing this habit. With the newer methods of labor, which teach promptness and system, and emphasize the worth of the beautiful, — the moral value of the well-painted house, and the fence with every paling and nail in its place, — we are bringing to bear upon the South an influence that is making it a new country in industry, education, and religion.

Source: *Atlantic Monthly*, 1886

HOW WELL DID YOU UNDERSTAND THIS SELECTION?

1. What is the Tuskegee System?

2. What does Washington think is the solution to the problems African Americans face in the South?

3. What influence does Washington maintain Tuskegee Institute has had on the South?

4. What does Washington think is the key to improving race relations?

5. Why does Washington advocate industrial rather than academic training for African Americans?

6. How does Washington think Tuskegee Institute has changed southern attitudes about labor?

OF THE TRAINING OF BLACK MEN" By W.E.B. Du Bois

W.E.B. Du Bois was an African-American leader who often criticized Booker T. Washington, especially his views on race and education. Du Bois disagrees with Washington's idea that industrial training is the most appropriate education for African Americans. He thinks African Americans are suited for higher education, especially college.

From the shimmering swirl of waters where many, many thoughts ago the slave-ship first saw the square tower of Jamestown have flowed down to our day three streams of thinking: one from the larger world here and over-seas, saying, the multiplying of human wants in culture lands calls for the world-wide co-operation of men in satisfying them. Hence arises a new human unity, pulling the ends of earth nearer, and all men, black, yellow, and white. The larger humanity strives to feel in this contact of living nations and sleeping hordes a thrill of new life in the world, crying, If the contact of Life and Sleep be Death, shame on such Life. To be sure, behind this thought lurks the afterthought of force and dominion, — the making of brown men to delve when the temptation of beads and red calico cloys. The second thought streaming from the death-ship and the curving river is the thought of the older South: the sincere and passionate belief that somewhere between men and cattle God created a *tertium quid*, and called it a Negro, — a clownish, simple creature, at times even lovable within its limitations, but straitly foreor-

306

dained to walk within the Veil. To be sure, behind the thought lurks the afterthought, — some of them with favoring chance might become men, but in sheer self-defense we dare not let them, and build about them walls so high, and hang between them and the light a veil so thick, that they shall not even think of breaking through. And last of all there trickles down that third and darker thought, the thought of the things themselves, the confused half-conscious mutter of men who are black and whitened, crying Liberty, Freedom, Opportunity — vouchsafe to us, O boastful World, the chance of living men! To be sure, behind the thought lurks the afterthought: suppose, after all, the World is right and we are less than men? Suppose this mad impulse within is all wrong, some mock mirage from the untrue?

So here we stand among thoughts of human unity, even through conquest and slavery; the inferiority of black men, even if forced by fraud; a shriek in the night for the freedom of men who themselves are not yet sure of their right to demand it. This is the tangle of thought and afterthought wherein we are called to solve the problem of training men for life. Behind all its curiousness, so attractive alike to sage and dilettante, lie its dim dangers, throwing across us shadows at once grotesque and awful. Plain it is to us that what the world seeks through desert and wild we have within our threshold; — a stalwart laboring force, suited to the semi-tropics; if, deaf to the voice of the Zeitgeist, we refuse to use and develop these men, we risk poverty and loss. If, on the other hand, seized by the brutal afterthought, we debauch the race thus caught in our talons, selfishly sucking their blood and brains in the future as in the past, what shall save us from national decadence? Only that saner selfishness which, education teaches men, can find the rights of all in the whirl of work.

Again, we may decry the color prejudice of the South, yet it remains a heavy fact. Such curious kinks of the human mind exist and must be reckoned with soberly. They cannot be laughed away, nor always successfully stormed at, nor easily abolished by act of legislature. And yet they cannot be encouraged by being let alone. They must be recognized as facts, but unpleasant facts; things that stand in the way of civilization and religion and common decency. They can be met in but one way: by the breadth and broadening of human reason, by catholicity of taste and culture. And so, too, the native ambition and aspiration of men, even though they be black, backward, and ungraceful, must not lightly be dealt with. To stimulate wildly weak and untrained minds is to play with mighty fires; to flout their striving idly is to welcome a harvest of brutish crime and shameless lethargy in our very laps. The guiding of thought and the deft coordination of deed is at once the path of honor and humanity.

And so, in this great question of reconciling three vast and partially contradictory streams of thought, the one panacea of Education leaps to the lips of all; such human training as will best use the labor of all men without enslaving or brutalizing; such training as will give us poise to encourage the prejudices that bulwark society, and stamp out those that in sheer barbarity deafen us to the wail of prisoned souls within the Veil, and the mounting fury of shackled men.

But when we have vaguely said Education will set this tangle straight, what have we uttered but a truism? Training for life teaches living; but what training for the profitable living together of black men and white? Two hundred years ago our task would have seemed easier. Then Dr. Johnson blandly assured us that education was needed solely for the embellishments of life, and was useless for ordinary vermin. Today we have climbed to heights where we would open at least the outer courts of knowledge to all, display its treasures to many, and select the few to whom its mystery of Truth is revealed, not wholly by truth or the accidents of the stock market, but at least in part according to deftness and aim, talent and character. This program, however, we are sorely puzzled in carrying out through that part of the land where the blight of slavery fell hardest, and where we are dealing with two backward peoples. To make here in human education that ever necessary combination of the permanent and the contingent — of the ideal and the practical in workable equilibrium — has been there, as it ever must be in every age and place, a matter of infinite experiment and frequent mistakes.

In rough approximation we may point out four varying decades of work in Southern education since the Civil War. From the close of the war until 1876 was the period of uncertain groping and temporary relief. There were army schools, mission schools, and schools of the Freedmen's Bureau in chaotic disarrangement, seeking system and cooperation. Then followed ten years of constructive definite effort toward the building of complete school systems in the South. Normal schools and colleges were founded for the freedmen, and teachers trained there to man the public schools. There was the inevitable tendency of war to underestimate the prejudice of the master and the ignorance of the slave, and all seemed clear sailing out of the wreckage of the storm. Meantime, starting in this decade yet especially developing from 1885 to 1895, began the industrial revolution of the South. The land saw glimpses of a new destiny and the stirring of new ideals. The educational system striving to complete itself saw new obstacles and a field of work ever broader and deeper. The Negro colleges, hurriedly founded, were inadequately equipped, illogically distributed, and of varying efficiency and grade; the normal and high schools were doing little more than common school work, and the common schools were training but a third of the children who ought to be in them, and training these too often poorly. At the same time the white South, by reason of its sudden conversion from the slavery ideal, by so much the more became set and strengthened in its racial prejudice, and crystallized it into harsh law and harsher custom; while the marvelous pushing forward of the poor white daily threatened to take even bread and butter from the mouths of the heavily handicapped sons of the freedmen. In the midst, then, of the larger problem of Negro education sprang up the more practical question of work, the inevitable economic quandary that faces a people in the transition from slavery to freedom, and especially those who make that change amid hate and prejudice, lawlessness and ruthless competition.

The industrial school springing to notice in this decade, but coming to full recognition in the decade beginning with 1895, was the proffered answer to this combined educational and economic crisis, and an answer of singular wisdom and timeliness. From the very first in nearly all the schools some attention had been given to training in handiwork, but now was this training first raised to a dignity that brought it in direct touch with the South's magnificent industrial development, and given an emphasis which reminded black folk that before the Temple of Knowledge swing the Gates of Toil.

Yet after all they are but gates, and when turning our eyes from the temporary and the contingent in the Negro problem to the broader question of the permanent uplifting and civilization of black men in America, we have a right to inquire, as this enthusiasm for material advancement mounts to its height, if after all the industrial school is the final and sufficient answer in the training of the Negro race; and to ask gently, but in all sincerity, the ever recurring query of the ages, Is not life more than meat, and the body more than raiment? And men ask this to-day all the more eagerly because of sinister signs in recent educational movements. The tendency is here born of slavery and quickened to renewed life by the crazy imperialism of the day, to regard human beings as among the material resources of a land to be trained with an eye single to future dividends. Race prejudices, which keep brown and black men in their "places," we are coming to regard as useful allies with such a theory, no matter how much they may dull the ambition and sicken the hearts of struggling human beings. And above all, we daily hear that an education that encourages aspiration, that sets the loftiest of ideals and seeks as an end culture and character than bread-winning, is the privilege of white men and the danger and delusion of black.

Especially has criticism been directed against the former educational efforts to aid the Negro. In the four periods I have mentioned, we find first boundless, planless enthusiasm and sacrifice; then the preparation of teachers for a vast public school system; then the launching and expansion of that school system amid increasing difficulties; and finally the training of workmen for the new and growing industries. This development has been sharply ridiculed as a logical anomaly and flat reversal of nature. Soothly we have been told that first industrial and manual training should have taught the Negro to work, then simple schools should have taught him to read and write, and finally, after years, high and normal schools could have completed the system, as intelligence and skill were demanded.

That a system logically so complete was historically impossible, it needs but a little thought to prove. Progress in human affairs is more often a pull than a push, surging forward of the exceptional man, and the lifting of his duller brethren slowly and painfully to his vantage ground. Thus it was no accident that gave birth to universities centuries before the common schools, that made fair Harvard the first flower of our wilderness. So in the South: the mass of the freedmen at the end of the war lacked the intelligence so necessary to modern workingmen. They must first have the common school to teach them to read, write, and cipher. The white teachers who flocked South went to establish such a common school system. They had no idea of founding colleges; they themselves at first would have laughed at the idea. But they faced, as all men since them have faced, that central paradox of the South, the social separation of the races. Then it was the sudden volcanic rupture of nearly all relations between black and white, in work and government and family life. Since then a new adjustment of relations in economic and political affairs has grown up, — an adjustment subtle and difficult to grasp, yet singularly ingenious, which leaves still that frightful chasm at the color line across which men pass at their peril. Thus, then and now, there stand in the South two separate worlds; and separate not simply in the higher realms of social intercourse, but also in church and school, on railway and street car, in hotels and theatres, in streets and city sections, in books and newspapers, in asylums and jails, in hospitals and graveyards. There is still enough of contact for large economic and group cooperation, but the separation is so thorough and deep, that it absolutely precludes for the present between the races anything like that sympathetic and effective group training and leadership of the one by the other, such as the American Negro and all backward peoples must have for effectual progress.

This the missionaries of '68 soon saw; and if effective industrial and trade schools were impractical before the establishment of a common school system, just as certainly no adequate common schools could be founded until there were teachers to teach them. Southern whites would not teach them; Northern whites in sufficient numbers could not be had. If the Negro was to learn, he must teach himself, and the most effective help that could be given him was the establishment of schools to train Negro teachers. This conclusion was slowly but surely reached by every student of the situation until simultaneously, in widely separated regions, without consultation or systematic plan, there arose a series of institutions designed to furnish teachers for the untaught. Above the sneers of critics at the obvious defects of this procedure must ever stand its one crushing rejoinder: in a single generation they put thirty thousand black teachers in the South; they wiped out the illiteracy of the majority of the black people of the land, and they made Tuskegee possible.

Such higher training schools tended naturally to deepen broader development: at first they were common and grammar schools, then some became high schools. And finally, by 1900, some thirty-four had one year or more of studies of college grade. This development was reached with different degrees of speed in different institutions: Hampton is still a high school, while Fisk University started her college in 1871, and Spelman Seminary about 1896. In all cases the aim was identical: to maintain the standards of the lower training by giving teachers and leaders the best practicable training; and above all to furnish the black world with adequate standards of human culture and lofty ideals of life. It was not enough that the teachers of teachers should be trained in technical normal methods; they must also, so far as possible, be broad-minded, cultured men and women, to scatter civilization among a people whose ignorance was not simply of letters, but of life itself.

It can thus be seen that the work of education in the South began with higher institutions of training, which threw off as their foliage common schools, and later industrial schools, and at the same time strove to shoot their roots ever deeper toward college and university training. That this was an inevitable and necessary development, sooner or later, goes without saying; but there has been, and still is, a question in many minds if the natural growth was not forced, and if the higher training was not either overdone or done with cheap and unsound methods. Among white Southerners this feeling is widespread and positive. A prominent Southern journal voiced this in a recent editorial: "The experiment that has been made to give the colored students classical training has not been satisfactory. Even though many were able to pursue the course, most of them did so in a parrot-like way, learning what was taught, but not seeming to appropriate the truth and import of their instruction, and graduating without sensible aim or valuable occupation for their future. The whole scheme has proved a waste of time, efforts, and the money of the state." While most far-minded men would recognize this as extreme and overdrawn, still without doubt many are asking, are there a sufficient number of Negroes ready for college training to warrant the undertaking? Are not too many students prematurely forced into this work? Does it not have the effect of dissatisfying the young Negro with his environment? And do these graduates succeed in real life? Such natural questions cannot be evaded, nor on the other hand must a nation naturally skeptical as to Negro ability assume an unfavorable answer without careful inquiry and patient openness to conviction. We must not forget that most Americans answer all queries regarding the Negro *a priori*, and that the least that human courtesy can do is to listen to evidence.

The advocates of the higher education of the Negro would be the last to deny the incompleteness and glaring defects of the present system: too many institutions have attempted to do college work, the work in some cases has not been thoroughly done, and quantity rather than quality has sometimes been sought. But all this can be said of higher education throughout the land: it is the almost inevitable incident of educational growth, and leaves the deeper question of the legitimate demand for the higher training of Negroes untouched. And this latter question can be settled in but one way — by a first-hand study of the facts. If we leave out of view all institutions which have not actually graduated students from a course higher than that of a New England high school, even though they be called colleges; if then we take the thirty-four remaining institutions, we may clear up many misapprehensions by asking searchingly, What kind of institutions are they, what do they teach, and what sort of men do they graduate?

From such schools about two thousand Negroes have gone forth with the bachelor's degree. The number in itself is enough to put at rest the argument that too large a proportion of Negroes are receiving higher training. If the ratio to population of all Negro students throughout the land, in both college and secondary training, be counted, Commissioner Harris assures us "it must be increased to five times its present average" to equal the average of the land.

Fifty years ago the ability of Negro students in any appreciable numbers to master a modern college course would have been difficult to prove. Today it is proved by the fact that four hundred Negroes, many of whom have been reported as brilliant students, have received the bachelor's degree from Harvard, Yale, Oberlin, and seventy other leading colleges. Here we have, then, nearly twenty-five hundred Negro graduates, of whom the crucial query must be made. How far did their training fit them for life? It is of course extremely difficult to collect satisfactory data on such a point, — difficult to reach the men, to get trustworthy testimony, and to gauge that testimony by any generally acceptable criterion of success. In 1900, the Conference at Atlanta University undertook to study these graduates, and published the results. First they sought to know what these graduates were doing, and succeeded in getting answers from nearly two thirds of the living. The direct testimony was in almost all cases corroborated by the reports of the colleges where they graduated, so that in the main the reports were worthy of credence. Fifty-three per cent of these graduates were teachers, — presidents of institutions, heads of normal schools, principals of city school systems, and the like. Seventeen per cent were clergymen; another seventeen per cent were in the professions, chiefly as physicians. Over six per cent were merchants, farmers, and artisans, and four per cent were in the government civil service. Granting even that a considerable proportion of the third unheard from are unsuccessful, this is a record of usefulness. Personally I know many hundreds of these graduates and have corresponded with more than a thousand; through others I have followed carefully the life-work of scores; I have taught some of them and some of the pupils whom they have taught, lived in homes which they have built, and looked at life through their eyes. Comparing them as a class with my fellow students in New England and in Europe, I cannot hesitate in saying that nowhere have I met men and women with a broader spirit of helpfulness, with deeper devotion to their life-work, or with more consecrated determination to succeed in the face of bitter difficulties than among Negro college-bred men.

Strange to relate! for this is certain, no secure civilization can be built in the South with the Negro as an ignorant, turbulent proletariat. Suppose we seek to remedy this by making them laborers and nothing more: they are not fools, they have tasted of the Tree of Life, and they will not cease to think, will not cease attempting to read the riddle of the world. By taking away their best equipped teachers and leaders, by slamming the door of opportunity in the faces of their bolder and brighter minds, will you make them satisfied with their lot? Or will you not rather transfer their leading from the hands of men taught to think to the hands of untrained demagogues? We ought not to forget that despite the pressure of poverty, and despite the active discouragement and even ridicule of friends, the demand for higher training steadily increases among Negro youth: there were, in the years from 1875 to 1880, twenty-two Negro graduates from Northern colleges; from 1885 to 1895 there were forty-three, and from 1895 to 1900, nearly 100 graduates. From Southern Negro colleges there were, in the same three periods, 143, 413, and over 500 graduates. Here, then, is the plain thirst for training; by refusing to give this Talented Tenth the key to knowledge can any sane man imagine that they will lightly lay aside their yearning and contentedly become hewers of wood and drawers of water?

The function of the Negro college then is clear: it must maintain the standards of popular education, it must seek the social regeneration of the Negro, and it must help in the solution of problems of race contact and cooperation. And finally, beyond all this, it must develop men. Above our modern socialism, and out of the worship of the mass, must persist and evolve that higher individualism which the centers of culture protect; there must come a loftier respect for the sovereign human soul that seeks to know itself and the world about it; that seeks a freedom for expansion and self-development; that will love and hate and labor in its own way, untrammeled alike by old and new. Such souls aforetime have inspired and guided worlds, and if we be not wholly bewitched by our Rhine-gold, they shall again.

Source: *Atlantic Monthly*, 1902

HOW WELL DID YOU UNDERSTAND THIS SELECTION?

1. What type of education does Du Bois advocate for African Americans?

2. Compare and contrast the ideas of Du Bois and Booker T. Washington regarding education for African Americans. How do the two men differ? Are there any similarities between them? Explain?

3. What does Du Bois think the ultimate value of college education will be for African Americans?

4. Is Du Bois an optimist or a pessimist?

5. What does Du Bois believe will be the consequence for American society if African Americans continue to be denied the right to a college education?

6. How does Du Bois respond to the white charge that African Americans are criminal?

7. How does Du Bois justify allowing African Americans to receive college education?

8. What are Du Bois' ideas on race relations? What does he think is necessary before improvements in race relations can occur?

SELF TEST

MULTIPLE CHOICE: Circle the correct response. The correct answers are given at the end.

1. Who was Andrew Carnegie?
   a. An important financier of the American Revolutionary War.
   b. One of the leaders of the oil refining industry.
   c. A wealthy steel magnet who used vertical integration to control all aspects of his business.
   d. A leader of the Progressive Movement who demanded that government place curbs on big business.

2. Which of the following industries can best be described as the engine that drove the American Industrial Revolution?
   a. Steel.
   b. Railroads.
   c. Oil.
   d. Coal.

3. Which of the following statements best describes the conditions of African Americans during the industrial era?
   a. Most lived in the North and had high paying jobs.
   b. In both the North and South blacks worked in the lowest paying jobs in the worst possible conditions.
   c. Most lived in the West where they worked as cowboys.
   d. Many were able to attend public universities in the South where upon graduation they found high paying jobs.

4. How did big business generally respond to Unions during the Industrial Era?
   a. By refusing to bargain with Unions.
   b. By signing Union contracts beneficial to workers.
   c. By forming company unions that workers could join.
   d. By raising wages to keep union out of factories and mines.

5. How much did immigrant workers earn, on average, during the last decades of the nineteenth century?
   a. $25,000 per year.
   b. $5,000 per year.
   c. $2,500 per year.
   d. $250 to $300 per year.

6. What Presidential candidate in the 1872 election is described as a spiritualist who advocated free love?
   a. Grover Cleveland.
   b. Elizabeth Cady Stanton.
   c. Victoria Woodhull.
   d. Horace Greeley.

7. Why did Congress enact the Sherman Anti-Trust Act?
   a. To encourage companies to become monopolies.
   b. Because monopolies were restricting competition.
   c. Because workers were being abused by large corporations.
   d. So that American companies could expand into overseas markets.

8. One result of American industrialism was:
   a. Safe working conditions in factories.
   b. The location of factories in rural areas.
   c. High wages for women and children.
   d. Explosive population growth in cities.

9. Why did the United States go to war with Spain in 1898?
   a. Because Spain was a barbaric nation.
   b. Because Spain destroyed the American battleship Maine.
   c. Because Spain refused to liberate Cuba.
   d. Because the United States wanted Spanish colonial possessions like Puerto Rico and the Philippines.

10. What did the theory of Social Darwinism hold?
    a. That government should develop affirmative action programs to help minorities.
    b. That an agricultural lifestyle was superior to an industrial lifestyle.
    c. That it was inevitable that a few exceptional people would rise to the top of society.
    d. That the American gene pool was being strengthened by immigration.

ANSWERS:
  1-c; 2-b; 3-b; 4-a; 5-d; 6-c; 7-b; 8-d; 9-d; 10-c

ESSAYS:

1. Discuss the impact the Industrial Revolution had on American politics and government. Pay attention to foreign policy and race relations.

2. Compare and contrast the impact the Industrial Revolution had on farmers and workers. How did both groups respond to industrialism? How successful were workers and farmers in solving problems both groups faced?

3. Should the government have done more to regulate industrialism? Why or why not?

4. Why did Andrew Carnegie and others adopt ideas like the Social Gospel and Social Darwinism? Do these ideas reflect elitism and racism? Why or why not?

OPTIONAL ACTIVITIES: (Use your knowledge **and** imagination.)

1. You are an immigrant in a West Virginia labor camp. Write a letter to a friend in your native country about your experiences in America.

2. You are Booker T. Washington. As president of Tuskegee Institute, you need to hire a new faculty member. Devise a set of interview questions to ask job applicants that reflect your views on African-American education.

3. Read other books in the Oz series written by L. Frank Baum. See if you can find symbolism from other historical periods and events (hint, one Oz book is about feminism).

WEB SITE LISTINGS:

Tsongas Industrial History Center
Educational programs about the American Industrial Revolution. http://www.uml.edu/tsongas/

The Blackstone Valley
The song "Blackstone Valley," written by Charlie Ball and performed by Plainfolk, tells the tale of the river that launched the American Industrial Revolution. http://www.plainfolk.com/BSV.html

Lowell Visitors Bureau
Visit website for historical information on such things as the beginnings of the Industrial Revolution in America. http://www.lowell.org/

Industrial Revolution
(Letsfindout.com) http://www.letsfindout.com/subjects/america/industri.html

Industrial Revolution
(Encyclopedia.com) http://www.encyclopedia.com/articles/06349.html

Carnegie, Andrew
(Encarta® Concise Encyclopedia Article)
http://encarta.msn.com/index/conciseindex/19/019E0000.htm?z=1&pg=2&br=1

Carnegie, Andrew
(Encyclopedia.com) http://www.encyclopedia.com/articles/02322.html

Ford, Henry
http://www.encyclopedia.com/search.asp?target=@DOCTITLE%20Ford%20%20Henry

The Magic of Oz
L. Frank Baum http://sailor.gutenberg.org/etext96/magoz10.txt

Lowell National Historical Park
The official expanded NPS website. Lowell National Historical Park preserves and interprets the history of the American Industrial Revolution in Lowell, MA. The park includes historic cotton textile mills, 5.6 miles of canals, operating gatehouses, and worker housing. http://www.nps.gov/lowe/home.htm

A Historical View of U.S. Immigration Policy
...the U.S. passed the **National Origins Act**. This **act**... www.missouri.edu/~socbrent/immigr.htm

Spotlight Biography: Labor Reformers
As the power and scale of American industry grew during the 19th century, working conditions for most Americans underwent radical change. Mechanized, large-scale factories staffed by unskilled laborers gradually came to replace specialized craftsmen and small workshops. Samuel Gompers, more than any other individual, helped to modernize the unions, organize them on a national scale, and open their doors to unskilled as well as skilled workers. http://educate.si.edu/spotlight/labor.html

United Mine Workers of America
(Encarta® Concise Encyclopedia Article)
http://encarta.msn.com/index/conciseindex/49/0494B000.htm?z=1&pg=2&br=1

The Homestead and Pullman Strikes

In light of the recent depression, the voters of 1896 were concerned with keeping money in their pockets. Within recent public memory lay two major events that led to this unease—the Homestead strike of 1892 and the Pullman Railroad strike of 1894. These two conflicts brought to the surface the deeper issues at work in an age of industrial progress. http://iberia.vassar.edu/1896/strikes.html

Haymarket Square

(Encyclopedia.com) http://www.encyclopedia.com/articles/05722.html

Haymarket Square Riot

(Encarta® Concise Encyclopedia Article)
http://www.encyclopedia.com/search.asp?target=@DOCTITLE%20Haymarket%20Square%20riot

Chapter Fourteen

THE TRANS-MISSOURI
WEST: The Last Frontier

Life west of the Mississippi River was vastly different for people living there than it was for people living east of the Mississippi River before the twentieth century. Native Americans were being forced onto reservations and conflict erupted when whites took Native American land by measures such as the Dawes Act. Native American leaders such as Red Cloud and W.C. Duncan protested before Congress and the American public but their words generally fell on deaf ears. After the Civil War thousands of farmers, miners, and outlaws went west seeking their fortune. These people did not care whether they took land from Native Americans; after all, they viewed Indians as standing in the way of progress. This migration was made possible in part by completion of the Transcontinental Railroad after the federal government offered huge subsidies to railroad companies willing to build this line. Life, for most, was difficult. Social mobility was no easier out West than it was back East. Individuals who came west with money had a much better chance of becoming wealthy than poor people. The West was, however, something of a melting pot as people from all over the world intermingled. Despite the multicultural nature of western society, ethnic minorities in western territories faced racism, prejudice, and discrimination. Congress passed the Chinese Exclusion Act to prevent more Chinese immigrants from settling in the West. Tejanos in Texas and other western states saw their land taken by white settlers. Conflict sometimes broke out between whites and Hispanics, between sheep ranchers and cattle barons, between miners and corporations, and between farmers and ranchers. During this time many myths about the West were created and passed down to future generations of Americans. The lonely cowboy, the gun-fighter, the rancher, etc. are all images Americans living today think of when the West is mentioned. While the western myth has some validity, most of it is not true. Ironically, at the very time the western myth was being created, the West was ending. In 1880 the United States Census Bureau declared the frontier to be officially closed.

The Populist Party arose in the West and made a mark on the American political landscape. Its candidate, William Jennings Bryan, ran a spirited campaign in 1896 when he and western farmers indicted the Republicans for standing behind the gold standard. In many respects the 1896 election represents a clash between the old America, a land of farms, ranchers, and independent individuals, with the new America, a land of corporate monoliths, workers enslaved to the factory, and robber barons who made vast fortunes from the sweat of millions of ordinary laborers.

IDENTIFICATION: Briefly describe each term.

Chief Joseph

Buffalo Bill Cody

Blackfeet

Little Crow

Sioux

Quaker Policy

Heroes of Sand Creek

George Armstrong Custer

Crazy Horse

Sitting Bull

Geronimo

Wounded Knee

Ghost Dance

Dawes Act

Chinese Exclusion Act

Workingmen's Party

Santa Fe Ring

Texas Rangers

Exodusters

Buffalo Soldiers

Comstock Lode

Western Federation of Miners

Joseph McCoy

Johnson County War

Code of the West

Lincoln County War

O.K. Coral

Leland Stanford

Homestead Act of 1862

Defeated Legion

Morrill Act

Grange (Patrons of Husbandry)

Wabash Case

Interstate Commerce Commission

Populist Movement

William McKinley

William Jennings Bryan

Yellowstone National Park

Annie Oakley

Mark Twain

THINK ABOUT:

1. Describe Native American societies in the West. What importance did the buffalo play in these societies? What did the slaughter of the buffalo mean for Native Americans living in the West? What role did government policy play in the decline of Native American societies?

2. Describe your life as a Chinese immigrant? How do you feel about your treatment at the hands of the American government?

3. Examine the views of the Grangers, the Populist, and the Republicans. How were they different? How were they similar?

4. How did life in the West differ from life in the East?

5. Describe your life as a homesteader in the West. What process did you have to follow to acquire land?

THE HOMESTEAD ACT

Passage of the Homestead Act by Congress in 1862 created the first program for making public lands available to ordinary Americans. Thousands of Americans went west in search of new lands. By the time the Civil War had ended, about 15,000 homestead claims had been filed with the government. Thousands of additional claims were filed during the two decades following the war. Most people filing claims were poor farmers from the East and Midwest; city dwellers generally lacked the resources and knowledge to farm in the West. The Homestead Act was responsible for Native Americans losing most of their land from 1862 until 1890. Americans who homesteaded in western states usually faced countless hardships, ranging from periodic droughts to erosion and violence. Some preserved while others gave up and went back east.

An act to secure homesteads to actual settlers on the public domain.

Be it enacted, that any person who is the head of a family, or who has arrived at the age of twenty-one years, and is a citizen of the United States, or who shall have filed his declaration of intention to become such, as required by the naturalization laws of the United States, and who has never born arms against the United States Government or given aid and comfort to its enemies, shall, from and after the first of January, eighteen hundred and sixty-three, be entitled to enter one quarter-section or a less quantity of unappropriated public lands, upon which said person may have filed a pre-emption claim, or which may, at the time the application is made be subject to pre-emption at one dollar and twenty-five cents, or less, per acre; or eighty acres or less of such unappropriated lands, at two dollars and fifty cents per acre, to be located in a body, in conformity to the legal subdivisions of the public lands, and after the same shall have been surveyed; Provided, that any person owning or residing on land may, under the provisions of this act, enter other land lying contiguous to his or her said land, which shall not, with the land so already owned and occupied, exceed in the aggregate one hundred and sixty acres.

Section 2. That the person applying for the benefit of this act shall, upon application to the register of the land office in which he or she is about to make such entry, make affidavit before the said register or receiver that he or she is the head of a family, or is twenty-one or more years of age, or shall have performed service in the Army or Navy of the United States, and that he has never born arms against the Government of the United States or given aid and comfort to its enemies, and that such application is made for his or her exclusive use and benefit, and that said entry is made for the purpose of actual settlement and cultivation, and not, either directly or indirectly, for the use or benefit of any other person or persons whomsoever; and upon filing the said affidavit with the register or receiver, and on payment of ten dollars, he or she shall thereupon be permitted to enter the quantity of land specified: Provided, however, that no certificate shall be given or patent issued therefore until the expiration of five years from the date of such entry; and if, at the expiration of such time, or at any time within two years thereafter, the person making such entry—or if he be dead, his widow; or in case of her death, his heirs or devisee; or in case of a widow making such entry, her heirs or devise, in case of her death—shall prove by two credible witnesses that he, she, or they have resided upon or cultivated the same for the term of five years immediately succeeding the time of filing the affidavit aforesaid, and shall make affidavit that no part of said land has been alienated, and that he has born true allegiance to the Government of the United States; then, in such case, he, she, or they, if at that time a citizen of the United States, shall be entitled to a patent, as in other cases provided for by law; And provided, further, that in case of the death of both father and mother, leaving an infant child or children under twenty-one years of age, the right and fee shall inure to the benefit of said infant child or children; and the executor, administrator, or guardian may, at any time within two years after the death of the surviving parent, and in accordance with the laws of the State in which such children for the time being have their domicile, sell said land for the benefit of said infants, but for no other purpose; and the purchaser shall acquire the absolute title by the purchase, and be entitled to a patent from the United States, on payment of the office fees and sum of money herein specified....

Source: U.S. Statutes at Large, Vol. 12

HOW WELL DID YOU UNDERSTAND THIS SELECTION?

1. Why did Congress enact the Homestead Act?

2. How much land could the head of a family acquire?

3. How much did the land cost the homesteader?

4. What effect did the Homestead Act have on settlement in the West? On Native Americans?

Perhaps the most important development in the history of the American West was construction of the transcontinental railroad. This railroad, which connected the East to the West, made it possible for western farmers and ranchers to get their crops and livestock to market. The transcontinental railroad would not likely have been built had the government not given tremendous subsidies to companies engaged in building the railway. The Pacific Railway Act, passed by Congress on July 1, 1862, made possible the construction of a railroad and telegraph line from the Missouri River to the Pacific Ocean.

Section 1. Be it enacted, That...five commissioners to be appointed by the Secretary of the Interior...are...erected into a body corporate...by the name of..."The Union Pacific Railroad Company"...and the...corporation is hereby authorized...to lay out, locate, construct, furnish, maintain and enjoy a continuous railroad and telegraph...from a point on the one hundredth meridian of longitude west from Greenwich, between the south margin of the valley of the Republican River and the north margin of the valley of the Platte River, to the western boundary of Nevada Territory, upon the route and terms hereinafter provided...

Section 2. That the right of way through...public lands be...granted to said company for the construction of said railroad and telegraph line; and the right...is hereby given to said company to take from the public lands adjacent to the line of said road, earth, stone, timber, and other materials for the construction thereof; said right of way is granted to said railroad to the extent of two hundred feet in width on each side of said railroad when it may pass over the public lands, including all necessary grounds, for stations, buildings, workshops, and depots, machine shops, switches, side tracks, turn tables, and water stations. The United States shall extinguish as rapidly as may be the Indian titles to all lands falling under the operation of this act...

Section 3. That there be...granted...for the purpose of aiding in the construction of...railroad and telegraph line, and to secure the safe and speedy transportation of mail, troops, munitions of war, and public stores thereon, every alternate section of public land, designated by odd numbers, to the amount of five alternate sections per mile on each side of said railroad, on the line thereof, and within the limits of ten miles on each side of...road... Provided That all mineral lands shall be excepted from the operation of act; but where the same shall contain timber, the timber thereon is...granted to said company...

Section 5. That for the purposes herein mentioned the Secretary of the Treasury shall...in accordance with the provisions of this act, issue to said company bonds of the United States of one thousand dollars each, payable in thirty years after date, paying six per centum per annum interest...to the amount of sixteen of said bonds per mile for each section of forty miles; and to secure the repayment to the United States...of the amount of said bonds...the issue of said bonds...shall ipso facto constitute a first mortgage on the whole line of the railroad and telegraph...

Section 9. That the Leavenworth, Pawnee and Western Railroad Company of Kansas are hereby authorized to construct a railroad and telegraph line...upon the same terms and conditions in all respects as are provided.... The Central Pacific Railroad Company of California is hereby authorized to construct a railroad and telegraph line from the Pacific coast...to the eastern boundaries of California, upon the same terms and conditions in all respects.

Section 10. ...And the Central Pacific Railroad Company of California after completing its road...is authorized to continue...construction...through the Territories of the United States to the Missouri River...upon the terms and conditions provided in this act...until said roads shall...connect...

Section 11. That for three hundred miles of said road most mountainous and difficult of construction, to wit: one hundred and fifty miles westerly from the eastern base of the Rocky Mountains, and one hundred and fifty miles eastwardly from the western base of the Sierra Nevada mountains...the bonds to be issued to aid in the construction thereof shall be treble the number per mile herein before provided...and between the sections last named of one hundred and fifty miles each, the bonds to be issued to aid in the constructions...shall be double the number per mile first mentioned...

Source: U.S. Statutes at Large, Vol. 12

HOW WELL DID YOU UNDERSTAND THIS SELECTION?

1. Why did Congress enact the Pacific Railway Act?

2. What incentives are railroads given to lay track across the West?

3. How did the government plan to finance the building of the transcontinental railroad?

4. What do you think would be the Populist Party's reaction to the fact that the government gave railroads so much western land? Why?

RED CLOUD SPEECH AT COOPER UNION, NEW YORK

Chief Red Cloud was one of the most important leaders of the Lakota Sioux. He was born in 1822 near the forks of the Platte River near what is now North Platte, Nebraska and died in 1909. Much of his early life was spent fighting whites and other Native American tribes in the West. His exploits as a warrior gave him enormous prominence within the Lakota nation. In 1866 Red Cloud led the Sioux in a war against the United States that represents the most successful conflict ever by a Native American tribe against the American government. The trouble began when the United States Army constructed forts along the Bozeman Trail in Wyoming to protect settlers and miners going to Montana and Colorado. Red Cloud attacked theses forts and defeated American forces, which caused the United States government in 1868 to sign the Fort Laramie Treaty, mandating that the United States would abandon its forts along the Bozeman Trail and guarantee the Lakota possession of the western half of South Dakota.

My brethren and my friends who are here before me this day. God Almighty has made us all, and He is here to bless what I have to say to you today. The Good Spirit made us both. He gave you lands and he gave us lands; he gave us these lands. You came in here, and we respected you as brothers. God Almighty made you but made you all white and clothed you. When he made us he made us with red skins and poor; now you have come.

When you first came we were very many, and you were few. Now you are many, and we are getting very few, and we are poor. You do not know who appears before you today to speak. I am a representative of the original American race, the first people of this continent. We are good and not bad. The reports that you hear concerning us are all on one side. We are always well disposed to them. You are here told that we are traitors and thieves, and it is not so. We have given you nearly all our lands, and if we had any more land to give we would be very glad to give it. We have nothing more. We are driven into a very little land, and we want you now, as our dear friends, to help us with the government of the United States.

The Great Father made us poor and ignorant—made you rich and wise and more skillful in these things that we know nothing about. The Great Father, the Good Father in heaven, made you all to eat tame food—made us to eat wild food—gives us the wild food. You ask anybody who has gone through our country to California; ask those who have settled there and in Utah, and you will find that we have treated them always well. You have children. We have children. You want to raise your children and make them happy and prosperous. We want to raise [ours] and make them happy and prosperous. We ask you to help us to do it.

At the mouth of the Horse Creek, in 1852, the Great Father made a treaty with us by which we agreed to let all that country open for fifty-five years for the transit of those who were going through. We kept this treaty. We never treated any man wrong. We never committed any murder or depredation until after the troops were sent into that country, and the troops killed our people and ill-treated them, and thus war and trouble arose, but before the troops were sent there we were quiet and peaceable, and there was no disturbance. Since that time there have been various goods sent from time to time to us, the only ones that ever reached us. After they reached us the government took them away. You, as good men, ought to help us to these goods.

Colonel Fitzpatrick of the government said we must all go to farm, and some of the people went to Fort Laramie and were badly treated. I only want to do that which is peaceful, and the Great Fathers know it, and also the Great Father who made us both. I came to Washington to see the Great Father in order to have peace and in order to have peace continue. That is all we want, and that is the reason why we are here now.

In 1868 men came out and brought papers. We are ignorant and do not read papers and they did not tell us right what was in these papers. We wanted them to take away their forts, leave our country, would not make war, and give our traders something. They said we had bound ourselves to trade on the Missouri, and we said, no, we did not want that. The interpreters deceived us. When I went to Washington I saw the Great Father. The Great Father showed me what the treaties were; he showed me all these points and showed me that the interpreters had deceived me and did not let me know what the right side of the treaty was. All I want is right and justice.... I represent the Sioux Nation, they will be governed by what I say and what I represent.

Look at me. I am poor and naked, but I am the chief of the Nation. We do not want riches, we do not ask for riches, but we want our children properly trained and brought up. We look to you for your sympathy. Our riches will ... do us no good; we cannot take away into the other world anything we have—we want to have love and peace.... We would like to know why commissioners are sent out there to do nothing but rob [us] and get the riches of this world away from us?

I was brought up among the traders and those who came out there in those early times. I had a good time for they treated us nicely and well. They taught me how to wear clothes and use tobacco, and to use firearms and ammunition, and all went on very well until the Great Father sent out another kind of men—men who drank whisky. He sent out whisky men, men who drank and quarreled, men who were so bad that he could not keep them at home, and so he sent them out there.

I have sent a great many words to the Great Father, but I don't know that they ever reach the Great Father. They were drowned on the way, therefore I was a little offended with it. The words I told the Great Father lately would never come to him, so I thought I would come and tell you myself.

And I am going to leave you today, and I am going back to my home. I want to tell the people that we cannot trust his agents and superintendents. I don't want strange people that we know nothing about. I am very glad that you belong to us. I am very glad that we have come here and found you and that we can understand one another. I don't want any more such men sent out there, who are so poor that when they come out there their first thoughts are how they can fill their own pockets.

We want preserves in our reserves. We want honest men, and we want you to help to keep us in the lands that belong to us so that we may not be a prey to those who are viciously disposed. I am going back home. I am very glad that you have listened to me, and I wish you good-bye and give you an affectionate farewell.

Source: *The New York Times*, July 17, 1870

HOW WELL DID YOU UNDERSTAND THIS SELECTION?

1. How does Red Cloud describe Native Americans?

2. How does Red Cloud describe whites?

3. What similarities and differences does Red Cloud see in whites and Native Americans?

4. How does Red Cloud describe relations between Native Americans and the United States government?

5. Who is Red Cloud? What does he want? What is he doing?

THE DAWES ACT

The Dawes Act, passed by Congress in 1887 was designed to impose assimilation on all Native American tribes and enable land-hungry whites to take lands delegated to Indian peoples. By the 1880s most Native Americans were living on reservations. Many whites believed that the reservations were too large and wanted thousands of acres of land encompassed in these reservations taken away from Native Americans and given to white farmers. Congress, bowing to pressure from farmers and ranchers, passed the General Allotment Act (Dawes Act), which gave individual Indian families 160 acres of land. The hundreds of thousands of acres remaining were then sold at bargain prices to whites, many of whom were land speculators. Native Americans felt cheated again by the United States government. The land most were left with was not large enough to support a family. The Dawes Act is partly responsible for the poverty Native Americans living on reservations experienced during the nineteenth and twentieth centuries.

Be it enacted. That in all cases where any tribe or band of Indians has been, or shall hereafter be, located upon any reservation created for their use, either by treaty stipulation or by virtue of an act of Congress or executive order setting apart the same for their use, the President of the United States be, and he hereby is, authorized, whenever in his opinion any reservation or any part thereof of such Indians is advantageous for agriculture and grazing purposes to cause said reservation, or any part thereof, to be surveyed, or resurveyed if necessary, and to allot the lands in said reservation in severally to any Indian located thereon in quantities as follows: To each head of a family, one-quarter of a section; To each single person over eighteen years of age, one-eighth of a section; To each orphan child under eighteen years of age, one-eight of a section; and, To each other single person under eighteen years now living, or who may be born prior to the date of the order of the President directing an allotment of the lands embraced in any reservation, one-sixteenth of a section: .. .

That upon the approval of the allotments provided for in this act by the Secretary of the Interior, he shall ... declare that the United States does and will hold the land thus allotted, for the period of twenty-five years, in trust for the sole use and benefit of the Indian to whom such allotment shall have been made, ... and that at the expiration of said period the United States will convey the same by patent to said Indian, or his heirs as aforesaid, in fee, discharged of such trust and free of all charge or encumbrance whatsoever:...

That upon the completion of said allotments and the patenting of the lands to said allottees, each and every member of the respective bands or tribes of Indians to whom allotments have been made shall have the benefit of and be subject to the laws, both civil and criminal, of the State or Territory in which they may reside, ... And every Indian born within the territorial limits of the United States to whom allotments shall have been made under the provisions of this act or under any law or treaty, and every Indian born within the territorial limits of the United States who has voluntarily taken up, within said limits, his residence separate and apart from any tribe of Indians therein, and has adopted the habits of civilized life, is hereby declared to be a citizen of the United States, and is entitled to all the rights, privileges, and immunities of such citizens, whether said Indian has been or not, by birth or otherwise, a member of any tribe of Indians within the territorial limits of the United States without in any manner impairing or otherwise affecting the right of any such Indian to tribal or other property....

Source: United States Statutes at Large, Vol. 24

HOW WELL DID YOU UNDERSTAND THIS SELECTION?

1. What was the primary purpose of the Dawes Act?

2. How much land did Native Americans receive under the Dawes Act?

3. What effect do you think the Dawes Act had on Native Americans?

4. If you were a Native American, how would you have felt about the Dawes Act?

D. W. C. Duncan was a Cherokee Indian who testified before a United States Senate Committee in 1906 investigating the condition of Native Americans in the West. He testified against the General Allottment Act (the Dawes Act), which took land from Native Americans and allowed land speculators and white farmers to buy it at cheap prices from the government. His testimony provides a valuable record of the effect the Dawes Act had on Native Americans in the West. As his testimony makes clear, Native Americans were impoverished by this law.

Senators, just let me present to you a picture; I know this is a little digression, but let me present it. Suppose the Federal Government should send a survey company into the midst of some of your central counties of Kansas or Colorado or Connecticut and run off the surface of the earth into sections and quarter sections and quarter quarter sections and set apart to each one of the inhabitants of that county 60 acres, rescinding and annulling all title to every inch of the earth's surface which was not included in that 60 acres, would the State of Connecticut submit to it? Would Colorado submit to it? Would Kansas brook such an outrage? No! It would be ruin, immeasurable ruin—devastation. There is not an American citizen in any one of those states would submit to it, if it cost him every drop of his heart's blood. That, my Senators, permit me—I am honest, candid, and fraternal in my feelings—but let me ask a question? Who is that hastened on this terrible destruction upon these Cherokee people? Pardon me, it was the Federal Government. It is a fact; and, old as I am, I am not capable of indulging in euphemisms.

Before this allotment scheme was put in effect in the Cherokee Nation we were a prosperous people. We had farms. Every Indian in this nation that needed one and felt that he needed one had it. Orchards and gardens—everything that promoted the comforts of private life was ours, even as you—probably not so extensively—so far as we went, even as you in the States. The result has been, which I now want to illustrate, as I set out, by my own personal experience.

Under our old Cherokee regime I spent the early days of my life on the farm up here of 300 acres, and arranged to be comfortable in my old age, but the allotment scheme came along and struck me during the crop season while my corn was ripening in full ear. I was looking forward to the crop of corn hopefully for some comforts to be derived from it during the months of the winter. When I was assigned to that 60 acres, and I could take no more under the inexorable law of allotment enforced upon us Cherokees, I had to relinquish every inch of my premises outside of that little 60 acres. What is the result? There is a great scramble of persons to find land—the office was located here in our town— to file upon. Some of the friends in here, especially a white intermarried citizen, goes up and files upon a part of my farm—on a part of my growing crop, upon the crop upon which I had spent my labor and my money, and upon which I had based my hopes. I remonstrated with him. I said to him, "Sir, you don't want to treat me that way. We are neighbors and friends. You can't afford to take my property that way. Of course the Dawes Commission and the Curtis law will give you the land, although I have subdued it, and I have fenced it, and cultivated it. But for God's sake, my friend, don't take my crop." "Well," says he, "I had to surrender my crop to a fellow down here. He allotted on me, and I don't know why I should be any more lenient on you than others are on me. If you don't let that corn alone, I will go to the court and get an order." That was new to me, but when I came to examine the Curtis law, and investigated the orders and rules established by the Dawes Commission, I just folded my hands and said, "I give it up." Away went my crop, and if the same rule had been established in your counties in your State you would have lost your dwelling house, you would have lost your improvements. Now, that is what has been done to these Cherokees.

What a condition, I have 60 acres of land left me, the balance is all gone. I am an old man, not able to follow the plow as I used to when a boy. What am I going to do with it? For the last few years, since I have had my allotment, I have gone out there on that farm day after day I have used the ax, the hoe, the spade, the plow, hour for hour, until fatigue would throw me exhausted upon the ground. Next day I repeated the operation, and let me tell you, Senators, I have exerted all my ability, all industry, all my intelligence, if I have any, my will, my ambition, the love of my wife, all these agencies, I have employed to make my living out of that 60 acres, and God be my judge, I have not been able to do it. I am not able to do it. I can't do it. I have not been able to clear expenses. It will take every ear of the bounteous crop on that 60 acres, for this year is a pretty good crop year, it will take every bushel of it to satisfy the debts that I have incurred to eke out a living during the meager years just passed. And I am here today, a poor man upon the verge of starvation, my muscular energy gone. Hope gone I have nothing to charge my calamity to but the unwise legislation of Congress in reference to my Cherokee people.

I am in that fix. Senators, you will not forget now that when I use the word I, I mean the whole Cherokee people. I am in that fix. What am I to do? I have a piece of property that doesn't support me, and is not worth a cent to me under the same inexorable cruel provisions of the Curtis law that swept away our treaties, our system of nationality, our every existence, and wrested out of our possession our vast territory. The same provisions of that Curtis law that ought to have been satisfied with these achievements didn't stop there. The law goes on and that 60 acres of land, it says, shall not be worth one cent to me, although the Curtis law has given me 60 acres as the only inheritance I have in God's world, even that shall not be worth anything. Let me explain.

If you had a horse that you couldn't use, and some competent power ordained that that horse should have no value in any market on the face of the earth, and at the same time you should be compelled to keep that horse as long as he should live, or at least twenty-five years, at your expense, now, in the name of common sense, what would you do with that horse? He is not worth anything, his services are not worth anything to me, I can't ride him, I can't use him. There is no man in the world that will give me a cent for him, the law won't allow me to sell him. I would get rid of that horse somehow sure.

The point I am making here is applicable to every species of property, whether real or personal. Prevent the property from being purchasable in open market and you destroy it. Upon the same principle, my allotment up here is absolutely destroyed. What am I going to do with it? What can any Indian do with his allotment under similar circumstances?

Let me allude to myself again. It is not egotism I will tell you what I am going to do with my allotment. I sat down one day and wrote out my application for the removal of my restrictions. I went to work and pushed it through all the Federal machinery up to the Secretary of the Interior and back again, and a few days ago I was notified my restrictions were raised. Now for the next step. What am I going to do with that worthless piece of properly? I am going to hold it—how long I don't know—but I am going to wait until the white population becomes a little more multitudinous, when the price of real estate will rise. When I can get anything like an adequate value for my farm I am going to sell it. It is worthless to me.

The Government of the United States knows that these allotments of the Indians are not sufficient. Congress recognizes the fact forcibly, by implication, that these allotments are not sufficient. Why, one American citizen goes out on the western plain in North Dakota to make a home. What is the amount of land allotted to him? Isn't it 160 acres? Why, it is the general consensus all over the country that nothing less would be sufficient to support any family, and there are many years when you think, too, that 160 acres is not sufficient. Since this country has been split up, the Cherokee government abolished, and the allotments attained, immigration has come in from the surrounding States, consisting of persons of different kinds. I have tested them, and know what I am talking about, personally. Persons in pursuit of a sufficient quantity of land upon which to rear their families and take care of themselves, I have interrogated them time and again. I have said to them. "Look here, my friend, where are you going?" "To Indian Territory." "What for?" "To get a piece of land." "Did you have any land in Missouri or Kansas?" "Yes, sir; I had some up there, but it was too small and wasn't sufficient." "How much was it?" "Eighty or one hundred acres," as the case may be. "I have leased out my land up there to parties, and thought I would come down here and get a larger piece of ground." Well, now, that is the state of the case. I think, gentlemen, when you investigate the case fully you will find that these people have been put off with a piece of land that is absolutely inadequate for their needs.

Source: U.S. Senate Report 5013, 59th Congress, 2nd Session

HOW WELL DID YOU UNDERSTAND THIS SELECTION?

1. Who is Duncan? What is he reacting to?

2. How does Duncan describe Cherokee life before the Curtis Law took effect?

3. What happened to Duncan as a result of the Curtis Law?

4. What does Duncan want Congress to do?

REPORT ON WOUNDED KNEE MASSACRE, By Benjamin Harrison

Wounded Knee was the last battle fought between American forces and Native Americans in the West. On December 29, 1890, the Seventh Calvary (the unit massacred at Little Big Horn) of the United States Army and a group of Sioux Indians engaged in a skirmish that resulted in 64 casualties. In addition, 51 Indians, most of whom were women and children, were wounded. The battle was precipitated when the Sioux began to follow the prophet Wovoka and perform the Ghost Dance, which they believed would restore the tribe to its former glory. Settlers and Indian agents feared that this dancing might lead to renewed conflict and tried to suppress it. In the suppression the aging chief, Sitting Bull, was killed. The army feared that his death might cause an Indian uprising, and the Seventh Cavalry rounded up over three hundred Sioux who had left the reservation and camped at Wounded Knee, South Dakota. After the army had began the process of disarming the Sioux, one Indian, intentionally or unintentionally (the evidence is unclear) fired a hidden gun. The troops, fearing they were under attack, opened fire on the Sioux. Indians who had not yet been disarmed returned fire at the troops, killing 25 members of the Seventh Calvary. Bodies of the dead Sioux were buried in a mass grave and the wounded were carried to a local missionary church where they lay beneath a banner proclaiming "Peace on Earth; Good Will to Men." President Harrison addressed Congress about the Battle of Wounded Knee on December 9, 1891.

The outbreak among the Sioux which occurred in December last is as to its causes and incidents fully reported upon by the War Department and the Department of the Interior. That these Indians had some just complaints, especially in the matter of the reduction of the appropriation for rations and in the delays attending the enactment of laws to enable the Department to perform the engagements entered into with them, is probably true; but the Sioux tribes are naturally warlike and turbulent, and their warriors were excited by their medicine men and chiefs, who preached the coming of an Indian messiah who was to give them power to destroy their enemies. In view of the alarm that prevailed among the white settlers near the reservation and of the fatal consequences that would have resulted from an Indian incursion, I placed at the disposal of General Miles, commanding the Division of the Missouri, all such forces as we thought by him to be required. He is entitled to the credit of having given thorough protection to the settlers and of bringing the hostiles into subjection with the least possible loss of life. . . .

Since March 4, 1889, about 23,000,000 acres have been separated from Indian reservations and added to the public domain for the use of those who desired to secure free homes under our beneficent laws. It is difficult to estimate the increase of wealth which will result from the conversion of these waste lands into farms, but it is more difficult to estimate the betterment which will result to the families that have found renewed hope and courage in the ownership of a home and the assurance of a comfortable subsistence under free and healthful conditions. It is also gratifying to be able to feel, as we may, that this work has proceeded upon lines of justice toward the Indian, and that he may now, if he will, secure to himself the good influences of a settled habitation, the fruits of industry, and the security of citizenship.
Source: Third Annual Message to Congress, Dec. 9, 1891

HOW WELL DID YOU UNDERSTAND THIS SELECTION?

1. How does Harrison view the Sioux? Did Americans view all Native Americans in this light? Why or Why not?

2. What reason did the Sioux have for fighting American forces at Wounded Knee?

3. What does American policy attempt to force Native Americans to do?

BRYAN'S CROSS OF GOLD SPEECH

William Jennings Bryan was the Populist/Democratic candidate for president in 1896 and again in 1900. He was noted as a spectacular orator. In 1896 he criss-crossed the United States and made hundreds of speeches in attempt to convince voters to support him against William McKinley in the presidential election. He captured the Democratic presidential nomination in 1896 with his famous "Cross of Gold" speech in which he supported inflation of the American currency through the free coinage of silver. This position was important to Westerners, as most silver produced in the United States was mined in the West and farmers and ranchers living west of the Missouri River faced economic difficulties they believed inflation would solve. Bryan did not win the presidency, but the "Cross of Gold" speech is considered one of the best examples of political oratory in American political history.

Mr. Chairman and Gentlemen of the Convention I would be presumptuous, indeed, to present myself against the distinguished gentlemen to whom you have listened if this were a mere measuring of abilities, but this is not a contest between persons. The humblest citizen in all the land, when clad in the armor of a righteous cause, is stronger than all the hosts of error. I come to speak to you in defense of a cause as holy as the cause of liberty—the cause of humanity.

Never before in the history of this country has there been witnessed such a contest as that through which we have just passed. Never before in the history of American politics has a great issue been fought out as this issue has been, by the voters of a great party. With a zeal approaching the zeal which inspired the crusaders who followed Peter the hermit, our silver Democrats went forth from victory unto victory until they are now assembled, not to discuss, not to debate, but to enter up the judgment already rendered by the plain people of this country. In this contest brother has been arrayed against brother, father against son, the warmest ties of love, acquaintance and association have been disregarded, old leaders have been cast aside when they have refused to give expression to the sentiments of those whom they would lead, and new leaders have sprung up to give direction to the cause of truth.

Thus has the contest been waged, and we have assembled here under as binding and solemn instructions as were ever imposed upon representatives of the people.

The gentleman who preceded me [Governor Russell, the former governor of MA.) spoke of the State of Massachusetts, let me assure him that not one present in all this convention entertains the least hostility to the people of the State of Massachusetts, but we stand here representing people who are the equals, before the law, of the greatest citizens in the State of Massachusetts. When you [the gold delegates] come before us and tell us that we are about to disturb your business interests, we reply that you have disturbed our business interests by your course.

We say to you that you have made the definition of a business man too limited in its application. The man who is employed for wages is as much a business man as his employer, the attorney in a country town is as much a business man as the corporation counsel in a great metropolis, the merchant at the cross-roads store is as much a business man as the merchant of New York, the farmer who goes forth in the morning and toils all day—who begins in the spring and toils all summer—and who by the application of brain and muscle to the natural resources of the country creates wealth, is as much a business man as the man who goes upon the board of trade and bets upon the price of grain, the miners who go down a thousand feet into the earth, or climb two thousand feet upon the cliffs, and bring forth from their hiding places the precious metals to be poured into the channels of trade are as much business men as the few financial magnates who, in a back room, corner the money of the world. We come to speak for this broader class of businessmen.

Ah, my friends, we say not one word against those who live upon the Atlantic coast, but the hardy pioneers who have braved all the dangers of the wilderness, who have made the desert to blossom as the rose—the pioneers away out there [in the West], who rear their children near to nature's heart, where they can mingle their voices with the voices of the birds—out there where they have erected schoolhouses for the education of their young, churches where they praise their Creator, and cemeteries where rest the ashes of their dead—these people, we say, are as deserving of the consideration of our party as any people in this country. It is for these that we speak. We do not come as aggressors. Our war is not a war of conquest, we are fighting in the defense of our homes, our families, and posterity. We have petitioned, and our petitions have been scorned, we have entreated, and our entreaties have been disregarded, we have begged, and they have mocked when our calamity came. We beg no longer, we entreat no more, we petition no more. We defy them.

The gentleman [Senator Vilas] from Wisconsin has said that he fears a Robespierre. My friends, in this land of the free you need not fear that a tyrant will spring up from among the people. What we need is an Andrew Jackson to stand, as Jackson stood, against the encroachments of organized wealth.

They tell us that this platform was made to catch votes. We reply to them that changing conditions make new issues, that the principles upon which democracy rests are as everlasting as the hills, but that they must be applied to new conditions as they arise. Conditions have arisen, and we are here to meet those conditions. They tell us that the income tax ought not to be brought in here, that it is a new idea. They criticize us for our criticism of the Supreme Court of the United States. My friends, we have not criticized, we have simply called attention to what you already know. If you want criticisms, read the dissenting opinions of the court. There you will find criticisms. They say that we passed an unconstitutional law, we deny it. The income tax law was not unconstitutional when it was passed, it was not unconstitutional when it went before the Supreme Court for the first time, it did not become unconstitutional until one of the judges changed his mind, and we cannot be expected to know when a judge will change his mind. The income tax is just. It simply intends to put the burdens of government justly upon the backs of the people. I am in favor of an income tax. When I find a man who is not willing to bear his share of the burdens of the government which protects him, I find a man who is unworthy to enjoy the blessings of a government like ours.

They say that we are opposing national bank currency, it is true. If you will read what Thomas Benton said, you will find he said that, in searching history, he could find but one parallel to Andrew Jackson, that was Cicero, who destroyed the conspiracy of Cataline and saved Rome. Benton said that Cicero only did for Rome what Jackson did for us when he destroyed the bank conspiracy and saved America. We say in our platform that we believe that the right to coin and issue money is a function of government. We believe it. We believe that it is a part of sovereignty, and can no more with safety be delegated to private individuals than we could afford to delegate to private individuals the power to make penal statutes or levy taxes. Mr. Jefferson, who was once regarded as good Democratic authority, seems to have differed in opinion from the gentleman who has addressed us on the part of the minority. Those who are opposed to this proposition tell us that the issue of paper money is a function of the bank, and that the Government ought to go out of the banking business. I stand with Jefferson rather than with them, and tell them, as he did, that the issue of money is a function of government, and that the banks ought to go out of the governing business.

They complain about the plank, which declares against life tenure in office. They have tried to strain it to mean that which it does not mean. What we oppose by that plank is the life tenure, which is being built up in Washington, and which excludes from participation in official benefits the humbler members of society.

Let me call your attention to two or three important things. The gentleman from New York says that he will propose an amendment to the platform providing that the proposed change in our monetary system shall not affect contracts already made. Let me remind you that there is no intention of affecting those contracts which according to present laws are made payable in gold, but if he means to say that we cannot change our monetary system without protecting those who have loaned money before the change was made, I desire to ask him where, in law or in morals, he can find justification for not protecting the debtors when the act of 1873 was passed, if he now insists that we must protect the creditors.

He says he will also propose an amendment, which will provide for the suspension of free coinage if we fail to maintain the parity within a year. We reply that when we advocate a policy which we believe will be successful, we are not compelled to raise a doubt as to our own sincerity by suggesting what we shall do if we fail. I ask him, if he would apply his logic to us, why he does not apply it to himself. He says he wants this country to try to secure an international agreement. Why does he not tell us what he is going to do if he fails to secure an international agreement? There is more reason for him to do that than there is for us to provide against the failure to maintain the parity. Our opponents have tried for twenty years to secure an international agreement, and those are waiting for it most patiently who do not want it at all.

And now, my friends, let me come to the paramount issue. If they ask us why it is that we say more on the money question than we say upon the tariff question, I reply that, if protection has slain its thousands, the gold standard has slain its tens of thousands. If they ask us why we do not embody in our platform all the things that we believe in, we reply that when we have restored the money of the Constitution all other necessary reforms will be possible, but that until this is done there is no other reform that can be accomplished.

Why is it that within three months such a change has come over the country? Three months ago, when it was confidently asserted that those who believe in the gold standard would frame our platform and nominate our candidates, even the advocates of the gold standard did not think that we could elect a president. And they had good reason for their doubt, because there is scarcely a state here today asking for the gold standard, which is not in the absolute control of the Republican Party. But note the change. Mr. McKinley was nominated at St. Louis upon a platform, which declared for the maintenance of the gold standard until it can be changed into bimetallism by international agreement. Mr. McKinley was the most popular man among the Republicans, and three months ago everybody in the Republican Party prophesied his election. How is it today? Why, the man who was once pleased to think that he looked like Napoleon—that man shudders today when he remembers that he was nominated on the anniversary of the battle of Waterloo. Not only that, but as he listens he can hear with ever-increasing distinctness the sound of the waves as they beat upon the lonely shores of St. Helena.

Why this change? Ah, my friends, is not the reason for the change evident to any one who will look at the matter? No private character, however pure, no personal popularity, however great, can protect from the avenging wrath of an indignant people a man who will declare that he is in favor of fastening the gold standard upon this country, or who is willing to surrender the right of self-government and place the legislative control of our affairs in the hands of foreign potentates and powers.

We go forth confident that we shall win. Why? Because upon the paramount issue of this campaign there is not a spot of ground upon which the enemy will dare to challenge battle. If they tell us that the gold standard is a good thing, we shall point to their platform and tell them that their platform pledges the party to get rid of the gold standard and substitute bimetallism. If the gold standard is a good thing, why try to get rid of it? I call your attention to the fact that some of the very people who are in this convention today and who tell us that we ought to declare in favor of international bimetallism— thereby declaring that the gold standard is wrong and that the principle of bimetallism is better—these very people four months ago were open and avowed advocates of the gold standard, and were then telling us that we could not legislate two metals together, even with the aid of all the world. If the gold standard is a good thing, we ought to declare in favor of its retention and not in favor of abandoning it, and if the gold standard is a bad thing why should we wait until other nations are willing to help us to let go? Here is the line of battle, and we care not upon which issue they force the fight, we are prepared to meet them on either issue or on both. If they tell us that the gold standard is the standard of civilization, we reply to them that this, the most enlightened of all the nations of the earth, has never declared for a gold standard and that both the great parties this year are declaring against it. If the gold standard is the standard of civilization, why, my friends, should we not have it? If they come to meet us on that issue we can present the history of our nation. More than that, we can tell them that they will search the pages of history in vain to find a single instance where the common people of any land have ever declared themselves in favor of the gold standard. They can find where the holders of the fixed investments have declared for a gold standard, but not where the masses have.

Mr. Carlisle said in 1878 that this was a struggle between "the idle holders of idle capital" and "the struggling masses, who produce the wealth and pay the taxes of the country," and, my friends, the question we are to decide is upon which side will the Democratic party fight; upon the side of "the idle holders of idle capital" or upon the side of "the struggling masses?" That is the question, which the party must answer first, and then it must be answered by each individual hereafter. The sympathies of the Democratic Party, as shown by the platform, are on the side of the struggling masses who have ever been the foundation of the Democratic Party. There are two ideas of government. There are those who believe that, if you will only legislate to make the well to do prosperous, their prosperity will leak through on those below. The Democratic idea, however, has been that if you legislate to make the masses prosperous, their prosperity will find its way up through every class, which rests upon them.

You come to us and tell us that the great cities are in favor of the gold standard, we reply that the great cities rest upon our broad and fertile prairies. Burn down your cities and leave our farms, and your cities will spring up again as if by magic, but destroy our farms and the grass will grow in the streets of every city in the country.

My friends, we declare that this nation is able to legislate for its own people on every question, without waiting for the aid or consent of any other nation on earth, and upon that issue we expect to carry every State in the Union. I shall not slander the inhabitants of the fair State of Massachusetts nor the inhabitants of the State of New York by saying that, when they are confronted with the proposition, they will declare that this nation is not able to attend to its own business. It is the issue of 1776 over again. Our ancestors, when but three millions in number, had the courage to declare their political independence of every other nation, shall we, their descendants, when we have grown to seventy millions, declare that we are less independent than our forefathers? No, my friends, that will never be the verdict of our people. Therefore, we care not upon what lines the battle is fought. If they say bimetallism is good, but that we cannot have it until other nations help us, we reply that, instead of having a gold standard because England has, we will restore bimetallism, and then let England have bimetallism because the United States has it. If they dare to come out in the open field and defend the gold standard as a good thing, we will fight them to the uttermost.

Having behind us the producing masses of this nation and the world, supported by the commercial interests, the laboring interests, and the toilers everywhere, we will answer their demand for a gold standard by saying to them: You shall not press down upon the brow of labor this crown of thorns, you shall not crucify mankind upon a cross of gold.

Source: William Jennings Bryan, *The First Battle: A Story of the Campaign of 1896*, Chicago 1897

HOW WELL DID YOU UNDERSTAND THIS SELECTION?

1. Who was William Jennings Bryan? What does he advocate in the "Cross of Gold" speech?

2. Why was his message in the "Cross of Gold" speech so appealing to many Americans in 1896?

3. What is the gold standard? What is bimetallism?

4. What have critics said about Bryan's ideas? How does he answer the critics?

THE PAGE LAW

The Page Law, passed on March 3, 1875, was designed to prohibit immigration of Chinese women for the purpose of prostitution. This act was part of the racism present in the American West against Asian immigrants. While untrue, it was widely believed by Westerners in cities like San Francisco that Chinese "pimps" were importing Chinese women to supply prostitution services to Asian and American laborers.

Be it enacted by the Senate and House of Representatives of the United States of America in Congress-assembled,

That in determining whether the immigration of any subject of China, Japan, or any Oriental country, to the United States, is free and voluntary, as provided by section two thousand one hundred and sixty two of the Revised Code, title "Immigration," it shall be the duty of the consul-general or consul of the United States residing at the port from which it is proposed to convey such subjects, in any vessels enrolled or licensed in the United States, or any port within the same, before delivering to the masters of any such vessels the permit or certificate provided for in such section, in ascertain for a term of service within the United States, for lewd and immoral purposes; and if there be such contract or agreement, the said consul-general or consul shall not deliver the required permit or certificate....

SEC.3. That the importation into the United States of women for the purposes of prostitution is hereby forbidden; and all contracts and agreements in relation thereto, made in advance or in pursuance of illegal importation and purposes, are hereby declared void; and whoever shall knowingly and willfully hold, or attempt to hold, any woman to such purposes, in pursuance of such illegal importation and contract or agreement, shall be deemed guilty of a felony, and, on conviction thereof, shall be imprisoned not exceeding five years and pay a fine not exceeding five thousand dollars....

SEC.5. That it shall be unlawful for aliens of the following classes to immigrate into the United States, namely, persons who are undergoing sentence for conviction in their own country of felonious crimes other than political or growing out of or the result of such political offenses, and women "imported for the purposes of prostitution." Every vessel arriving in the United States may be inspected under the direction of the collector of the port at which it arrives, if he shall have reason to believe that such obnoxious persons are on board; and the officer making such inspection shall certify the result thereof to the master or other person in charge of such vessel, designating in such certificate are person or persons, if any there be, ascertained by him to be of either of the classes whose importation is hereby forbidden.....

Source: Proceedings of the Forty-third Congress, Second Session

HOW WELL DID YOU UNDERSTAND THIS SELECTION?

1. What does the Page Law do?

2. Why would the American government pass such a law?

3. How does the Page Law fit into the pattern of racism against Chinese immigrants in the United States?

CHINESE EXCLUSION ACT

Passage of the Chinese Exclusion Act represents the first real attempt by the United States government to close its doors to immigrants from any ethnic group. This law was enacted because a small but vocal minority of white Americans, primarily from the Western states, was racist. Westerners who wanted to prevent further immigration of Chinese to the United States were reacting to economic and labor problems that gripped the West during the 1870s and 1880s. White Americans in the West feared that Chinese laborers, who were highly sought after as miners and railroad workers, would take jobs from them. Chinese immigrants made easy scapegoats for western economic problems because, like Native Americans, they were different.

WHEREAS, in the opinion of the Government of the United States the coming of Chinese laborers to this country endangers the good order of certain localities within the territory thereof, Therefore, Be it enacted. That from and after the expiration of ninety days next after the passage of this act, and until the expiration often years next after the passage of this act, the coming of Chinese laborers to the Untied States be, suspended, and during such suspension it shall not be lawful for any Chinese laborer to come, or, having so come after the expiration of said ninety days, to remain within the United States.

SEC 2: That the master of any vessel who shall knowingly bring within the United States on such vessel, and land or permit to be landed, any Chinese laborer, from any foreign port or place, shall be deemed guilty of a misdemeanor, and on conviction thereof shall be punished by a fine of not more than five hundred dollars for each and every such Chinese laborer so brought, and may be also imprisoned for a term not exceeding one year.

SEC 3: That the two foregoing sections shall not apply to Chinese laborers who were in the United States on the seventeenth day of November, eighteen hundred and eighty, or who shall have come into the same before the expiration of ninety days next after the passage of this act,

SEC 6: That in order to the faithful execution of articles one and two of the treaty in this act before mentioned, every Chinese person other than a laborer who may be entitled by said treaty and this act to come within the United States, and who shall be about to come to the United States, shall be identified as so entitled by the Chinese Government in each case, such identity to be evidenced by a certificate issued under the authority of said government, which certificate shall be in the English language or (if not in the English language) accompanied by a translation into English, stating such right to come, and which certificate shall state the name, title, or official rank, if any, the age, height, and all physical peculiarities former and present occupation or profession and place of residence in China of the person to whom the certificate is issued and that such person is entitled conformably to the treaty in this act mentioned to come within the Untied States.

Source: United States Statutes at Large, Vol. 22

HOW WELL DID YOU UNDERSTAND THIS SELECTION?

1. What does the Chinese Exclusion Act do?

2. What penalties will be assessed against violators of the law?

3. What did non-laborers from China have to do to come to the United States?

4. Is the Chinese Exclusion Act racist? Why or why not?

REPUBLICAN PARTY PLATFORM

The 1896 presidential election was a pivotal one in American history. There was a clear difference between the parties and their stand on the issues. The Republican Party represented big business, imperialism, and the gold standard. The Republican candidate, William McKinley, ran a traditional campaign. Rather than crossing the country to ask for votes, he stayed at home in Ohio and let other Republicans, like Theodore Roosevelt, campaign for him. The issues he and his Republican campaigners stressed are summarized in the Republican Party Platform adopted at their St. Louis convention on June 16, 1896.

The Republicans of the United States, assembled by their representatives in National Convention, appealing for the popular and historical justification of their claims to the matchless achievements of thirty years of Republican rule, earnestly and confidently address themselves to the awakened intelligence, experience, and conscience of their countrymen in the following declaration of facts and principles:

For the first time since the Civil War the American people have witnessed the calamitous consequences of full and unrestricted Democratic control of the Government. It has been a record of unparalleled incapacity, dishonor and disaster. In administrative management it has ruthlessly sacrificed indispensable revenue, entailed an unceasing deficit, eked out ordinary current expenses with borrowed money, piled up the public debt by $262,000,000 in time of peace, forced an adverse balance of trade, kept a perpetual menace hanging over the redemption fund, pawned American credit to alien syndicates, and reversed all the measures and results of successful Republican rule. In the broad effect of its policy it has precipitated panic, blighted industry and trade with prolonged depression, closed factories, reduced work and wages, halted enterprise and crippled American production, while stimulating foreign production for the American market. Every consideration of public safety and individual interest demands that the Government shall be rescued from the hands of those who have shown themselves incapable of conducting it without disaster at home and dishonor abroad, and shall be restored to the party which for thirty years administered it with unequalled success and prosperity. And in this connection we heartily endorse the wisdom, patriotism and the success of the Administration of President Harrison.

Allegiance to <u>Protection</u> Renewed.
We renew and emphasize our allegiance to the policy of Protection as the bulwark of American industrial independence and the foundation of American development and prosperity. This true American policy taxes foreign products and encourages home industry; it puts the burden of revenue on foreign goods; it secures the American market for the American producer; it upholds the American standard of wages for the American workingman; it puts the factory by the side of the farm, and makes the American farmer less dependent on foreign demand and prices; it diffuses general thrift and founds the strength of all on the strength of each. In its reasonable application it is just, far and impartial, equally opposed to foreign control and domestic monopoly, to sectional discrimination and individual favoritism.

We denounce the present Democratic tariff as sectional, injurious to the public credit and destructive to business enterprise. We demand such an equitable tariff on foreign imports which come into competition with American products, as will not only furnish adequate revenue for the necessary expenses of the Government, but will protect American labor from degradation to the wage level of other lands. We are not pledged to any particular schedules. The question of rates is a practical question, to be governed by the conditions of the time and of production; the ruling and uncompromising principle is the protection and development of American labor and industry. The country demands a right settlement, and then it wants rest.

Reciprocity Demanded.
We believe the repeal of the reciprocity arrangements negotiated by the last Republican Administration was a national calamity, and we demand their renewal and extension on such terms as will equalize our trade with other nations, remove the restrictions which now obstruct the sale of American products in the ports of other countries, and secure enlarged markets for the products of our farms, forests and factories.

Protection and reciprocity are twin measures of Republican policy and go hand in hand. Democratic rule has recklessly struck down both, and both must be re-established. Protection for what we produce, free admission for the necessaries of life which we do not produce; reciprocal agreements of mutual interest which gain open markets for us in return for our open market to others. Protection builds up domestic industry and trade and secures our own market for ourselves; reciprocity builds up foreign trade and finds an outlet for our surplus.

We condemn the present Administration for not keeping faith with the sugar producers of this country; the Republican party favors such protection as will lead to the production on American soil of all the sugar which the American people use and for which they pay other countries more than $ 100,000,000 annually. To all our products--to those of the mine and the field, as well as those of the shop and the factory--to hemp, to wool, the product of the great industry of sheep husbandry, as well as to the finished woolens of the mill--we promise the most ample protection.

Merchant Marine.

We favor restoring the early American policy of discriminating duties for the upbuilding of our merchant marine and the protection of our shipping in the foreign carrying trade, so that American ships--the product of American labor, employed in American shipyards, sailing under the Stars and Stripes, and manned, officered and owned by Americans--can regain the carrying of our foreign commerce.

The Currency Plank.

The Republican Party is unreservedly for sound money. It caused the enactment of the law providing for the resumption of specie payment in 1879; since then every dollar has been as good as gold.

We are unalterably opposed to every measure calculated to debase our currency or impair the credit of our country. We are, therefore, opposed to the free coinage of silver, except by international agreement with the leading commercial nations of the world, which we pledge ourselves to promote, and, until such agreement can be obtained, the existing gold standard must be preserved. All our silver and paper currency must be maintained at parity with gold, and we favor all measures designed to maintain inviolable the obligations of the United States and all our money, whether coin or paper, at the present standard, the standard of the most enlightened nations of the earth.

Justice to Veterans.

The veterans of the Union armies deserve and should receive fair treatment and generous recognition. Whenever practicable, they should be given the preference in the matter of employment, and they are entitled to the enactment of such laws as are best calculated to secure the fulfillment of the pledges made to them in the dark days of the country in peril. We denounce the practice in the Pension Bureau, so recklessly and unjustly carried on by the present administration, of reducing pensions and arbitrarily dropping names from the rolls, as deserving the severest condemnation of the American people.

Foreign Relations.

Our foreign policy should be at all times firm, vigorous and dignified, and all our interests in the Western hemisphere carefully watched and guarded. The Hawaiian Islands should be controlled by the United States, and no foreign Power should be permitted to interfere with them; the Nicaragua Canal should be built, owned, and operated by the United States, and, by the purchase of the Danish Islands, we should secure a seaport and much-needed naval station in the West Indies.

The massacres in Armenia have aroused the deep sympathy and just indignation of the American people, and we believe that the United States should exercise all the influence it can properly exert to bring these atrocities to an end. In Turkey, American residents have been exposed to the gravest dangers, and American property destroyed. There, and everywhere, American citizens and American property must be absolutely protected at all hazards and at any cost.

We reassert the Monroe Doctrine in its full extent, and we reaffirm the right of the United States to give the doctrine effect by responding to the appeals of any American State for friendly intervention in case of European encroachment. We have not interfered, and shall not interfere, with the existing possessions of any European Power in this hemisphere, but those possessions must not, on any pretext, be extended. We hopefully look forward to the eventual withdrawal of the European Powers from this hemisphere, and to the ultimate union of all the English-speaking part of the continent by the free consent of its inhabitants.

Suffering Cuba.

From the hour of achieving their own independence, the people of the United States have regarded with sympathy the struggles of other American peoples to free themselves from European domination. We watch with deep and abiding interest the heroic battle of the Cuban patriots against cruelty and oppression, and our best hopes go out for the full success of their determined contest for liberty. The Government of Spain, having lost control of Cuba, and being unable to protect the property or lives of resident American citizens, or to comply with its treaty obligations, we believe that the Government of the United States should actively use its influence and good offices to restore peace and give independence to the island.

The Navy.

The peace and security of the Republic, and the maintenance of its rightful influence among the nations of the earth, demand a naval power commensurate with its position and responsibility. We therefore favor the continued enlargement of the navy and a complete system of harbor and seacoast defenses.

Foreign Immigration.

For the protection of the equality of our American citizenship and of the wages of our workingmen against the fatal competition of low-priced labor, we demand that the immigration laws be thoroughly enforced and so extended as to exclude from entrance to the United States those who can neither read nor write.

Civil Service.

The Civil Service law was placed on the statute book by the Republican Party, which has always sustained it, and we renew our repeated declarations that it shall be thoroughly and honestly enforced and extended wherever practicable.

Free Ballot.

We demand that every citizen of the United States shall be allowed to cast one free and unrestricted ballot, and that such ballot shall be counted and returned as cast.

Lynchings.

We proclaim our unqualified condemnation of the uncivilized and barbarous practices well known as lynching and killing of human beings, suspected or charged with crime, without process of law.

National Arbitration.

We favor the creation of a National Board of Arbitration to settle and adjust differences which may arise between employers and employed engaged in inter-State commerce.

Homesteads.

We believe in an immediate return to the free homestead policy of the Republican party, and urge the passage by Congress of the satisfactory free homestead measure which has already passed the House and is now pending in the Senate.

Territories.

We favor the admission of the remaining Territories at the earliest practicable date, having due regard to the interests of the people of the Territories and of the United States. All the Federal officers appointed for the Territories should be selected from bona fide residents thereof, and the right of self-government should be accorded as far as practicable.

We believe the citizens of Alaska should have representation in the Congress of the United States, to the end that needful legislation may be intelligently enacted.

Temperance and the Rights of Women.

We sympathize with all wise and legitimate efforts to lessen and prevent the evils of intemperance and promote morality.

The Republican Party is mindful of the rights and interests of women. Protection of American industries includes equal opportunities, equal pay for equal work, and protection to the home. We favor the admission of women to wider spheres of usefulness, and welcome their co-operation in rescuing the country from Democratic and Populistic mismanagement and misrule.

Such are the principles and policies of the Republican Party. By these principles we will abide, and these policies we will put into execution. We ask for them the considerate judgment of the American people. Confident alike in the history of our great party and in the justice of our cause, we present our platform and our candidates in the full assurance that the election will bring victory to the Republican party and prosperity to the people of the United States.

Source: Proceedings of the Republican National Convention, 1896

HOW WELL DID YOU UNDERSTAND THIS SELECTION?

1. How does the Republican Party Platform criticize the Democratic-controlled government?

2. Identify the various planks within the Republican Party Platform.

3. Does the Republican Party Platform favor business? Why or why not?

4. Does the Republican Party favor giving women the right to vote? Why or why not? What is the Republican stand on the women's rights movement?

5. Discuss Republican views on foreign policy.

The Populist or People's Party was one of the most successful third parties in American history. It elected candidates to many positions in the 1880s and 1890s, including the United States Congress, state governors, and state legislatures. In 1892 and 1896 the Populist Party ran candidates for president. Most supporters of the Populist Party came from the South and West because those states were largely agricultural, and the Populist Party was clearly the party of farmers. The Populist Party largely disappeared after the 1896 election because the Democratic Party "stole" its issues and presidential candidate (William Jennings Bryan) in that year. Even though the People's Party disappeared, most issues it advocated later became law. These issues are summarized in the Populist Platform adopted at its convention in St. Louis on July 24, 1896.

The People's party, assembled in National Convention, reaffirms its allegiance to the principles declared by the founders of the Republic, and also to the fundamental principles of just government as enunciated in the platform of the party in 1892. We recognize that, through the connivance of the present and preceding. Administrations, the country has reached a crisis in its national life as predicted in our declaration four years ago, and that prompt and patriotic action is the supreme duty of the hour. We realize that, while we have political independence, our financial and industrial independence is yet to be attained by restoring to our country the constitutional control and exercise of the functions necessary to a people's government, which functions have been basely surrendered by our public servant to corporate monopolies. The influence of European money changers has been more potent in shaping legislation than the voice of the American people. Executive power and patronage have been used to corrupt our Legislatures and defeat the will of the people, and plutocracy has thereby been enthroned upon the ruins of Democracy. To restore the Government intended by the fathers and for the welfare and prosperity of this and future generations, we demand the establishment of an economic and financial system, which shall make us masters of our own affairs and independent of European control by the adoption of the following:

Declaration of Principles.

FIRST. We demand a national money, safe and sound, issued by the General Government only, without the intervention of banks of issue, to be a full legal tender for all debts, public and private, a just, equitable, and efficient means of distribution direct to the people and through the lawful disbursements of the Government.

SECOND. We demand the free and unrestricted coinage of silver and gold at the present ratio of 16 to 1, without waiting for the consent of foreign nations.

THIRD. We demand the volume of circulating medium be speedily increased to an amount sufficient to meet the demands of the business and population and to restore the just level of prices of labor and production.

FOURTH. We denounce the sale of bonds and the increase of the public interest-bearing debt made by the present Administration as unnecessary and without authority of law, and demand that no more bonds be issued except by specific act of Congress.

FIFTH. We demand such legislation as will prevent the demonetization of the lawful money of the United States by private contract.

SIXTH. We demand that the Government, in payment of its obligations, shall use its option as to the kind of lawful money in which they are to be paid, and we denounce the present and preceding Administrations for surrendering this option to the holders of Government obligations.

SEVENTH. We demand a graduated income tax to the end that aggregated wealth shall bear its just proportion of taxation, and we regard the recent decision of the Supreme Court relative to the Income Tax law as a misinterpretation of the Constitution and an invasion of the rightful powers of Congress over the subject of taxation.

EIGHTH. We demand that postal savings banks be established by the Government for the safe deposit of the savings of the people and to facilitate exchange.

Transportation.

FIRST. Transportation being a means of exchange and a public necessity, the Government should own and operate the railroads in the interest of the people and on a non-partisan basis, to the end that all may be accorded the same treatment in transportation and that the tyranny and political power now exercised by the great railroad corporations, which result in the impairment if not the destruction of the political rights and personal liberties of the citizen, may be destroyed. Such ownership is to be accomplished gradually, in a manner consistent with sound public policy.

SECOND. The interest of the United States in the public highways built with public moneys and the proceeds of extensive grants of land to the Pacific Railroads should never be alienated, mortgaged, or sold, but guarded and protected for the general welfare as provided by the laws organizing such railroads. The foreclosure of existing liens of the United States on these roads should at once follow default in the payment thereof by the debtor companies, and at the foreclosure sales of said roads the Government shall purchase the same if it becomes necessary to protect its interests therein, or if they can be purchased at a reasonable price, and the Government shall operate said railroads as public highways for the benefit of the whole people and not in the interest of the few under suitable provisions for protection of life and property, giving to all transportation interests equal privileges and equal rates for fares and freights.

THIRD. We denounce the present infamous schemes for refunding these debts, and demand that the laws now applicable thereto be executed and administered according to their interest and spirit.

Telegraph.

The telegraph, like the Post-office system, being a necessity for the transmission of news, should be owned and operated by the Government in the interest of the people.

Land.

FIRST. True policy demands that the National and State legislation shall be such as will ultimately enable every prudent and industrious citizen to secure a home, and, therefore, the land should not be monopolized for speculative purposes. All lands now held by railroads and other corporations in excess of their actual needs, should by lawful means be reclaimed by the Government and held for natural settlers only, and private land monopoly as well as alien ownership should be prohibited.

SECOND. We condemn the frauds by which the land grant Pacific Railroad Companies have, through the connivance of the Interior Department, robbed multitudes of actual bona fide settlers of their homes and miners of their claims, and we demand legislation by Congress which will enforce the exception of mineral land from such grants after as well as before the patent.

THIRD. We demand that bona fide settlers on all public lands be granted free homes, as provided in the National Homestead law, and that no exception be made in the case of Indian reservations when opened for settlement, and that all lands not now patented come under this demand.

Direct Legislation.

We favor a system of direct legislation, through the initiative and referendum, under proper constitutional safeguards.

General Propositions.

FIRST. We demand the election of President, Vice-President, and United States Senators by a direct vote of the people.

SECOND. We tender to the patriotic people of the country our deepest sympathies in their heroic struggle for political freedom and independence, and we believe the time has come when the United States, the great Republic of the world, should recognize that Cuba is and of right ought to be a free and independent State.

THIRD. We favor home rule in the Territories and the District of Columbia, and the early admission of the Territories as States.

FOURTH. All public salaries should be made to correspond to the price of labor and its products.

FIFTH. In times of great industrial depression idle labor should be employed on public works as far as practicable.

SIXTH. The arbitrary course of the courts in assuming to imprison citizens for indirect contempt, and ruling them by injunction, should be prevented by proper legislation.

SEVENTH. We favor just pensions for our disabled Union soldiers.

EIGHTH. Believing that the elective franchise and an untrammeled ballot are essential to government of, for, and by the people, the People's party condemn the wholesale system of disfranchisement adopted in some of the States as unrepublican and undemocratic, and we declare it to be the duty of the several State Legislatures to take such action as will secure a full, free and fair ballot and honest count.

NINTH. While the foregoing propositions constitute the platform upon which our party stands, and for the vindication of which its organization will be maintained, we recognize that the real and pressing issue of the pending campaign, upon which the present election will turn, is the financial question, and upon this great and specific issue between the parties we cordially invite the aid and co-operation of all organizations and citizens agreeing with us upon this vital question.

Source: Proceedings of People's Party (Populist) Convention, 1896

HOW WELL DID YOU UNDERSTAND THIS SELECTION?

1. What does the Populist Party appear to be reacting against?

2. Identify the various planks in the Populist Party Platform.

3. Contrast Populist views with those of Republicans in the 1896 election.

4. What is the most significant issue in the Populist Party Platform?

SELF TEST:

MULTIPLE CHOICE: Circle the correct response. The correct answers are given at the end.

1. How much land did the Dawes Act provide for each head of a Native American family?
   a. Three acres.
   b. 140 acres.
   c. 160
   d. one-quarter section (60 acres).

2. What does William Jennings Bryan advocated in the "Cross of Gold" speech?
   a. A strict gold standard.
   b. A currency that is deflated.
   c. Government policies that will help corporations but discriminate against agriculture.
   d. Inflation through the coinage of silver.

3. The final battle between whites and Native Americans in the West was
   a. Wounded Knee.
   b. Little Big Horn
   c. Custer's Last Stand
   d. Sand's Creek.

4. What was the most significant factor in the destruction of the Plains Tribes?
   a. Introduction of the horse.
   b. Destruction of the Buffalo.
   c. The demise of Salmon populations in the Pacific Northwest.
   d. The coming of the Railroad into western territories.

5. Why did the United States want to limit Chinese immigration to the United States?
   a. Because of racist views in the United States.
   b. Because China was traditionally an enemy of the United States.
   c. Because there was not enough work for Chinese laborers to do in the United States.
   d. Because Chinese immigrants were put on the welfare rolls in higher numbers than were other immigrant groups.

6. What was the African-American settlement in northwestern Kansas called?
   a. Exoduster.
   b. Deadeye Dick.
   c. Isom Dart.
   d. Nicodemus.

7. Which of the following did William McKinley and the Republican Party favor in the 1896 election?
   a. The free coinage of silver to create inflation.
   b. Giving 18 year old citizens the right to vote in national elections.
   c. Making Hawaii an independent nation.
   d. Tariffs, big business, and the gold standard.

8. Which of the following was not part of the Populist Party Platform in 1896?
   a. Direct election of United States Senators.
   b. A graduated income tax.
   c. A strict gold standard.
   d. The free coinage of silver.

9. The first great economic boom in the Far West occurred in which of the following industries?
   a. Petroleum.
   b. Farming.
   c. Cattle ranching.
   d. Mining.

10. What was perhaps the worst problem women who lived in the Great Plains faced?
    a. Loneliness and isolation.
    b. Hard labor.
    c. Indian attacks.
    d. Few men to serve as mates.

ANSWERS: 1-c; 2-d; 3-a; 4-b; 5-a; 6-d; 7-d; 8-c; 9-d; 10-a

ESSAYS:

1. There are many myths prevalent in American society about the West. Identify some of these myths and examine their validity.

2. Compare and contrast the views of the Populist Party with those of the Republican Party in the 1896 election.

3. Discuss the mistreatment of Native Americans. How could this mistreatment have been avoided?

4. Examine the racism present in the United States against minority ethnic groups. Why were Americans so racist? How can racism be overcome?

5. Examine the effect the Homestead Act had on the West. What happened to most of the land that was filed on? How was the act abused?

OPTIONAL ACTIVITIES: (Use your knowledge **and** imagination.)

1. You are a Native American confined to a reservation in the West. Keep a diary for the semester in which you compare and contrast your life before and after life on the reservation.

2. You are a member of a United States Senate Committee investigating conditions and events that led to the massacre at Wounded Knee. Write a report that summarizes the findings of your committee.

3. You have just been nominated by the Populist Party to run for Congress in a district from South Dakota in 1896. Write and deliver a campaign speech to your class that reflects your views on the issues dominant in American politics in 1896.

WEB SITE LISTINGS:

Populist Party

> http://www.encyclopedia.com/search.asp?target=@DOCTITLE%20Populist%20party
> (Encyclopedia.com)
> http://www.encyclopedia.com/searchpool.asp?target=@DOCTITLE%20Populist%20party

CyberSoup's Wild West

> Colorful educational site covering Western legends and Native Americans. http://www.thewildwest.org/

Bryan, William Jennings

> Essays and speeches about imperialism (1898-1913) by one of the most influential leaders of the Democratic Party during the late 19th and early 20th centuries. http://www.boondocksnet.com/ail/bryan.html

Bryan, William Jennings

> (Encarta® Concise Encyclopedia Article)
> http://encarta.msn.com/index/conciseindex/0C/00C50000.htm?z=1&pg=2&br=1

Biography of Jesse James

> In-depth article about the legendary outlaw and gunman
> http://www.crimelibrary.com/americana/jesse/index.htm

Angel Island Immigration Station

> Historical information about Angel Island State Park in California, site of the Immigration Station, a National Historic Landmark, which played a role in the Chinese Exclusion Act of 1882.
> http://www.angelisland.org/immigr02.html

Women of the West Museum

> An educational organization that traces and interprets the history, contributions, and roles of women of all cultures—past, present, and future in the American West. http://www.wowmuseum.org/

American West Heritage Center

> dedicated to honoring, celebrating, and re-creating the heritage and culture of the American West from the period of 1820 to 1920 http://www.americanwestcenter.org/

Legends of the American West - Wyatt Earp & the Gunfighters

> Reviews on Legends of the American West - Wyatt Earp & the Gunfighters written by consumers at Epinions.com. http://www.epinions.com/mvie_mu-1037468

Ghost Town Museum

> A complete and authentic old western town built from the very buildings abandoned after the Pikes Peak Region's gold mining era and straight out of the days of America's frontier.
> http://www.ghosttownmuseum.com/

Buffalo Soldiers and Indian Wars

> Sixteen photographs of Buffalo Soldiers, 14 of their legendary Native American foes, two mini-videos and 24 story/page links are displayed. Buffalo Soldier battles, skirmishes and background events are given. http://www.buffalosoldier.net

The Buffalo Soldiers on the Western Frontier

> History of the 9th and 10th Cavalry
> http://www.imh.org/imh/buf/buftoc.html

CHAPTER NOTES

Chapter One

EUROPEANS REACT TO THE CULTURES THEY ENCOUNTERED IN NORTH AMERICA

1.   Marston Bates, *Gluttons and Libertines: Human Problems of Being Natural* (New York: Vintage Books, 1958), 14.

2.   William Hilton Graves, "The Evolution of American Indian Policy: From Colonial Times To The Florida Treaty (1819)" (Florida State University, Ph.D. dissertation, 1982), 7.

3.   Gary B. Nash, *Red, White and Black: The Peoples of Early America* (Englewood Cliffs, N.J.: Prentice-Hall, Inc., 1974), 35,38.

4.   James Axtell, "Colonial America Without the Indians: Counterfactual Reflections," *The Journal of American History* 73 (March 1987): 992.

5.   Robert F. Berkhofer, Jr., *The White Man's Indian: Images of the American Indian from Columbus to the Present* (New York: Alfred A. Knopf, 1978), xv.

6.   Nash, *Red, White and Black,* 30.

7.   Olive Patricia Dickason, *The Myth of the Savage: And the Beginnings of French Colonialism in the Americas* (Edmonton, Alberta: The University of Alberta Press, 1984),30.

8.   Don Juan de Onate to the Court of Spain, March 2, 1599 as reprinted *in New Mexico in 1602: Juan de Montoya's Relation of the Discovery of New Mexico,* eds. George P. Hammond and Agapito Rey, Quivira Society Publications, Volume 3 (Albuquerque: University of New Mexico Press, 1938), 45.

9.   Gonzalo Fernandez de Oviedo, *La Historia General y Natural de las Indias,* as reprinted in The Discovery of New Spain in 1518 by Juan de *Grijalva, trans.* Henry R. Wagner (Pasadena, CA: Val Trafz Press, 1942), 101.

10.   Bernal Diaz del Castillo, *The Conquest of New Spain,* ed. J.M. Cohen (Harmondsworth, Middlesex, England: Penguin Books, Ltd., 1963), 62.

11.   Friar Diego de Landa, Yucatan: *Before and After the Conquest, With Other Related Documents, Maps and Illustrations,* translated and edited by William Gates (New York: Dover Publications, Inc., 1978), 30.

12.   Alvar Nunez Cabeza de Vaca, "The Narrative of Alvar Nunez Cabeza de Vaca," ed. Frederick W. Hodge, in *Spanish Explorers in the Southern United States* 1528-1543, eds. Frederick W. Hodge and Theodore H. Lewis (New York: Barnes & Noble, Inc., 1946), 21.

13.   A Portugal gentleman of Elvas, *Virginia Richly Valued, By the Description of the Maine Land of Florida, Her Next Neighbor,* trans. Richard Hakluyt (London: Felix Kyngston for Matthew Lownes, 1609), 23.

14.   Pedro de Castaneda of Najera, "The Narrative of the Expedition of Coronado by Castaneda," ed. F.W. Hodge, as reprinted in *Spanish Explorers in the Southern United States 1528-1543,* 344.

15.   Albert H. Schroeder and Dan S. Matson, *A Colony on the Move: Gaspar Cantano de Sosa's Journal 1590-1591* (Salt Lake City: Alphabet Printing Co., School of American Research, 1965), 118.

16.   Francis Fletcher, *The World Encompassed by Sir Francis Drake, carefully Collected out of the notes of Master Francis Flethcher, Preacher in this Imployment, and divers other his followers (London, 1628), reprinted in Early English and French Voyages: Chiefly from Hakluyt,* 1534-1608, ed. Henry S. Burrage (New York: Charles Scriber's Sons, 1930), 169.

17.   Arthur Barlowe, "The First Voyage to the Coasts of America, with Two Barks, Wherein Were Captains M{aster} Arthur Barlowe, Who Discovered Part of the Country Now Called Virginia, Anno 1584," in Richard Hakluyt, *Hakluyt's Voyages of the New World,* ed. David Freeman Hawke (Indianapolis: The Bobbs-Merrill Company, Inc., 1972), 89.

18.   Richard Hakluyt, "A shorte and briefe narration of the Navigation made by the commandment of the King of France, to the islands of Canada, Hochelaga, Saguenay, and divers others which now are called New France," in *Early English and French Voyages,* 66-67.

19.   Dickason, *The Myth of the Savage,* 31.

20.   Hernando de Alarcon, "Relation of the Navigation and Discovery Undertaken by Captain Hernando de Alarcon by Order of His Excellency, Don Antonio de Mendoza, Viceroy of New Spain, Given at Colima, a Harbor of New Spain," in *Narratives of Coronado Expedition* 1540-1542, eds. George P. Hammond and Agapito Rey (Albuquerque: University of New Mexico Press, 1940), 135.

21.   Hernando de Alvarado, "Account of What Hernando de Alavardo and Fray Juan de Padilla Discovered While in Search of the South Sea," in *Narratives of the Coronado Expedition,* 184.

22.   Francisco Vasquez de Coronado to Antonio de Mendoza, August 3, 1540, in *Narratives of the Coronado Expedition*, 175.

23.   Nicolas Le Challeux, "Nicholas Le Challeux's narrative of Captain Jean Ribaut's last voyage in 1565, undertaken at the King's command to an island in the Indies commonly called Florida," *in The New World: The First Pictures of America*, ed. Stefan Lorant (New York: Duell, Sloan, & Pearce, 1946), 96.

24.   De Landa, *Yucatan*, 43, 45-46; Dickason, *The Myth of the Savage*, 31.

25.   Ibid., 46-47.

26.   Ibid., 8.

27.   Thomas Hariot, *A Carolina Heritage Reprint of: A Briefe and True Report of the New Found Land of Virginia* (Reproduced in Facsimile from the First Edition of 1588), intro. Luther S. Livingston (Murfreesboro, N.C.: Johnson Publishing Co.), E2-E4.

28.   Bartoleme de Las Casas, *Historia de las Indias in The Discovery of New Spain in 1518 by Juan de Grijalva,* 151.

29.   Bartoleme do Las Casas, *Tears of the Indians*, trans. J. Phillips {(London, 1956) reprint ed. Williamstown, Massachusetts: The John Lilburne Company, Publishers, 1970}, 8.

30.   Dickason, *The Myth of the Savage*, 21-22.

31.   Fernandez de Oviedo, *La Historia General in The Discovery of New Spain*, 114.

32.   Ibid., 128.

33.   Diaz, *The Conquest of New Spain*, 38.

34.   Ibid., 96.

35.   De Landa, *Yucatan*, 91.

36.   Elvas, *Virginia Richly Valued*, 23.

37.   Diaz, *The Conquest of New Spain*, 229.

38.   De Landa, *Yucatan*, 47-48.

39.   Alarcon, "Relation of the Navigation and Discovery," in *Narratives of the Coronado Expedition*, 135.

40.   Castaneda, "The Narrative of the Expedition of Coronado," in *Spanish Explorers in the Southern United States*, 346.

41.   Dickason, *The Myth of the Savage*, 50.

42.   Castaneda, "The Narrator of the Expedition of Coronado," in *Spanish Explorers in the Southern United States*, 346.

43.   Elvas, *Virginia Richly Valued*, 21.

44.   Cabeza de Vaca, "The Narrative," in *Spanish Explorers in the Southern United States*, 54.

45.   De Landa, *Yucatan*, 8-9.

46.   Barlowe, *Hakluyt's Voyages of the New World*, 88.

47.   Fletcher, "The World Encompassed by Sir Francis Drake," in *Early English and French Voyages*, 160.

48.   Richard Hakluyts, "The First Relation of Jaques Cartheire of S. Malo of the New Land called New France." In *Early English and French Voyages*, 23.

49.   Hakluyts, "A Shorte and Briefe Narration," as reprinted in *Early English and French Voyages*, 67.

50.   Jacques le Moyne, "The Narrative of Jacques le Moyne de Morgues, an Artist Who Accompanied the French Expedition to Florida under Rene de Laudonniere in the Year 1564," in *The New World*, 56.

51.   Alarcon, "Relation of the Navigation and Discovery," in *Narratives of the Coronado Expedition*, 129.

52.   Elvas, *Virginia Richly Valued*, 42.

53.   Schroeder and Matson *A Colony on the Move*, 100,.

54.   Juan de Montoya, "Account of the Discovery of New Mexico and Many Other Provinces and Cities Newly Found, Sent From the Indies to Spain and Thence to Rome," in *New Mexico in 1602,* 38.

55.   Barlowe, *Hakluyt's Voyages of the New World*, 82.

56.   Le Challeux, "Nicholas Le Challeux's Narrative," in *The New World*, 94.

57.   Le Moyne, "The Narrative of Jacques le Moyne," in *The New World*, 38.

58.   Alarcon, "Relation of the Navigation and Discovery," in *Narratives of the Coronado Expedition*, 129.

59.   De Landa, *Yucatan*, 33. (It is essential to add that the Mayan are remarkably short in stature, even today.)

60.   Francisco Vasquez de Coronado to His Majesty, Emperor Charles V, Oct. 20, 1541, in *Narratives of the Coronado Expedition*, 188.

61.   Neal Salisbury, *Manitou and Providence: Indians, Europeans, and the Making of New England 1500-1643* (Oxford: Oxford University Press, 1982), 52; Elvas, *Virginia Richly Valued*, 53; Cabeza de Vaca, "The Narrative," in *Spanish Explorers in the Southern United States*, 50.

62. Diaz, *The Conquest of New Spain,* 125.

63. Ibid., 224-225.

64. Vincente de Zaldibar Mendoza to Governor Onate, Sept. 15, 1588 {actually 1598}, in *New Mexico in 1602,* 57.

65. Fletcher, "The World Encompassed by Sir Francis Drake," in *Early English and French Voyages,* 170.

66. Cabeza de Vaca, "The Narrative," in *Spanish Explorers in the Southern United States,* 86.

67. Hakluyts, "A Shorte and Briefe Narration," in *Early English and French Voyages,* 68-69.

68. Las Casas, *Tears of the Indians,* 7-8.

69. Lewis Hanke, "The Cultural Contribution of Bishop Juan de Zummarrage to Mexican Culture," *The Americas* 5 (1948), 276-277, in Dickason, *The Myth of the Savage,* 31-32.

70. Fernandez de Oviedo, *La Historia General,* in *The Discovery of New Spain,* 129.

71. Diaz, *The Conquest of New Spain,* 19, 122, 224-225.

72. Cabeza de Vaca, "The Narrative," in *Spanish Explorers in the Southern United States,* 88.

73. Alarcon, "Relation of the Navigation and Discovery," in *Narratives of the Coronado Expedition,* 147-148.

74. De Landa, *Yucatan,* 33.

75. Castaneda, "The Narrative of the Expedition of Coronado," in *Spanish Explorers in the Southern United States,* 346, 344, 344-345, 348, 346, 354.

76. Alarcon, "Relations of the Navigation and Discovery," in *Narratives of the Coronado Expedition,* 148.

77. Hakluyts, "A Shorte and Briefe Narration," in *Early English and French Voyages,* 67-68.

78. De Landa, Yucatan, 29.

79. Cabeza de Vaca, "The Narrative," in *Spanish Explorers in the Southern United States,* 83.

80. De Landa, *Yucatan,* 54.

81. Le Challeux, "Nicholas Le Challeux's narrative," in *The New World,* 94.

82. Cabeza de Vaca, "The Narrative," in *Spanish Explorers in the Southern United States,* 51.

83. Ibid., 64-65.

84. Alarcon, "Relation of the Navigation," in *Narratives of the Coronado Expedition,* 139.

85. Fernandez de Oviedo, *La Historia General,* in *The Discovery of New Spain,* 124.

86. Diaz, *The Conquest of New Spain,* 70, 143, 149.

87. Elvas, *Virginia Richly Valued,* 20, 77.

88. Schroeder and Matson, *A Colony on the Move,* 87.

89. De Landa, *Yucatan,* 25.

90. Cabeza de Vaca, "The Narrative," in *Spanish Explorers in the Southern United States,* 84.

91. Ralph Lane, "Ralph Lane's Report to Sir Walter Raleigh Concerning the English Colony which had been left in Virginia by Sir Richard Grenville," in *The New World: The First Pictures of America,* ed. Stefan Lorant (New York: Duell, Sloan & Pearce, 1946), 145.

92. Hariot, *A Briefe and True Report,* E2.

93. Las Casas, *Tears of the Indians,* 7.

94. Cabeza de Vaca, "The Narrative," in *Spanish Explorers in the Southern United States,* 50-51.

95. Las Casas, *Tears of the Indians,* 48.

96. Barlowe, *Hakluyt's Voyages of the New World,* 85.

97. Castaneda, "The Narrative of the Expedition of Coronado," in *Spanish Explorers in the Southern United States,* 362-363.

98. Frat Marcos de Niza to Don Antonio de Mendoza, Sept. 2, 1539, in *Narratives of the Coronado Expedition,* 73-74.

99. Fletcher, "The World Encompassed by Sir Francis Drake," in *Early English and French Voyages,* 170, 161-162.

100. Cabeza de Vaca, "The Narrative," in *Spanish Explorers in the Southern United States,* 66.

101. Diaz, *The Conquest of New Spain,* 242.

102. Lane, "Ralph Lane's Report to Sir Walter Raleigh," in *The New World,* 143.

103. Richard Hakluyt, "The Third Voyage of Discovery Made by Captaine Jaques Cartier, 1540 {1541} unto the Countreys of Canada, Hochelaga, and Saguenay," in *Early English and French Voyages,* 101.

104. Le Moyne, "The narrative of Jacques le Moyne," in *The New World,* 60.

105. Hariot, *A Briefe and True Report,* E2.

106. Nash, *Red, White and Black,* 44.

107. Lane, "Ralph Lane's report to Sir Walter Raleigh," in *The New World,* 136.

108. Castaneda, "The Narrative of the Expedition of Coronado," in *Spanish Explorers in the Southern United States,* 307.

109. Hakluyts, "A Shorte and Briefe Narration," in *Early English and French Voyages*, 69.

110. Lewis Hanke, *All Mankind is One: A Study of the Disputation Between Bartolome de Las Casas and Juan Gives de Sepulveda in 1550 on the Intelletual and Religious Capacity of the American Indians* (De Kalb: Northern Illinois University Press, 1974), 85. Even though Sepulveda never visited America, his comment does reflect the attitude of some of the Spanish settlers in the Yucatan.

111. De Landa, *Yucatan*, 82.

112. Cabeza de Vaca, "The Narrative," in *Spanish Explorers in the Southern United States*, 52-53.

113. Hariot, *A Briefe and True Report*, F2.

114. De Landa, *Yucatan*, 8.

115. Diaz, *The Conquest of New Spain*, 214, 235.

116. Nash, *Red, White and Black*, 11.

117. Francisco Vasquez de Coronado to Antonio de Mendoza, August 3, 1540, in *Narratives of the Coronado Expedition*, 171.

118. Don Juan de Onate to the Court of Spain, March 2, 1599, in *New Mexico in 1602*, 49.

119. Schroeder and Matson, *A Colony on the Move*, 117.

120. Castaneda, "The Narrative of the Expedition of Coronado," in *Spanish Explorers in the Southern United States*, 351.

Chapter Two

"NEW ENGLAND'S ANNOYANCES"

[1] Harrison T. Meserole, ed., *Seventeenth Century American Poetry* (Garden City: Anchor Books, 1968), pp. 503-05.

[2] Patch upon patch.

Chapter Six

DISCRIMIATION IN OHIO DURING THE EARLY REPUBLIC

1. Seventh Annual Report of the American Colonization Society (1824), p.260, Records of the American Colonization Society, Series 5, vol. 7, Library of Congress, Washington, D.C.

2. Leon F. Litwach, North of Slavery: The Negro in the Free States, 1790-1860 (Chicago, 1961), p.64

3. Leodard GIttings, "A Study of the Motives, Attitudes, Achievements and Decline of the American Colonization Society From Its Inception to 1840" (Doctoral these, Loyola University of Chicago, 1956), pp.154-155.

4. Ibid.

5. Frederic Bancoft, "The Colonization of American Negroes," in Jacob E. Cooke, Frederick Bancroft: Historian (Nornan, Oklahoma, 1957), pp.154-155.

6. Charles Thomas Hickok, "The Negro in Ohio" (Doctoral thesis, Western Reserve University, 1896), p.39.

7. See Hickok, p.34. Hickok indicates that there was considerable debate with regard to the franchise. An attempt was made by the "friends of the black man" to grant the ballot to blacks who were residents of Ohio. The proposal was initially approved by the Convention but was voted down when the President cast the deciding vote against it after the second reading.

8. Hickok, pp.40-42; Frank U. Quillin, The Color Line in Ohio: A History of Race Prejudice in a Typical Northern State (Ann Arbor, Michigan, 1913), pp.21-22; Eugene H. Berwanger, The Frontier Against Slavery: Western Anti-Negro Predjudice and the Slavery Extension Controversy (Urbana, Illinois, 1971), pp.22-23.

9. B. Griffiths, Jr., Two Years' Residence in the New Settlements of Ohio (London, 1835), pp. 83-84, In Ray Allen Billington, America's Frontier Heritage (San Francisco, 1966), p. 78.

10. Quillin, p.45.

11. Berwanger, p.31.

12. Eugene H. Roseboom & Francis Weisenburger, A History of Ohio, 2nd edition, ed. James H. Rodabaugh (Columbus, 1976), p.152.

13. The Supporter (Chillicothe), June 16, 1819; Quillin, pp. 28-29.

14. Wm. Graham to R.R. Gurley, February 10, 1827, A.C.S. Records, series 1, vol.3.

15. African Repository, vol. 10, 41, in Peter Kent Opper, "Mind of the White Participant in the African Colonization Movement, 1816-1840" (Doctoral dissertation, University of North Carolina at Chapel Hill, 1972), pp.86.

16. Charles J. Wilson, "The Negro in Early Ohio." Ohio Archeological & Historical Society Quarterly, 39 (1930), p. 724.

17. T. Watkins to Charles Hammond, July 14, 1828, Charles Hammond Collection, box 2, folder 6, Ohio Historical Society, Columbus, Ohio.

18. Ohio State Journal (Columbus), December 19, 1827.

19. Ohio State Journal, February 1, 1832.

20. Ohio State Journal, December 6, 1827.

21. Ohio State Journal, September 18, 1828.

22. See Roseboom & Weisenburger, p. 152. Roseboom & Weisenburger estimate 2,258 blacks in a total population of 24,000.

23. Berwanger, p. 34.

24. Richard C. Wade, "The Negro in Cincinnati, 1800-1830, "The Journal of Negro History, 39 (1954) p. 46.

25. Litwack, p. 72.

26. Litwack tended to portray the Riot of 1829 in dramatic terms. "Impatient for results, white mobs roamed through Cincinnati's Negro quarters, spreading terror and destruction." Richard C. Wade, however, tended to play down the significance of the event in "The Negro in Cincinnati." According the Wade, the so called riot was more in the nature of "sporadic fighting." He acknowledged that a large number of blacks did leave the city, but maintained "they left to escape the enforcement of 'black laws' and not in fear of violence." (p.51) Wade also pointed out that what violence did occur actually brought sympathy to the plight of Cincinnati's black community "leading many whites to review the situation and reexamine their position." (p.55) Peter Kent Opper, in "The Mind of the White Participant," noted that the importance of the attempt by Cincinnati to enforce the Ohio Black Laws in stimulating Ohio blacks to migrate to Canada's "Wilberforce Colony." (p.153)

27. Wilson, p. 719.

28. Quillin, pp. 53-54.

29. The Supporter, February 9, 1820.

30. The Scioto Gazzette and Fredonian Chronical (Chillicothe), January 14, 1820.

31. The Scioto Gazzette and Fredonian Chronicle, February 17, 1820.

32. John Sloane to Henry Clay, October 16, '822, The Papers of Henry Clay, ed. James F. Hopkins (Lexington, Kentucky, 1963), vol.3 p. 294.

33. The Supporter & Scioto Gazetta, December 20, 1823.

34. The Supporter & Scioto Gazette, January 10, 1824.

35. Annuals of Congress of The United States: Eighteenth Congress - First Session (Washington, D.C. 1856), p. 1428.

36. Secretary of State Mississippi to Governor Morrow, January 24, 1826, Jeremiah morrow Papers, Ohio Historical Society, Columbus, Ohio.

37. J. Staudenraus, The African Colonization Movement, 1816-1865 (New York, 1961), p. 170.